9-02
16.00
VER

W9-DBE-725

JK 1764 .C38 2000
Casper, Barry M.
Lost in Washington : finding the way back to
democracy in America.
   3 0366 1000 0867 0

Lost in Washington

Lost in Washington

Finding the Way Back to Democracy in America

Barry M. Casper

University of Massachusetts Press
Amherst

To Jay, Kaarin, Daniel, Aaron, Ben, and Michael

Copyright © 2000 by
University of Massachusetts Press
All rights reserved

Printed in the United States of America
LC 00-055176
ISBN 1-55849-246-1 (cloth); 247-X (paper)
Designed by Dennis Anderson
Set in Sabon by Graphic Composition, Inc.
Printed and bound by Sheridan Books, Inc.

Library of Congress Cataloging-in-Publication Data

Casper, Barry M.
   Lost in Washington : finding the way back to democracy in America / Barry M. Casper.
      p. cm.
   Includes bibliographical references and index.
   ISBN 1-55849-246-1 (cloth : alk. paper)—ISBN 1-55849-247-X (pbk. : alk. paper)
      1. Political participation—United States. 2. Democracy—United States. 3. Business and
   politics—United States.   I. Title.

JK1764.C38 2000
323'.042'0973—dc21

                                                                            00-055176

British Library Cataloguing in Publication data are available.

Contents

Acknowledgments

When Paul Wellstone took office as U.S. Senator from Minnesota in 1991, I was his first policy adviser in Washington and it was already clear that three especially timely and highly contentious issues would be debated during his first term in the Senate: (1) a national energy strategy, (2) campaign finance reform, and (3) health care reform. In each case, joining with national public interest groups and organizing inside and outside of Washington, we developed policy proposals and strategies to mobilize support for them. I want to thank everyone who helped to map out the overall vision and specific goals and strategies for each of these three important debates.

In the case of the national energy strategy, powerful private and public institutions favoring the status quo dependence on nuclear power and fossil fuels initially held the high ground. But by the 1990s, opinion surveys showed that proponents of an alternative "sustainable energy" paradigm had won the support of a great majority of the American people. Still, given the disposition of political power in Washington, the outcome of this debate remained very much in doubt. I personally am much indebted to members of a superb Energy Policy Advisory Group, assembled by Wellstone aide Scott Adams, including George Crocker, John Dunlop, J. Drake Hamilton, Anne Hunt, Diane Jensen, David Morris, Michael Noble, Carol Overland, Lola Schoenrich, and Marie Zellar. They pointed the way to the Wellstone Sustainable Energy Transition Act and kept me on track, in the process sensitizing me to powerful socializing forces faced by senators and staffers alike. I also learned a great deal from many friends in Washington's environmental lobbying community, including Carol Werner, Ken Bossong, Bill Magavern, Dave Hamilton, Jeff Genzer, Brooks Yeager, Mike Matz, and Dan Becker. Thanks also to Senate staffers Linda Lance (Bryan), Gene Peters (Bradley), and Katie McGinty (Gore), who welcomed us and pointed the way through the political thickets to a surprising if not entirely successful outcome. And most of all, thanks to my wise and creative collaborators in this debate, Karl Gawell, Norman Vig, and Henry Kelly.

When Paul decided to run for the Senate against the two-term incumbent, Republican Rudy Boschwitz, it was obvious that he would be outspent many times over, so five of us did a careful study of his opponent's fund-raising. In the process, we learned some surprising things that enabled us to turn Boschwitz's enormous financial advantage into a liability by election day. More generally, we came away from this exercise with a much enhanced understanding of how campaign fund-raising is carried out. I am indebted to Gina Campbell, Loren Haskins, Marilyn Schuster, and Leah Langworthy for their fine work on this study. Later another group of five, including Ben Senturia, Marty Jezer, Randy Kehler, and Danny Cramer wrote the Clean Money Campaign Reform proposal and model legislation, which demonstrated how full public financing can be applied to state and congressional election campaigns. Two Carleton College students, Nick Corson and Bert Johnson, also contributed in important ways, as did Public Citizen Lobbyists/Organizers Donna Edwards and Craig MacDonald, along with the grassroots network of the Working Group on Electoral Democracy and three key individuals: Ellen Miller and Nick Nyhart of Public Campaign and Larry Makinson of the Center for Responsive Politics.

As he planned his run for the Senate in 1989, Paul had endorsed a universal health care insurance system based on the Canadian model. Physicians for a National Health Program led by two Cambridge, Massachusetts, doctors, David Himmelstein and Steffie Woolhandler, had long promoted such a "single-payer" system, and they had mapped out its essential features and how the transition could occur. My understanding of functional and dysfunctional single-payer interest group politics in 1993–94 was greatly informed by candid accounts from the preeminent Washington single-payer organizer in that period, Public Citizen's Sara Nichols. In 1993, I began working with Kip Sullivan, whose nationally recognized research on single-payer and managed care programs has made him a highly respected contributor to the U.S. health care reform debate.

Under the leadership of physician Ken Frisof and executive director Diane

Lardie, the Cleveland-based network known as Universal Health Care Action Network (UHCAN) was established to promote the single-payer movement in the United States. Another arm of that network, Single Payer Across the Nation (SPAN), directed by Barbara Otto, was established to promote single-payer during the great health care debate of 1993–94. Because the Clinton administration and Senate Majority Leader George Mitchell were promoting "managed competition" and waged a successful campaign to take "single-payer" off the table in Washington, our only chance to get a fair debate of single-payer was to take the proposal to California and collect the million signatures necessary to put it on the ballot in the nation's largest state. That is just what the grassroots organization Neighbor-to-Neighbor decided to do, and along the way I had an opportunity to learn about both the substantial positive and the substantial negative features of the ballot initiative process. Several leaders of Californians for Health Security became good friends, including Donald Cohen, Glen Schneider, and Paul Milne along with Jeanne Ertle and Stephanie Jennings, who became key leaders of the San Diego single-payer campaign.

Political scientist Sanford Lakoff, one of the nation's leading scholars of democracy, had agreed to be my host at the University of California, San Diego, and I was privileged to have him critique my book manuscript carefully and insightfully. Sandy and his wife Evelyn soon became close friends; they could not have been more hospitable to me. Harvey and Norma Mader also became very dear friends while this work was in progress. Harvey continually bombarded me with books, magazines, and other published works that I invariably found extremely useful. Pat Travaglio, my landlady in San Diego, was wonderfully welcoming. Doug Foxgrover, technology wizard of Carleton College's physics and astronomy department, repeatedly bailed me out with ingenious technical assistance.

Once again, it has been a pleasure to work with the University of Massachusetts Press. My editor, Clark Dougan, saw promise in this probably overly ambitious project and dedicated himself to making sure it came to fruition. For that I will be forever grateful. My copy editor, Ella Kusnetz, was looking over my shoulder all the way, polishing the manuscript, clarifying the language, and otherwise improving every page. I'll never be able to thank her enough for all she has done for this book. I also want to express my great appreciation to Carol Oliver for creating the index.

Paul Wellstone got me into this. The National Science Foundation's EVIST Program, headed by Rachelle Hollander, gave me a grant to write a book in 1990. Each of the three stories in the book was an exciting and instructive adventure. My wife Nancy stayed with it all the way to the end of what proved to be nearly a decade-long project. Without her love and support, *Lost in Washington* would never have been completed. To her I owe my deepest thanks.

B. M. C.

Abbreviations

AEC	Atomic Energy Commission
ANWR	Arctic National Wildlife Refuge
APS	American Physical Society
AARP	American Association of Retired People
CAFE	Corporate Average Fuel Economy
CAPA	California Physicians Alliance
CEA	Council of Economic Advisors (president's)
CEE	Customer Energy Efficiency (utilities' programs)
CMCR	Clean Money Campaign Reform
CNA	California Nurses Association
CURE	Consumers United for Rail Equity
DFL	Democratic Farmer Labor Party
DNC	Democratic National Committee
DoE	Department of Energy
DPC	Democratic Policy Committee
EWG	Exempt Wholesale Generator
FERC	Federal Energy Regulatory Commission
FEC	Federal Elections Commission
FECA	Federal Elections Campaign Act
GOTV	Get Out the Vote
HIAA	Health Insurance Association of America
JCAE	Joint Committee on Atomic Energy
LWV	League of Women Voters

L.A.	Legislative Aide
LCV	League of Conservation Voters
NASEO	National Association of State Energy Offices
NCI	National Citizens Initiative
NES	National Energy Strategy
NESA 1991	National Energy Security Act of 1991
NOTA	None of the Above
NPOC	Nuclear Power Oversight Committee
NRSC	National Republican Senatorial Committee
N2N	Neighbor-to-Neighbor
OCS	Outer Continental Shelf
OMB	Office of Management and Budget (White House)
OTA	Office of Technology Assessment
PAC	Political Action Committee
PNHP	Physicians for a National Health Program
PG&E	Pacific Gas & Electric
PUCs	Public Utility Commissions (state)
PUHCA	Public Utility Holding Company Act
SEIU	Service Employees International Union
SLC	State Legislative Committee, AARP
SERI	Solar Energy Research Institute
SETA	Sustainable Energy Transition Act
TAGT	Taxpayers Against the Government Takeover

LOST IN WASHINGTON

Has American Democracy Lost Its Way?

Lost in Washington

Opinion surveys confirm pervasive anecdotal evidence that over the past three decades there has been an alarming decline of public confidence in American democracy in general and elected representatives in particular. For instance, when asked, "can [you] trust the government to do what's right always or most of the time?" of those who responded to a 1964 national survey 76 percent answered yes; by 1984 the positive response was down to 44 percent; and by 1994 it had dropped to an astonishing 19 percent. In the 1994 poll, 84 percent indicated that officials in Washington were "heavily influenced by special interests" and "out of touch with the average person." Only 19 percent believed they were "honest."[1]

The trends in economic inequality in the United States are comparably striking. In 1976 the wealthiest 1 percent of America's households held 20 percent of the wealth; in the next twenty years that figure zoomed up to over 40 percent, the greatest concentration of wealth since the eve of the stock market crash in 1929. From 1983 to 1989, 62 percent of the wealth gain went to the richest 1 percent of households and 99 percent went to the richest 20 percent.[2]

The decline in public confidence in democracy and the growth in economic inequality are connected. The ability of incumbent politicians to stay in office depends to a large extent on campaign contributions from a relatively few very wealthy individuals and lobbying coalitions. Opportunities for the rich to become richer depend to a large extent on federal tax, monetary, and regulatory policies. These dynamics naturally invite the

3

antidemocratic symbioses that infest Washington. Lost in the resulting politics of power and greed are American ideals of political equality and economic and social justice.

What can be done to revive a once promising political system and restore confidence that our elected officials are truly dedicated to government of, by, and for the people? An unexpected opportunity to address that question was offered to me in 1990 when my longtime friend and closest professional collaborator, Democrat Paul Wellstone, was elected to the U.S. Senate from Minnesota in a stunning upset over the heavily favored incumbent, Republican Rudy Boschwitz. A college professor, political activist, and community organizer allied with financially beleaguered family farmers, blue-collar workers, welfare mothers, and others struggling to survive, Wellstone won by waging a populist campaign. Minnesota has a venerable history of progressive-populist politics, in which ordinary citizens have mobilized against exploitation and injustice to demand social and political reform. The midwestern farmers' revolt of the 1890s and the rise to power of the Minnesota Farmer-Labor party in the 1930s are notable examples.

Like so many members of Congress, Wellstone's opponent had gone off to Washington and become caught up in that city's power and money games. During the 1989–90 campaign, I led a year-and-a-half study that documented the millions of dollars Boschwitz had solicited from very rich people and special interest PACs. That became a decisive issue in the 1990 election as Wellstone's populist commitment and message struck a resonant chord among Minnesota voters; his victory was an early signal to Washington of the depth of anti-incumbent sentiment abroad in America in the 1990s.

After Wellstone took office, I served for a time as his first senior policy advisor. As a direct and indirect consequence of that connection, I became deeply immersed in three important public policy debates: over a national energy strategy, arguably the preeminent environmental policy issue of the 1990s; over campaign finance reform, the essential first step in making government accountable to the people; and over health care reform, perhaps the most urgent economic and social justice issue facing our nation. Plunged into the United States Senate, a quasi-feudal culture with powerful socializing forces and elite-serving definitions of what is "politically realistic," I saw how agents of progressive change, reform-minded public servants and public interest groups alike, can lose their way in Washington. In particular, I watched with dismay a major political party, the Democrats, in the process of becoming lost, as a primary commitment to getting reelected and maintaining congressional control proved to be an uncertain political and moral compass. At the same time, I participated in the three efforts described in this book, which planted some constructive seeds of populist reform that may soon blossom to redirect our nation's course on those three important public policy issues.

Three Initiatives for Change

The Wellstone office developed legislative initiatives which would have produced fundamental changes in energy and related environmental policy, campaign financing, and health care. Each had the potential for substantial popular support, but instead each was decisively thwarted in Washington by powerful legislators and interest groups before the public debate began. At this propitious moment, these three remarkably parallel stories can help disenchanted Americans differentiate between the kinds of changes in the rules of the political game that really would make a difference from those Washington often prefers to serve up: soothing, symbolic, fundamentally phony reforms.

In the stories of these three policy initiatives are clear indications of the most telling antidemocratic features in the way Washington works, as well as compelling hints of what it would take to change a system that has become largely of, by, and for the wealthy.

A Sustainable National Energy Strategy

Two weeks after Paul Wellstone was sworn in on January 3, 1991, the Persian Gulf War began, underscoring our nation's energy vulnerability. Wellstone had chosen to serve on the Senate Energy Committee (the Senate Committee on Energy and Natural Resources) because we knew that in 1991 the long-awaited national energy strategy debate was about to begin. We developed sustainable energy transition legislation, aimed at moving away from fossil fuels and nuclear power and toward efficient energy use and renewable energy sources. Opinion surveys showed overwhelming public support for such a change in policy.

But before we arrived in Washington, the issue had been framed in such a way that a sustainable energy transition strategy was effectively ruled out. The powerful Democratic chair of the Senate Energy Committee, J. Bennett Johnston, with the backing of the Republican president, George Bush, had put his enormous influence squarely behind a bill that one of the most respected members of the committee, Bill Bradley, would later aptly describe as "a wish list for the energy industries."

Our natural allies, the environmental groups, were well-organized and well-prepared. Recognizing the chairman's power, however, most were initially resigned to accepting the chairman's framework and trying "make it a better bill." A few of us decided to push instead for what insiders at first thought was a hopeless goal—to block the bill and substitute a sustainable energy transition alternative. Eventually that became the strategy of most of the national environmental groups and their grassroots members and what began as a small nucleus of senators and their staffs. As the effort mushroomed, the chairman called out a veritable army of energy industry lobbyists and a major battle ensued. Up to the moment of the Senate vote, virtually everyone expected the chairman to prevail. But on November 1, 1991, the Senate shocked the nation by refusing to consider his bill. Arguably, no one in the Congress was more responsible for that decision than the freshman senator from Minnesota. There was great rejoicing in the environmental community and considerable hope that an alternative energy strategy package, including the Sustainable Energy Transition Act we had written, would become the new rallying point for support in Washington and around the nation. But as we shall see, that was not to be.

Congressional Campaign Finance Reform

Anger and apathy in the electorate are fueled by a widely held perception that many Washington lawmakers are beholden to the wealthy people and PACs whose campaign contributions fund their reelections. Paul Wellstone's 1990 campaign typified what a difficult, degrading experience it is for a challenger to raise the enormous amount of money necessary to become a credible candidate and what a relatively comfortable, though time-consuming, experience that can be for incumbents. Later, during the 1991 Senate energy strategy debate, some off-hours research verified what I suspected: members of the Senate Energy Committee had been soliciting large amounts of money from energy industry lobbying coalitions at the very time they were making decisions worth hundreds of millions of dollars to those industries.

It was not difficult to conceive of an approach to funding congressional campaigns that would avoid both the appearance and the reality of corruption. In two years, a Wellstone working group consisting of an unusual mix of respected campaign finance experts and superb grassroots organizers hammered out the details of a pathbreaking plan that would cut the big money links between lawmakers and lobbying coalitions by offering full public financing of congressional campaigns. We called it the proposal for Democratically Financed Elections; later it would become renowned as the Clean Elections Option or Clean Money Campaign Reform.

Years of local education and agitation by public interest groups with large grassroots memberships, including Common Cause and the League of Women Voters, had forced campaign finance reform onto the national political agenda. As a candidate, Bill Clinton had pledged to make that issue one of his highest priorities. As the 103rd Congress convened in January 1993 with a Democratic president and a Democratic congressional leadership joining the public interest groups in calling for "real reform", the stage seemed set for an historic change in congressional campaign finance rules.

But behind the scenes in Congress, the incumbents tended not to be overly upset with the lopsided financial advantage incumbents enjoyed. And the new president agreed to leave the terms of the legislation up to the Democratic leaders of the House and Senate. The only hope for significant campaign finance reform would have been enormous grassroots pressure, with the public alerted by national public interest groups not to be taken in by the sweet-sounding but ineffectual proposals the Democrats had put on the table. For reasons that offer valuable insight into the Washington political culture, however, that did not happen.

Health Care Reform

Wellstone was the Senate sponsor of the Canadian-style "single-payer" bill establishing a system of universal health insurance administered by the states and funded through progressive taxes. I served on the steering committee of the grassroots coalition, Single-Payer Across the Nation. During his 1992 campaign, Bill Clinton had endorsed an alternative concept known as "managed competition," and after his election Hillary Rodham Clinton led a task force that developed a detailed legislative proposal. Using their White House podium effectively, the Clintons sold the American people on the necessity of universal coverage and cost containment. They also lined up early support for their plan from a politically potent coalition, ranging from major labor unions and public interest groups to health care corporations and the largest health insurance companies.

The Clintons had a problem, however. Several authoritative studies had demonstrated that the administratively simple and economically efficient single-payer approach would achieve all the Clinton health care goals at a much lower cost. In fact, they showed that such a plan would save enough money to fund comprehensive health insurance for the tens of millions of Americans currently uninsured or underinsured and provide effective cost containment as well.

Despite the fact that the single-payer plan had over ninety cosponsors in the House, the Clintons and their congressional and interest group allies launched an inside-the-Beltway campaign to dismiss it as "politically unfeasible." That notion soon became the conventional wisdom in Washington's insider circles, and by processes that should concern all who appreciate the importance of an informed electorate in a democratic society, it soon became the conventional wisdom in press circles as well. Throughout the subsequent debate, there was a veritable blackout of the single-payer reform proposal in the mainstream media.

The best chance to win affordable universal coverage during the great health care debate of 1993–94 emerged not in Washington, but rather in California. With the support of a National Science Foundation research fellowship, I spent the first eight months of 1992 and 1993 at the University of California, San Diego, in order to work on this book, and my wife, Nancy, and I became deeply involved in the San Diego single-payer movement. In 1994, as the Clinton plan was dismantled and slowly sunk in Congress under an insurance industry barrage, a statewide citizens' coalition in California astounded political insiders by gathering the million signatures needed to put a single-payer initiative on the November 1994 ballot. In contrast to what happened in Washington, ordinary citizens were able to force single-payer onto the political agenda in California.

By the end of April 1994 when the signatures were submitted, a volunteer army of thousands of California single-payer activists had been mobilized, and the initiative had tremendous momentum and enthusiasm as we headed into the ballot campaign. But something happened between April and the statewide vote in November. Having experienced the positive side of popular initiatives for change, we soon experienced the downside as well.

None of these debates is over. Well-conceived and potentially popular proposals may have been thwarted initially, but the critical underlying problems remain. They continue to fester, posing serious threats to our nation's future. America has not seen the last of the Sustainable Energy Transition Act, clean money campaign reform, or single-payer health care reform.

Ordinary Citizens Shut Out

A striking feature of the three policy debates described here is that each issue became one that Congress could not ignore because of popular unrest. It was grassroots agitation and education by well-organized environmentalists about the consequences of continued reliance on fossil fuels and nuclear power that led to the 1991 national energy strategy debate. It was public anger born of a widely held perception that many politicians were bought by special interests, as well as effective grassroots organizing by Common Cause and other public interest groups, that sparked the campaign finance reform debate. And it was concern in the electorate about gaping holes in health insurance coverage, fear of losing coverage, and rapidly escalating costs that made health care reform an issue the politicians had to face.

Social change is a dialectical process led by movements composed of a spectrum of individuals and groups, from local grassroots activists to Washington's insider elites. For the eventual compromise on any particular issue to constitute significant social change, grassroots pressure must pry open considerable space between policies that represent the status quo and the policy demands of the movement. At present, however, the rules of America's political game have been shaped to insure that ordinary citizens are routinely shut out of effective involvement in debates on issues once the focus shifts to decision-making forums in Washington.

Three features of the current political game stand out as principal contributors to the citizen shutouts in the stories recounted here.

The Incumbent Addiction Problem

Most elected representatives are driven into financial dependence on special interest lobbying coalitions for the periodic fixes of large amounts of campaign cash they depend on to stay in office. As a consequence, aside from infrequent occasions when many constituents are watching them closely, most incumbents are far more responsive to the lobbying coalitions than they are to the people they are supposed to represent.

The obvious solution is to change the way political campaigns are financed. The question is how.

The Elite Framing Problem

A striking feature of issue politics in Washington is the often decisive role of elite collaborations among legislative lords with more power than democracy can bear, lobbying coalitions prepared to spend whatever is necessary, and executive branch allies. Meeting in private before the public debate begins, these three groups set the agenda for virtually every important congressional policy debate. And often the most important result of these Washington framing forums is that policy proposals that would be the most attractive focuses for grassroots organizing efforts are eliminated.

Elite framing that effectively eliminates proposals from the public debate has two crippling consequences for American democracy: The first is that negative, oppositional protest goals are often all that is left for people to organize behind when positive proposals have been taken off the table in Washington. It is far more satisfying, of course, to work for programs and policies that are effective responses to problems. If such options are repeatedly foreclosed at the outset of policy debates, the second consequence in the long run inevitably is dampened enthusiasm for public participation in the process. Even the most fervent believers in representative democracy can be worn down by a steady diet of positive options foreclosed and symbolic politics substituted.

In each of the three stories recounted in this book, the preemptive narrowing of the frame by elite forums decisively affected the course and outcome of the Washington debate. A debate over energy strategy inspired by the environmentalists' vision of a sustainable energy future was derailed by a framing process that focused instead on tearing down environmental protection barriers that hindered the traditional energy industries. Likewise in a health care debate sparked by consumer concerns, the framing process consigned the single-payer plan to the "politically unfeasible" scrap pile and brought the Clinton managed competition proposal to the fore; the result was a debate whose most lasting effect was to facilitate the corporate takeover of American medicine. And while it was anger in the electorate about incumbents' soliciting money from wealthy interest groups that prompted serious efforts for campaign finance reform, the legislation that was framed might aptly be termed the Incumbent and Special Interest Protection Bill. In each instance, the institutions whose troubling behavior prompted public concern played central roles in framing the legislative debate.

The Challengers' Resource Problem

The imbalance of resources, especially money, tilts policy decision-making enormously toward the preferences of a few elite individuals and institutions. Obviously the access and influence that large campaign contributions buy is one important part of the problem. But every bit as important is the work of the lobbying coalitions, which tend to be closely allied with powerful legislators. The legislative process is conducted in a sea of highly knowledgable, politically astute, well-connected lobbyists with loads of money at their disposal. They are the community organizers of Washington politics, gathering timely intelligence, developing and implementing political strategies, arranging public relations campaigns, bringing blandishments and pressures to bear on targeted legislators, and working the White House and the agencies that implement legislation. In contrast, grassroots citizen organizing efforts that challenge the elite networks are usually starved for the money they need for organizers, networking, and public education, rarely coming close to raising the amounts necessary to compete with their well-heeled opponents. At the same time, commercial media and government information channels fail miserably in performing the vital tasks of fostering the informed citizenry and public debate our representative democracy requires.

In this regard, a major irony of the current discussions of political reform is the way the "free speech" issue has been defined. In the protracted Washington debate over campaign finance reform, there has been much hand-wringing about "free speech" by those who claim it means untrammeled ability of the wealthy to spend as much as they wish in influencing election outcomes. But there is a much more fundamental issue of "free speech" that should be at the heart of the political reform debate. With privately owned news media the principal channel for conveying the information most people receive about controversial public policy issues, citizen-challengers to the status quo find it difficult, at times nearly impossible, to get their messages out. Solving the problem of providing the American electorate with a free marketplace of ideas in electoral and issue politics is probably the most momentous challenge our democracy faces today.

Changing the Rules

Legislators traditionally play compromiser roles. On most issues, most of the time, incremental change makes sense and those compromisers perform valuable service. But every so often, as in the case of the three issues discussed in this book, an aroused citizenry can create a moment ripe for much more than compromise. As Senator Wellstone and I prepared to go to Washington, I envisioned us as agents of progressive change, with the senator traveling the country using his highly visible office to become a national leader of struggles for economic and social justice and political equality: to assure comprehensive, affordable health insurance for all Americans; to build sustainable energy systems that will not devastate our planet's environment; and to exorcise the crippling influence of great concentrations of wealth on our elections. Overcoming the powerful opposition of entrenched interests would require building countervailing power bases in the form of countrywide grassroots movements. Such a role would play to Paul Wellstone's strengths—his energizing oratorical gift and his grassroots organizing genius.

But assuming that role proved far more difficult than I imagined. With notable exceptions, public interest group leaders and reform-minded legislators and their staffs tend over time to become creatures of the Washington culture. And as noted, ordinary citizens are usually shut out of effective participation in the issues that most affect their lives when policies to deal with those issues are decided in Washington.

A basic question is whether it is possible to conceive of changes in America's political game that would invite ordinary citizens in, not shut them out. One clear lesson from the three stories in this book is that citizen movements for change tend to be thwarted from the start if they do not have the tools they need to force their policy ideas onto the agenda of the nation's public policy debates.

The most obvious tool is a standard part of state ballot initiatives. The petition drive to qualify an initiative for the ballot can be an outstanding way of getting citizens involved and energized. However, the ballot initiative experience in California and other states inspires caution. Given the news media's frequent abdication of its duty to inform the public fully, the ballot phase of citizen initiatives for change are the most vulnerable to manipulative media propaganda campaigns. It is far easier for initiative opponents to plant doubts and fears in voters' minds than it is for initiative proponents to allay those doubts and fears and inspire confidence.

An unexpected conceptual breakthrough occurred when I realized there is a way to modify the initiative so as to retain its best features, while strengthening, not supplanting, our system of representative democracy. Surprisingly, the introduction of this modified initiative process and a corollary campaign finance reform would *naturally* create a robust new framework for an American politics from the bottom up. As discussed in detail at the end of this book, ordinary citizens would be invited in and many institutions, from political parties to public interest organizations to local citizens groups, would find important new democracy-enhancing purpose.

A Propitious Time for a Progressive Populism

In America at the close of the twentieth century, "populist" politicians are springing up in every quarter. They all claim to be for the little guy and against the special interests. Political consultants, with their polls and focus groups, have discovered that is what the voters want to hear. However, historically populism has taken two very different paths. The reactionary-populist path has often featured demagogic leaders who rise to prominence in times of economic adversity and incite ordinary people to fight among themselves for a shrinking portion of the economic pie, scapegoat others, and fail to challenge the hegemony of wealthy and powerful elites. The progressive-populist path, on the other hand, has featured politicians like William Jennings Bryan and Robert M. LaFollette, whose visions of political democracy and economic justice mobilized ordinary people to confront extreme concentrations of wealth and wealth determinants of political power. As the twenty-first century begins, it is not at all clear which path America will choose. That choice promises to be at the cutting edge of a monumental struggle for the heart and soul of our nation.

Some signs point down the dark path. The opportunities and rewards for mean-spirited demagoguery are apparent. The recent targetting of poor people, immigrants, and other minority groups is just a hint of the scapegoating that could flare up on a much grander scale. Other signs are more promising. In many respects this is a propitious moment to launch an American progressive-populist movement for egalitarian ideals, the kind we teach in school, such as "one person, one vote" and "equal opportunity for all." Most Americans are disgusted with the functioning of our political system and disenchanted with politicians of both major political parties.

At the same time, wealth and income inequality in America have reached extraordinary proportions with disastrous consequences for tens of millions of families and severe economic stress for many more. By 1997, the richest 1 percent, about one million of America's roughly one hundred million households, had about 40 percent of the wealth (net worth); the richest 5 percent of households about 62 percent and the richest 20 percent of the households totalled 85 percent, leaving only 15 percent of the wealth for the remaining eighty million households to share.[3]

Real wages (adjusted for inflation) peaked in 1973 and have stagnated or declined ever since. Corporations are merging at a record pace, cutting salaries and benefits, laying off longtime workers, and pulling out of communities that depend on them. The economist Lester Thurow has put the phenomenon in historical perspective and suggested what is at stake for our nation: "Since accurate data have been kept, beginning in 1929, America has never experienced falling real wages for a majority of its work force while its per-capita G.D.P. was rising. . . . No one can know what will happen if inequality continues to rise and a majority of our families experience falling real incomes. But if capitalism does not deliver rising real wages in a period when the total economic pie is expanding, its hold on the political allegiance of the population will be threatened. Similarly, if the democratic political process cannot reverse the trend to inequality, democracy will eventually be discredited."[4]

Not only are the ideals of representative democracy lost in the process, but also lost is a commitment to American ideals of economic justice. Without a doubt, we as a society have sufficient financial resources to assure that every family has adequate food, clothing, shelter, and health care. The most basic facts about wealth in America make that abundantly clear. In 1996, the roughly one hundred million households in the United States had total wealth (assets minus debts) amounting to about $25 trillion.[5] If that total household wealth were distributed equally, each American household would have an astounding $250,000.

Of course, the wealth distribution is far from equal. In the richest country on earth, over forty million people have no health insurance; tens of millions lack adequate food, clothing, and housing; our public education system is severely underfunded; and many middle-class families are experiencing increasing economic insecurity. At this writing, the net worth of the wealthiest one million households ranges from around $2½ million to $60 billion. The redistribution of even a modest proportion of that wealth, in ways that would not affect at all how any of those privileged families live, could wipe out poverty in America and change the face of our society.

Wealth redistribution engineered by governmental action is hardly "un-American." United States government policies between 1976 and 1996, most notably the changes in the tax code in the 1980s, were central contributors to an enormous transfer of wealth in that period to the wealthiest households. The capital gains and inheritance tax law changes in the Clinton-Gingrich balanced budget agreement tilted the balance to the rich even further. The 1980s federal tax changes emanated from a Democratic House of Representatives and were signed by a Republican president, while the 1997 balanced budget agreement was passed by a Republican Congress and signed by a Democratic president. Support for those "Reverse-Robin-Hood" tax policies was truly bipartisan.

Lester Thurow has aptly described this politics of greed as something like "a pressure cooker" that has been placed "on the stove over a full flame and waiting to see how long it takes to explode."[6] America needs a safety valve. People must to be able to work effectively for equitable policies that make sense for us all. But elites are keeping the lid on, thwarting that possibility. As a consequence, the United States today is a fertile field for a populist reaction. The challenge is to channel the public pressure down the progressive path, with the anger and frustration of ordinary people mobilized behind changing the rules of the now wealth-dominated political and economic games.

"We Don't Let Strangers In"

2

Prototypical Strangers

When California's Barbara Boxer first ran for the Senate in 1992, she liked to tell about a conversation she once had with a senior senator in which he informed her bluntly, "We don't let strangers in." That story rings true to me. Individual senators, even junior ones, have significant power. Naturally, there would be concern among the power brokers about letting in people they regard as strangers, even though for most candidates the typical path to the U.S. Senate involves considerable experience in politics, government, and elective office.

But if ever there was a "stranger" elected to the Senate, Paul Wellstone was he. A college professor who had never held elected office, from his earliest days at Carleton College in Northfield, Minnesota, he was drawn frequently to confrontation and controversy. His 1960s doctoral work at the University of North Carolina about the Civil Rights movement had taught him what kind of political scientist he wanted to be. In his words, "I came out of that experience determined to use the tools of scholarship and my understanding of political power to make a difference in the lives of people, determined not to decouple my values from my work—not to stand back as a dispassionate observer, but to step forward and stand with people struggling for justice and equality."

Since coming to Minnesota, Paul had been a leader in many such struggles. Twice he was arrested in protest demonstrations: in the early seventies on the steps of the Federal Building in Minneapolis, with students protesting the

Vietnam war, and again in the mid-eighties at a rural bank in west-central Minnesota, with farmers trying to block the foreclosure of a family farm.

With its progressive-populist tradition, Minnesota has been a spawning ground for vital communities of political activists. Paul had been an influential participant in many of their battles for over twenty years and he inspired many students by his example. Soon after he joined the faculty at Carleton College, his students began doing studies of low-income housing, food stamps, and health care in our rural county, working with welfare mothers in the nearby county seat to establish an effective, combative welfare rights organization. He later chronicled the struggles and successes of that group in his first book, published in 1978, *How the Rural Poor Got Power: Narrative of a Grassroots Organizer.*[1] In his preface to Paul's book, the noted Harvard psychiatrist, educator, and author Robert Coles wrote, "if only there were [more] participant observers around like this book's author, . . . our academic life would be less cloistered, less smug and insulated, more in touch with the realities of this life. . . ." In the classroom, Paul challenged his students to think about their values and to incorporate those values in their work: in his words, "to act on what they believe in." As one former student put it, "the real issue with Paul is, don't stand on the sidelines." Many went on to be outstanding community organizers themselves. Paul had more long-term impact on the lives of his students than any other college teacher I have known.

Sometimes, to the dismay of a succession of Carleton College presidents, this led to confrontations on the campus. From the Vietnam War to South Africa divestment, student demonstrations shook the civility of Northfield's ivory tower. The presidents always suspected Paul was behind the demonstrations.

His lack of enthusiasm for doing conventional academic research and his preference for grassroots activism nearly got him fired in 1974. Initially, he was denied tenure. But a firestorm of student reaction and compelling allegations of serious irregularities in the process by which his work had been evaluated triggered a review of the decision. Two well-known political scientists were brought to the campus as outside evaluators. They were so effusive in their praise that the college had to relent and grant him tenure.

I had been teaching physics at Carleton for three years when Paul arrived in 1969. It was the height of the Vietnam War and at a succession of early faculty meetings that year I clashed with the college president, urging the college to take a stand against the war. Sensing a kindred spirit, Paul sought me out and a very fruitful twenty-year collaboration began.

In the beginning, we tended to work on different issues in different arenas. Paul had the instincts of a community organizer, focusing on issues in and about communities he could reach directly. My emphasis then tended to be national issues, with a Washington focus, including nuclear arms control, energy, and the environment. We became good friends, regularly running long distances together over the noon hour, talking and strategizing as we ran. When my wife, Nancy, and I were married in 1979, Paul was the best man at our wedding.

Our first professional collaboration was the book we published in 1981, *Powerline: The First Battle of America's Energy War*.[2] My involvement in the powerline controversy, probably Minnesota's most heated energy and environmental policy dispute ever, drew me away from the national policy focus of my previous work and toward grassroots activism in Minnesota. It turned out to be an invaluable introduction to progressive-populist politics.

I came to that dispute via an unlikely route. It began when I received a research fellowship to spend the 1975–76 academic year at two bastions of establishment thinking and Washington orientation, Harvard University and the Brookings Institution. At Harvard, political scientist Anne Cahn and I led a seminar entitled "Scientists, Government, Politics—Entangled Webs" in the Kennedy School of Government's Institute of Politics. Every week we invited guest speakers to lead the discussion. One of our speakers was Arthur Kantrowitz, a well-known physicist who had been appointed to President Gerald Ford's science advisory committee and who, in that capacity, was promoting an idea, the use of "science courts" to mediate technology policy disputes.

Kantrowitz described the concept to our seminar. First, the court would identify the significant questions of science and technology associated with a controversial public policy issue. Second, a panel of impartial scientist-judges would preside over an adversary proceeding in which scientific experts would testify and scientist advocates would cross-examine them. Third, the judges would issue their decision on the scientific facts pertaining to the disputed technical questions. I was quite skeptical about the idea on several fundamental grounds and published an article in the journal *Science* explaining my reservations.[3] When Jimmy Carter became president in 1977, the White House task force that Kantrowitz headed was dissolved, and the President's Science Advisory Committee never undertook a science court experiment.

But when I returned home the next year, Minnesota was embroiled in the controversial construction of a 430-mile high voltage powerline that drew thousands of Minnesota farmers, two electric utilities, and a governor into a protracted, explosive confrontation. Public sentiment was with the farmers, who were resisting construction of the line, and Governor Rudy Perpich, finding himself uncomfortably in the middle, proposed organizing a science court to mediate the dispute.

In many ways, this was a cutting-edge struggle between continuing the traditional energy policy approach of building more and more fossil fuel and nuclear power plants to meet electricity demand and a new "sustainable energy" approach that gained currency in the 1970s. Paul was the person who got me involved. He and one of his students, Monte Tarbox, had been out to meet with the farmers to offer their support. What made this confrontation so intriguing and important was that it was the first major test of several new Minnesota environmental laws that had been passed in the mid-1970s, including a "certificate of need" process to decide whether a proposed energy project was really necessary and, if so, to establish a siting process to minimize adverse environmental impacts. In the case of the powerline, these processes had revealed quite clearly cozy relationships between the power companies and the state energy planners and environmental regulators.

Some health and safety questions had been raised about the powerline that a science court could consider, but those had not been the main reasons for the farmers' opposition. More than anything else, they objected to the taking of their land without their consent for a project they were convinced was not needed by a process that they viewed as rigged against them. That the process was rigged was soon confirmed. When farmers participating in the hearings to site the line convinced the authorities in one county to refuse the necessary permits, the siting procedure was abruptly changed and the state Environmental Quality Board assumed authority.

When the governor surprised the farmers with the science court proposal, they were not sure what to make of it. One morning Paul called from western Minnesota, asking if I would come out and talk with the farmers about how to respond to the governor. I anticipated a small meeting at the farm of the protest leaders, John and Alice Tripp, but instead we drove to a fire station in the town of Lowry, which had become the center of the protest. Instead of a small group, there were several hundred farmers in the auditorium waiting to hear about the science court.

I explained that the science court had never been tried; with no precedent as a guide, the participants could feel free to negotiate the scope and terms of the proceeding. The farmers wanted no part of a science court restricted to health and safety questions; that would have been an all too *fitting* climax to a chain of statutory and procedural restrictions that had channeled them away from their basic concerns about the powerline. They decided to tell the governor that they would participate in a science court only if its scope were broadened to reopen such questions as whether the project was needed and whether the process had been stacked against them from the start.

Noting that this was really a political issue, the farmers demanded that an accountable public official make the judgment; they demanded that the governor not delegate his responsibility to "experts" and proposed instead that he himself be the judge. When they told this to the governor the next morning, he was taken aback; after two weeks of thinking about what to do, he announced he was no longer interested. That was the end of what would have been the nation's first experiment with a "science court."[4]

But it was by no means the end of our relationship with the farmers. Paul and I kept in close touch with them as the struggle continued, occasionally offering advice. In the summer of 1978, Alice Tripp decided to run against Governor Perpich in the Democratic-Farmer-Labor (DFL) primary to seek public support for the farmers' position and to call attention to the cozy connection between the state agencies and the power companies. She wanted Paul or me to be her running mate. When Paul demurred, I found myself running for lieutenant governor of Minnesota.

That race turned out to be a remarkably rewarding and pleasurable experience. To dramatize our commitment to a sustainable energy future, we swept the state in an old pickup truck powered by gasohol, with a loudspeaker powered by solar cells. Outgoing, articulate, blunt-spoken Alice had great rapport with people and the press. Our campaign treasurer and balladeer, Patty Kakac, a young farmwoman with a beautiful voice, provided crowd-pleasing musical accompaniment. And I tagged along in the background, developing campaign themes, writing press releases, and so forth. In the end we lost decisively, though we got 20 percent of the statewide Democratic primary vote.

In trying to capture the essence of the farmers' outrage about the close relationship they had discovered between the state agencies and the power companies and to generalize that message to include other important issues, I rediscovered the populism that had spread like wildfire across the midwestern prairies in the late nineteenth century. Our basic campaign theme was captured in the questions, "Who Benefits? Who Sacrifices? Who Decides?" Only much later would I learn that an issue that was at the center of the agrarian populist revolt of the 1880s and 1890s, fiat currency versus

VC LIBRARY

gold-based currency, had been subjected to the same analysis by the farmers of that day. Expansion of the money supply by government fiat would have resulted in inflation and helped agrarian debtors; a fixed money supply tied to gold would have served the interest of bankers, financiers, and other creditors. The struggle then, as in modern times, basically was not a matter subject to resolution by technical analyses, though such analyses are relevant. Rather, the struggle had everything to do with the de facto accountability of a supposedly democratic government to wealthy elites, rather than to ordinary people. Such a populist perspective, it seemed to me, was just as apt today.

Throughout the 1980s Paul and I collaborated on a series of projects, as I was drawn to issues with a Minnesota focus and he became increasingly interested in running for high public office. In 1982 he ran a populist campaign for state auditor, the only position open on the DFL ticket. Paul is a very competitive person, and I kidded that he was running for auditor because I had run for lieutenant governor. He responded that mine had been merely a symbolic "protest candidacy"; his was going to be a "serious" effort, aimed at winning. No doubt he was a much better politician. His skill as an orator and his love of talking to people and learning from them suited beautifully the enterprise of running for public office. In the beginning, few took him seriously, but soon his impassioned and energizing speeches were capturing the imagination of county party conventions around the state. He swept to the DFL nomination and made a surprisingly strong showing, even though he lost to the most popular candidate on the Republican ticket, the incumbent auditor, later the governor, Arne Carlson.

In the process Paul became renowned as Minnesota's most powerful stump speaker since Humbert Humphrey, honing this talent by studying the speeches and writings of two great political orators of the past, Martin Luther King Jr. and Eugene V. Debs. We both knew he would run for political office again. The next Christmas he gave me a book he had just read, a volume in Robert Caro's biography of Lyndon Johnson, *The Path to Power*. The inscription reads, "To Mike, I've learned all the lessons about the path to power and I'm ready to go!"

During the 1980s Paul and I made complementary, mutually supportive contributions to several Minnesota policy issues. In a fall 1982 project, seven students and I designated ourselves the "Energy Policy Planning Task Force for the Next Governor," and early the next year we presented our ideas, first to a special hearing of the state Senate Energy Committee and later in a lengthy meeting with Governor Perpich in his office. Perpich was especially taken with one proposal. That fall he named Paul his special assistant to direct what in his hands became the highly successful Governor's Community Energy Program, as he traveled the state to initiate energy conservation efforts in dozens of Minnesota towns. During its period of maximum political impact in 1983–84, Paul was on the board of the Minnesota Nuclear Weapons Freeze Campaign, and at his prodding I became its executive director. From 1985 to 1988, the height of the Midwest's farm financial crisis, Paul was an influential figure in the policy debate on several levels: he was a leading strategist in Groundswell, the statewide farmers movement that sparked protest activity against farm foreclosures; he helped organize a massive demonstration of farmers at the state capital; and he and I promoted a moratorium on farm foreclosures that nearly passed the legislature. Through Paul's connections, a farm-debt restructuring proposal my students and I had developed, the Fair Credit Plan, gained the support of the National Farmers Fair Credit Campaign and became an important part of the congressional debate in Washington.

At the same time Paul was active in Democratic party politics. From 1984 to 1990 he served on the Democratic National Committee. In 1986 he founded the "Minnesota 33% Campaign"; with help from his old friends Frances Fox Piven and Richard Cloward, well-known scholars of poverty and welfare in America, he provided key research, testimony, and leadership in prompting the Minnesota legislature to pass the nation's most progressive voter registration law, including election day registration and "motor-voter" registration with drivers' license renewals. In 1988 Paul became a prominent figure in Minnesota presidential politics, co-chairing the state's Jesse Jackson campaign. Jackson did very well in the Minnesota caucuses, and Paul made a name for himself as a conciliatory force in a divisive Middle East policy debate at the state DFL convention and in the Minnesota delegation at the Democratic national convention. Later Paul cochaired the Minnesota Dukakis campaign, where he was an important influence in bringing divided elements of the state DFL party back together for the November election and helping Dukakis to carry the state.

Money in Politics

All this set the stage for Paul Wellstone's run for the Senate against the popular incumbent, Rudy Boschwitz. I will not describe here how Paul surprised everyone, first by gaining the DFL party endorsement by out-organizing his better known opponents; then defying the polls and winning the DFL primary in ironic fashion by cultivating a "feel-good" image built around an old school bus he traveled in and amusing television spots projecting that image; and finally by coming from far behind in the last few days to win a very close election despite Boschwitz's enormous financial advantage. Paul's populist message matched the mood of the electorate and his grassroots organizing paid off. At the last minute a scandal involving the Republican gubernatorial candidate created turmoil, and a desperate Boschwitz mailing backfired. Two Minnesota reporters Dennis McGrath and Dane Smith, have written an excellent book chronicling that exciting year and a half, *Professor Wellstone Goes to Washington: The Inside Story of a Grassroots U.S. Senate Campaign.*[5]

One aspect of the campaign became my particular interest, laying the groundwork for an issue we would address when we got to Washington: the often decisive and fundamentally undemocratic role of money in American politics today. Paul's campaign had barely begun when the barring of "strangers" from running for public office was brought home to me. A few weeks after Paul announced his candidacy, he and his wife, Sheila, took a brief break from the campaign and rented a cabin on Madeline Island, in Lake Superior off the coast of Wisconsin. For the last couple of days, Nancy and I drove up to join them. Very early the next morning Paul handed me a magazine article he had just read by Ed Garvey about his 1986 experience running for the Senate in Wisconsin against the Republican incumbent.[6]

At the beginning, people kept telling Garvey they liked him and his issue positions, but it was too early to give him money. When he finally won the Democratic primary, however, they told him it was too late. He got some contributions, but not nearly enough to counter the blitz of television spots his incumbent opponent could afford. As I finished reading the article, Paul and I looked at each other and smiled sheepishly. We both sensed that Paul was very likely to have exactly the same experience—even if he did everything right.

That is precisely what happened. Paul learned immediately that he had to become preoccupied with fund-raising. To get the campaign off the ground and keep it going, he had to spend several hours a day on the phone calling rich people he didn't know and asking them for money. In many campaigns, the most important function of the candidate is to solicit large chunks of cash from fat cats and political action committees. When Paul's campaign manager, Jeff Blodgett, returned from a Washington seminar on directing a campaign, he reported having learned that *his* most important function was to make sure Paul made those calls.

During the summer of 1989, I did some informal probing for money in Washington at the Democratic Senatorial Campaign Committee and among a few friends who were funders and fund-raisers. I knew most of those I spoke with shared Paul's politics; I naively assumed that they would be excited to know someone like him was running and eager to help his campaign get started.

Not at all. What surprised me most was the lack of interest even among these people in why Paul was running and what he stood for. Instead, the immediate question in almost every conversation was "Can he win?" You might say that is surely a legitimate primary concern for any potential financial backer. Is this guy a serious candidate, with a plausible prospect of winning? But what became abundantly clear from the conversations was that the question, "Can he win?" meant something much more specific. It had a simple, direct translation: "Can he raise the millions of dollars necessary to win a Senate seat?" If the answer to that question was demonstrably yes, they would take him seriously.

Of course at that early stage, when the campaign needed money the most, the answer was not demonstrably yes. Generally speaking, at that stage the candidates for whom the answer is convincingly yes are either incumbents or millionaires.

And it was not just early on that money was the overriding question. A year later, after Paul had won the DFL endorsement at the state convention in June 1990, we went to the Washington office of a well-known liberal campaign funding group that I had supported for many years. Besides the group's giving money itself, its enthusiastic endorsement in a mailing to members can result in a contribution of tens of thousands of dollars. It would be hard to imagine a candidate more admirable than Paul in terms of the issues the organization and its supporters cared about, and Paul did a superb job laying out his case to the director. I could scarcely contain myself when I realized from the skeptical questions about Paul's prospects of winning that he wasn't going to get the time of day, much less tens of thousands of dollars.

From Paul's experience, I became sensitized to how big-money donors—wealthy individuals and special interest PACs, especially lobbying coalitions that can package large bundles of individual and PAC contributions—have become gatekeepers of our politics, in effect determining who gets to run for high public office and who does not. John Bonifaz and Jamie Raskin, legal experts on the subject of campaign finance reform, have developed an apt analogy; they call it the "wealth primary."[7]

From the beginning, it seemed that Paul's Republican opponent, Rudy Boschwitz, would have two enormous advantages over any Democratic challenger: his name recognition and popularity as an incumbent senator and his fund-raising prowess as the outgoing chair of the national Republican Senatorial Campaign Committee. Especially imposing was the financial challenge. In the first six months of 1989, with a year and a half still to go, Boschwitz had already raised nearly two and a half million dollars. The conventional wisdom was that he would amass ten million dollars or so by election day. That money would be used to buy an avalanche of television ads to bury Paul at the end of the campaign. I felt that a central objective of the Wellstone campaign strategy should be to turn those two Boschwitz advantages, incumbency and money, on their head—to make them liabilities by election day. A few Minnesota friends and I set out to do just that.

One way to turn Boschwitz's incumbency and money into liabilities would be to hammer away at the theme that incumbents in Washington had lost touch with the constituents to whom they are supposed to be accountable; that instead, on many issues they had become much more responsive to special interest lobbying coalitions, their "cash constituents," on whom they depend for reelection money. So we launched a study of where Rudy Boschwitz got his millions of dollars in campaign contributions. He often talked about the money coming from what he called "Skinny Cats," individual contributors who gave less than one hundred dollars. But first with laborious hand tabulations by two Carleton students, Gina Campbell and Leah Langworthy, and later with Paul's good friend Marilyn Schuster doing data entry and statistician Loren Haskins supervising the computer programming, we found there was much more to the story. In the process, I became familiar with the Federal Election Commission data bases and the campaign finance literature. The more I learned, the more disturbed I became about how our election campaigns are funded.

The first thing that jumped out of the Boschwitz data was that most of his early contributors were anything but Skinny Cats. In fact, the bulk of his early money came from a surprisingly few individual donors and corporate PACs. What was particularly striking was how much came from individuals who had given one thousand dollars or more, whom we dubbed "Very Fat Cats." Of the $2.4 million dollars Boschwitz had raised from January to June 1989, nearly a million dollars had come from 756 Very Fat Cats and the next largest sum, over half a million dollars, came from 256 political action committees. Less than 10 percent came from Skinny Cats and about

62 percent came from that remarkably small number of Very Fat Cats and PACs. Also noteworthy was that 86 percent of those Very Fat Cats and 92 percent of the PACs were from outside Minnesota.

Reading though the FEC lists day after day brought me vicariously to places I had never been. It was like traveling around the country with Rudy Boschwitz and looking on as millionaires showered him with money. For the last week in March 1989, for instance, he went to Florida for a series of fundraisers where 121 wealthy Floridians wrote out one thousand–dollar checks so that he would be reelected senator from Minnesota. In that six-month period a year and a half before the election, Boschwitz picked up more money from his fat cat and PAC friends than Paul would raise during his entire campaign.

The contrast between this and Paul's continually scraping for a few bucks and having doors closed in his face was stark. Especially for challengers, it is humiliating to have to call wealthy strangers on the phone and, in effect, beg for money. The DFL candidate for the Senate in 1988, Hubert H. (Skip) Humphrey III, had told me during his campaign that he absolutely hated that part of running for office.

Incumbents and challengers alike spend far too much time foraging for money. Many incumbent senators report that during the last two years before their election, they are preoccupied with fund-raising. That was certainly true of Rudy Boschwitz in 1989–90. In the summer of 1990, Senate Majority Leader George Mitchell felt compelled to complain that so many senators were spending so much time raising money that it was interfering seriously with the work of the Senate. It is even worse for House incumbents, who are *always* in the last two years before reelection. In the course of the study, I began to feel strongly that the system we now use to finance campaigns with private contributions must be changed fundamentally. The advantage it gives to incumbents and the way it pulls them away from their work are two significant problems, but there are other important ways it undermines our representative democracy.

I can illustrate the problems with Rudy Boschwitz as an example. The first problem was the emergence of a shadow Boschwitz constituency. A few hundred individuals and PACs, mostly non-Minnesotans, had a special relationship with our senator, who was supposed to be accountable to us. In 1985 Boschwitz achieved a certain notoriety when a *Wall Street Journal* story pointed out that he was telling potential donors they would receive ten blue stamps to ensure preferential access to him if they would promise to contribute one thousand dollars to his 1990 reelection campaign. And, of course, there is always the suspicion that what campaign contributions buy goes beyond just "access."

Second, it was supposed to be a Minnesotans' election, but outside money had poured in to influence how we voted. I realized that the interest of most of the donors in supporting Boschwitz went beyond access and special favors. They were confident that he would be "their kind of senator," someone they would like to see in the Senate because of his views on issues they cared about.

Third were the important, possibly decisive, ways the outside money would be used to influence our election. In large measure, it be would be used to buy television ads. What many Minnesotans would remember most about Rudy Boschwitz when it came time to vote would be the pleasing, memorable myths they saw in his television spots. With compelling images and stirring music, he appeared as a protector of the environment and a supporter of children. This bore little relation to his voting record in the Senate, where the year before the election the League of Conservation Voters had given him a 40 percent rating and the Children's Defense Fund had given him a zero.

For representative democracy to function, a key requirement is accountability of the representative to his or her constituents. We now have a system in which money buys strong accountability links to nonconstituents, while that same money is used for misleading television ads to seriously weaken the election-based accountability to constituents.

We wrote up an extensive report of our findings, "Where Rudy Boschwitz Got His Crucial Early Money," which Paul released at a press conference at the State Capitol in St. Paul.[8] The initial media coverage was quite disappointing, however; a major competing political story happened to break at the same time, so only a few reporters showed up. And their attitude seemed to be "so what?" as typified by one reporter's question to Paul: "What's wrong with Boschwitz going to Florida and New York and California for most of his money? That's where most of the money *is!*"

We had better luck in another quarter. I personally delivered copies of the report to the editorial page editors of the two major Twin Cities newspapers and briefed them about it. In a small way, this careful study may have helped to lend credibility to the campaign among some people whose endorsement would later be very important to Paul.

It also planted a seed that blossomed a year later. Less than a week before the election, the *Minneapolis Star Tribune,* Minnesota's widest circulation newspaper, decided to run an op-ed piece detailing the findings of our study. Headlined "To Wealthy Out-of-Staters, Boschwitz Fits Bill," it was prominently displayed alongside a cartoon depicting Rudy Boschwitz wearing clothes that were a montage of money.[9] In the concluding sentence, I vented my unhappiness with the senator and the system: "Boschwitz' fund-raising preoccupation and prowess epitomize a serious problem with American politics today, where too often the measure of a senator is the money he can raise and getting reelected is his highest purpose." The 1992 *Almanac of American Politics,* which gives a history of every senator's career attests that this arduous effort did eventually pay off. In the Wellstone biography, it notes, "Wellstone turned Boschwitz's financial advantage into a disadvantage. . . . He had raised huge sums of money from PACs and political insiders, and now found it a liability."[10]

A Sobering Message

In mid-December 1990, I sat in on a Washington meeting between Paul and Ralph Nader and some of his associates, including Joan Claybrook, president of the Nader organization Public Citizen, a principal backer of the Canadian-style national health insurance program known as "single-payer." After hearing Paul out, Claybrook said she was impressed with what he had to say, but cautioned that she'd heard it plenty of times before; there had been other senators who had come in planning to be different and shake the place up, but somehow they never ended up doing so. At that point Nader added: "They all say 'I don't have time to think.'"

I found Claybrook's remark sobering, though I thought to myself there couldn't have been many senators with a community organizing background like Paul's. What I didn't begin to appreciate until later was that it is not only the senators who are tamed by the Washington insider culture; the same kind of acculturation can affect leaders of Washington-based public interest groups as well.

Of course, Paul was about to become a U.S. senator and in most respects his mode of operation would necessarily change. But I was committed in one major way to helping him use his office to be a different kind of senator. What I could encourage was a continuation in the Senate of how we had worked together in Minnesota for many years: anticipating important policy opportunities, working with citizen groups to develop policy initiatives, and helping to expand the grassroots constituency by assisting local organizing in support of policy initiatives. Paul could use his position as senator to be an agent of change, a leader of grassroots movements nationwide on behalf of initiatives for economic justice, environmental protection, and representative democracy.

I was struck by Nader's comment that previous would-be agents of change lamented that they didn't have time to think. I already knew from encounters with the Senate that senators often dash around frantically and that their staffers are also overwhelmed with too many responsibilities. With time to think, I could help to develop a program of timely legislative initiatives and associated organizing strategies. With foresight, Paul, despite his lack of seniority, could make a significant impact at the very outset of his Senate career.

It was clear what some of the important targets of opportunity would be: campaign finance reform was already prominent on the agenda of the 102nd Congress; during his campaign, Paul had pledged to pursue the single-payer approach to health care reform; and we were about to discover that an enormous battle was shaping up in an arena in which both Paul and I had significant experience.

THE SENATE ENERGY WAR

Into the Realm of
a Legislative Lord

3

A Fateful Call

The day after Paul's election my phone nearly rang off the hook, with friends wanting to share their elation. One of the callers was Ben Cooper, a physicist with some intriguing news. A few months before, Ben had been named staff director of the Senate Energy Committee, probably the most powerful staff position on energy policy in the Congress. He was very pleased Paul had won and hoped he would consider joining the committee. He wanted us to know that soon after the next Congress began, the Energy Committee was going to take up historic national energy legislation that would shape America's energy future. He urged me to come to Washington with Paul and assured me that if I did, I would be in for a very interesting time.

In the early 1970s, a committee I chaired had proposed that the American Physical Society (APS), the professional society of physicists, join with the American Association for the Advancement of Science in launching a Congressional Science Fellowship Program to send scientists to work for a year in Senate or House offices. At the time there were very few congressional staffers with any training in science or engineering and only two with doctoral degrees. Beginning with five fellows from those two professional societies in 1973, the program has flourished over the years, with twenty-eight science and engineering societies sponsoring fellows by 1998. During those twenty-five years, a total of 669 scientists and engineers served as fellows.

Ben Cooper was one of the two APS fellows chosen that first year. Eager to get the program off to a good start and hearing excellent things about him, I had driven down to Iowa State University to encourage Ben to apply and, as a member of the selection committee, I had vigorously advocated his selection.

Since 1973 was the year of the Arab oil embargo, energy policy was a very hot issue and Ben, like so many of the early fellows, was drawn to work on energy policy. A prime place for that in the Congress was the Senate Interior Committee, chaired by Henry ("Scoop") Jackson from Washington state. Ben became a part of the core group of Jackson staffers, led by the committee's chief counsel, Bill Van Ness, which was the hub of energy policy initiatives in the Senate in those exciting times. That same year, a very capable, politically astute young freshman senator from Louisiana, J. Bennett Johnston, also joined the committee and soon became Jackson's protégé. When Paul took office a little over seventeen years later, Senator Johnston was the powerful chair of the renamed Energy and Natural Resources Committee, Ben Cooper was its new staff director, and Bill Van Ness and his law firm were leading the lobbying efforts for many of the most controversial features of the chairman's comprehensive energy policy bill.

In the 1970s, the environmental movement had blossomed and some of the most important environmental protection issues related to energy policies were developed. A series of studies in that decade laid the foundations for a "sustainable" energy policy paradigm, emphasizing investments in renewable energy sources and in increasing the efficiency of energy-using devices. By the end of the decade, this vision of America's energy future had begun to draw serious support away from the dominant post–World War II energy paradigm which emphasized long-term reliance on nuclear power and fossil fuels. Physicists made significant contributions to the development of that new paradigm and to its practical implementation. A 1974 summer study on the physics of efficient energy use at Princeton University which I helped to organize produced insights into where the greatest gains in energy efficiency were likely to be realized and helped to create a critical mass of innovative physicist-practitioners.

I spent the summer of 1976 based at the Brookings Institution in Washington, interviewing dozens of the scientist-fellows and writing about their experiences on the Hill.[1] That was remarkable preparation for my own work in the Senate fifteen years later. For instance, two early fellows with the Senate Commerce Committee, Allan Hoffman, a physicist, and Barry Hyman, a mechanical engineer, had been responsible for what was the most effective and far-reaching energy policy initiative of the 1970s. Cars and trucks were the major users of the energy source of greatest concern, petroleum, and they were not using it at all efficiently. The average fuel economy of new automobiles sold in America in 1975 was less than 14 miles per gallon.

Hoffman and Hyman drafted the principal response to this problem, a Corporate Average Fuel Economy (CAFE) standard. Beginning in 1976, each major automobile manufacturer would be required to increase the average fuel economy of the cars it sold to 27.5 miles per gallon over the next ten years. The auto manufacturers strongly opposed the measure, arguing that such increases in gas mileage could not be accomplished except by building much smaller, unsafe cars that could not satisfy the Clean Air Act auto emission standards. With his technical competence, Hoffman was able to determine that this was not the case. With technologies like the catalytic converter to reduce polluting emissions, auto fuel economy was not directly coupled to emission control. The CAFE standard could be met without sacrifice in safety or emissions reduction.

The fruit of Hoffman's and Hyman's labors, the Auto Fuel Economy and Research and Development Act of 1975, which passed the Senate in July 1975, was the basis for mandatory standards that resulted in far greater savings of oil than any other measure the Congress passed. By 1986, every one of the major manufacturers had reached the 27.5 mpg standard, halving the oil consumption per mile traveled of the cars on the American road.

One other early physicist-fellow deserves special mention as background to this story. Henry Kelly had used his fellowship in 1974 to join the staff of a newly created arm of the Congress, the Office of Technology Assessment (OTA). I had first met Kelly years before, when I was doing my Ph.D. work at Cornell University and he was a student in my freshman physics lab. We renewed our acquaintance around the time he began working at OTA and soon became good friends. As a technology policy analyst, Kelly has few peers. A succession of OTA directors came to recognize the power of his intellect and the insights of his studies. When the director of OTA, Jack Gibbons, was appointed Presidential Science Advisor in 1993, it was no surprise that he asked Kelly to come with him to the White House.

When the Department of Energy's Solar Energy Research Institute (SERI) began operating in 1978, Kelly was tapped by its director, Denis Hayes, to be his associate director and the technical leader of the operation. While at SERI, Kelly led what is widely regarded as the preeminent technical study in the 1970s of the potential of energy efficiency and renewable energy sources in the United States. Entitled *Building a Sustainable Future* and finally published in 1981, it is commonly known simply as the "SERI Report."[2] That study involved many of the most prominent physicists active in energy policy and charted the new sustainable energy paradigm in compelling detail. It showed very clearly that in many instances, saving energy was substantially less expensive than generating it. From that follows the revolutionary insight that throughout our nation's energy systems, the most cost-effective investments were in "saved energy" via more efficient energy-using devices, such as higher gas mileage cars and more efficient furnaces, refrigerators, air conditioners, and light bulbs. Every barrel of oil, cubic foot of natural gas, or kilowatt-hour of electricity saved would be available for other tasks. It just costs less to produce them through energy efficiency investments than it does via conventional energy supply investments.

Kelly illustrated this new paradigm succinctly in the executive summary of the SERI Report: "One would not commonly think of an investment in building insulation as an alternative to an investment in an oil well, but the two kinds of investments have precisely the same outcome. For example, the equivalent of about 8.1 million barrels of oil per day (MBD) can be "produced" from existing buildings and new residential and commercial buildings at an average cost that is about half the cost of providing electricity, oil and/or gas to these buildings from new conventional sources" (1:18).

The project task leader, whom Kelly recruited to administer the SERI study, was a politically sophisticated young man named Karl Gawell. Kelly and Gawell would later become two of my closest allies in the war in the Senate over a National Energy Strategy in 1991. In an ironic twist, Ben Cooper and his boss, Bennett Johnson, turned out to be our chief adversaries, as freshman Sen. Paul Wellstone and his staff were among the ones who threw sand in their gears and led the fight to derail their bill.

Joining the Energy Committee

For Paul, one of his two major committee preferences was obvious. The Labor and Human Resources Committee had jurisdiction over many issues about which he cared the most and was quite knowledgeable, such as education, health care, and welfare reform. The other choice was much less clear. One possibility was the Energy Committee, a choice that had some very positive features but some quite negative ones as well.

The chief attraction, of course, was the prospect of being at the center of a struggle to shape our nation's energy future. Decades of federal government policies had been instrumental in leading America down the "hard path," featuring fossil fuels and increasing reliance on nuclear power. By 1991 public disaffection with that approach and support of the "soft path" of sustainable energy had created the political conditions for a monumental fight in the U.S. Senate. Another attraction was that Paul and I had considerable background on these issues. The Minnesota powerline fight that we had chronicled was in important measure a struggle over which energy path to follow. And the program Paul had led in 1983–84, the Minnesota Governor's Community Energy Program, was a model of how a state could promote effective involvement of its citizens in seeking sustainable energy solutions.

But there were major drawbacks as well. In contrast to Paul's other primary committee assignment on Labor and Human Resources, the Energy Committee was not likely to be a friendly place. It had a long history of domination by senators from energy-producing states, who joined to protect and enhance their energy supply industries and public lands projects back home.

Another reason the Energy Committee was not likely to be friendly to a "soft-path" advocate was the "cozy triangle" phenomenon. On many issues, there tends to be built up over time a sympathetic, supportive relationship between the congressional committees, the executive agencies they oversee, and the corporations with whose interests they deal. Identifying these is a good first step to understanding the locus of power in Washington. Within these cozy three-cornered symbiotic relationships, the congressional committees, and especially their powerful chairs, occupy very influential positions. Normally the Congress goes along with what the committees decide so their members, particularly the chairs and their committee staffs, are like bright flames attracting the ardent attention of federal agency and corporate lobbying moths.

Nowhere has the cozy triangle phenomenon been more evident than in the post–World War II history of federal energy research and development. National energy research and development priorities were dominated by the influence of an alliance of the Atomic Energy Commission (AEC) and its national laboratories, the nuclear reactor industry, and, at the top of the triangle, Congress's Joint Committee on Atomic Energy (JCAE). For nearly twenty-five years after the war, two-thirds or more of the government's energy R&D spending had been directed to nuclear fission reactors and, adding nuclear fusion research, about three-quarters of all government energy R&D spending was for nuclear technologies under the aegis of the JCAE and the AEC.[3]

The cozy triangle concept informed my thinking about the Senate Energy and Natural Resources Committee when that committee was formally created in 1977 as part of a comprehensive reorganization of congressional committee jurisdictions. The regulatory part of the old Atomic Energy Commission had been separated off as the Nuclear Regulatory Commission, and the Carter administration was on the verge of consolidating all energy R&D in one agency, the (new) Department of Energy. In the Senate, a new committee with jurisdiction over all energy issues was being proposed.

I worried that those who supported this seemingly rational idea might not get what they bargained for. In a short article, I warned of dangerous unintended consequences of creating "super energy committees" in the Senate and House for the long-term politics of energy:

> On paper, consolidating energy research and development jurisdictions looks eminently sensible; it seems to bring order out of congressional chaos, at last permitting Congress to deal with energy in a unified, coherent way. But what looks sensible on an organization chart may not be wise in terms of its practical impact on the disposition of political power. . . .
>
> As Congress prepares to reform the way it deals with energy, it should not ignore this central lesson of the Joint Committee experience. In the absence of a national consensus on what energy policies to pursue, an appropriate objective for Congress is to promote public debate of alternative energy strategies and provide effective access to a broad spectrum of advocates and interests. It will be ironic if one reform necessary for achieving this objective, abolishing the Joint Committee or stripping it of its legislative authority, is coupled to the creation of super energy committees. If history is any guide, before long they will be in bed with Jimmy Carter's new energy agency and the big energy companies; it will be the joint committee-AEC-nuclear industry alliance all over again, but on a grander scale.[4]

Little did I realize that fourteen years later I would find myself supporting an environmentalist challenge to sweeping changes in national energy policies proposed by the chair of the Senate's "super energy committee" and struggling against the immense power of the grand alliances I had warned against.

But the biggest minus for Paul as he contemplated joining the Energy Committee was surely the chairman. When I called around to staffers who knew the scene, I was told that serving on that committee would be a real challenge. Not only was Bennett Johnston unsympathetic to our view of a desirable energy future, but as I wrote in a memo to Paul, "He rules the committee with an iron fist. . . . I am told [Ohio Sen. Howard] Metzenbaum tried to be an independent voice on the committee, but eventually left in frustration."

That was definitely a mixed review. A very important debate was about to begin. The visibility of the issue would be very high. The environmental groups were gearing up. I would likely be able to arrange for strong technical support from working groups in Washington and Minnesota. But promoting policies to support a sustainable energy transition from Bennett Johnston's committee was not going to be easy.

Welcomed to the Senate

One thing I had difficulty anticipating was the kind of reception Paul, the ultimate "stranger," would receive from his colleagues. Entering the Senate is like moving into a *very* small community, where you have to live for at least six years. In my 1970s interviews with the scientist-fellows, the thing that had disturbed me the most were tales of the rapid socialization of staffers by their offices, even when that meant significant shifts in policy preferences. If you were to be taken seriously in the Senate, you had to understand the prevailing notion of what was "realistic" and adapt to your immediate political environment. I was told that in some cases quite striking changes in outlook were evident in a matter of months. I knew that Paul would face powerful socialization pressures too. Some would pull him away from using his office to become a national leader in grassroots struggles for economic and social justice and political democracy. As we prepared to go to Washington, resisting those pressures was a central element of my vision and my hope.

But that vision was clearly in serious tension with some basic mores of the place to which we were headed. The U.S. Senate is populated by individuals who tend to put reelection above other principles or purposes, to the point that if Senator A tells Senator B that a certain vote or action, no matter how noble or important, might adversely affect A's reelection chances, that is all that needs to be said. A bedrock principle of the place is reelection above all else. A corollary to that principle is that incumbents tend not to do anything directly that might adversely affect the reelection prospects of their colleagues. In order for us to compete with the entrenched Washington interests, we would have to work with groups organizing in the states of other senators, sometimes in opposition to the senators' positions and in ways that might hurt their reelection chances. Paul surely would encounter pressures that would strongly discourage such activity—pressures that turned out to be very difficult to resist.

A socializing source of especially great concern was the media. Before he ever got to Washington, many Minnesotans, including his supporters, worried publicly that the biggest question mark about Paul Wellstone was whether or not he could be "effective" in the Senate. According to the conventional wisdom, this would depend on his ability to get along with his colleagues in a body where personal relationships, willingness to compromise, and patterns of reciprocal favors are crucial. Fear of being labeled "ineffective" and marginalized by the media was no small matter to any freshman senator. It could adversely affect his ability to be a respected and influential political leader.

A second important source of socialization pressure was Paul's "community" in the Senate, the Democratic Caucus, headed by Majority Leader George Mitchell. My hunch was that Mitchell would approach Paul warily, waiting to find out if this "stranger" was willing to play the game. That's an indication of how little I knew about how Washington deals with would-be agents of change. Instead of keeping Paul at arms' length until he passed some tests of good behavior, the majority leader reached out and embraced him as his welcomer, friend, and benefactor. Mitchell would prove to be a significant constraining influence on Paul during his early years in the Senate.

It was clear that Mitchell was extremely nervous about a serious problem looming, the possibility that the Democrats might lose control of the Senate in the 1992 election. Although they held a substantial 56–44 Senate majority in the 102nd Congress, there was good reason for the Democrats to be concerned. They had regained control of the Senate in the 1986 election when eleven new Democratic senators had won. Those eleven were up for reelection in 1992 and that first reelection race is typically the time of maximum vulnerability for an incumbent. Add to that the many signs already apparent in 1991 of a strong anti-incumbent mood in the electorate, and George Mitchell had good reason to be worried.

One thing is certain: It is much more rewarding to be a senator if your party is in control. All the committee and subcommittee chairmanships go to members of the majority, while the minority party, generally speaking, plays only a secondary, reactive role in the Congress. I remember vividly a scene in the immediate aftermath of the November 1980 election, the previous time the Democrats had lost their long-time control of the Senate. From time to time over the years, I would stop by the Senate to see Ben Cooper when I was in Washington. In December 1980 the office was dim and the mood somber. Ben and another senior staffer had an enormous trash bin in the middle of their office and they were sorting through the volumes of reports on their bookshelves and throwing many away. Now that they were in the minority, they were being moved out of their relatively spacious office into much smaller and less desirable quarters. And it was not just the office they were losing. As minority staff, they would soon be at the mercy of the

Republican majority staffers who would assume control of the committee. Ben's plaintive comment to his colleague at that moment stuck in my mind: "I sure hope they don't treat us like we treated them," he said.

Not all of the important socializing pressures constraining Senator Wellstone's behavior came from outside his office. Beginning the day he was elected, I worried that any senator with too much of an eye on reelection would have difficulty taking the risks that would come with the leadership-for-change role I hoped Paul would take on. Soon after his 1990 election, I suggested a way of thinking about his tenure in office that I intuitively felt was crucial to his ability to resist the pressures and fulfill his promise to be a different kind of senator. It was fine for him to plan on running for a second term and to announce that intention publicly. But in his day-to-day decisions about what he should or should not do, he should think of himself as a one-term senator. Only in that way could he insulate himself from the overly cautious and often perverse reelection calculations that insinuate themselves into the decisions that most senators make every day.

A senator's staff tends to reinforce the senator's own reelection imperative. A senator is more than just an individual; he or she is the center of an institution with forty or more very talented and often ambitious employees in Washington and back home. Their future rides on the success, especially the reelection success, of their senator, and the reelection concern tends to breed caution in their behavior. Since key staffers have a great deal of influence, built into the office is an aversion to the courage, risk-taking, and boat-rocking that is necessary for a senator to assume leadership of movements for change.

Perhaps because I was not planning to stay for long, I may have been more immune to those aversions and anxious to help Paul establish himself as a risk-taking, boat-rocking leader of such movements. Naturally, I went looking for allies. In late January, my Carleton colleague, political scientist Norm Vig, who would take my place as Paul's policy advisor that fall, had come to Washington to begin to get acquainted with the issues the Energy Committee would take up. We went first to the office of what we thought would be our most likely ally on the committee, Sen. Tim Wirth of Colorado, and met with one of his energy aides.

We began by explaining our backgrounds in energy and environmental policy and acknowledging that Senator Wirth was a leader in the Senate on energy efficiency and renewables. Our purpose, we told Wirth's aide, was to inquire how we could work together on these issues. Were there some initiatives we might work on that would complement what Senator Wirth was planning to do? Perhaps we could work together on a critique of the antici-pated emphasis on fossil fuels and nuclear fission in Bennett Johnston's bill.

On this first visit to the office of the leading environmentalist on the Energy Committee, we were taken aback by the response. What we got from Wirth's aide was a lecture about how you have to "go along if you want to get along" in the Senate. Specifically he told us that Wirth had managed to establish good rapport with Bennett Johnston and how he expected to be able to work with the chairman on improving the energy strategy bill. He also told us about the public lands plums that had accrued to Wirth's home state of Colorado as a consequence of that relationship and suggested that we, too, should be alert to the special opportunity Paul had as a member of the Energy Committee to get public lands projects for Minnesota.

It was not a propitious beginning. Paul would later remind me more than once that I had gotten him into this frequently uncomfortable assignment. For better or for worse, we had cast our lot with the Energy Committee.

How the Energy Strategy Debate Was Framed

4

The President's Plan

From the moment the public debate began with the introduction of the Johnston-Wallop bill, S.341, on February 5, 1991, I felt as if I were straining to get out of a box. The way the debate had been framed did not permit the most fundamental, most contentious, issues about a national energy strategy to be addressed. Namely, what kind of energy future made sense for America and what policies would it take to get there?

The framing of public policy debates by closed elite circles in Washington is a prime contributor to the antidemocratic nature of contemporary American politics. In many ways, as a Senate staffer involved in this debate I had the same frustrations I had repeatedly experienced as an ordinary citizen going to Washington to support policy changes—being told, in effect, that it was too late to consider the options we advocated. What we wanted was "unrealistic" given the decisions that had already been made about the terms of the debate.

Nearly everyone involved claimed to agree on the objectives of a national energy strategy. The three central objectives were energy security, environmental protection, and economic strength. Energy security was shorthand for reducing our national vulnerability to disruptions in the oil supply and price fluctuations stemming from America's increasing dependence on foreign oil. Environmental protection in this context referred to many energy-related problems, including air and water pollution, toxic waste disposal (including radioactive waste), acid rain, and, of especially great concern, global warming resulting from carbon dioxide and other greenhouse gases emitted when fossil fuels are burned. The long-term economic strength of our nation has many connections to energy policy choices, such as jobs that energy-related industries produce, energy costs to manufacturing and other businesses, and excessive reliance on energy sources and technologies that may prove vulnerable in the future—for example, in the wake of radioactive releases from a catastrophic nuclear power plant accident or suddenly reduced access to major foreign sources of petroleum.

To arrive at a comprehensive, coherent package of programs that would be an "energy strategy," a natural first step would be a national debate over where we want to end up twenty, thirty, or forty years down the road—a vision of our nation's energy future. Of course, any energy strategy must be viewed as only the beginning of a process that will require many midcourse corrections. But it was essential to begin by thinking hard about where we want to go. Given the natural inclination of institutions to survive and prosper, there would be powerful pressures simply to keep going in the direction in which we were already heading.

A central concept of previous influential energy strategy studies, such as the 1974 Ford Foundation study, the 1979 National Academy of Sciences study, and the 1981 SERI Report, was a *transition* focus, emphasizing the importance of deciding where we want to go and concentrating on how to get there.[1] Had such a debate taken place in 1991, it is not hard to imagine alternative visions that would have been emphasized, such as the future of electric power and the future of transportation in America. In the case of electric power, supply-side issues would include the desirable mix of sources among fossil fuels, nuclear fission, and renewables and the relative emphasis on large centralized sources and smaller distributed sources. Demand-side issues include identifying technologically ambitious and economically practicable targets and timetables for increasing the efficiency of electrical devices like refrigerators, air conditioners, computers, and light bulbs. In the case of transportation, supply-side issues include choices among alternative fuel substitutes for petroleum and the relative R&D emphasis on fuel-cell-powered and battery-powered electric vehicles.[2] Demand-side issues include identifying technologically ambitious and economically practicable targets and timetables for increasing the fuel economy of vehicles and reducing vehicle miles traveled through such devices as car-pooling incentives and urban mass transit.

The Sustainable Energy Vision

One vision that surely would have been seriously considered is a sustainable energy future, an emphasis on efficient electrical devices, electricity from renewable sources—solar, wind, and biomass—and transportation based on highly efficient electric vehicles powered by fuel cells operating on renewable fuels such as alcohols and hydrogen. The bridge to that future would include heavy investments in energy efficiency and increased use of natural gas as a transition fuel for both electric power generation and for transportation.

Such a vision was strongly supported by all the major environmental organizations and articulated most forcefully and persuasively in *America's Energy Choices: Investing in a Strong Economy and a Clean Environment,* a study commissioned by four leading environmental groups and published in late 1991.[3] Among the conclusions of that study were that if current energy production policies and energy consumption trends continued until 2030, national energy consumption would rise by over 40 percent and renewable energy sources would make only a very modest contribution to the energy supply mix. Especially ominous were projections that in this business-as-usual scenario, petroleum consumption would grow by 16 percent, increasing America's vulnerability to oil supply disruptions, and carbon dioxide emissions would grow by nearly 60 percent, greatly exacerbating the problem of global warming.

The study also examined three other scenarios involving more or less rapid introduction of energy efficient devices and renewable energy sources. The most aggressive, in which the U.S. was assumed to participate in an international effort to limit global warming by decreasing its carbon dioxide emissions, would reduce national energy consumption by 2030 to half of that in the business-as-usual case. Renewable energy sources would be providing half of America's energy, and petroleum consumption would have declined to one-third its current level.

A national energy strategy aimed at shaping a transition to a sustainable energy future would involve a conscious tilt toward energy efficiency and renewables through use of a number of government policy instruments. It would require dramatic changes in research and development priorities, in tax policies directed toward the energy industries, requiring far greater federal support for state and regional conservation and renewable programs.

Opinion surveys at the time suggested strong public support for moving in such a direction. For instance, on the eve of the debate in January 1991, a poll conducted by Vincent Breglio and Celinda Lake, prominent

Republican and Democratic pollsters respectively, asked "If you were the person responsible for funding research and development in the Department of Energy, what would be your top priority for energy R&D funding?" Seventy-five percent chose renewables or energy conservation, 12 percent coal and oil, and 10 percent nuclear energy.[4]

That same poll probed the degree of public support for specific policies. One that ranked exceptionally high was a renewed upward push in the automobile fuel economy standard, which had leveled off at about 27.5 miles per gallon for passenger cars after nearly doubling in the 1976–86 period as a result of the 1976 CAFE legislation. Eighty-six percent of those polled supported a CAFE increase to 40 miles per gallon by the year 2000, and 89 percent said they would still favor it even if it meant a new car would cost them five-hundred dollars more.

The Traditional Post–World War II Vision

An alternative vision was the one that had dominated U.S. energy policy planning in the post–World War II era and which was still the clear choice of the major energy industries. It envisioned electricity from nuclear fission and possibly nuclear fusion in the long run, with an extended transition period emphasizing "clean coal technologies" and increased use of natural gas. The nuclear power industry, which had begun no new nuclear generating plant construction since 1978, was promoting a new strategy for revitalizing nuclear power that would feature a streamlined "one-step" nuclear plant licensing process, a new generation of standardized, supposedly "inherently safe," reactors, and the establishment of a national repository for high level radioactive waste. Many industries, from the electric utilities to the nuclear power plant manufacturers to the natural gas pipeline companies were salivating at the prospect of building large numbers of new nuclear and fossil fuel–fired electric generating plants in the coming decades.

For transportation, different industries had different ideas. The electric utilities were promoting rechargable battery–powered vehicles and the automobile manufacturers had already joined together in a large project with federal support to try to develop appropriate batteries. The oil and natural gas producers and the natural gas pipeline companies were touting natural gas and methanol as transportation fuels and some of the major producers were already building large methanol-from-natural-gas production facilities in the Middle East. Ethanol was the choice of midwestern corn growers and, especially, the country's dominant producer of ethanol, the giant Archer Daniels Midland Corporation.

From my vantage point in the office of an energy committee senator, I became well aware of the corporate enthusiasm for the traditional vision of our energy future. During my eight months in the Senate, dozens of industry lobbyists called, came by my office, invited me to lunch, and sometimes suggested all-expense-paid trips to places like San Francisco, Alaska, Puerto Rico, and North Dakota so I could better appreciate their perspectives. Almost to a person, I found these people likeable, attractive, and very well-informed.

They all presented arguments from their employers' perspectives, and I often found them quite educational. But something bothered me about our conversations that I couldn't pin down for quite a while. I finally realized what it was—the absence of ethical arguments, with one notable exception: they all wanted "a level playing field." Of course, that was disingenuous. Their businesses already depended on enormous tilts—toward them. The oil companies had their depletion allowances and their passive loss credits. The coal companies had their billions of dollars in clean coal R&D funds. The nuclear industry had its forty years of government sponsored R&D, its government guaranteed Price-Anderson reactor accident liability insurance, and so forth. They and lobbyists before them had engineered the tilts. Their job was to keep it tilted.

I do not minimize the importance of the concerns of these industries— for themselves, for their employees, and for the nation. But these concerns tend to be the product of relatively short-term calculations, and each has a perspective that focuses on a fairly narrow range of the whole energy policy spectrum. To the extent that these institutional concerns dominate decision-making, the policies that emerge are likely to be short-term and piecemeal rather than long-term and comprehensive, reflecting the goals and values of corporations and thereby failing to incorporate some of the most important goals and values of the American people. It made no sense to me to approach a national energy strategy in 1991 without first focusing on careful analyses of alternative visions and strategies. But I found myself thwarted for reasons going back to the previous year and a half when the national energy strategy debate had been framed.

Soon after he took office on July 26, 1989, George Bush, who said he wanted to be known as the "environmental President," instructed his energy secretary, Admiral James Watkins, to undertake a major reexamination of U.S. energy policies aimed at producing a National Energy Strategy (NES). The result, released in February 1991, was a thick, slick document with politically appealing pictures on the front cover of photovoltaic arrays, modern wind turbines, and solar power plants.[5] But between the covers was a very different plan. What happened is a revealing story of who gets invited in and who gets left out in the most critical phase of the Washington policy-making process—the framing phase.

Watkins had brought in as top advisors several talented women who had worked with him at his previous post as chair of the President's Commission on AIDS, led by Polly L. Gault, who became his chief of staff at the Department of Energy (DoE). He also hired Linda Stuntz from the staff of the House Energy and Power subcommittee to be the department's deputy undersecretary for policy, planning, and analysis and to lead the National Energy Strategy project.

As an aside, it should be noted that much of what the Department of Energy does is not related to civilian energy, but rather to military weapons, a direct consequence of its origins as the Atomic Energy Commission, created after World War II primarily to build nuclear bombs and secondarily to develop nuclear power reactors. This bureaucratic connection between two very different objectives had profound effects on post–World War II energy policy because federal money flows most freely to government agencies responsible for military projects. The principal consequence was abundant funding for the development of nuclear fission reactors and the U.S. choice of a particular kind, light water reactors, initially designed for nuclear submarine propulsion. Another consequence was the enormously greater funding that was poured into nuclear fusion reactor R&D compared to the paltry amount invested in solar energy R&D, despite the long-recognized fact that both had huge energy potential.

The NES exercise began in what seemed to be a most promising manner. Watkins and his former AIDS commission staffers set the tone by vowing to repeat what they had done to so much acclaim on AIDS policy. Without preconceptions, they would go around the country to learn what knowledgable and concerned people were thinking. Then they would go back to Washington and hammer out a hard-hitting report with strong policy recommendations. To open the process, Watkins held public hearings around the country. By the end, the DoE boasted that 499 witnesses from forty-three states had testified at eighteen hearings. Nevertheless, environmentalists were apprehensive because the hearings seemed to have been stacked in favor of witnesses from oil, natural gas, nuclear power, and electric utility interests.

One NES staffer confidentially echoed that view, but stressed that the hearings had not succeeded in screening out other voices and opinions: "Although there were lots of hearings in oil and coal country, the overwhelming testimony was still in favor of renewables and conservation." The April 1990 NES Interim Report summarizing the hearing findings contained a clear signal of what they had heard, "The loudest single message was to increase energy efficiency in every sector of energy use. Energy efficiency was seen as a way to reduce pollution, reduce dependence on imports, and reduce the cost of energy."[6]

Beyond that conclusion, however, the report was a compendium of basic energy information, along with over seven hundred policies that had been proposed by witnesses at the hearings. It invited feedback: "We need response, reaction, and public debate based on this Interim Report." But that posed a problem. Had the report contained tentative policy recommendations rather than a laundry list of policy options, then a real debate would have been possible. Failing that, there was no clear focus for a public debate. People close to the process said that President Bush's White House Chief of Staff, John Sununu, had, as one reliable source put it, "intervened pretty heavy handedly," ordering Admiral Watkins to make it a laundry list, not a draft policy report.

Sununu evidently did not like where Secretary Watkins's public process was taking them. The NES staff had originally planned two months of "public comment and review" after the first draft of the strategy, including specific policy recommendations, had been prepared. Instead, from April 1990, when the Interim Report was issued, to February 1991, when the proposed National Energy Strategy was released, the process went on behind closed doors. That was the period when many important decisions were made and the subsequent energy strategy debate was framed.

In June 1990 the Economic Policy Council Working Group on the NES, an interagency body closely connected with Sununu and his White House Domestic Policy Council, began to ride herd on the NES. Twenty-one executive branch departments and agencies were involved and three of them, the White House Office of Management and Budget (OMB), the Treasury Department, and the President's Council of Economic Advisors (CEA), began overseeing the process. Their heads, Richard Darman of OMB, Nicholas Brady at Treasury, and Michael Boskin, chair of the CEA—known to insiders as the "troika"—kept a close watch on what policy proposals would emerge in the National Energy Strategy.

A June memo from a Treasury Department official to the NES staffer leading the effort to assign priorities to the proposed policy options described the White House's unease with the direction in which Secretary Watkins's open process to involve the public was heading:

> The options handed out yesterday in almost every case suggest the current
> energy policy is wrong, and needs to be fixed, preferably by government. . . .
> The list leaves an impression that we are headed toward more, not less, inter-
> vention in the markets. This interventionist approach is glaringly inconsistent
> with Administration policies. . . . The NES process continues to rely exces-
> sively on Secretary Watkins' public hearing process. . . . I suggest we abandon
> the current plan and not base the analysis solely on options presented in the
> public hearings. . . .

The memo added a warning: "I understand you have your orders from the
Secretary. But he should know that Treasury will very likely oppose any energy strategy that looks like the current list of options, whether they came
from the public hearings or not."[7]

In testimony before Congress, Vito Stagliano, the deputy to NES director
Stuntz, later asserted, "I believe the process for developing the NES was as
open and comprehensive as we could make it."[8] However, it is evident that
once the process went behind closed doors, the interim report, with all its
public input, ended up being just window dressing, peripheral to the decisions that set the specific policies in and the conceptual structure of the National Energy Strategy.

For instance, "the loudest single message" that emerged from the nationwide public hearings, "to increase energy efficiency in every sector of energy
use," was simply disregarded. According to one NES insider who wished to
remain anonymous, "There was a huge list of stuff [concerning policies to
promote energy efficiency] in the comments that came in from the public.
None of them got analyzed; none of them was ever seriously put into the process." Instead, he noted, three fundamental principles governed the decision-
making process: "no regulations; no new taxes; and it can't be anything
Jimmy Carter had talked about."

Those involved in the energy strategy exercise claimed to employ "objective" quantitative methods in evaluating alternative options, including computer modeling of the impacts of various policies on future energy supply
and demand and associated cost/benefit analyses. Of course, what comes
out of quantitative studies depends on the assumptions built into them. One
internal struggle, for example, focused on whether or not to include so-
called externalities, most notably the costs of environmental impact, such as
global warming or acid rain from fossil fuel–fired electric generating plants,
in the *cost/benefit* analyses that were instrumental in assigning NES policy
priorities. A large working group was established, and after much pseudo-
objective discussion it was decided that *no externalities* would be included.

Henry Kelly, a physicist who is one of the nation's most respected authorities on sustainable energy, had been detailed from Congress's Office of Technology Assessment to the NES project to work on energy conservation and efficient energy as part of a national energy strategy. On arriving at the DoE, he was dismayed to find the conservation and renewables policy staff in disarray. There were a few outstanding individuals in the office, to be sure, but eight years of the Reagan administration, which had sought to abolish the Department of Energy, had left it with much of its expertise gone, its morale low, and its analytical capabilities poor.

It soon became clear what a daunting task it would be to replace the DoE's outdated computer models with the kind of energy modeling capability the NES would need in order to evaluate various policy alternatives. In the end, the National Energy Strategy relied on the old computer models. While NES officials would later tell Congress things like, "The Interagency analytical process was characterized by a high degree of analytical discipline and rigor," Kelly knew that some of the conclusions simply were wrong.[9] For example, he had been perplexed by the extremely small electricity savings the NES modelers, using their FOSSIL2 computer program, predicted would result from utility conservation and efficiency programs, far smaller than either his own calculations or those the utility industry had projected.

The reason for the discrepancy was not easy to track down, but Kelly finally discovered the problem. Two of the many input variables that were fed into the computer model were clearly wrong. As a consequence, while the model fit the 1990 electricity data, its predictions beyond 1990, most notably a miniscule reduction in electricity consumption from energy conservation and efficiency measures, were demonstrably incorrect. Computer modelers have a name for this common kind of error, "garbage in, garbage out" or "gigo" for short. Kelly pointed this out, but it was too late. The NES study results were published with authoritative-looking graphs going out to the year 2030, but they were quite misleading. They were used to buttress the almost total neglect of electric energy efficiency and conservation in the NES policy recommendations.

An amusing nod was made in the direction of "public comment and review." Seven workshops were scheduled and selected members of the "public" were invited to attend. For example, when NES policies relating to nuclear power were discussed on October 24, 1990, the public attendees were five representatives of the nuclear industry, who met with six employees from the DoE's Office of Nuclear Energy. It would be hard to imagine more of a charade. One of the "public representatives" was Sherwood Smith, chairman and president of Carolina Power and Light Company, who chaired the nuclear industry's Nuclear Power Oversight Committee (NPOC) which was just completing an influential document, "Strategic Plan for Building New Nuclear Plants," that mapped out the very policies that were written into the National Energy Strategy. The other "public participants" were lobbyists for nuclear power advocacy groups that had contributed to the NPOC policies. The people from DoE's Nuclear Energy Office had also worked hand-in-glove with NPOC as that document was developed.

Similar workshops were held with industrial energy users, utility industry people, and auto industry lobbyists. Representatives of environmental organizations were brought in for two sessions, but their inclusion clearly was pro forma, a smart political move to prevent any claims that they had been completely shut out. However, they did learn at those October 1990 meetings that some substantial sustainable energy policy proposals were still on the table, including energy efficiency standards for buildings and for many kinds of electrical devices, from transformers and motors to heating, ventilating, and air conditioning equipment to computers and light bulbs. A modest CAFE standard was also being considered, along with a proposal promoted by the Solar Energy Industries Association, providing renewable energy production tax credits for solar, wind, geothermal, and biomass electricity production. Kelly recalled, however, that by the time the NES policy recommendations were sent from the Department of Energy to the White House, "all that was left was light bulbs." That, and the proposal for renewable electric energy production tax credits.

But even the tax credit proposal was in vain. In early February 1991, before the NES report was published, House Speaker Tom Foley demanded that the White House send him a copy of the recommendations. Someone complied with remarkable haste, simply xeroxing the copy that the Department of Energy had sent to the president, with White House revisions from Sununu and his associates scribbled in. This draft achieved wide circulation and instant notoriety among congressional energy policy staffers. Within hours we all had copies. It was impossible to miss the huge handwritten X's through the already depleted sections on "Energy Conservation Standards" and "Renewable Energy." Later, NES director Stuntz's deputy made an unusually candid admission before a congressional committee that illuminated what the task of the Interagency Working Group had become under the watchful eyes of the troika: "First, *the interagency staff identified barriers and disincentives to efficient resource development or use. Then they exam-*

ined policies, procedures, and methodologies that could be used to remove or reduce the barriers or eliminate market distortions." [10]

The upshot was that many energy and auto industry lobbying coalitions gained access to the framing process with proposals for eliminating barriers their industries faced. Those barrier-busting proposals sailed through the NES filters and into the National Energy Strategy that was unveiled to the public as the congressional debate began in February 1991. The public and public advocacy groups had been left outside the closed decision-making circles and their vision of a sustainable energy future ended up outside the national energy strategy frame. As a result, in the midst of a war over access to oil, the DoE came out with an NES that contained virtually nothing to reduce American petroleum consumption.

The Chairman's Bill

In mid-February, the National Energy Strategy was released with great fanfare by the Department of Energy. Linda Stuntz and her deputies came up to the Hill and briefed us at great length about its contents. A few days later, the president sent over his energy strategy legislation. But that particular bill was never the focus of the congressional debate. Instead, the focus was S.341, The National Energy Security Act of 1991, based on a draft prepared by Ben Cooper and the energy committee staff for Chairman Bennett Johnston.[11] It contained the major proposals of the NES and more.

From the beginning, Johnston, a Democrat, adopted a strategy of allying himself with the Republicans on the twenty-member committee. Johnston took his NES-inspired draft to Wyoming Sen. Malcolm Wallop, the ranking Republican, who enlisted the support of the committee's other eight Republicans. With the backing of Alabama's Dick Shelby, already a Democrat in name only (he officially changed parties immediately after the Republicans gained control of the Senate in the 1994 election), and using his considerable leverage to bring along some other Democrats, Johnston had a solid majority behind the bill from the start.

S.341, jointly sponsored by Johnston and Wallop, was introduced on February 5, two weeks before the NES was officially released. But Johnston was known to be coordinating his bill with the Department of Energy's and to be in close touch with the White House. In fact, the Republican president referred to this bill as *his* energy strategy.

The Johnston-Wallop bill was 285 pages and fifteen titles long. Each title was a detailed, complex set of propositions and proposals. The bill obviously would have a major impact on every sector of the American energy enterprise. Understanding them was a daunting, difficult task. One evening near the end of January, Henry Kelly, who was still at the DoE, gathered a few thoughtful energy policy analysts from the Washington environmental community for a brainstorming session at our office. I was looking for a niche for Paul in the upcoming debate and for energy policy initiatives we might develop and introduce. The Johnston-Wallop bill was full of subtle details about issues I understood only superficially, and replete with obscure references to previous legislation it sought to change. However, as I studied the various titles I spotted disquieting signs that hidden in the technical prose were very far-reaching, probably quite controversial, modifications of many laws.

During the 1970s and 1980s the traditional energy supply industries had encountered a variety of barriers to the policies they wished to pursue, principally regulations to safeguard the environment or to protect consumers. The industry lobbying coalitions and their congressional allies saw this new legislation as an opportunity to dismantle old barriers and prevent new ones, and while they were at it, to see how much they could shake loose from the federal money tree to subsidize their future plans.

I would soon learn that Chairman Johnston had built an impressive network of cozy connections with major energy industry lobbying coalitions, which were poised to launch an all-out effort to pass the Johnston-Wallop bill. The biggest barrier buster in the entire bill was the provision for opening up the Arctic National Wildlife Refuge (ANWR) to drilling for oil and natural gas. The environmental community was up in arms and organizing nationwide opposition through the Alaska Coalition, headquartered in the Sierra Club's Washington office. The chance to drill was coveted by many of the major oil companies, especially those already involved in Alaska oil exploration and associated with the Trans-Alaska pipeline corporation, Alyeska. A local Eskimo tribe also stood to garner an immense fortune if oil exploration were permitted on the ANWR coastal plain and oil in amounts approaching the very large estimate by the Interior Department were discovered. For years, Bill Van Ness, of the Georgetown law and lobbying firm Van Ness, Feldman, and Curtis, had been the Washington lobbyist for the Arctic Slope Regional Corporation representing the tribe, and he had organized the "Coalition for American Energy Security," a major lobbying coalition in favor of ANWR drilling. Van Ness also had been chief counsel of the Senate Interior Committee and a close confidant of Bennett Johnston when Johnston was its rising young star, as well as Ben Cooper's immediate supervisor when Ben came to work for the committee in 1973.

A second oil title concerned off-shore drilling on the outer continental shelf (OCS). It mandated a report assessing the long-term prospects for OCS leasing and drilling and also included what I suspected was a great deal of money, 37.5 percent of new OCS revenues as "impact aid to coastal states and communities affected by OCS leasing and development." My suspicion on reading that title was that it might be a kind of bribe to overcome local opposition to off-shore drilling, although at the time, I did not realize how much off-shore drilling had already been curtailed by local opposition that had led to the moratoriums at prime sites, especially off the coasts of California and Florida. This meant a principal beneficiary of the impact assistance revenues would be Bennett Johnston's home state of Louisiana.

The third oil title would impose a 9 percent "oil security premium" (not a "tax," we were assured) on every barrel of imported oil, with the proceeds going to increase the amount of oil held in the Louisiana-based Strategic Petroleum Reserve from a little over half a billion barrels to a billion barrels. That seemed to me to be a useful buffer to reduce our nation's vulnerability to foreign oil supply disruptions. At the time, I did not appreciate that another consequence of the 9 percent premium on imported oil would be about a 9 percent rise in world oil prices, resulting in huge windfall profits to domestic oil producers.

Three titles were aimed at revitalizing the moribund nuclear power industry. One provided for a very controversial "streamlining" of the nuclear power plant licensing process. The current two-step licensing was said to be a major barrier to investors, who faced the possibility that after putting up huge sums for construction, the power plant operating license could later be denied. Another title of the bill provided very large amounts of government funding for a program to develop, demonstrate, and help commercialize new "advanced nuclear reactor" designs that would be "inherently safe," economically competitive, not conducive to nuclear weapons proliferation but suitable to standardized design, construction, and licensing procedures. It too was aimed at reducing the likelihood of glitches in the licensing process and it also was meant to address qualms people had about nuclear power. One of the lobbyists for the nuclear industry's principal trade group, the American Nuclear Energy Council, and for some major nuclear industry and nuclear electric utilities was Bennett Johnston's close friend and former chief of staff, Charlie McBride.

A third title called for restructuring the U.S. uranium enrichment enterprise, which had long been under the Department of Energy, by creating a "wholly-owned government corporation" to take over the work and the DoE facilities and enrich uranium on a profit-making basis. At the time, I had no idea of the reasons for this change or its major consequences. Later there would be revelations that in the changeover billions of dollars owed to the government by electric utilities with nuclear power plants would be canceled and very large costs for decontaminating and decommissioning old uranium enrichment facilities would be assumed by the government.

Other provisions of this title directed the new corporation to institute an "overfeed" program that would stimulate the use of more uranium in the enrichment enterprise. It would restrict government purchases of uranium to that mined in the U.S. and purchased from domestic uranium producers. It also established a National Strategic Uranium Reserve which would stockpile substantial amounts of domestically produced uranium. The director of the Uranium Producers of America was Johnston's former Senate Energy Committee staff director, Grenville Garside, operating out of Van Ness, Feldman, and Curtis.

By far the most contentious nuclear power issue of all was addressed in a separate bill before the committee, aimed at moving forward with siting a national repository to store high-level radioactive waste from commercial nuclear power plants. Several years before, Bennett Johnston had been instrumental in instituting a repository site selection process that resulted in the choice of Yucca Mountain in Nevada. But powerful statewide citizen and Nevada government opposition had stalled its progress. This loomed as potentially the greatest impediment to further deployment of nuclear power plants in the United States.

Another Johnston-Wallop title had to do with the construction of natural gas pipelines and with the natural gas prices that pipeline companies could charge. It provided several ways for "streamlining" the regulatory procedures for pipeline construction and for transferring some regulatory authority from the states to the Federal Energy Regulatory Commission. The articulate young Energy Committee counsel, Don Santa, who was so well versed in the intricacies of natural gas law, had recently come over to the committee from Van Ness, Feldman, and Curtis to handle this title of the bill and other natural gas–related issues. The famous revolving door between the lobbying community, Capitol Hill, and the executive branch had temporarily deposited him on the Senate Energy Committee staff, on his way to a seat on the Federal Energy Regulatory Commission in 1993.

Another title of the Johnston-Wallop bill was known as PUHCA reform.

The summary the committee staff circulated to us contained a one-sentence description of its contents: "Removes impediments to independent power production contained in the Public Utility Holding Company Act of 1935." Even before the committee met for the first time, I was getting strong signals from lobbyists that this was *very* important and *very* controversial. Analyses like those in the National Energy Strategy report were predicting that hundreds of new electric generating plants would be built in the next twenty or thirty years, with the construction of each one a lucrative enterprise. If this title were passed, many more companies than were presently eligible could compete to build them. For instance, natural gas pipeline companies were lobbying heavily for it; they hoped to become major players in constructing and operating natural gas–fired electric generating plants. At the first meeting of staffers working with the Energy Committee and its members, the committee staffer responsible for PUHCA reform, Bill Conway, (another import from Van Ness), took me aside and explained how much this reform was needed.

The very large electric utilities were in a barrier-busting mood. They supported PUHCA reform, which would allow them to compete to sell electricity to utilities far beyond their previously assigned service areas. They also pressed for one-step nuclear licensing and the Yucca Mountain nuclear waste repository, wanted their coal-fired electric generating plants to be exempted from provisions from the Clean Air Act as amended in 1990, opposed measures to counter global warming such as a carbon tax, mandatory reductions in carbon dioxide emissions and begged for federal R&D subsidies to develop "inherently safe" nuclear power plants and "clean coal technologies" that would reduce sulfur and nitrogen oxide emissions from coal-burning power plants.

From the Van Ness office, former Interior Committee staffer Ben Yamagata directed the "Clean Coal Technology Coalition," representing nearly a hundred coal mining companies, power plant manufacturers, and electric utilities. Former Johnston legislative assistant Bob Szabo directed another lobbying coalition from the Van Ness office, called "Consumers United for Rail Equity" (CURE), representing over 150 electric utilities that were heavy users of coal.

The automobile manufacturers were adamantly opposed to another decade or more of mandated CAFE increases, but the Bryan bill, with its 40 percent increase in ten years, was expected to breeze through the Senate Commerce Committee again and to command strong support when it reached the Senate floor. The Johnston-Wallop bill had its own, very different, CAFE title, which left it up to the Secretary of Transportation to decide how much of an increase to require. Given that the Department of Transportation had already expressed its opposition to any mandatory CAFE increases, that was a prescription for non-action on automobile fuel economy.

The committee's ranking minority member, Sen. Malcolm Wallop of Wyoming, had insisted on this extremely weak CAFE language and Johnston was forced to accept it, at least for the time being, to get Wallop to sign on as cosponsor of his bill. Johnston was already worried that many senators who supported Bryan would find this sufficient cause to oppose the entire Johnston-Wallop bill.

Other energy efficiency and renewable energy programs were also very weak. An analysis by the highly regarded American Council for an Energy-Efficient Economy demonstrated pitifully small energy savings would result from the residential, commercial, and industrial energy efficiency provisions of the Johnston-Wallop bill. The renewables title provided little support for solar, wind, and biomass technologies. One section that dealt with hydropower seemed to include significant changes in the regulatory rules, transferring some authority from the states to the Federal Energy Regulatory Commission and removing small hydropower plants from federal regulation. Only later would I learn that those changes were very controversial.

Obviously the Johnston-Wallop bill had enormous scope. It had the potential to profoundly affect virtually every energy industry in America. By mid-February 1991, as the Persian Gulf War was nearing its climax, Bennett Johnston and his staff were geared up and ready to go. So were the industry lobbyists and the Department of Energy. At that point, I had only a very imperfect understanding of the bill's contents and consequences and was just beginning to bring into focus Johnston's impressive network of energy industry lobbying coalitions, but I would soon rectify that.

The Johnston Juggernaut 5

Running It By the Interests

The public phase of the national energy strategy debate began in February 1991 with the release of the National Energy Strategy report and the introduction of the Johnston-Wallop bill. Even before they were unveiled, I had begun to receive signals of what some of the most controversial issues and most active interest groups would be.

Given that we were at that very moment involved in a war over access to oil in the Persian Gulf, the most salient issues concerned the nation's vulnerability to oil supply disruptions and price fluctuations resulting from our increasing dependence on foreign sources of oil. There were two obvious approaches to dealing with that problem. One was to increase domestic oil production by extracting it more efficiently or by finding new oil. The second was to reduce America's consumption of oil by using it more efficiently or by substituting alternative fuels. In the debate over Johnston-Wallop, two specific proposals, each with a four-letter acronym, came to symbolize these two approaches. One was ANWR, exploring for oil on the off-limits coastal plain of the Arctic National Wildlife Refuge, the other was CAFE, increasing the corporate average fuel economy, of new automobiles and "light trucks" (vans, pickup trucks, and sports utility vehicles).

On February 1 staffers from the Energy Committee and its members' offices were invited to lunch by nine large oil companies at a posh Capitol Hill restaurant, Le Monocle. I had an enlightening conversation about oil drilling in Alaska with British Petroleum lobbyist Roger Herrera and lunch at an AMOCO lobbyist's table before we all were briefed on ANWR by Herrera.

For me the briefing was quite educational. I found out exactly where ANWR was located (in the northeast corner of Alaska) and at least part of the reason the oil companies thought there might be lots of oil there. Along the north coast just to the west of ANWR was the largest Alaska oil field discovered so far, Prudhoe Bay, and just to the east was another major oil field; geological surveys had disclosed several promising "traps" beneath the wildlife refuge that might hold oil or natural gas, including two enormous ones. In the unlikely event that either was full of oil, ANWR would be a bonanza. Chevron had drilled an exploratory well into the largest of these traps in 1985, but wouldn't tell what was found.

How much oil really is there was evidently quite uncertain. The figure usually cited was 3.6 billion barrels, but it might be zero or it might be much more. According to a 1987 Interior Department estimate, there was a one-in-five chance that ANWR held commercial quantities of oil. A further reason for oil company interest in that particular spot was that the huge Prudhoe Bay field, which is the source of oil for the trans-Alaska pipeline, was already past its peak production and an adjacent ANWR field would be a convenient new source of oil to feed it. I could certainly understand the companies' enthusiasm for further drilling. Although the chances were fairly small, a major find would mean lots of money, as a crude estimate makes clear: 3.6 billion barrels times twenty dollars per barrel is *seventy-two billion dollars*.

Soon thereafter, a Chevron lobbyist invited me to lunch. He wanted to follow up the briefing and get a sense of whether Paul might support drilling in ANWR. The answer was no. Our view began with the fact that U.S. domestic oil production had peaked in 1970 and had been declining more or less steadily ever since. The optimistic estimate of 3.6 billion barrels of ANWR oil would supply the U.S. at its current consumption rate for only about two-hundred days, so even in the event of such a large discovery, ANWR would be only a brief blip in the oil supply picture and would not alter our long-term downward trend in domestic supply and our increasing dependence on foreign oil.

The percentage of oil we import had been increasing to the point that by 1990 it was about 50 percent and by 2010, if the current trend continued, it would be about 70 percent. The three or four billion barrels that might be found in ANWR under an optimistic scenario were only 1 percent of the Middle East's proven reserves. The effect of such a major ANWR find would be to reduce the percentage of oil we would import in 2010 by only a small amount, from 70 percent to 67 percent, and a decade after that the oil would be gone.

From that perspective, if we were really going to get serious about the energy security problem, the emphasis in our policies had to be on using oil more efficiently, most notably in transportation vehicles, and on moving as rapidly as possible to introduce alternatives to oil, particularly in transportation fuels. In the politics of this issue, those pressing that position most strongly were the environmentalists, who would soon become our close allies in the energy strategy debate.

The other most visible and controversial proposal was CAFE. Requiring the automakers to double the corporate average fuel economy of their new car fleets in the ten years following 1975 had proved remarkably effective. Despite all the arguments by the companies that it couldn't be done and that it would result in unsafe cars, by 1985 the major manufacturers had achieved the prescribed 27.5 MPG standard without sacrifice of safety.

A couple of years after the standards in the original CAFE law had been achieved, however, the upward trend in automobile fuel economy stalled. In fact, there was even some retrenchment as both American and Japanese auto manufacturers began to change their production mixes toward more luxury cars with lower mileage and greater profits. The fleet average for all new passenger cars sold in the United States peaked at 28.8 MPG in the 1988 model year, declining to 28.2 MPG by 1991. And the increase in sales of light trucks brought the overall average for new cars and light trucks down from a 1987 peak of 26.2 MPG to 25.5 MPG in 1991. Imported cars averaged about three to four MPG more than domestically produced cars.[1]

The CAFE bill introduced by Sen. Richard Bryan of Nevada in 1990 would have put automobile energy efficiency back on the upward track. It required the fuel economy average of cars and light trucks sold in the U.S. by each manufacturer to increase by at least 20 percent in five years and 40 percent in ten years. For the big three American manufacturers, that would mean increasing CAFE for automobiles to about 39 MPG, and for the leading Japanese manufacturers, who were already producing more fuel efficient vehicles, it would mean about 43 MPG.

The auto manufacturers and the Bush administration opposed the bill, saying it was economically unfeasible and would result in lost jobs. They also claimed that higher gas mileage standards would require lighter and therefore less safe cars. Proponents of a new CAFE mandate countered that the industry had made the same arguments fifteen years before; they had been fallacious then and they were still fallacious. They pointed to a DoE study that found that greater fuel economy could be achieved though technological advances, not necessarily lighter cars.

In September 1990, led by Michigan's Sen. Don Riegle, opponents filibustered to keep the Bryan bill from coming to the floor, but the Senate stopped the filibuster by a 68 to 28 vote. However, the auto industry and the Bush Administration lobbied heavily and eleven days later, in the midst of another filibuster, another cloture vote was taken; it fell 3 votes short of the necessary 60, 57 to 42, thus killing the legislation. A similar bill in the House never made it out of committee.

In 1991, soon after we arrived, Bryan introduced his CAFE bill again, now numbered S.279.[2] Much of what I knew about the new CAFE proposal I learned from the woman behind the Bryan legislation, Commerce Committee staffer Linda Lance. In contrast to so many other staff members I had met in the strikingly insular Senate, she was quite helpful and very interested in our working together. She explained what had happened the year before and what she expected in 1991. The Bryan bill had passed the Commerce Committee by a 13 to 5 vote, but the auto industry was going all out, to defeat it and she could already detect some erosion in Senate support.

While ANWR and CAFE were the two most visible issues, lobbyists were telling me there would also be fights over the PUHCA reform title, the nuclear licensing and uranium enrichment titles, and some natural gas pipeline provisions, as well as attempts to strengthen the energy efficiency and renewable energy titles.

Surprisingly, the lobbyist who best fit my stereotype of how one would look and act represented the Solar Energy Industries Association. He invited me to lunch at La Colline, a fancy Capitol Hill restaurant. It was my first lunch with a lobbyist. Outgoing, friendly, garrulous, he informed me expansively that I could order anything on the menu and he proceeded to regale me with stories about the trials and tribulations of the fledgling solar industries. He also gave me a clever new solar-powered device.

When I returned to the office, however, my story produced considerable consternation. I was informed by a colleague that I had violated the Wellstone rules regarding lunches with lobbyists, which turned out to be much more stringent than the Senate rules I had studied. Wellstone staffers were supposed to pay for their own meals and accept no gifts from lobbyists. I had evidently been the first in the office to encounter temptation and I had succumbed miserably. My misadventure became an object lesson for us all on how not to behave. After that I always bought my own lunch and accepted no gifts.

What I found is that you can learn a great deal from lobbyists, but you only get one side of the story. Given my state of ignorance, I really needed to hear debates among articulate spokespersons for different sides of these contentious issues. Congressional hearings, when they are well conceived, can foster such illuminating debates. In the past, when working on controversial legislative issues, I had often found congressional hearing records by far the best source of information and argument to enable me to get rapidly up to speed. I was very much looking forward to the hearings on Johnston-Wallop, although little did I know what surprises Bennett Johnston and Ben Cooper had in store.

Struggling to Keep Up

A *National Journal* profile of Cooper in March emphasized the urgency he and Johnston felt in pushing rapidly for passage of the Johnston-Wallop bill: "During the recent Persian Gulf crisis, Cooper has been at the center of the action on the Energy Committee. The speed with which the panel is moving is grounded in the time-honored congressional rule that in politics, timing is everything," Cooper said. "You can make energy policy at a time when the country is in a crisis," he noted. "When there's no crisis, when energy is cheap, there's no reason to act."[3]

When the committee hearings began on February 21, with Energy Secretary Watkins presenting the National Energy Strategy, Johnston was ready to move amazingly rapidly. In four weeks, he held seventeen hearings, rushing through the entire Johnston-Wallop bill. I called it the "Johnston Juggernaut."

Many of the Johnston-Wallop titles could easily have been separate bills, each deserving several days of hearings. But rarely was any given more than a half-day hearing. Johnston and his staff were in command, orchestrating the process, shaping the agenda, choosing the witnesses, and managing the flow of information to committee members. Throughout the process and particularly during the "markup" that followed the hearings, when amendments to the bill were considered by the committee, we would often receive written testimony and other materials at the very last minute. Frequently in the markup we would not even be sure what topics would be taken up until we arrived at the hearing room. Johnston rushed the process along, deliberately keeping the rest of us in the dark and seemingly trying to leave us in his wake.

Johnston benefited from an enormous advantage over the other members of the committee. In effect he had his own "think tank," headed by Cooper, with seventeen professional staffers and a comparable number of additional support staff working for and reporting directly to him. They had divided up the titles of the bill, with each specializing on one or two and, with months of preparation, they were raring to go. In contrast, the other committee members had one or, at most, two staffers trying to come to grips with the entire bill.

I found myself constantly struggling to keep up. Typically we would receive the transcripts of the next day's testimony the afternoon before. I would have to get up at an ungodly early hour to finish reading the testimony, figure out the major implications of the provisions under discussion that day, prepare questions for Paul to ask the witnesses, and then brief him between 6:00 and 7:00 A.M. while we ran together around the mall between the Capitol and the Washington Monument.

It was a crash course in energy policy, but not one that made sorting out the issues and understanding the full implications of the proposals easy. For his hearings, Johnston had in mind something very different from fostering an illuminating public debate. Time after time, the hearings would consist of one-sided propaganda to buttress the provisions of the Johnston-Wallop bill. At the end of a long program, one or two token witnesses might present dissenting opinions, but only rarely was there anything approaching genuine debate. I often found myself angry about the abuse of power I was witnessing. Throughout the February and March hearings, I never felt I had command of the bill and there were several important provisions about which I wasn't really sure what to think.

Energy Secretary Watkins opened the hearings with a presentation of the National Energy Strategy on February 21, and he announced that President Bush would veto any energy strategy bill that did not include drilling for oil in ANWR, the Arctic National Wildlife Refuge. Then the hearings turned to the provisions of S.341, the Johnston-Wallop bill.

At the hearing on energy efficiency, I was particularly intrigued by one of the presentations, by Greg Rueger, senior vice president and general manager of the Electric Supply Division of Pacific Gas and Electric Company (PG&E), the nation's largest utility, which serves much of northern California. He explained that PG&E did not plan to build any more electric generating capacity in the 1990s; instead, it would invest heavily in consumer energy efficiency and peak load management programs to buy time so that in the post-2000 period, with anticipated advances in renewable sources, it could invest in them cost effectively. I was interested in learning more about what the company had done already in both efficiency and renewables and eager to learn more about why they seemed more open than other utilities to incorporate seriously efficiency and renewable programs in their future plans.[4]

Two hearings were held on the most important energy efficiency provision, CAFE, and Johnston's clear intent was to try to discredit the Bryan bill.[5] At the first hearing, on February 28, only one of the eleven witnesses supported Bryan and the second, on March 20, was monopolized by the testimony of two Bryan critics, with only one token supporter heard at the very end. In the process, there was no direct debate of the issues.

The big three American automakers all testified that the Bryan-mandated 20 percent CAFE increase in the first five years was totally unrealistic; they claimed they already were virtually locked in to 1996 models and that 40 percent in ten years, as required by the Bryan bill, couldn't be done. They applauded the Johnston-Wallop bill's approach of asking the Secretary of Transportation to set the CAFE standard to be the "maximum feasible fuel economy." They warned that performance and safety would be sacrificed if the CAFE standard were increased substantially.

Two technical experts, Steve Plotkin from the Office of Technology Assessment and a consultant to his office, K. G. Duleep, were the focus of attention in the CAFE hearings. Johnston loved what they had to say. Their basic conclusion was that very little CAFE increase was possible in the first five years. The companies were already pretty well locked in to their 1996 designs. The American automakers could probably get to an actual 29 MPG average by 1996, which would translate, with "alternative fuel credits" (mostly an additional 1.2 MPG that would be credited to so-called flexi-fuel cars which could run on *both* gasoline and an alternative, such as ethanol, methanol, natural gas, an electric battery, or a fuel cell), into CAFE's of 30 or 31 MPG for the American manufacturers.

By 2001, much more was possible in terms of actual increases in fuel economy, Duleep reported; the maximum technically feasible changes could get American manufacturers to about 38 MPG in ten years. Plotkin emphasized that by then manufacturers might well be selling many more "dedicated" alternative fuel vehicles, which run exclusively on nonpetroleum fuels, for which they would get substantial CAFE credits. (According to the politically determined rules, a car that goes thirty miles on a fuel input whose energy content is equal to that of one gallon of gasoline is assigned a CAFE rating of 30 MPG if it runs exclusively on gasoline, 200 MPG if it runs exclusively on natural gas, 145 MPG if it runs exclusively on ethanol, 137 MPG if it runs exclusively on electricity, and 105 MPG if it runs exclusively on methanol.) These CAFE-based incentives to build alternatively fueled vehicles could enable manufacturers to reach a CAFE of about 40 MPG. But that would mean auto manufacturers would have to abandon product lines before their normal replacement times, so the practicable technological potential under existing market conditions was probably somewhat less, Plotkin testified.

Duleep, whose testimony struck me as more straightforward and less political than most of the other witnesses, suggested that if one looked beyond ten years, much higher mileage vehicles were possible if the auto manufacturers made that a priority. Intrigued by hints in this testimony of what might be in Duleep's technical analyses, I obtained a lengthy primer he had written about different ways automobile fuel economy could be increased and studied it carefully.

Before the second CAFE hearing, I stopped by the Commerce Committee offices to talk with Linda Lance about some of the ideas in Plotkin's and Duleep's testimony at the first hearing and my tentative thoughts about sensible modifications or additions to the Bryan bill. She was open to considering changes and agreed, among other things, that the 1996 deadline in Bryan's CAFE bill for 20 percent increase in fuel economy was too soon.

At that hearing, Duleep said that enormous gas mileage increases were possible by 2010. He warned, however, that the use of alternative fuel and other "CAFE credits" could enable auto manufacturers to comply with CAFE standards without actually achieving anywhere near the nominal increases in fuel economy. Several prototype vehicles with very high actual fuel economies had already been built and tested. For instance, General Motors "Impact" prototypes were already achieving greater than 70 MPG, either as an electric car or powered by an efficient gasoline engine.

Henry Kelly and I developed a package of four proposals which, on the one hand, would signal the manufacturers they had to increase fuel economy aggressively and, on the other hand, assist them in doing so. Its practical expression was in four CAFE amendments which: (1) set a 40 MPG CAFE standard for 2003, with 10 percent of each manufacturer's fleet getting at least 70 MPG; (2) set a 2013 CAFE standard of 60 MPG; (3) subsidized a major new advanced vehicle R&D program; and (4) allowed states to set higher CAFE standards than the federal government in case the Congress passed weak or no new CAFE standards. Johnston was hurrying the hearings along so fast, we decided to hold off until the markup to introduce those amendments. But by the time of the markup discussion of CAFE we could see it would be an exercise in futility in the context of the Energy Committee.

The one hearing that was held on ANWR was not very helpful because the oil companies and the environmental groups talked past each other. The oil companies emphasized that ANWR might be an important new domestic source that might yield billions of barrels of oil. They obviously hoped to maintain the Trans-Alaska pipeline as an economical operation. Where the oil companies and the environmentalists disagreed was on the likely environmental impact of the drilling and on the availability of alternative exploration sites in Alaska. However, the two environmentalist witnesses, the Alaska Coalition's Mike Matz and the Audubon Society's Brooks Yeager, appeared together near the end of the hearing and these disagreements were not effectively explored.[6]

Along with ANWR and CAFE, the most contentious issue was PUHCA reform, the precursor of a looming battle over utility deregulation. The Public Utility Holding Company Act (PUHCA) had been enacted in 1935 to curb abuses by public utilities that were taking unfair advantage of their monopoly status. The proposed 1991 PUHCA reform would allow the creation of new electric power producing entities called Exempt Wholesale Generators (EWGs) that could compete with local utilities in building new generating plants and selling electricity wholesale to other utilities. Proponents said the 1935 act was outmoded; what was needed in the 1990s was competition in the electric power industry.

But that was just the first step. The largest electric utilities and natural gas pipeline companies were already viewing PUHCA reform as the opening wedge to deregulation of the electric power industry. First, large electric utilities and natural gas pipelines would build power plants far beyond their traditional service areas and compete to sell electricity wholesale. Next would come their holy grail—direct retail sales. The dream of large electric utilities and natural gas pipelines was to sell directly to exceptionally heavy users of retail electricity, such as large manufacturing firms. They aimed to take advantage of economies of scale to land choice retail customers with offers of very low rates. The big losers would be residential and small business customers, who would find their rates skyrocketing, and small local utilities, who might well find themselves unable to compete.

The lobbying was heavier on this issue than on any other in the Johnston-Wallop bill. PUHCA reform was being promoted strongly by the PUHCA Reform Coordinating Council, a powerful coalition of large utilities and natural gas pipeline companies nationwide, led by Pacific Gas and Electric and Southern California Edison and including Northern States Power (NSP), the giant of Minnesota's electric utilities. NSP was clearly hoping to sell its electricity retail to Chicago/Milwaukee industrial customers.

On the other hand, PUHCA reform was opposed vigorously by many smaller utilities, who had united in a forty-four-member Washington-based lobbying consortium known as the Electric Reliability Coalition. Minnesota Power and Light sent three different lobbyists to my office to urge that Paul oppose this provision. They feared that the very largest utilities would subsidize their generating plant construction with profits from other parts of their businesses, allowing them to win bids for building new plants around the nation. And since the largest utilities owned the bulk of the large transmission lines, they might use that control to give them unfair advantage in the competition for the lucrative, preferred retail customers.

As I thought about PUHCA reform, I was concerned that it might have other implications as well. In particular, I worried that it would affect adversely the prospects for a shift to a sustainable energy transition. Given the inefficient and profligate ways we use electricity, the potential for energy savings is enormous. By substituting efficient electrical devices alone, U.S. electricity use could be cut by as much as half without in any way affecting how Americans live. This meant that concerted, vigorous efficiency and conservation programs on the part of utilities could delay for a decade or more the necessity of building many of the new power plants now in the planning stages. That could buy time for development of cost-effective renewable alternatives to new large power plants. But once such large plants are built, they have a lifetime of forty years or more.

Several foreseeable advances in sustainable energy make for a compelling argument that prudent U.S. energy planning would avoid as much as possible those forty-year commitments to coal and nuclear plants: the promise of economical solar, wind, and biomass technologies for electric power generation in the early twenty-first century; the strong possibility that global warming and other environmental problems will necessitate a move away from fossil fuels; and the likelihood that high costs and public concerns about radioactive waste disposal, catastrophic reactor accidents, routine reactor emissions, and nuclear weapons proliferation will lead to a move away from nuclear power.

My initially vague concern about PUHCA reform came to focus on the possibility that the introduction of Exempt Wholesale Generators might tilt the balance in the American utility business toward building many new large power plants and away from vigorously pursuing saved-energy programs and renewable electricity generation. That vague concern was boosted to genuine worry by a conversation I had with the manager of Pacific Gas and Electric's Energy Efficiency Services. Within the utility business, PG&E has cultivated a reputation as a leader in saved-energy and renewable energy programs. When he came by my office, I asked him what PG&E would do if PUHCA reform passed. I expected him to tell me about how his company's experience with making saved energy a profitable business could be put to good use in helping other utilities establish similarly profitable enterprises. His answer made me realize my naïveté. Under PUHCA reform, he said, PG&E, working in the partnership it had established with the Bechtel Corporation, would be bidding to build new coal- and natural gas–fired generating plants around the nation. Not a word about saved energy. Not a word about wind or solar.

I realized that PG&E's pioneering work on energy efficiency, wind power, and photovoltaic cells was in significant measure a result of its being confined to its California service territory, where the regulatory framework was very different from that of the rest of the country. Regulatory rules framed by the California Energy Commission in the 1970s strongly militated against the building of new coal-fired and nuclear power plants in their service territories and rewarded saved-energy programs. I strongly suspected that building new generating plants and selling their power would be much more lucrative for PG&E than its saved-energy programs, no matter how much its officials proclaimed their commitment to them. If it could only be released from its California shackles and allowed to roam the country, PG&E, too, would participate in the building of new generating plants in less environmentally sensitive parts of the nation and in selling electricity outside its present service area.

It was not until the Energy Committee held hearings on PUHCA reform that I found that consumer advocacy groups like the Consumer Federation of America shared my concern. I also began to hear from public interest lobbyists that several factors would be crucial in deciding whether it would be more or less likely that saved-energy and renewable-generated electricity could thrive and prosper against the big utilities who wanted to build coal, natural gas, and nuclear power plants in the proposed brave new world of electricity competition.

Especially helpful in my education about this matter was Leon Lowery, an Environmental Action lobbyist who specialized in utility issues. He explained that two troubling problems with Exempt Wholesale Generators (EWGs) in the proposed new PUHCA regime were self-dealing and cross-subsidization. Self-dealing pertains to financial shell games that could be played between a utility and an EWG it had set up in which, for example, the price that the EWG charged the utility for electricity might be set to make it cost less than saved energy, a requirement for building new generating capacity in states with "least-cost planning." Cross-subsidization refers to similar shell games wherein an EWG set up by a large utility or natural gas or other kind of company is subsidized temporarily by proceeds from other operations of the company to allow it to underbid smaller utilities in the competition to build new generating plants.

On March 14 the committee held two hearings on PUHCA Reform.[7] As government witnesses testified enthusiastically in favor, I began to understand better how this change in the rules would give the Federal Energy Regulatory Commission (FERC) a much larger role in determining utility policies as significant regulatory power flowed to it from state regulatory commissions. But FERC had a long-standing reputation for cozy relationships with the big energy corporations, while many state public utility commissions (PUCs) were the driving force behind "least-cost planning." We were assured by utility witnesses that the PUCs would retain all of their authority over local utilities' policies, but I had a feeling this proposed "reform" would nevertheless end up creating a strong new bias in the system toward what the big companies wanted—to build new power plants.

In questioning the witnesses, Paul probed the likely impacts of the proposed PUHCA changes on utilities' programs to promote energy efficiency and state PUCs' attempts to institute least-cost energy programs. His concern that PUHCA reform would weaken the ability of state PUCs to promote sustainable energy initiatives and tilt the balance back toward conventional electric generation prompted an enlightening discussion. I began to think we were onto something important, an impression reinforced a few days later when I was invited to lunch by the chief Washington lobbyists of several natural gas producers: the pipeline giant ENRON, Interstate Natural Gas, NSP, and PG&E. PUHCA reform was clearly a very important issue for big players in energy game. These are examples of the well-heeled players who were going all out for PUHCA reform.

For those developing a strategy to revive the nuclear industry, three issues loomed large. One was the uncertainty inherent in two-step licensing, whereby a new nuclear plant underwent scrutiny in two stages, each involving local citizen participation. First, a construction license had to be granted, and second, an operating license had to be granted years later after construction was completed. Industry advocates claimed that investors were very reluctant to put up the roughly one billion dollars required for construction of a large nuclear plant, knowing that it was possible an operating permit would later be denied. They had convinced the Nuclear Regulatory Commission (NRC) to issue a rule prescribing a new process involving only one step, a combined construction and operating license before construction began.

Citizen intervention after construction would only rarely be possible and then only on sharply circumscribed issues. A public advocacy group, the Nuclear Information and Resource Service and its lawyer, Eric Glitzenstein, had successfully contested the rule in court, so Johnston was trying to write one-step licensing into the law.

Clearly, that would be a step backward in citizen participation, but what consequences was it likely to have in practice? This was one case for which a debate of sorts was arranged.[8] The initial plan was to have only six witnesses, all nuclear proponents, testify. Only at the last minute did Johnston allow Glitzenstein to participate. It happened at the very end of the March 5 hearing, when most of the senators had left. Glitzenstein was matched against former NRC chair, Marcus Rowden. It was a magnificent, informative debate with both side very ably represented, from which I came away with a strong sense that the proposed procedure would preclude a second hearing in many situations when it was clearly in the public interest to have one.

Two days later, uranium enrichment was the topic. This was a particularly stacked hearing, with no opponents at all testifying. I was surprised because the National Taxpayers Union had issued a compelling critique of this title, arguing that it would be a "ten billion dollar giveaway." During a break in the hearing, I spotted Jill Lancelot of the Taxpayers Union in the back of the hearing room. She said she had requested the opportunity to testify but had been turned down.

The hearing on a third nuclear power issue, the disposal of high-level radioactive waste from nuclear power plants, was a fascinating contrast to all the others in that the anti-Johnston position was articulated forcefully by a veritable army of credible opponents of the plan that Johnston had previously guided into law—storage of the waste at Yucca Mountain in Nevada. The hearing began with the case for the Yucca Mountain repository from the DoE's biggest gun, Secretary Watkins. My journal described what happened after that in this most memorable hearing.

"The fireworks begin when the governor and the entire Nevada congressional delegation, including Senators Bryan and Reid and both Congresspersons, show up to argue with extraordinary vehemence against what Senator Reid and the governor call the 'Screw Nevada Bill.' They are all adamantly opposed to Yucca Mountain and they are furious with the Congress and the DoE for shoving it down their throats.

"They are here to make it clear that they will fight this project with all their might. They are not sure the repository will be safe for the people of

Nevada and they do not trust the DoE to make a fair assessment of its safety. They believe instead that there are larger forces at work, political forces that will override any 'objective' attempt at 'scientific' assessment. They know that nuclear power proponents (industry, Congress, DoE) desperately need a waste repository and they know Nevada has been chosen as the place.

"Much of the discussion on the DoE side is about scientific assessment: 'All we are asking is to go on the site and find out for sure what's there,' says Watkins. And Johnston speaks of establishing an answer 'with scientific certainty.'

"From the Nevada side there is *some* discussion of scientific evidence that calls into question the long-term safety of the repository, but mostly there is discussion of why they don't trust the process; mostly history—the misleading assurances the soldiers at the Nevada atomic bomb tests were given; the more recent revelations of leaking radioactive waste from storage tanks near the plutonium production reactors at Hanford, Washington; and new evidence of an unexpectedly high incidence of leukemia among Oak Ridge, Tennessee, workers.

"Paul has a protracted exchange with Secretary Watkins about why the level of distrust is so high and what might be the implications of this distrust not only for siting a nuclear waste repository, but also for siting the hundreds of new nuclear power plants the National Energy Strategy report forecasts. Watkins admits the public had a right to be skeptical before he took over, but insists that has all changed and new procedures will engender public trust. Paul's and my sense is that given the history, public trust is unlikely, and with good reason!"

Why Not an Alternative?   6

Rescued from the Washington Mind-Set

On Saturday, March 2, I was back in Minnesota for the first time since January. What an intellectually liberating experience that turned out to be. Paul's energy policy aide in Minnesota, Scott Adams, had arranged for me to meet at the Wellstone office with an energy policy working group he had assembled. That splendid group included my Carleton colleague Norm Vig, David Morris of the Institute for Local Self-Reliance, Dean Abrahamson of the University of Minnesota's Humphrey Institute of Public Affairs, John Dunlop of the Minnesota Department of Public Service, Diane Jensen of Clean Water Action, Michael Noble of Minnesotans for an Energy Efficient Economy, and Anne Hunt of the St. Paul Neighborhood Energy Consortium. Vig, Morris and Abrahamson are known nationally for their energy and environmental policy work, and Dunlop, Jensen, Noble, Hunt, and others in the group are leaders of pathbreaking efforts to promote sustainable energy in Minnesota.

I spoke for an hour, describing the structure and major provisions of the Johnston-Wallop bill and explaining that it would be the vehicle for defining a new national energy strategy. Then I discussed my early thinking about initiatives Paul might sponsor. The group reacted in a surprising way. I may be overstating their dismay a bit, but basically their message was, "My gosh, you've only been there for two months and here you are giving us the Washington view of what is realistic. How could you have changed so fast?"

To put it mildly, they didn't like the Johnston-Wallop bill and didn't think it was an appropriate framework for charting our nation's energy future.

They suggested instead a vision of an energy-independent Minnesota, with Congress providing federal funds for investments in energy efficiency and renewables. That would help the state move in the right direction—toward energy efficient buildings and indigenous renewable supplies like windpower and biomass for electricity and ethanol and hydrogen for transportation and, in the longer term, wind and solar photovoltaic-generated hydrogen. They pointed out that Minnesota imports nearly all its energy, paying out billions of dollars every year to energy companies in the energy-producing states.

It wasn't that I didn't know this. After two months in Washington, I suppose I had become resigned to thinking that whatever would be done would necessarily occur within the framework of the Johnston-Wallop bill. In telling the Minnesota group what was possible, I was no longer looking beyond my new world, the Senate Energy Committee. Not long before, in speaking and writing I had been saying just what they were telling me that day.

In just a short time in the Senate, I had begun to lose my way. That meeting rescued me from the seductive Washington mind-set and set me back on course.

Trying to "Make It a Better Bill"

I was not the only one seduced by the Washington view of what is possible. Those who want to be "serious players" in the Capitol Hill policy games are socialized into thinking there is no alternative to accepting the ground rules laid down by powerful chairmen like Bennett Johnston. That's what happened at first to me. That, it seemed, was also what happened at first in the national energy strategy debate to many members of the Washington environmental community.

Before Paul's election, by late autumn 1990, many Washington-based environmental groups and their lobbyists had become concerned with what might be in the National Energy Strategy legislation. At that point, each group was pursuing its own particular interests, some focused on ANWR, some on CAFE, others on energy efficiency more generally. There were some cooperative efforts to fight against opening ANWR for oil exploration, such as that of the Alaska Coalition, headquartered in the Sierra Club and also including the Wilderness Society, the Audubon Society, and the National Wildlife Federation. A CAFE Working Group, involving representatives of U.S. PIRG (a national network of state public interest research group founded by Ralph Nader), the Sierra Club, the National Wildlife Federation,

VC LIBRARY

the Union of Concerned Scientists, and the Energy Conservation Coalition, was also meeting regularly.

Another effort known as the National Energy Strategy Working Group had been organized by the Union of Concerned Scientists, the Alliance to Save Energy, the American Council for an Energy Efficient Economy, and the Natural Resources Defense Council. Their principal focus was commissioning a study to compare four long-term energy policy scenarios: (1) continuing present policies and trends; (2) minimizing consumer energy costs; (3) adding environmental costs to a cost-minimizing model; and (4) reducing carbon dioxide emissions to stabilize climatic effects. Representatives from the four groups helped design a computer modeling study that was carried out at the Boston-based Tellus Institute and became the basis for the influential report, *America's Energy Choices*.[1]

In November 1990, with the release of the Bush National Energy Strategy proposal drawing near, the membership of the NES Working Group was greatly expanded to include all interested environmental organizations and it began meeting every week at the Wilderness Society. By attending these very large meetings, the groups were able to keep abreast of the latest intelligence about the NES and Johnston-Wallop bill and they began to plan cooperative efforts to influence the outcome of the energy strategy debate. One such project was to join with the public-interest public relations firm, the Communications Consortium, to inform the press nationwide of the environmental community's views about the energy strategy proposals. Phil Sparks, codirector of the consortium, led that effort.

The message was simple: the Bush plan put far too much emphasis on investing in traditional energy supplies while giving short shrift to efficient energy use and renewable energy sources. A poll that Sparks had commissioned demonstrated conclusively that the vast majority of Americans favored investments in conservation and renewables, rather than fossil fuels and nuclear power. When the NES was released, editors around the nation, alerted by consortium-prepared press packets, echoed these sentiments in critical editorials with such headlines as "Energy Policy: Oil Producers are Big Winners in Bush's New Plans" (the *Arizona Daily Star*); "Plan Slights Energy Efficiency" (*Daytona Beach News-Journal*); "Energy Policy: Bush Proposal Ignores Conservation" (the *Ft. Worth Star-Telegram*); "A Backward Energy Policy" (the *Chattanooga Times*); "A Bad Energy Plan" (*Burlington [Vt.] Free Press*); "Conserve Before Drilling" (the *Providence Journal*); "That's No Energy Policy" (*Indianapolis News*); and even "The Plan Stinks" (*Mobile Beacon-Alabama Citizen*).

As the environmentalists pressed their case to the American people, ANWR became the symbol of energy producers' seeking to circumvent environmental protections and CAFE became the symbol of environmentally benign energy efficiency and conservation alternatives. Meanwhile, the environmental groups were trying to figure out a strategy to deal with the Johnston juggernaut. Given that the Johnston-Wallop bill was the central focus of the Senate Energy Committee that year, the most natural response was to try to amend that bill by deleting the ANWR title, strengthening the CAFE and energy efficiency titles, and safeguarding against self-dealing and cross-subsidies in the PUHCA title.

As the committee hearings began, the Senate office most closely in touch with the environmentalists was that of Sen. Tim Wirth of Colorado. As chair of the Alliance to Save Energy, Wirth was a member of the NES Working Group. He was also chair of the Regulation and Conservation Subcommittee of the Energy Committee. Some of the environmentalists regarded him as their "agent" on the Energy Committee; others were suspicious about what he was up to with regard to the NES. Within the NES Working Group, the Alliance to Save Energy's executive director, Jim Wolf, often spoke for Wirth.

One suggestion that was made early on in the NES Working Group was that someone introduce a "good bill." On March 21, the last day of the Energy Committee hearings, Wirth introduced S.742, "The National Energy Efficiency and Development Act of 1991." The seven-title bill called for identifying a mix of policies that would result in a 20 percent reduction in carbon dioxide emissions by 2005, modest levels of federal funding for energy efficiency and renewables R&D and innovative state implementation programs, and significantly higher levels of federal funding for solar photovoltaic demonstration projects and for alternatives to petroleum fuels and vehicles powered by those fuels. It also mandated the Bryan CAFE standards, appliance efficiency standards, and least-cost-planning for state-regulated utilities. While not representing a radical shift in direction of U.S. energy policy, this was an important package of proposals not included in the Bush energy strategy or the Johnston-Wallop bill.

The last title, "Measures to Promote the Use of Natural Gas," however, read as though it had been written by natural gas industry lobbyists. Of course, Wirth was from Colorado, a major natural gas–producing state, and he was a genuine natural gas enthusiast, frequently regaling the Energy Committee with the pleasures of driving his natural gas–powered car. Another title had generated even more controversy. Many of the environmental groups were adamently opposed to including support of nuclear power in the bill and Wirth was forced to take it out.

At the time of the Energy Committee hearings, the environmentalists' strategy was not clear to me. Were they hoping to make Johnston-Wallop into a better bill by amending pieces of it? Or were they planning to oppose Johnston-Wallop altogether and back an alternative? After I got to know many of the environmental lobbyists, I learned that at that time they had not yet been able to reach a consensus on that crucial question. For instance, there was a split within the Sierra Club about both goals and tactics. I was told by one observer, "Some people cared about the Arctic and nothing else and other people cared about CAFE and nuclear power and efficiency standards. . . . Some people thought there was one thing we could win: we could strip ANWR from the bill. Other people thought we could offer killer amendments that would blow up Johnston's coalition. Maybe it would be PUHCA, maybe CAFE, maybe taking out ANWR. The idea would be to anger one constituency so much that the bill would die."

But many factors were pushing the environmentalists toward trying to make Johnston-Wallop a better bill. Within certain limits, that is probably what Bennett Johnston expected and would support. From the environmentalists' perspective, Wirth was the only member of the Senate who might have introduced a comprehensive alternative energy strategy bill that could have served at the grassroots as a substitute for Johnston-Wallop. But Wirth decided instead to play ball with his chairman and constructively amend the Johnston-Wallop bill. When Norm Vig and I had first gone by his office in January, Wirth's aide had made it clear that the senator did not intend to challenge Bennett Johnston. Rather, he planned to get along by going along and, as a consequence, he would be granted permission to add provisions to strengthen the efficiency, renewables, and natural gas titles of the Johnston-Wallop bill.

So, Wirth did not put together a comprehensive package that promoted a competing vision of a sustainable energy future. With the support of the Alliance to Save Energy, an attempt was made to mobilize grassroots criticism of the Johnston-Wallop bill on grounds that its energy efficiency and renewable provisions were weak or nonexistent. But that effort was laying the groundwork for making Johnston-Wallop a better bill by adding Wirth's provisions during the committee markup or on the Senate floor.

Two weeks before the Wirth bill was introduced, a hint appeared in the press that Tim Wirth already had a hunch about how the most contentious issues in the energy strategy debate would ultimately be resolved. A March

9, 1991, a *National Journal* article headlined "Showdown Over Arctic Oil" suggested that Bennett Johnston's hope was a "political swap": at some point, he would accept a strengthened CAFE provision in exchange for drilling in ANWR. However, the article ended with an intriguing alternative prediction from Jim Wolf, Wirth's spokesperson in the environmental community: "More likely, however, Congress will opt for the easy way out, said James L. Wolf, executive director of the Alliance to Save Energy: 'We will have an energy bill here, but probably without CAFE or ANWR.'"[2]

In terms of substance, such a compromise would make no sense. I could see the logic of Johnston's arguing for a compromise that would include both production (ANWR) and efficiency (CAFE), the environmentalists' arguing for giving priority in the strategy to efficiency and renewable measures, or the oil companies' arguing for giving priority to increasing domestic oil production. But I couldn't see the sense of a so-called compromise that would do neither. The logic I could detect existed entirely in the realm of political maneuvering.

First Glimmers of a Wellstone Energy Initiative

The Minnesota meeting had jolted me into thinking about energy the way I had before I went to Washington. Back in 1982–83, in a project entitled "Planning for Minnesota's Energy Future," my students and I had designated ourselves the "Energy Policy Planning Task Force for the New Governor" and we had three recommendations for Gov. Rudy Perpich when he took office in January 1983. One of them was that he call together the governors of the other energy-importing states to organize a coalition aimed at changing the politics of energy in the country.

Paul and I had published an op-ed piece in the March 5, 1983, *Minneapolis Star Tribune* explaining this idea:

> The importing states have in common an energy-dollar drain that threatens their people and saps their economies. Minnesota epitomizes the problem: We import 99% of our fuel. We are vulnerable to supply interruptions, and we have no control over energy prices. . . . Minnesota's wholesale energy budget is larger than the state budget. Most of that money leaves the state, never to return. And with those dollars go economic activity and jobs.
>
> State energy efficiency programs are the key to stemming this energy dollar drain. Despite conservation, we have barely tapped Minnesota's energy saving potential. . . . For less than $5,000, weatherization specialists can halve the energy consumption of even supposedly well-insulated homes. And weatheri-

zation is labor intensive; no other energy strategy produces so many jobs per dollar invested. Further, saving energy in Minnesota and other energy-importing states makes sense from a national perspective. It costs less to save a gallon of oil or a thousand cubic feet of natural gas in Minnesota than it does to drill for them in Texas.

An all-out effort to weatherize Minnesota would cost about $800 million in 10 years. The big question is how to pay for the effort. In tight times, the money required is not available within the state. All energy-importing states share Minnesota's dilemma. They have the opportunity to achieve large savings, but lack the money to finance the work.[3]

What we recommended was that the importing state governors get behind federal energy taxes "that reach to the other end of the pipelines and bring back revenues for the importing states' energy investments." But, we noted, "Initiative for these actions will have to come from a coalition of energy-importing states. If we rely on a President and Congress beholden to the oil and gas interests, we will not get our fair share [of such taxes]."

That op-ed piece turned out to be a significant step in the process that led to a major conference in January 1984 that brought about a hundred state energy officials and energy specialists to Minnesota from fifteen cold-weather states under the cosponsorship of the Northeast-Midwest Congressional Coalition and hosted by Governor Perpich. They came to share common energy policy concerns and discuss concerted political action.

The Minnesota meeting in 1991 jarred me out of the Washington mindset and back to my own long-held convictions about reforming energy policy. The objective in the 1990s, moreover, was a national energy strategy that would benefit the entire nation, not just Minnesota and the other energy-importing states. Programs organized by states or regional consortia had to be a central part of the sustainable energy transition strategy and could be the key to nationwide support and legislation.

There are several reasons why regional, state, and local programs are particularly important in promoting energy efficiency and renewables. Different regions of the country have different climates and different indigenous renewable resources, giving rise to very different regionally specific transition strategies. During the 1970s and '80s many states and consortia of states demonstrated impressive results in saving energy and developing renewable resources. As a result, the expertise, the experience, and the intellectual resources needed to design and direct programs sensitive to local conditions are to be found at the state and local levels. The policy and regulatory authority is also there. And the strongest motivation is there as well—economic vitality and energy vulnerability are state and local concerns closely tied to future developments in energy.

But as in Minnesota, by 1991 most state energy programs were languishing for lack of sufficient financial resources. The most important thing the federal government could do would be to raise the money through a tiny energy tax and then distribute that money to states that demonstrated they had serious, sensible long-term sustainable energy transition plans.

Those were the key ideas in the Wellstone energy initiative, which later became the proposed Sustainable Energy Transition Act (SETA). Small energy taxes would feed a Sustainable Energy Transition trust fund that the Department of Energy would use to finance grants aimed at prompting each state to prepare and execute a comprehensive plan to exploit cost-effective energy efficiency opportunities and to support the development and commercialization of indigenous renewable energy resources. If such plans were implemented in all fifty states with adequate funding, not only would energy efficiency and renewables programs blossom and flourish, but a nationwide constituency also would be created behind a sustainable energy transition, perhaps powerful enough to challenge the hegemony of the currently dominant energy interests.

In March 1991, as the Johnston-Wallop bill was moving rapidly toward markup in Johnston's Energy Committee, this was just a glimmer in my mind's eye, not a formal proposal. The immediate question was how we could interject such a sustainable energy transition proposal into congressional consideration. One possibility would be to try to attach it to the Johnston-Wallop bill. Paul first floated our idea in public in mid-March in a statement at an Energy Committee hearing about alternative automobile fuels. A few days later, however, Ben Cooper pointed out that since our proposal involved an energy tax, it would have to go to the Finance Committee rather than the Energy Committee.

At about the same time, what seemed at first to be a far more promising avenue opened up. In early March, Majority Leader George Mitchell made the surprise announcement that he had named a special Energy Policy Task Force of Democratic senators to look into what should be the ingredients of a national energy strategy. Included on the task force were Mitchell and Bennett Johnston, along with several potential critics of the Johnston-Wallop bill. Some of those were from other committees, including Environment and Public Works Committee members Max Baucus of Montana, Joe Lieberman of Connecticut, and Howard Metzenbaum of Ohio, along with Commerce Committee member Dick Bryan of Nevada. And several were from the

Energy Committee, including Bill Bradley of New Jersey, Dale Bumpers of Arkansas, Wyche Fowler of Georgia and Tim Wirth of Colorado. To our disappointment, Paul was not named. Almost immediately, however, Metzenbaum's energy aide, Ken Rynne, called to say he would like to meet with me and that he would be glad to introduce our ideas into the task force's deliberations.

While rumors abounded, no one I knew was sure of the real purpose of the Mitchell task force. The optimistic theory was that Mitchell wanted a fundamentally different bill that would be a Democratic alternative to the Bush administration's National Energy Strategy and the Republican-backed Johnston-Wallop proposal. As his 1991 book, *World on Fire: Saving An Endangered Earth,* demonstrates, Mitchell is a committed environmentalist, with strong views on global climate change and environmental protection.[4]

A less optimistic theory was that Mitchell was afraid that a nasty, divisive public fight among Senate Democrats was shaping up. He could foresee that such an intraparty struggle would prevent passage of legislation on an issue as vital and visible as national energy policy. At the least, he was worried that the Democrats, who controlled the Congress, would appear seriously divided. According to the pessimists, the purpose of the task force was to work out the differences among Democrats in private so they could present a united front on the Senate floor; it was not aimed at dramatically altering the Johnston-Wallop approach.

Some members of the task force obviously *were* interested in a dramatic departure from Johnston-Wallop. After its first meeting, Montana's Sen. Max Baucus, a leading member of the Environment Committee, circulated a memo proposing that the task force state its opposition to the National Energy Strategy. He also proposed that the Democrats commit themselves to an alternative energy strategy with the Bryan CAFE bill the "first essential element. . . ."

The Wellstone Sustainable Energy Transition Act concept clearly fitted that alternative focus. So, with plenty of feedback from my energy-wise friends in Washington and Minnesota, I drew up a lengthy memo describing the proposal and circulated it among all members of the task force. The memo explained why it was attractive on both substantive and political grounds. It emphasized the benefits to the energy-producing states as well as the energy-importing states. It emphasized that sustainable energy programs, particularly energy conservation and energy efficiency programs, are highly labor intensive. It would be difficult to conceive of a more cost-effective, more socially useful, way of investing federal dollars to create large numbers of new jobs throughout the nation. In those regions rich in renewable resources as well as fossil fuels, sustainable energy transition planning would include the establishment of new sustainable energy industries, the retraining of workers, and so forth. For states whose economies were heavily dependent on fossil fuel production, diminishing resource bases as well as any future global warming policies would necessitate the development of sustainable substitutes; organizing an orderly economic transition and otherwise protecting the people of the region was an important goal of the government.

To our disappointment, one of the majority leader's first actions regarding the task force strongly hinted at which of the two theories about his intent was correct: he named Bennett Johnston to chair the group. And when Kari Moe, then Paul's legislative director, approached Mitchell's chief of staff to inquire how best to introduce our proposal into the task force deliberations, he told her we should work through Ben Cooper and the Energy Committee staff.

Whatever Mitchell's intent, it was all for naught. With Johnston at the helm, the task force went nowhere.

Nevertheless, though the Wellstone bill would not be completed until much later that year, we now had formulated the basic elements of his energy initiative. I became convinced that SETA could be the centerpiece of a package of proposals to replace the Johnston-Wallop approach, and the Wellstone challenge became the principal preoccupation of my remaining time in Washington. I'll continue with that story after one digression to relate some evidence I gathered under questionable circumstances that further convinced me state programs were key to a sustainable energy transition.

The circumstances were my first encounter with what happens when special interest lobbyists take congressional staffers on all-expense-paid trips to exotic places. From Tuesday, March 26 to Friday, March 29, 1991, eighteen congressional staffers and I were the guests of Pacific Gas and Electric Company, first in San Francisco and then down the coast at a fancy resort near Carmel.

I agreed to go on this trip for several reasons. First, I was curious about what happens on such an expedition. Second, I looked forward to seeing first hand what PG&E, one of the utility leaders in saved-energy programs, in wind power generation, and in research on photovoltaics and electric and natural gas-powered vehicles, was doing. But I was perhaps most curious about PG&E as a leader in the movement for PUHCA reform, which would permit it to compete to build new power plants. I hoped to understand what accounted for this apparent contradiction—that it eschewed new power plants in California, pursuing energy efficiency as vigorously as any utility in the country, and that just as vigorously it was urging changes in the utility regulatory rules that would enable it to build new power plants and sell electricity outside of its long-standing Northern California service area.

The invitation I received promised us a good time and said that Tuesday evening, we would "enjoy a hearty dinner with PG&E executives in a well-known San Francisco restaurant." PG&E was certainly good to its word. They put us up at a plush hotel, the Galleria Park, and treated us to a fine meal at Bentley's, an elegant restaurant in the hotel, hosted by the PG&E's congressional lobbying director, Bob Testa, who had been one of those bending my ear about PUHCA reform in Washington the week before.

The next morning we met at PG&E headquarters in downtown San Francisco and heard from several top executives, including the chairman and CEO, Dick Clarke, about PG&E's commitment to energy efficiency and environmental protection. Clarke proudly described PG&E's plan to meet 75 percent of its anticipated near-term increased energy demand, which would have required 2500 megawatts of new generating capacity by the turn of the century, by reducing the demand with customer energy efficiency (CEE) programs instead. A famous 1990 California "Collaborative Agreement" that had resulted from intense negotiations among environmentalists, utility executives, and state officials contained a formula whereby the regulatory rules could be changed so that a utility, as well as its ratepayers, would profit from saving energy. Out of nearly $1 billion dollars in PG&E earnings from its regulated business in 1990, $9 million came from the customer energy efficiency programs, which Clarke described as "not a lot, but not a little." He also plugged PUHCA Reform, "so we can compete in building new generating capacity."

Howard Golub, vice president and general counsel, was evidently a dedicated environmentalist. He enthusiastically noted that in the 1990s PG&E would avoid building any large new power plants. Its hope was to use that decade to develop renewable technologies for after the turn of the century. A new coal or gas power plant was not just for the present, said Golub—its impacts would be felt for forty years. I saw the philosophy of buying time in the 1990s with intensive energy efficiency, conservation, and renewable development efforts as an important feature of a state's sustainable energy transition plan, and this discussion helped to sharpen my thinking.

Next we went downstairs to the Energy Control Center to see where PG&E coordinates its multitude of power sources to meet changing demand for electricity. The center's manager gave us several insights in his briefing. One thing he explained was that even though wind power is quite variable, PG&E had been surprised to find it could be used almost like base-load generating capacity. With many separate wind machines, the output available is fairly predictable many hours in advance. Combined with rapid access to hydropower reserves in the Pacific Northwest and gas-fired backup generators that can be brought on line in a few minutes, wind was an important and dependable contributor to PG&E's generating capacity.

Then on to the San Ramon laboratory, where I had a fascinating conversation with PG&E's research director Carl Weinberg, one of the pioneering utility thinkers about saved energy and renewables. A luncheon talk about PG&E's strong interest in natural gas and electric vehicles gave me some understanding of how the oil companies' early edge in promoting methanol as California's preferred alternative automotive fuel was being countered by political forces behind natural gas and electricity.

After that our bus went on to the Altamont Pass Wind Farms. For some reason, I expected the scene to be an unaesthetic, ugly cacophony. But to my surprise, I found the arrays of wind turbines turning together as far as the eye could see across an agricultural landscape memorably picturesque and not unpleasantly noisy.

Then came a long drive down the coast to Carmel and the elegant Quail Lodge, where each of us was assigned an opulent suite alongside fountains and a golf course. That's when I began to get a little nervous about what I was doing there.

The next day consisted of wall-to-wall briefings, all excellent, very well prepared, but including almost too much information to handle. Greg Rueger, whose presentation before the Energy Committee had impressed me, gave an instructive overview of the utility business and elaborated in great detail on PG&E's plans for the next twenty years. Then Mason Willrich, president and CEO of PG&E's cooperative effort with Bechtel, PG&E Enterprises, gave the pitch for PUHCA reform. I sensed that promoting PUHCA reform was PG&E's most important hidden agenda for this trip. Willrich's presentation and the answers to the questions I raised did nothing to assuage my fear that the net result of this far-reaching change with difficult-to-predict outcomes would be to tilt the balance in the utility business away from saved energy and toward new power plants in most of the rest of the country outside California.

To assuage my guilt, I begged off the next morning's program and drove off from Quail Lodge before daybreak in a rental car to Berkeley, where physicist Art Rosenfeld had arranged for me to meet with a group at Lawrence Berkeley Laboratory interested in our Sustainable Energy Transition legislation. The meeting was fairly short, but very stimulating. Art and his colleagues had done much to contribute to the remarkable tilt toward saved energy in California.

All in all, I found the trip very useful. I learned a great deal about conserving electricity, deploying renewables, and operating a utility; I also found much in California to reinforce my enthusiasm for developing the Wellstone sustainable energy transition initiative; and I remained very skeptical of PUHCA reform.

The Tide Turns 7

The Wellstone Team

With the Johnston-Wallop markup rapidly approaching in early April, a formidable Wellstone energy team was taking shape. Norman Vig made several opportune visits in preparation for replacing me as Paul's policy advisor the following September. I began looking for an energy legislative aide (L.A.) in mid-February and hit the jackpot with Karl Gawell, who had been project manager for the Solar Energy Research Institute's influential study *Building a Sustainable Future.*[1]

The 1981 SERI report was a seminal work, drawing together in one document the experience and insights of the 1970s experiments with energy efficiency and renewables. Using innovative analytical tools, the report demonstrated that many approaches to saving energy in residential and commercial buildings and in using electricity were already cost effective. It made a compelling case that a sustainable energy future built around energy efficiency and solar and other renewables held far greater potential for economically attractive investments far sooner than the conventional wisdom of the time posited.

However, as this study was completed, Ronald Reagan was elected president. A monumental struggle broke out when Reagan appointees took over at the Department of Energy and tried to suppress publication of the SERI report. The press got wind of the struggle, portions of the report were leaked, and eventually it was published. But the dark ages of energy policy in the Reagan years set in and federal government R&D and other support of energy efficiency and renewable energy were squelched.

I had known of Gawell's excellent reputation even before I met him. He came to work as the Wellstone energy and environment L. A. on April 3 and soon proved to be everything we could have hoped for. In addition to supervising the SERI study, he had worked over the years on energy and environmental policy in two House offices and later as congressional lobbyist on those issues for the National Wildlife Federation. He brought to our office a broad knowledge of energy policy, a sophisticated understanding of how Congress works, many valuable contacts in the Washington environmental community, and a work ethic that was truly exceptional, even when judged by Capitol Hill's ridiculously high expectations.

From the moment he arrived, Karl was a fount of creative ideas. He suggested that an apt way to think about the fifteen-title Johnston-Wallop bill was as a menu of delectable items that made Bennett Johnston's and his energy industry friends' mouths water. Presumably, though, Bennett had his favorites and he would probably trade some items away if necessary to get the ones he wanted most. This bill was an ideal starting point for a consummate wheeler-dealer.

The conventional wisdom was that the one item Johnston wanted more than any other was ANWR. He had gone out of his way to say so repeatedly, and he had made ANWR revenues the funding source for all the new programs in his bill, a clever move designed to create very difficult problems if ANWR were removed. But Karl had a provocative thought. What if ANWR were a giant Johnston head-fake? That one proposal had become the lightning rod for the best organized and most aggressive grassroots environmentalist opposition. There were other environmental outrages in the bill, but ANWR had attracted the most criticism. Suppose Johnston were deliberately setting this up, Karl suggested, planning that later if his controversial bill encountered trouble, he could drop the ANWR provision at just the right moment? The opposition would be disarmed and the rest of his bill would pass easily.

The "Giant Johnston Head-Fake Theory" is a good example of the stimulating thinking Karl brought to the Wellstone office. My own view was that there was good reason to believe that Bennett Johnston sincerely wanted ANWR and was not planning to remove it. But what became obvious in our discussions was that by making ANWR the issue that symbolized their opposition to the bill, the environmentalists had made their position vulnerable.

Besides Norm and Karl, an important, though informal, consultant to the team was Henry Kelly, one of the nation's foremost authorities on energy efficiency and renewables. Henry had been the associate director of the Solar

Energy Research Institute during Karl's tenure there, and the sustainable energy transition goal that had been laid out most effectively in the 1981 SERI report coincided with our own current position. I felt that after ten years of political exile, the SERI program deserved national recognition and a hero's welcome back to guide our country's energy policy. With these three strong allies, I no longer felt so outgunned by Johnston's forces as the opening of the Johnston-Wallop bill markup approached.

Sand in the Gears

At a meeting of committee member staffers in the Energy Committee library, Ben Cooper announced that the markup would begin on April 16 and he distributed thirteen volumes of transcripts, covering all the hearings on the Johnston-Wallop bill. That was an amazingly rapid publication turnaround. Ben told us the chairman hoped the entire markup could be completed in the two weeks before the next recess began on April 26. Johnston evidently planned to ram this comprehensive, far-reaching legislation through the committee and get it quickly to the Senate floor.

Karl and I decided that our first task would be to throw sand in the gears and try to slow the juggernaut down. We needed time to build Johnston-Wallop opposition coalitions on the Energy Committee, in the Senate, and within the environmental community and to strategize and work with them. We hoped to use the markup period to signal the full Senate and the press that there were many provisions of the bill that were very controversial and strongly opposed by influential senators and respected national environmental organizations. Given Chairman Johnston's proven ability to control the agenda and reward and punish members, he would surely get his way in the committee. But if a large number—we hoped a majority—of Democrats on the committee could be lined up, with the support of prestigious public interest groups, against the controversial provisions, that would signal that the bill was in for a stiff fight on the Senate floor.

At our suggestion, Mike Matz, director of the Alaska Coalition, arranged a meeting in Sen. Tim Wirth's office with staffers of members who might conceivably join in this effort. Matz and Brooks Yeager of the Audubon Society led a strategy discussion with Tracy Thornton from Sen. Wyche Fowler's office, Gene Peters from Sen. Bill Bradley's office, Russ Shay and Dave Harwood from Sen. Wirth's office, and Karl and me. We agreed that we would each prepare tough opening statements for the first day of the markup and cooperate in challenging every controversial provision of the bill and forcing protracted, contentious debate. In my journal, I noted, "It is promising to see Senate offices talking about organizing together, but I'll believe it when it happens. The senators are all such prima donnas, with their own personal agendas, that they rarely work together. Still, the meeting was a hopeful event."

Next, we prepared our part of the opening salvo of that campaign, Paul's opening statement. Two days before the markup began, Norm and I mapped out its contents. Within an hour, Norm whipped up an excellent detailed outline. By the morning the markup began, Norm had written and Karl and I had refined a powerful opening statement.

In retrospect, that Tuesday morning was a defining moment. Norm and I went up to the Labor Committee to pick up Paul and arrived at the Energy Committee hearing room at 9:45. Although the markup was scheduled to start at 9:30, we were unconcerned. The hearings had always begun a bit late; I was confident Johnston would still be in the preamble of his statement and it would be a very long time before Paul—nineteenth in seniority on the committee—would get his chance to speak.

When we entered the hearing room, however, we were in for a big surprise. Johnston had announced there would be no opening statements. The markup had begun at precisely 9:30 and committee staffers were already testifying about the renewable energy title of the bill and proposing amendments. Other committee members, who shared our expectations, were just beginning to arrive and similarly were taken aback to find the markup rushing along in high gear.

As Paul took his seat, we conferred briefly. He must not let Johnston get away with it! Paul interrupted and demanded to make his statement. Johnston responded impatiently that the markup was already in progress. But Paul insisted that he and probably others wanted to lay out their concerns with the bill at the beginning. Again Johnston tried to brush him aside. The mood in the room was tense. A freshman senator defying the chairman like that just wasn't done. One knowledgable friend in the audience, an environmental lobbyist, later told me she was nervous about the likely consequences, as if Paul were committing senatorial suicide in terms of effective participation on the Energy Committee.

But Paul refused to back down and Johnston was forced, reluctantly, to let him speak. The statement was not brief and throughout his delivery the tension in the hearing room was palpable. What he said was a hard-hitting criticism of the chairman's bill in both general and specific terms. First, he was blunt in his overall appraisal.

The legislation before us, unfortunately, just does not take us in the right direction. It does not alter our basic course. We have a fundamental choice to make here: we can continue to go down the fossil fuel and nuclear path we're on, and perhaps smooth it out a bit by raising efficiency standards and mitigating some of the obvious side-effects such as air pollution and nuclear proliferation; or we can choose to head down a different path that takes us in the long-term direction I believe we must go—the direction of maximal energy efficiency and conservation, of temporarily shifting to transition fuels that don't add so much to the carbon dioxide buildup, and of serious development of new, renewable supplies of energy that will both meet our needs and maintain the stability of the planet in the next century.

Then he elaborated on his objections to specific provisions of the Johnston-Wallop bill: drilling for oil in a unique and priceless wilderness area; reducing citizen participation in nuclear power plant licensing; undermining the trend toward utility investments in energy efficiency; making a mockery of required increases in automobile fuel economy; and on and on through the titles of the bill. To move toward a sustainable energy future, he concluded, state and regional transition plans and programs, funded by federal Sustainable Energy Transition Grants and aided by appropriate federal sustainable energy research and development, could lead the way.

When Paul finished, Johnston gave him an icy look and made a scornful crack about the 75 miles-per-gallon cars that Paul had said should be in production in substantial numbers in ten years. By then most of the senators had arrived and we expected several to follow with statements of their own concerns about the bill. But no one backed Paul up. Tim Wirth made a few desultory remarks about energy taxes. Johnston said he didn't wish to discuss that now; maybe they could take up his concerns at the end of the markup. And that was it. Paul had started the markup on just the right note, but if we were going to have success in getting the press to report on the defects of the bill, there would have to be much more controversy and many more confrontations on the committee. Where was the support we had expected from other senators? And why had the audience snickered at his mention of 75 miles-per-gallon cars. (Two years later, getting 80 MPG cars on the road in large numbers in the same time frame would become the centerpiece of the Clinton administration's billion-dollar "Clean Car Initiative" in partnership with the major American auto manufacturers.) Paul was angry and upset, even though to my mind this had been one of his finest hours in Washington.

In any case, the immediate problem was Bennett Johnston and his attempt to rush his bill through the Energy Committee and onto the Senate floor. As in the hearings, Chairman Johnston controlled the markup agenda. It soon became apparent that he did not plan simply to begin with Title I and then move systematically through the bill. Rather, he would decide the order of topics, often giving the rest of us little advance notice and generally keeping us off balance. His markup strategy, it was rumored, was to start with the less contentious titles, establishing a spirit of cooperation and accommodation within the committee, and later move to the more controversial provisions.

After the first markup session, a meeting of the supposedly dissident group was held in the office of Sen. Dale Bumpers (D., Arkansas) to plan for the Wednesday session. By then the environmentalists were sounding the alarm, especially since Johnston's staff had just circulated proposed new language pertaining to the regulation of hydropower projects that was more controversial than ever. Staffers present expressed concern. "But there is little cohesion in the group and little evidence of backbone," I noted in my journal.

The amendment Johnston's staff was circulating at the last minute provided for the states to assume regulatory authority over small hydropower dams. The small print made it clear that some important federal environmental protections would be lost in the transition, those included in the Wild and Scenic Rivers Act, the National Environmental Policy Act, and the Endangered Species Act. What is more, only about fifteen of the fifty states had carried out the sort of comprehensive assessments of their river systems that suggested they were prepared to protect their river environments from serious adverse effects of hydropower development.

Karl took responsibility for developing an appropriate response. That evening in our office he and the two witnesses who had most effectively criticized the Johnston-Wallop approach at the committee's hydropower hearing drew up two amendments. One preserved the federal environmental protections and the other required states to do appropriate statewide river assessments before they assumed hydropower regulatory authority.

The result was extensive, contentious debate in the committee, alerting the press to negative, far-reaching consequences of the Johnston proposal. While his amendments did not pass, Paul had succeeded in slowing up the process and publicizing serious problems with the bill. From the beginning, he had let it be known that he was going to make a fuss about the barriers the energy industries hoped to tear down with this legislation. He was underscoring the controversial issues and laying the groundwork for the challenges that would come later on the Senate floor and in the House. To Paul's credit, a topic Johnston had probably thought would be disposed of amicably in an hour or so had taken two full days. A new tone had been introduced.

Another fight broke out at the next markup session over a package of natural gas pipeline amendments introduced by Tim Wirth. One involved changing natural gas pricing rules to help domestic pipeline companies compete with Canadian natural gas; another involved an automatic eminent domain option for pipeline projects, circumventing citizen participation in public hearings. The day before the markup, a team of lobbyists came by our office for separate conversations with Karl and with me, introducing themselves by saying Wirth's office had suggested they drop by and talk with us about the Canadian gas pricing issue. They assured us that Minnesota consumers as well as domestic pipeline companies would benefit from the Wirth amendment. But Karl was skeptical. He called the Public Utility Commission staff in Minnesota to check and was told that the lobbyists were dead wrong. The next day Paul supported Bill Bradley in an attempt to drop that amendment, although the challenge was defeated 13–7.

Otherwise our campaign to slow things down had mixed results. Wirth and Johnston had similarly comfortable committee support on the natural gas pipeline eminent domain provision. Many of the Democrats seemed inclined to join with the Republicans and the chairman on even the most contentious votes. Some items passed with surprisingly little debate. For instance, the committee authorized tens, perhaps hundreds, of millions of dollars in compensation for residents of those states where oil spills and other consequences of offshore drilling required cleanup operations and other measures. My journal described what happened: "Two minutes maximum. No one present, besides Johnston, a couple of staffers and some lobbyists, has any idea of what was just given away in a few short moments! This will probably result in an enormous windfall of benefits to Louisiana residents and to oil companies."

But we had more success on the nuclear power front. First, we were involved in maneuvering to buy time for grassroots citizens groups to lobby against one-step nuclear licensing. Johnston was evidently planning to speed that provision through the committee before the one-week Senate recess. Several of the environmental groups wanted to use the recess to lobby committee members heavily on this issue. We decided on a delaying tactic, circulating a letter indicating that Paul was planning to introduce two amendments—one to allow individual states to pre-empt the federal government and set stronger nuclear power plant safety standards and the other to strike the entire one-step licensing title. But Paul did not show up at the beginning of the last markup session before the recess. Ben and his associates kept asking me anxiously where he was. I assured them he would be there eventually, that he had another important committee hearing and then had to preside over the Senate. Meanwhile, Karl kept watch outside the hearing room door to be sure Paul did not show up until quite late. When he finally did arrive, it was near the end of the session, with insufficient time for the nuclear licensing issue to be dealt with. The environmental groups would have the week they wanted to lobby against the one-step licensing proposal.

The upshot of these efforts, at any rate, was that even at the supposedly uncontentious beginning, the markup moved much more slowly and much less smoothly than Johnston had hoped. By the end of the two weeks in which Ben had said the chairman wanted to complete the markup of the entire bill, all we had completed was renewables, natural gas and off-shore drilling.

By this time, apparently, the environmental groups had made a conscious decision to accept the Johnston-Wallop bill as the framework for the energy strategy debate and to try to make it a better bill by eliminating its most objectionable provisions, such as ANWR drilling, and strengthening its weakest provisions, most notably its energy efficiency and renewables titles. They also seemed to have decided not to spend too much time and effort trying to bring about those changes in the Energy Committee, in part because it seemed so hopeless a venue. They would save their powder for fights on the Senate floor and in the House.

While I understood the reason for their decision, I nevertheless found it frustrating. We would have appreciated more help. Soon after the markup began, I remarked in my journal, "Karl and I are both disappointed with the environmental lobby for failing to press hard in the Energy Committee and expose what is going on. Their strategy is evidently to make the real fight on the floor; in the meantime, they wouldn't mind some really bad stuff being put in the bill—to be exposed later. And believe me, there is already very bad stuff—removing citizen participation rights in pipeline siting and nuclear licensing and hydro projects, giving away power to the energy companies right and left."

Time to Think, Time to Act

Political scientist Sanford Lakoff was to be my host for a sabbatical year at the University of California at San Diego that had been scheduled to begin in January 1991. When Paul was elected and I called to tell Sandy my arrival would be delayed, he was very supportive, but made me promise that either Paul or I would give a talk at the university in April, during a congressional recess. I'm sure he hoped for Paul, but he got me instead.

The topic of my April 30 talk was "Congress and a National Energy Strategy." Armed with the thirteen volumes of Energy Committee hearings, I spent five days closeted in the Lakoffs' guest room overlooking the Pacific. What a pleasure it was to have time to think. By the time of the talk, I finally felt for the first time that I had a real sense of the Johnston-Wallop bill as a whole. With this overview, I could see not only the specific problems I had previously spotted, but also very disturbing patterns of problems in the bill.

The most striking pattern was one I have already highlighted: major energy industries had obviously encountered serious government regulation barriers, most of them the product of twenty years of environmental legislation. For example, the oil and gas producers found themselves unable to drill for oil on the coastal plain of ANWR and in choice spots on the outer continental shelf off Florida and California; the nuclear power industry had been stymied by public distrust and investor reluctance stemming from such issues as nuclear reactor safety, radioactive waste disposal, and uncertain, soaring costs; the coal companies had found that their principal customers, coal-fired generating plants, had been forced to clean up or shut down, and they worried what the government might do in response to the prospect of global warming; the American automakers feared that once again they would be required to increase fuel economy; the natural gas pipelines faced delays in acquiring land and competition from Canadian gas and they ached to be allowed to join in the lucrative construction of gas-fired electric power plants; and many of the largest electric utilities were itching to build new power plants around the country but were limited to their local service areas.

When the National Energy Strategy and the Johnston-Wallop bill were framed, many policies had been proposed, but the proposals had been selectively filtered. For my University of California, San Diego, talk, I prepared some transparencies to illustrate this process and its outcomes. One showed the original broad spectrum of policy proposals that Secretary Watkins had elicited in his public hearings encountering a series of filters from the Department of Energy, from the White House, and from the Energy Committee staff, with only the industry-backed proposals flying through unimpeded to emerge in the National Energy Strategy and the Johnston-Wallop bill. I ended by showing another cartoon depicting the Johnston-Wallop bill as a Christmas tree bedecked with a large number of individually labeled gifts for the energy industries.

With this perspective and numerous examples to back it up, I returned to

Washington in May with a new sense of purpose. I had become convinced that the Johnston-Wallop bill was beyond fixing. It did not make sense to try to make it a better bill. We should try instead to defeat it, and I had to develop a concrete strategy to propose to the environmental groups.

This led almost immediately to my first sense of significant accomplishment since I got to Washington—at a meeting one week after the UCSD talk. Carol Werner of the Environment and Energy Studies Institute, a long-time friend and one of the most respected environmental leaders in Washington, arranged two seminars in a Senate hearing room, one on energy taxes and the other on renewable energy supplies. The first attracted many Hill staffers, the second mostly environmental group representatives. Karl and I did not make a formal presentation, but we found the environmentalists generally receptive to the notion that we join together to develop a strategy to organize against the Johnston-Wallop bill as a whole. This was a partial misperception, however, which Carol pointed out to us later that day. The Alliance to Save Energy, the American Council for an Energy Efficient Economy, and some other organizations were committed in fact to making Johnston-Wallop a better bill, not to opposing it.

That evening I mused in my journal about elements of an insider/outsider strategy:

> First, we have to get the story out. We should begin with one-page briefing papers on each of the Christmas tree adornments that Johnston-Wallop is giving away to the energy interests. Everything they have wanted for years is attached to this bill. For that we need to develop themes: This is no strategy; it's not long-range, not comprehensive. It has been rushed through with inadequate, unbalanced hearings. It is designed to overcome barriers many energy industries face, including environmental protections and citizen participation mechanisms. It is riddled with billion-dollar giveaways to the energy companies. And loads of money is pouring in in the form of campaign contributions to members of the Senate Energy Committee from the oil, gas, coal, nuclear and utility companies. That is quite a story, beginning with Bennett Johnston himself. Second, we need to sow seeds of opposition in the Senate outside the Johnston-prone Energy Committee; as a member of that committee who is willing to speak out, Paul could play a major role in such an effort. Third, we need a grassroots reaction. In many respects, energy policy is *the* central environmental issue. Local environmental groups should be up in arms against this bill. Fourth, we need an alternative energy strategy package, a positive alternative which inside and outside efforts can rally around.

A week later, at a meeting of the Media Committee of the NES Working Group at the Communications Consortium office, I had an opportunity to make an appeal to the environmentalists to change their strategy. Among those present were the cochairs of the committee, Phil Sparks (Communications Consortium) and Eileen Quinn (Union of Concerned Scientists), and a dozen or so others representing a broad spectrum of prominent environmental organizations in the coalition. I handed out a list of fifteen serious objections to the bill, along with a copy of the last visual from my UCSD talk, the Christmas tree adorned with "giveaway" presents.

I explained that I was convinced they could not make Johnston-Wallop good enough to support and urged that they launch an all-out attack on the bill. They themselves had effectively made the case that it lacked sufficient energy efficiency and renewable programs; and they had also focused public attention on ANWR and CAFE. But there were many other scandalous stories: enormous giveaways to corporate interests amounting to tens of billions of tax dollars, and rollbacks of the fruits of twenty years of citizen participation that had established a bulwark of environmental, public health, and consumer protections.

I asked them to flesh out that list of fifteen egregious giveaways and rollbacks into compelling stories aimed at attracting attention in the media and providing ammunition for mobilizing grassroots support. I also offered to help in documenting connections between the aims of the industry lobbyists swarming around key titles of the bill and the large campaign contributions that members of the Senate Energy Committee were successfully soliciting at the same time from the oil, gas, coal, nuclear, and utility lobbying coalitions.

This approach seemed to light a spark. They seemed ready to shift gears away from a make-it-a-better-bill approach and to concentrate instead on a comprehensive strategy to defeat the Johnston-Wallop bill. Ken Bossong of Public Citizen volunteered to write a first draft of a letter to be signed by all the major environmental groups, making the case I had outlined and urging nationwide opposition to the bill. Energy Committee senators also would be urged to use the remaining markup period to attract attention to the many defects in the bill and to take advantage of their prerogative to add minority views to the committee report that would lay out detailed criticisms of the bill's worst features. Bossong asked for help from others in drawing up short briefing papers on each problem.

That was the beginning of a very exciting week, in which I began to feel we might have a chance to make a real impact. On May 8, the Energy Committee resumed marking up the Johnston-Wallop bill. Given a week's recess, Karl was very well-prepared; with considerable help from environmentalist friends, he was loaded with ammunition for Paul, including briefing materials on the two nuclear power amendments—one to allow states to set higher safety standards, the other to delete one-step licensing entirely. My journal reported what happened:

> Despite a week to prepare, Energy Committee documents on nuclear licensing and advanced nuclear reactors are delivered to our office at 7:30 in the evening, the day before the markup! This is getting ridiculous! Other offices are beginning to react too—Gene Peters, Bradley's guy, erupted yesterday about our difficulty in finding out when items are scheduled to come up at the markup.
>
> As the hearing begins at 9:30, Johnston pulls another fast one. Instead of taking up energy efficiency first as everyone expected, he announces the committee will begin with advanced nuclear reactors! Before Karl arrives with Paul, Johnston *almost* has claimed unanimous consent for the entire advanced reactor section, including authorization now for whatever advanced reactor design the Secretary of Energy chooses in 1996! . . . Paul barely arrives in time to stop him. He proposes waiting until after R&D to authorize building the reactors. . . . An extended exchange ensues, but he gets no help from other senators, most of whom have not arrived, not knowing this was going to come up. Johnston wins.
>
> Nuclear licensing is different. Debate on Paul's amendment to strike one-step licensing from the bill goes on for more than two hours. Wyche Fowler of Georgia strongly supports Paul; so does Bumpers. Apart from Wallop, the Republicans hardly open their mouths. Johnston loses the argument, but wins the vote 13–6. . . . Conrad and Wirth vote with Johnston to limit citizen participation. An excellent showing for Paul, but a decisive loss in the vote.

Paul had also introduced his other nuclear licensing amendment, to allow states to apply stricter protection standards than the federal government. This amendment was defeated 14–5.

While the vote outcomes were lopsidedly against us, the exchanges that took place were important insofar as they changed the mood of the markup. Johnston might have the votes in his committee, but the serious, substantive opposition to provisions of his bill in his own domain held promise of serious, substantive debates on the Senate floor, possibly with different outcomes. Instead of smooth passage through the committee, there would be a fight over this bill and committee members would have to go on record on every contentious issue.

In fact, although the members of the committee did not realize it at the time, they *were* going on record with their markup votes. A striking feature of congressional markups is that while they are the proceedings in which members make what are usually the most important votes that occur on any particular issue—those on amendments—neither their votes nor their remarks are ever made public. A transcript of the Energy Committee markup, including the vote tallies, was kept in the committee office and available only to committee members and their staffs. When I wanted to see it I had to go down to the office and read it there. Furthermore, I could not make a copy of it. During Paul's 1990 campaign, I had encountered the same kind of secrecy when I tried to track down what his opponent, Sen. Rudy Boschwitz, had done in sessions of the Agriculture and Foreign Relations committees.

This kind of secrecy is endemic to Washington. Until 1970, even the full House of Representatives had treated all floor votes on amendments the same way. The final vote on a bill by each House member was made public, but the crucial votes that shaped the legislation, on amendments, were not released. That summer, however, when an important environmental bill came to the floor of the House, a group of environmentalists sat in the gallery, recorded how each member voted on the amendments, and sent a press release back home to their congressional districts. What an embarrassment that proved to be for many lawmakers! Within a very short time the House decided that from then on amendment votes would be recorded and published in the *Congressional Record*.

In the 1970s, when Ben Cooper and the other early scientist-fellows went to the Congress, the markup sessions themselves had been held in private, with only committee members, staffers, and selected lobbyists allowed in the room. A reform in the mid-'70s opened up the sessions to the public, although, not surprisingly, the so-called public attendees were usually paid lobbyists.

In the case of the Johnston-Wallop bill markup, an environmental watchdog group, the League of Conservation Voters, a coalition of the major environmental organizations, decided to send its staff to attend the Energy Committee sessions, record how each committee member voted on eight key issues, and release a vote "scorecard" for the entire committee, along with an environmental rating for each senator based on those votes. Of course, this scorecard created the potential for embarrassment among the senators, who were being forced, in insiders' terminology, to "walk the plank." On May 9, nine days after my UCSD talk, the National Energy Strategy Working Group, now representing twenty-two environmental and consumer organizations, voted to oppose the Johnston-Wallop bill. There was excitement in the air and Paul was praised; in fact, when his name was mentioned, there was spontaneous applause for his performance in the committee on nuclear licensing the day before. The groups discussed plans to take a strong public stand in opposition to the Johnston-Wallop bill and they scheduled a press conference for the next week. They decided to emphasize all the alarming features, not just ANWR and CAFE: the many giveaways, the rollbacks of citizen participation, the threats to environmental and consumer protection. A few weeks later one of the cochairs of the NES Working Group's media committee said my comments at the meeting had sparked the decision to oppose the bill and that my handouts had shaped the anti-bill approach. That evening I wrote in my journal, "It's nice to feel I've accomplished *something* down here."

Norm and I decided that he should draw up revisions to the environmentalists' draft letter, help prepare for their press conference, prepare a similar letter from the groups to Majority Leader Mitchell, and prepare a Wellstone op-ed piece. Norm wrote a beautiful piece that became the heart of a letter sent on May 16 to almost three thousand editorial writers and columnists nationwide signed by the twenty-two environmental and consumer groups. Suddenly we were in a very interesting fight and Bennett Johnston was not the only one with powerful resources behind him.

Of course, it was a foregone conclusion that the Energy Committee would pass the Johnston-Wallop bill. The Republicans were behind it because it included all the major elements of the Bush administration's National Energy Strategy. The Democratic chairman had his leverage over almost all the members of the committee, who in turn had their own reasons to go along with Chairman Johnston. He had positioned himself as chair of both the Committee on Energy and Natural Resources, which authorizes funds for energy, water, and public lands projects, and the Subcommittee on Energy and Water Development of the Senate Appropriations Committee, which decides how much of the authorized money is actually spent. In this way, Bennett Johnston ruled the Senate roost in everything connected to energy, water, and public lands. Almost all the members of the Energy Committee came from states where those issues were of vital economic importance. And the public lands plums dangled before us at the first staff meeting in January were only a small part of the favors the chairman could dispense or deny. Add to that the fact that most of the members expected to serve on the Energy Committee for years to come. How rewarding an experience that would be would depend more than anything else on their relations with the lord of that realm.

From my vantage point, I could see hints of Johnston's leverage in gaining support for his bill. Some provisions were especially important to individual committee senators; for instance, Johnston had agreed to incorporate uranium enrichment provisions of particular interest to Sen. Wendell Ford of Kentucky, and Sen. Tim Wirth's constituents stood to benefit from the natural gas amendments. Sen. Frank Murkowski of Alaska coveted ANWR; Sen. Daniel Akaka of Hawaii hoped his electric vehicle R&D proposal and a separate strategic petroleum reserve for his island state would be added to the bill; California's Sen. John Seymour, facing election in 1992, wanted to be able to tell the voters back home that he had added to the bill a long-term moratorium on oil drilling off the California coast; Sen. Kent Conrad of North Dakota wanted legislative fixes to serious problems encountered by his state's lignite coal industry as a consequence of the previous year's Clean Air Act amendments; Oregon's Sen. Mark Hatfield had an Old Growth Forest bill; Bill Bradley, chair of the Water and Power Subcommittee of the Senate Energy and Natural Resources Committee hoped to pass a historic change in the California water allocation law; and so on. Each required the chairman's support.

Beyond that were the chairman's close connections to, and coordination with, the actions of many of the industry lobbying coalitions that were heavily engaged in promoting provisions of the Johnston-Wallop bill. They were in a position to help or hinder significantly the political fortunes of many members of the committee. Still, those of us who were committed to opposing the bill had used the markup as the stage to set the scene for a fight on the Senate floor. The markup story could no longer be about a bill that had sailed through committee. It was now public knowledge that many of its provisions were very controversial and sharply challenged.

Bennett Johnston's Car Problem

The automobile fuel economy title of the Johnston-Wallop bill posed a serious dilemma for Chairman Johnston. He had reluctantly accepted this provision in the initial version of the bill, which in effect would result in no mandated CAFE increase, but he was not comfortable with the political consequences of that decision. He was pushing for ANWR drilling as the key response to the nation's oil vulnerability, but it was clear that even modest increases in auto fuel economy would have far greater effect. Kent Conrad of North Dakota, a backer of the Bryan bill the previous year, had already announced that he could not support ANWR drilling unless the bill also contained some sort of mandated schedule of annual CAFE increases. It was likely that other senators would adopt the same position when the bill came to the floor. So Johnston was torn by his need for cooperation from Wallop and the other Republicans on his committee and his desire for a bill the Senate would pass.

Also, some insiders were saying that Johnston had another strong motive for including a CAFE mandate in his bill. CAFE would give him leverage at the end of the legislative process when members of the Senate and the House met in a conference committee to reconcile the bills the individual bodies had passed. The dominant figure in the House on energy matters was Rep. John Dingell of Michigan, chair of the House Energy and Commerce Committee, whose congressional district included Dearborn, home of the Ford Motor Company. Dingell strongly opposed any CAFE mandate and Johnston presumably assumed that if the Senate bill had some sort of CAFE mandate and the House bill none, he would be able to extract concessions from Dingell in the conference negotiations.

In the meantime, the automobile industry had created the "Coalition for Vehicle Choice" to launch a $10 million media advertising and congressional lobbying campaign designed to discredit the Bryan CAFE proposal. The thrust of the campaign was that if the Bryan bill passed, the American people would be forced to buy small, unsafe cars. The most spectacular television ad showed a 4,000-pound luxury car crushing a 2,300-pound subcompact as a voiceover intoned, "While smaller cars can save you gas, they could cost you something far more precious."

The Wellstone office was among the targets of this campaign. Paul received nearly identical letters from many Minnesota auto dealers, each on its own stationery and each saying in the same words that if Congress forced auto manufacturers to build 40 miles-per-gallon cars, there would be a serious downturn. "Customers will stay away from the showroom in droves. . . . A lot of dealers will go under." Paul also received a personal note from the chairman of the Ford Motor Company, reminding him that Ford had a large manufacturing plant in St. Paul and expressing displeasure with Paul's CAFE votes in markup.

Recall that the CAFE debate in the Senate revolved around three proposals, which I'll refer to as "Strong CAFE," "No CAFE," and "Weak CAFE." "Strong CAFE" was the Bryan bill, backed by the environmental organizations, which would have increased the CAFE mandate to about 40 MPG over a ten-year period; a furious counteroffensive by the auto industry had resulted in sufficient erosion in Senate support to make it vulnerable to a filibuster.

"No CAFE" was the proposal backed by the auto industry worldwide that the ranking Republican member of the Energy Committee, Malcolm Wallop, had forced Chairman Johnston to incorporate in the Johnston-Wallop bill; it would let the Secretary of Transportation decide, but the secretary had already announced his opposition to any further CAFE mandate. Johnston knew that the "No CAFE" provision was a poison pill that would render the entire Johnston-Wallop bill unpassable; it would have to be replaced by a stronger CAFE mandate, but one that was sufficiently weak that the auto-makers would accept it.

Johnston sprang the "Weak CAFE" proposal on us at the end of the May 14 markup session. Although Johnston called it "the maximum feasible" schedule of CAFE increases, in fact it was appallingly modest. Beginning with the 1990 CAFE level of 28.1 MPG for passenger cars, it mandated an increase to about 30 MPG by 1996, 34 MPG by 2001, and 37 MPG by 2006. To lend authoritative support to this allegedly maximum feasible schedule, Johnston's aides circulated an official looking graph and explained that he had consulted closely with K. G. Duleep, the man he had annointed the world's CAFE guru.

The Johnston schedule of required CAFE increases had at least one *very* peculiar feature. The small increase in the first five years may have been reasonable, but after that the schedule made no sense, especially to anyone familiar with Duleep's testimony before the committee or who had read his paper about what CAFE increases were feasible in the next twenty years. In the second five years, the required CAFE increase was about 4 MPG, in itself surprisingly low. But what was really astounding was that in the next five years, during the 2001–2006 period when, according to Duleep, new technologies could result in very large CAFE increases, this "maximum feasible" schedule required only about a 3 MPG increase—even smaller than during the previous five years! Not only did Johnston's maximum feasible CAFE schedule fail to increase more rapidly in the post–2001 period as one would expect intuitively, but it was also inconsistent with the numerical conclusions of Duleep's analysis.

By the next morning, I had prepared a graph for Paul that demonstrated the inconsistency between Johnston's CAFE schedule and Duleep's analysis. When it was time to vote on the Johnston substitute "Weak CAFE" amendment, Tim Wirth immediately moved to table it. It soon became obvious that Johnston did not have the votes. He lost decisively, 13–7, with all nine Republicans voting against him. What's more, at the urging of the American automakers, the White House had decided to support the extremely extremely weak CAFE language already in the bill and asked the Republicans to stand firm against Johnston's proposed change.

Then followed some weird shenanigans. Wirth had been expected to propose substituting the Bryan bill language next. Nine members of the committee had consistently supported Bryan before, so a very close vote was anticipated. But when Wirth surveyed the committee, he found he didn't have anywhere near the votes he needed. So he announced he would not move to substitute Bryan. At that point, Johnston, still smarting from his defeat, said he would make Wirth's motion for him. The resulting vote was 15–5 against Bryan's CAFE. The session ended on a truly bizarre note when Johnston moved to strike the entire CAFE title from his bill and that lost too, 12–8. So Johnston was stuck with a CAFE title that he knew was too weak for his bill to pass the Senate.

The *Washington Post* story of May 16 showed a smiling Senator Dick Bryan and carried a headline, "Fuel Economy Measure Seems to Win by Losing." Dan Becker, a Sierra Club lobbyist was said to have called the votes "a train wreck" for the Johnston-Wallop bill, and the article said the bill would never pass with the CAFE provision the committee had left in. At the hearing that morning, Johnston seemed uptight and upset.

There was also behind-the-scenes intrigue on the part of Majority Leader George Mitchell. I attended a meeting organized by Sen. Kent Conrad's office to discuss possible CAFE compromises. Majority Leader Mitchell had sent one of his staffers to represent him. His mission soon became clear. Mitchell feared that we might come up with a CAFE compromise for Johnston-Wallop; the staffer was there to warn us off. At that point it was clear Mitchell wanted Johnston's bill to remain mortally wounded. The nominally neutral majority leader would play an important role behind the scenes as the Johnston-Wallop story unfolded.

On May 23, the very last day of the markup, Johnston finally addressed the most controversial provision in the bill, drilling for oil in the Arctic National Wildlife Refuge. From the beginning, Johnston had had 10 sure votes of the twenty members on the committee, so there was no chance of eliminating the ANWR title. However, John Seymour (R., California) was involved in an uphill election battle in his state where the environmental constituency was formidable. An embarrassing 10–10 tie in Johnston's own committee was not out of the question.

How Johnston got Seymour's vote was a rare public display of the kind of deals he was making throughout the markup. When the off-shore drilling title had been marked up four weeks earlier, Seymour had been absent, but one of the other Republican senators had indicated that Seymour would be introducing a California drilling moratorium amendment. Johnston held that amendment hostage right up to the day of the ANWR vote.

Early in that last markup session, Seymour announced he wished to introduce an amendment that would establish a moratorium in California on offshore oil exploration or leasing until 2000. Johnston replied, "the people in the oil industry think this amendment is an abomination. But I'm going to support it." In the ensuing discussion, Senator Wendell Ford of Kentucky asked Seymour if he were planning to vote for ANWR drilling. Seymour said indeed he was. He explained his decision by asking whether we should allow drilling where "tens of millions of people enjoy this natural resource called the California coast each and every year, or should we do it in an area where 150 to a maximum of 250 human beings a year enjoy another natural resource and a treasure? The answer for me is very simple." It was clear that this was the choice Johnston had given Seymour. ANWR drilling passed, 11–8.

The markup ended with the committee members voting on the entire Johnston-Wallop bill. The result was overwhelming support for the chairman and a crushing defeat for us: 17 ayes, including from several members we had expected to be our allies (Wirth, Fowler, Conrad, and Akaka); and 3 nayes (Bradley, Bumpers, and Wellstone). But the other two dissenters, Bradley and Bumpers, were both Energy Subcommittee chairs, among the most senior and highly respected members of the Committee. Those votes made waves in the Senate.

A Primer of Johnston-Wallop Horrors

We had planned all along to attach a Wellstone minority report to the majority report that would be printed with the revised bill that passed the Energy Committee. Although minority reports are typically just one or two pages, we had something much more substantial in mind because our purpose was different. Ours would be a title-by-title critique of the key provisions of the bill, aimed at laying out the case for opposing the bill as a whole. In the process, we hoped to produce a primer of Johnston-Wallop horrors that could serve as an educational tool and a rallying point for the opposition we hoped would emerge in the Congress and around the country. If we couldn't frame the legislation, we would try to frame the terms of the postcommittee discussion and debate.

Karl did most of the work, with considerable help on some sections from specialists among the environmental lobbyists. We were fairly certain that Johnston would move his "Weak CAFE" campaign to the floor of the Senate as the preferred alternative to the Bryan bill. We devoted the first chapter to a thorough critique of "Weak CAFE," the rationale for significant CAFE increases, and refutations of the anti-CAFE public relations campaign. The table of contents of this primer then went on to ANWR, Nuclear Power, PUHCA Reform, Natural Gas, Hydropower, Coal, Uranium Enrichment, and Energy Efficiency.

By the time I wrote the CAFE chapter, I had come to understand that Johnston's "Weak CAFE" was even weaker than I had previously realized. Johnston had claimed that his proposal would increase the required CAFE for new cars to 34 MPG in 2001. But he did not point out that CAFE MPG credits would be given for alternatively fueled vehicles (an estimated 2 MPG) and for cars with air bags (.5 MPG) and, in addition, that his bill gave the Secretary of Transportation discretion to lower the CAFE level by 2 MPG. The net effect was that instead of the advertised 34 MPG in 2001, the Johnston "Weak CAFE" proposal could actually mean a real fuel economy increase by 2001 to only

$$34 \text{ MPG} - 2 \text{ MPG} - .5 \text{ MPG} - 2 \text{ MPG} = 29.5 \text{ MPG}$$

Since the average fuel economy for new cars in 1988 had been 28.8 MPG, the actual increase in passenger car fuel economy under what Johnston was billing as "the maximum feasible CAFE" could be less than 1 MPG in thirteen years. The CAFE chapter of the Wellstone Minority Views had shown that Johnston's "Weak CAFE" mandate was very likely to be ridiculously weak in practice.

Our dissenting views were literally in their tenth revision as our noon deadline approached on June 3. We got them up to Ben Cooper's office with only minutes to spare. All in all, the twenty-eight page Wellstone primer on the Johnston-Wallop bill, turned out very well. The effect of reading the critiques was devastating: This bill is *really bad*.[1]

Next to our minority views in the committee's report about the amended Johnston-Wallop bill, now S.1220, was a much less specific, but still hard-hitting and effective minority view that Bill Bradley submitted. It described the bill as a "business as usual approach with little in the way of new thinking." The two pages of Bradley's critique closed with a pithy phrase that captured the essence of this legislation: "It reads like an industry wish list that in numerous cases is contrary to the public interest."[2]

Preparing for Battle

8

The Outside Opposition Mobilizes

The public interest groups initiated a two-pronged offensive to defeat the Johnston-Wallop bill. One major effort was Washington-oriented, focusing primarily on the Senate and aimed at educating senators beyond the Energy Committee about the defects of S.1220, the amended form that had passed the Energy Committee. The other major effort was directed toward the grass roots and aimed at educating the press and the public about the bill and mobilizing a nationwide network of local opposition.

The National Energy Strategy Working Group brought together representatives of the major environmental and consumer organizations every Thursday afternoon to coordinate the Washington strategy. By late spring, the Wellstone office was sending a representative to those meetings on a regular basis.

Karl and I attended the June 6 meeting, where we discussed possible elements of a strategy to combat passage of the bill. An immediate goal would be to delay bringing the bill to the Senate floor, so there would be time to organize opposition. One way of doing that would be to encourage appropriate committee and subcommittee chairs to send letters to Majority Leader George Mitchell requesting a "hold" on the bill, explaining that they had jurisdiction over important issues addressed by the bill and wanted an opportunity to hold hearings before the bill could be brought to the floor. For instance, the Commerce Committee might hold automobile fuel economy hearings on Johnston's proposed "Weak CAFE" since Johnston was almost certain to try to put it in his bill as an amendment once it reached the Senate floor; the Environment Committee might hold hearings on ANWR, nuclear licensing and off-shore drilling; the Banking Committee might hold hearings on PUHCA reform, and so forth.

At the same time the anti-Johnston-Wallop coalition groups would begin to lay the groundwork for an opposition campaign within the Senate. Audubon Society vice president and NES Working Group co-chair, Brooks Yeager, proposed the theme of the campaign: "There's only one thing worse than no national energy strategy and that's a *bad* national energy strategy." This forceful initial message would be followed by an intensive office-by-office campaign to educate senators and staff.

Within a week, every Senate office received a letter signed by eighteen major public interest organizations. Dated June 13, it detailed a long list of serious problems with S.1220 from environmental, consumer, and taxpayer perspectives, making clear that ANWR and CAFE were only two among many such problems. The letter concluded, "We ask that you carefully review the provisions of S.1220. We hope you will agree that far from assuring America's future energy security, it will only serve to insure the perpetuation of our reliance on environmentally hazardous fossil and nuclear fuels. We need a national energy policy, but we don't need S.1220. Please join us in opposing this legislation." This joint letter was soon followed by letters from individual groups offering detailed critiques of different titles of the bill.

At the regular NES Working Group meeting on June 13, Alaska Coalition leader Mike Matz of the Sierra Club announced that he had commitments from several senators for a filibuster on the floor, including Lieberman, Metzenbaum, Bryan, Bradley, and Wellstone. This was the first time that I had heard the word filibuster, explicitly mentioned.[1] I was intrigued and a bit worried to see that the person pushing it was the director of the Alaska Coalition, whose principal goal was removing ANWR from the bill. In a conversation with Matz ten days later, I became certain that what he had in mind was a filibuster of the Arctic portion. Of the senators he listed, however, Lieberman was the only one whose main concern was ANWR. While the others opposed the ANWR provision, they all had major objections to other provisions as well.

A letter to every senator from the Sierra Club's president, Phillip Berry, and executive director, Michael Fischer, dated June 21, 1991, also urged a filibuster, but made it clear that the target of the filibuster strategy was the entire bill. Describing the Johnston-Wallop bill as "an environmental disaster," and "a wish list of environmentally destructive changes which the oil, nuclear and coal industries have sought for years" that "weakens virtually every major national environmental law and policy," they urged senators "to defeat it." The letter's bottom line: "We specifically urge that you vote against a motion to invoke cloture in order to sustain a filibuster against S.1220."

A major part of the grassroots campaign against the bill also was carried on by the Sierra Club, whose Washington office sent a series of letters to thousands of energy activists and other letter-writing members nationwide, keeping them updated on the bill's current status and urging them to pressure swing senators. Dan Becker, their chief energy policy lobbyist, saw ANWR as the motivator and initial source of support for what would become a much larger effort: "The one thing everyone talks about is the Arctic," he said. "The Arctic was the rallying cry and the initial momentum giver to the campaign. . . . Later people jumped on board for other issues, nuclear power, offshore oil drilling, CAFE, etc."

The Communications Consortium, meanwhile, undertook a campaign to educate the media and through them the American people about the defects of the bill. The Washington-based consortium had begun its "Energy Efficiency Education Project" in 1988 under the leadership of codirector Phil Sparks. The initial project was a strategic media campaign to educate the public about sustainable energy and to cast energy policy as an environmental issue, with particular emphasis on how energy policy choices would impact global warming. This was a sophisticated operation that began with extensive opinion research. One notable finding was that the notion of "energy conservation" had negative connotations for many people—associated with "Jimmy Carter and freezing in the dark," said Sparks—but that "energy efficiency" had very positive connotations, ideas about "American technology leading the way."

In 1991, the Communications Consortium project became the media arm of the NES Working Group, with its initial goal to reframe the energy strategy debate as an environmental issue. They deliberately decided to delay making a push for the sustainable energy vision. As Sparks put it, "It was easy to organize around the Arctic issue." In the first five months of 1991, through Washington-based press conferences for reporters, nationwide informational mailings to five-hundred newspaper editorial page editors, distribution of op-ed articles by leading environmentalists, and the like, they had done an effective job of getting out the story that the NES and the Johnston-Wallop bill were bad energy policy. By the end of the markup, the foundation had been laid for a political battle. According to Sparks, after

May the press lost interest in the substance of the debate, and reporters began to focus instead on "the horse race story."

The formal announcement of a major grassroots campaign came on June 25 at a Capitol press conference packed with reporters. It was billed as the kickoff of a national petition and postcard drive "suporting safe, clean and affordable national energy policies and opposing the Bush/Sununu/Johnston national energy tragedy." Paul was among the featured speakers. The drive was a joint effort of several environmental groups, including the Sierra Club, the Safe Energy Communication Council, U.S. PIRG, Greenpeace, and Environmental Action. It had actually gotten underway some weeks before and over a hundred thousand postcards and petition signatures had already been collected.

By that time, the Wellstone office had developed an excellent working relationship with the environmental community. Although it was highly unusual for a senator's staff to work so closely with public interest groups, we were regular attendees at their NES Working Group and we exchanged information on a daily basis with many of their lobbyists. During the markup, when Johnston often kept everyone in the dark until very late, Karl had begun sending out fax alerts to environmentalist lobbyists as soon as we learned what would be on the next day's agenda. Of course, this budding relationship had been mutually supportive. Environmental lobbyists came in to brief Paul on such topics as CAFE and global warming and they helped us develop Wellstone amendments on such topics as hydropower, nuclear licensing, and PUHCA Reform.

Typical of such assistance was the legal advice I received from Jeff Genzer, counsel for the National Association of State Energy Offices, in drafting a state-option CAFE amendment. Jeff, along with Carol and Jack Werner and several other public interest group staffers, also collaborated with us in developing the Sustainable Energy Transition Act. In fact, Jeff and I wrote the first draft and Carol called the meeting at her Environmental and Energy Studies Institute which interested several of the public interest groups in that legislation.

In Washington, lobbyists, congressional committee staffers and executive agency staffers have time to think. Harried congressional office staffers like me were naturally drawn to look to them for support. I could not count on Johnston's committee staffers for help, but I did receive hints that had I remained in Washington for long, I would have developed close ties with sympathetic policy staff at the Department of Energy. Of course, we did have one such relationship, with Henry Kelly. He was of more help to us than anyone else in Washington. And even before the markup began, I had received an invitation from two other DoE staffers who were leaders of that agency's sustainable energy program suggesting we get together for a drink. It was such a hectic time that things kept coming up so we never did meet till after the markup was over. At the conclusion of a very pleasant conversation in early June, during which they suggested several ideas we might have introduced as amendments in the markup, I said I sure wished we had gotten together before. Their reply: "Well, that's what we've been trying to arrange for two months!" I was beginning to understand how cozy relationships naturally blossom among like-minded individuals at executive branch agencies, congressional committees, and lobbying coalitions.

The Wellstone office became very much engaged in planning and executing the Washington-focused part of the two-pronged organizing campaign to defeat the Johnston-Wallop bill. However, for reasons I didn't fully understand, we were much less connected to the grassroots part. With Paul's organizing skills and his ability to move people to undertake concerted action, he would have been a natural leader of a national movement for sustainable energy. But Paul had not arrived in time to put a sustainable energy transition initiative on the table by the beginning of the energy strategy debate. Later, when he introduced the Sustainable Energy Transition Act, I hoped Paul would have that opportunity. That vision spurred my work in developing a Wellstone bill. But I continued to wonder whether there were systemic reasons why Paul and perhaps a few other senators were not enlisted for that grassroots organizing role.

In late spring, Carol Werner called a meeting of many public interest group representatives to discuss an idea that Public Citizen was considering, to launch a nationwide campaign for sustainable energy development, beginning on a day in April 1992. Ken Bossong, the leader of the project, called it "Sun Day." Although the initial focus would be on one day, the emphasis would be on the campaign as a whole and it would continue in future years. It would emphasize projects at the state and local levels, with perhaps fifty state efforts aimed at increasing energy efficiency and renewable energy investments. The project eventually became known as "SUN DAY: Campaign for a Sustainable Energy Future." Since this concept closely complemented the document we had submitted to the Mitchell task force, I immediately sent a copy of our proposal to Ken Bossong. I could foresee this project as a way to develop a national constituency for our Sustainable Energy Transition Act.

The Inside Opposition Crystallizes

As the environmentalists were mobilizing an all-out attack on the Johnston-Wallop bill, there began to be stirrings of another kind of alliance toward that same end—in the normally insular world of the senators' offices.

I have described how Karl and I had been part of an effort to organize Energy Committee senators to speak out against the bill at the beginning of the markup. But that effort had fallen flat. And the overwhelming 17–3 margin by which the bill passed the committee was hardly the signal we had hoped to send to the American people. After the bill left his committee, however, Johnston no longer had control of events and we and the environmental groups could seek Senate allies less dependent on his favors and less fearful of his wrath.

The first stirrings of a Senate alliance to oppose Johnston-Wallop occurred on June 6, when Karl, Henry, and I ran into Linda Lance in the hall outside her Commerce Committee office. We had a long conversation that ran from our mutual unhappiness with the Johnston-Wallop bill to our ideas about how the Bryan bill might be modified to win the 60 votes it would need to overcome a filibuster on the floor. It turned out Linda was thinking along quite similar lines. Her boss, Dick Bryan, was feeling pressure from Johnston, who was pushing Majority Leader Mitchell very hard to get his bill, with its CAFE provision as Title I, onto the Senate floor. With his CAFE bill already reported out by another major committee, Bryan was a major obstacle in Johnston's rush to get his bill debated.

Linda agreed that we needed to organize a working group of staff from sympathetic Senate offices right away. The following Monday I spent most of the day on the phone to other Senate offices, trying to get a sense of the strength of opposition to the Johnston-Wallop bill and inviting selected staffers to a meeting in our office the next day to discuss how to modify the Bryan bill to garner the 60 votes required to overcome a possible filibuster of that bill.

I should mention there was one office with a strong competence in, and a similar attitude about, CAFE that we did not invite to our meeting, the staffers of Colorado Sen. Tim Wirth. Despite the fact that he was clearly the best informed and most articulate advocate of the Bryan bill on the Energy Committee, we were hearing from other staffers that he was likely to inform Johnston about what we were up to. A second office we did not invite was that of Sen. Kent Conrad of North Dakota. He was obviously playing along with Johnston and by June he had decided to support actively the CAFE "compromise" Johnston had proposed in committee. "Weak CAFE" soon became the Johnston-Conrad amendment.

By my reckoning, June 12 was the day the Senate opposition forces began to coalesce. Linda Lance (Bryan), Katie McGinty (Gore), Joyce Rechtshaffen (Lieberman), Brian Keefe (Jeffords), Karl, and I met in the Wellstone conference room. Ken Rynne (Metzenbaum) and Sally Yozell (Kerry) were supportive but unable to make the meeting. There was obviously genuine interest in finding a strong, winning CAFE along the lines we had discussed with Linda. I distributed a paper about the future of transportation that Henry Kelly had written for the occasion, along with a schematic diagram I had constructed, laying out major options for revising the Bryan bill. Gore aide Katie McGinty had some intriguing ideas that dovetailed with ours. I was encouraged by the cooperative spirit of the meeting and came away feeling we could put together a strong CAFE proposal that would respond to many of the criticisms Bryan had encountered, *if* we had time to develop it.

What lent a sense of urgency to that meeting was another one scheduled for the following day. Bryan and Johnston had been asked to meet with Mitchell in the majority leader's office to decide on an orderly process to deal with their CAFE proposals. At that meeting, Mitchell asked Bryan if he would be willing to let his bill, S.279, be proposed as an amendment to the CAFE title of the Johnston-Wallop bill, S.1220, on the Senate floor. Bryan refused. Mitchell then asked Johnston if he would agree to let the Bryan CAFE bill come to the floor first. After a discussion of conditions surrounding the debate (and expected filibuster) of the Bryan bill, Johnston said he would think about that.

Soon thereafter, Johnston sent a letter to Mitchell setting out his understanding of what had been proposed at the meeting: S.279, the Bryan bill, would come to the floor very soon and only two cloture votes would be permitted. If Bryan did not achieve the 60 votes necessary to cut off the filibuster of his bill on either of those votes, S.1220, the Johnston-Wallop bill, would come to the floor soon thereafter.

Obviously Johnston was anticipating that Bryan could not muster the 60 votes he needed. After two cloture votes, the Bryan CAFE bill would be dead. Then the Johnston-Wallop bill would come to the floor, where, presumably, Johnston would move to strengthen the CAFE title with the Johnston-Conrad "Weak CAFE" amendment.

Linda Lance told me that something else had come up at the meeting in Mitchell's office that required immediate attention. The majority leader had not, as we had hoped, received many letters from senators requesting a "hold" on the Johnston-Wallop bill. Mitchell, therefore, had not heard a groundswell of opposition to Johnston-Wallop, suggesting that we had to mount a concerted effort to create one. By June 19 Karl and I had drafted letters to Environment Committee chair Quentin Burdick and Environmental Protection Subcommittee chair Max Baucus requesting hearings to assess the environmental impacts of S.1220; a letter to Commerce Committee chair Fritz Hollings requesting hearings be held on the anticipated Johnston "Weak CAFE" amendment; and a letter to Majority Leader Mitchell asking for a hold on S.1220 until those hearings could be completed. We also drafted a S.279 (Bryan) hold letter arguing that a hearing on Johnston-Conrad "Weak CAFE" amendment must be held before the Bryan bill was debated, because it was likely that amendment would be proposed as a substitute for the Bryan bill.

I faxed the draft letters to Linda, and later on the phone she expressed confidence that Johnston would be foiled in his attempt to bring S.279 to the floor and kill it; Bryan simply could tell Mitchell that he did not want his bill to come to the floor for a while. Later that day Linda invited us to a meeting in Bryan's office to map out further strategy. That meeting, along with the CAFE strategy meeting we had held the week before, turned out to be the crucial beginning of organized opposition with the Senate, where it is so difficult to get the separate fiefdoms to cooperate and coordinate. The next afternoon, June 20, Karl and I attended the first in a series of anti-Johnston-Wallop bill strategy meetings in Bryan's office, chaired by Bryan's chief of staff, Jean Neal. That meeting sought to identify a core group of senators who could go public immediately with floor statements against the bill as a whole and possibly indicate to Mitchell that they would join together in filibustering against the motion to proceed to bring the Johnston-Wallop bill to the Senate floor. The other major priority was to identify additional senators who might join in opposing the bill and to get them involved.

Along with the senators who had committed themselves early on to a filibuster—Lieberman, Metzenbaum, Bryan, and Wellstone—Al Gore and John Kerry were certain to join. Michigan's Don Riegle was suggested as a likely immediate addition to the core group, and forty-two other senators were identified as potential allies. Bill Bradley was also a supporter, though his aide Gene Peters explained at that first meeting in Bryan's office that his senator could not cross Johnston while his California water bill was awaiting consideration by the Subcommittee on Energy and Water Appropriations, which Johnston chaired. As Gene put it from the back of the room, "The Energy and Water Appropriations bill is coming up and people are sensitive." Bradley could say, "No way on ANWR," but he wanted to be sure "there is no way Bennett Johnston can say 'You stuck a knife in my back.'" Nevertheless, on that day and subsequently, Gene Peters was an influential contributor to the strategy discussions and to efforts to contact other offices and expand the opposition group. Given that Bradley was one of three votes against the Johnston-Wallop bill on the Energy Committee, we knew he would eventually join the opposition group.

Besides gathering supporters to keep the Johnston-Wallop bill off the floor, we needed to anticipate what Mitchell would do. Johnston was pressing him to bring the bill to the floor before the month-long August recess. When Mitchell campaigned for majority leader in 1988, he had made a commitment to the committee chairs not to allow a few senators to put a bill on indefinite hold. His test for bringing contentious legislation to the floor was a credible demonstration by the bill's sponsor that the necessary 60 votes existed to defeat a filibuster. Someone at the meeting suggested that Mitchell was in a particularly sensitive spot in his relations with Johnston, who had challenged him for the position of majority leader in 1988. Now he wanted to avoid the appearance of being vindictive.

I ended my journal comments about this significant meeting on a worried note: "Both Karl and I were struck and somewhat daunted by the presence and active participation of one of Wirth's aides. We are put off by Wirth's telling people that that aside from ANWR and CAFE, the rest of the Johnston-Wallop bill was 'strong,' and we are worried about the role he might play, in public and behind the scenes, to negotiate changes that, at a crucial moment, would enable him to go public and label the bill 'acceptable.'"

Around this time, rumors of organized opposition to Johnston-Wallop began to spread on the Hill. For instance, a June 19 article in the trade publication *Energy Daily* headlined "Growing Senate Opposition to Johnston's Energy Bill" claimed that George Mitchell had already received letters from "nearly a dozen senators" asking him not to schedule a vote on S.1220 and that Bill Bradley and Joe Lieberman had warned they would lead a filibuster against the bill.[2] According to the article, Mitchell "asked some members to write to him about their dislikes in S.1220;" he "wants to go to Johnston with a packet of letters from other senators saying, 'I hate this bill and I don't want to have to vote on it.'" The article went on, "Senators who have met with Mitchell said he opposes Johnston's bill and wants to kill it." However, a spokesperson for Mitchell denied he had asked senators to write to him and said, "though Mitchell supports higher auto fuel efficiency stan-

dards and opposes oil and gas drilling in the Arctic National Wildlife Refuge, he has taken no position on Johnston's omnibus energy bill as a whole."

The second strategy meeting in Bryan's office the following week was very
promising. Staffers for Senators Bryan, Wellstone, Lieberman, Jeffords, Bradley, Kerry, Adams, Lautenberg, Gore, Kohl, Roth, Wirth, Harkin, Graham,
and others were there. Plans were made for a press conference with several
senators explaining why they had decided to oppose the bill and several
more distributing printed statements.

The day before our press conference, Johnston held one of his own. It was
heavily attended and Dan Becker, the Sierra Club lobbyist, reported that he
seemed defensive, nervous, and uncomfortable. The two most conservative
Republicans on the committee, Sen. Malcolm Wallop of Wyoming and Sen.
Larry Craig of Idaho, were with him. According to Becker, the session was
unfocused and reporters left wondering why he had called it. One bit of
welcome news: at the press conference, Johnston indicated his bill might
not come to the Senate floor before the August recess. The next morning's
Washington Post story began, "Sen. J. Bennett Johnston (D-La), renowned
on Capitol Hill as a backroom wheeler and dealer, went public yesterday to
seek allies in what he called a 'first class political fight' over the wide-ranging
energy bill he has championed. Johnston needs all of the allies he can get,
according to Senate sources and energy lobbyists, because he could be facing
one of the most damaging defeats of his long political career."[3]

Bradley's aide Gene Peters got a call from Ben Cooper just a half hour
before Wednesday afternoon's anti-1220 coalition meeting in Bryan's office.
Johnston was obviously fully apprised of everything the coalition was up to
and he was keeping the pressure on Bradley. Peters was superb at those meetings; he assured us Bradley would make a statement or at least reissue his
previous dissenting remarks.

At the meeting in Bryan's office that afternoon, I could sense our support
growing. The room was crowded with staffers. Bryan's chief of staff, Jean
Neal, filled us in on recent developments. Told eight to ten senators wanted
a block of floor time to speak against the bill Thursday morning, Majority
Leader Mitchell reportedly "chuckled at length." Johnston called Mitchell's
office soon thereafter to find out what was happening and demanded equal
time for statements from his supporters.

That was the background to a dramatic confrontation on the Senate
floor on June 27. It was like *High Noon,* the prelude to a gunfight. Bryan,
Lieberman, and Wellstone were on the floor at 9:00. So was Johnston,

accompanied by several aides, looking grim and determined. One by one his faithful gunslingers sidled in from the side aisles to join him—Republicans Wallop, Nickles, Murkowski and, surprisingly, one young, eager Democrat, North Dakota's Kent Conrad. Most of the other committee Democrats had been asked to come to support Johnston, but only Conrad agreed.

Bryan, Lieberman, and Wellstone spoke first. Then Johnston, responded, pointing out that his critics were mere "freshman Senators" and that he had been formulating energy policy for years. He presented charts and graphs and and stumbled for one memorable moment when he said, "We in the oil industry call this . . . " Though of course that slip never showed up in the *Congressional Record* since his staff had it excised.

Upstairs the anti-Johnston-Wallop senators held the planned press conference where Montana's Max Baucus announced he had sent Mitchell a letter requesting sequential referral to his Environmental Protection subcommittee so that it could hold hearings on the environmental implications of the bill before it come to the floor. He also requested prior notification before it was scheduled for full Senate consideration, thereby signaling he would filibuster against bringing it to the Senate floor for debate. Bryan, Lieberman, and Wellstone also spoke at the press conference and their floor statements and those of several other senators opposing S.1220 were distributed to reporters. Another surprise—presidential aspirant Tom Harkin issued a very strong and eloquent statement of opposition. So did Bradley, Metzenbaum, Lautenberg and several others.

A thought I had while watching our press conference: We needed to educate the opposition senators to feel comfortable debating the full range of serious problems with the bill; not just ANWR and CAFE, but also nuclear licensing, PUHCA Reform, the bill's emphasis on fossil fuels, its inadequate efficiency provisions, virtual vacuum on renewables, and so on. Otherwise we would be playing into Johnston's hands, practically inviting him to drop ANWR from his bill at a suitable moment and disarming the opposition. His opposition would fall apart and the rest of the bill would go through on greased wheels.

After the press conference, I went to the Energy Committee hearing room, which was filled with many senators' energy aides who had been invited in to be educated by the Senate Energy Committee staff about the real contents of S.1220. Ben Cooper presided over carefully orchestrated presentations, with questions and answers from the other committee staffers. From the audience, Bradley aide Gene Peters and I tried to plant seeds of doubt. I challenged Ben's characterization of Johnston's CAFE compromise, explaining how small an increase in auto fuel efficiency it actually called for. I urged the staffers to read Wellstone's minority remarks about the Johnston CAFE amendment and describing many other defects of S.1220. I also explained that one of the committee staffers had glossed over a huge controversy in his discussion of one-step nuclear reactor licensing. But the session as a whole was remarkable for its one-sided presentations, a continuation of Johnston's standard operating procedure.

That afternoon, I spent an hour at an Energy Committee hearing. Ben Cooper came over and sat down and chatted amiably. That's the Senate for you. An air of friendliness on the surface, but lots more going on out of view.

Warning Shots Across Their Bow

By the end of June, it was apparent that the Johnston-Wallop bill would not be brought to the Senate floor until after the August recess, giving us more time to prepare for the battle to come. On July 16, the League of Conservation Voters, which had monitored the Johnston-Wallop markup votes, released the scores of the twenty Energy Committee members at a press conference and sent out press releases to the media in each committee senator's state. Headed by former Arizona governor Bruce Babbitt, who later became Secretary of the Interior in the Clinton administration, the LCV was the election arm of the Washington-based environmental community, with the mission of "helping elect pro-environment candidates to federal office and working to defeat anti-conservation House and Senate incumbents."

For many members of the Committee, the LCV markup scores were a major embarrassment. Thirteen of the twenty senators received a failing mark of 50 or less. And five, Idaho's Larry Craig, New Mexico's Pete Dominici, Utah's Jake Garn, Alaska's Frank Murkowski, and Wyoming's Malcolm Wallop, all scored zero. Larry Craig's press secretary was so upset by the negative publicity that he complained, "the only one to get 100 percent was Paul Wellstone, a self-professed socialist." Craig soon issued a public apology.

Under attack from the environmentalists, seeing Senate opposition beginning to swell, and with the press beginning to pick up on the story that his bill might be in trouble, Johnston began to deliver lengthy statements from the Senate floor on different aspects of his bill, giving one virtually every day from July 16 to the end of the month. His staff assembled the printed texts of the statements from the *Congressional Record,* bound them together in book form and distributed them widely. Soon after Congress returned from its August recess, Johnston and Wallop distributed a document entitled

"Setting the Record Straight," intended, according to its preamble, to correct misinformation about their bill. It identified twenty-six allegedly erroneous allegations, although interestingly, the first claim the document denied was that "The bill was rushed through the legislative process, frustrating thorough examination and debate." In rebuttal, the document protested that the committee had held seventeen public hearings with testimony from about one hundred individuals, neglecting to mention, of course, how one-sided and misleading those hearings had been.

Once it was clear that the battle would not be joined until after Labor Day, both sides continued working on behind-the-scenes persuasion and other preparations for the debate. On our side, Nancy Hirsch of Environmental Action coordinated the writing of an excellent briefing book, explaining our concerns with the bill as a whole and with each of its titles, with different groups taking responsibility for different parts of the critique. By the end of July, virtually every Senate office had a copy and many senators had received a visit from representatives of the public interest groups. But impressive resources were arrayed against us. On August 5 Chairman Johnston announced to a gathering of 150 lobbyists that he had hired Anne Wexler to head a new lobbying consortium, the National Energy Security Coalition, to launch a pro-S.1220 public relations campaign and coordinate the actions of lobbyists working to pass the many diverse provisions of the bill. There was a guard at the door to the meeting, and we were not allowed in. And of course, one big difference between their campaign and ours was that they had lots of money at their disposal for campaign contributions.

Winning the Battle 9

An Opposition Strategy Takes Shape

By Labor Day, Nancy and I were back home in Minnesota, where I began teaching a class at Carleton called "Congress, Campaign Money, and a National Energy Strategy." My students joined me in keeping abreast of the fast-breaking, fascinating developments in Washington and contributing ideas and analyses on a daily basis.

As the Senate reconvened after Labor Day, the outside opposition groups were mobilized and important links had been forged among the opposition senators. What we still needed was a simple, clear strategy to provide a sharp focus for the lobbying efforts of the outsiders and for the organizing efforts of the insiders. In the Wellstone office, Norman Vig set about persuading Paul that he had to take a key leadership role, and for the next two months Johnston-Wallop became the number one priority of the office—no small accomplishment, given the diverse complement of "most important" demands on a senator's time.

In retrospect, Norm felt that the most important thing that Paul's office did was to organize the staff meetings that led to the meetings of the core group of senators who opposed the bill. The early meetings included Linda Lance representing Bryan, Ken Rynne representing Metzenbaum, Barb Cairns and Joyce Rechtschaffen representing Lieberman, Bob Davison representing Baucus, and Kate Kimball representing Mitchell—or so I thought. It turned out that although Kate Kimball worked closely with Majority Leader George Mitchell, she was officially employed as counsel to the Environmental Protection subcommittee of the Environment and Public Works Committee, chaired by Max Baucus. As Norm put it, she and Bob Davison worked for both Mitchell and Baucus, but whenever they came to these meetings, they stressed that "they were wearing their Baucus hats." In retrospect, however, Norm would conclude, "they were playing a game. . . . They were very important intermediaries in this whole thing, I think, keeping Mitchell well-informed about what was going on."

The immediate task was for the five core group senators to contact other senators on a target list, urging them to join in deferring action on the Johnston-Wallop bill at least until the next year. Initially, they decided to focus on Democrats, and the message, which Karl laid out in a memo entitled "Talking Points," was a politically partisan one:

> Scheduling floor time for this bill is likely to work to the White House's advantage: This bill is strongly endorsed by President Bush and John Sununu as the Administration's energy policy; *passing this bill will provide the White House with a major domestic victory* at a time when the Democrats are challenging the Republicans for not having a domestic policy agenda.

> Scheduling floor time for this bill is likely to work against Democrats: Without a clear Democratic counter-position, floor action is likely to *make Senate Democrats look disorganized and ineffectual;* if the Democrats and Republicans appear to support the same publicly unpopular energy policy, passage of this bill could *spur anti-incumbency voting,* which could threaten Democratic control of the Senate.

> Scheduling floor time this fall is likely to result in unnecessary political damage: Since the outlook for House action is uncertain due to conflicting Committee jurisdictional claims over key issues, the Senate would be *shedding blood over legislation that may never reach a Conference;* on the other hand, *if we let the House act first, it might provide Democrats an alternative position* supported by consumer and environmental groups (the House bill is not likely to have an Arctic Refuge drilling provision, for example).

> Would you be willing to: *Let the Majority Leader know you share these concerns* about scheduling floor time this fall? More importantly, *stand up in an upcoming Democratic Conference Lunch in support of not scheduling floor time* until either (1) the House has acted or (2) negotiations in the Senate produce a better "Democratic" starting point for floor action?

These arguments became the rallying cry and sparked a remarkably successful mobilizing of opposition to the Johnston-Wallop bill. The immediate goal was to have a majority of Senate Democrats tell the majority leader that they did not want the bill to come to the floor, although the door was left open for a "better 'Democratic' starting point," however that might be defined. This kind of close cooperation among Senate offices is quite unusual. Among the original five "core group" offices, the Bryan, Metzenbaum, and Wellstone staffers (Linda Lance, Ken Rynne, Karl and Norm) were enthusiastically behind the effort from the beginning. But the key to getting the effort off the ground was Sen. Max Baucus of Montana, the most senior senator represented and the most credible with his colleagues. Kate Kimball and Bob Davison were very important in getting Baucus committed and getting Baucus to call the meetings.

A basic problem with a strategy of keeping the bill from coming to the floor was Mitchell's view of his responsibility as majority leader to keep the Senate business moving along without undue delay. If the core group senators wanted to be sure of keeping the bill off the floor, their obvious option was a filibuster when the "motion to proceed" was offered. To make a filibuster threat credible enough for them to solicit commitments, they needed a critical mass of about ten or twelve senators supporting them from the start. Throughout October, the core group met regularly in Baucus's hideaway office in the Capitol, usually just prior to the Tuesday Senate Democratic Caucus luncheons. Baucus, the natural leader of the group, was an excellent chair—focusing on what had to be done, who had to talk to whom, what the pitch should be to particular senators, and so forth. What was striking, Norm noted, was how closely he stuck to the partisan pitch Karl Gawell had proposed.

At the same time, the environmental groups were rearranging their operations to join forces with the Senate core group. The regular NES Working Group meetings had been held downtown near the White House at the Wilderness Society. Near the end of September, the groups with full-time lobbyists—the National Wildlife Federation, the Audubon Society, U.S. PIRG, the Sierra Club, and others—decided they needed to coordinate their efforts closely with one another and also with the Senate core group offices. The meetings were moved to the Sierra Club on Capitol Hill, where they gathered at the end of every day. A key decision for these outside forces was an agreement to support the filibuster strategy. According to Bill Magavern, then a lobbyist for U.S. PIRG, until that moment there had been ambiguity about just exactly what they should be asking senators to do. Suddenly they had a focus and a mission—to enlist enough senators to participate in a filibuster and to convince others to vote against invoking cloture to stop it.

The opposition strategy had moved to a third stage: from the initial

"Make it a better bill" to the general "Oppose this bill," to the very specific, "Vote against cloture in order to sustain the filibuster and block consideration of the Johnston-Wallop bill." Typical of this approach was a letter the League of Conservation Voters (LCV) sent to all senators on October 2, saying, "We want to bring to your attention what may very well be the most critical pro-environment vote of this Congress. . . . In the event a cloture petition is filed to end this debate, *we will consider a vote opposing cloture as a critical pro-environment vote.*"

Tim Wirth also joined the core group during the second week of October. That was an important event because Wirth was widely respected in the Senate on energy and environmental issues. Both Bill Magavern and Dave Hamilton, U.S. PIRG's top-notch environmental lobbyists, saw Wirth's joining as crucial to the credibility of the filibuster effort. When I asked why Wirth had joined, however, they weren't sure. A Wirth aide who began coming to the core group staff meeting, an intellectually impressive and politically savvy young man, seemed to think that defeating Johnston was impossible, that failure was a foregone conclusion. And according to Magavern, Wirth himself became something of a disruptive force, always saying, "'Okay, what are we going to do when the filibuster loses?'"

Another big breakthrough occurred in early October when William Roth of Delaware, a very senior Republican, joined the filibuster group, and yet another came when Don Riegle of Michigan, chair of the Banking Committee, also joined. Roth, a member of the Environment Committee, was the chief sponsor of the bill (soon to pass the committee by a vote of 12–4) to designate the coastal plain of ANWR a wilderness area off-limits to oil exploration. He was also the first Republican to join, providing cover for other Republicans to follow. Riegle was a good friend of the auto industry and consequently an adamant opponent of any increase in CAFE standards, which he expected Johnston to push via an amendment on the Senate floor. From then on, it was a given in the core group that drilling for oil in ANWR and increasing the CAFE mandate were coupled; if one were removed from the bill the other would be also. Two other senior Democrats, Pat Leahy of Vermont, chair of the Agriculture Committee, and John Kerry of Massachusetts, joined about the same time. This was no longer a movement of freshmen; it was a force to be reckoned with.

Then on October 10, the day after Mitchell and the core group had agreed he would call for a vote in the October 15 Democratic Caucus, the Majority Leader suddenly announced that S.1220 was scheduled to come to the floor on October 16. Something quite unexpected had grabbed the attention of the Senate, changed the caucus agenda, and altered the political context of the vote: The day after our core group meeting, Anita Hill testified before the Senate Judiciary Committee, and the Senate put off its vote on the Clarence Thomas Supreme Court nomination until 6:00 P.M., October 15, several hours after the scheduled caucus meeting.

I speculated in my journal that the fate of Clarence Thomas and the fate of Johnston-Wallop might become intertwined: "The vote on whether to bring S.1220 to the floor is still expected at the Democratic Caucus luncheon tomorrow at 2:30, though the senators and staff will surely be preoccupied with the Thomas vote. I suspect that the politics of the energy debate are closely tied to the Thomas outcome. In particular, should Thomas win confirmation in a close, divisive vote, more Democrats may want to draw the line against Bush policies they don't believe in, as exemplified by S.1220; and more might be willing to support a dramatic move like a filibuster." The Thomas vote, occurring directly before the energy debate, created a context that reinforced the politically partisan anti-Johnston-Wallop argument Karl was making: Passage of S.1220 would be a domestic policy victory for George Bush. As Norm put it, "Dammit, the Republicans really made the Democrats look like asses on the Thomas vote; we're not going to give them another one. What does the Democratic party stand for anyway?"

In talking to environmental lobbyists afterward, I was intrigued to find they too were stressing Karl's argument when canvassing Democratic Senate offices and that they noted an almost immediate enhanced receptivity to it after the Thomas vote. For instance, Bill Magavern recalled, "We kept telling everybody this was Bush's energy bill. Why would you want to pass it? . . . Why do you want to give Bush a domestic policy victory a year before the election? That really caught fire after the Thomas hearings. . . . It made Democrats mad. Mad at Bush, mad at the Republicans, and frustrated at their own inability to present a Democratic alternative."

A Tempting Deal or Divisive Trap?

Representatives of seventeen Senate offices showed up on the morning of October 15 for a briefing organized by the Wellstone office, a promising indication of potential support for the filibuster. Not surprisingly, however, the senators at the luncheon were much more concerned with Clarence Thomas that day than they were with Johnston-Wallop. Bryan, Lieberman, and Wellstone spoke briefly, but no vote was taken on whether S.1220 should come to the floor.

Both sides scheduled press conferences for October 17. First, Johnston released an Office of Technology Assessment report, which he claimed supported the Johnston-Conrad proposed increase in the CAFE standard to 34 MPG in ten years. But Carol Werner's associate, Doug Howell, effectively challenged him from the audience, explaining that if the Secretary of Transportation were to use his discretionary authority under the Johnston amendment and if other "credits" were employed, the real fuel economy standard after ten years could be as low as 29.5 MPG. And Norm Vig pointed out that Johnston's amendment was inconsistent with the testimony of his own expert, Duleep, in terms of the technological potential for large fuel economy increases in the post-2000 period.

Then Tim Wirth arranged and orchestrated a press conference in the Senate Press Gallery for the core group senators. Wirth, Roth, Bryan, Baucus, Lieberman, and Wellstone all announced they intended to filibuster the motion to bring S.1220 to the floor. Gore, Leahy, and Metzenbaum were not there but sent supporting statements. Norm reported there were now seventeen senators behind the filibuster, including four Republicans. The only slightly discouraging note was sounded the next day in an oddly framed press release from Senator Wirth's office. The *Wall Street Journal* reported that "Opponents of the Johnston-Wallop measure announced plans to try to block the bill from coming to the floor through a filibuster. 'We are here to state that we will do whatever we can to stop the opening of the Arctic refuge from happening,' said Senator Timothy Wirth."

Dave Hamilton's reaction: "After raising all of those issues in the committee, [Wirth] came on strictly on the Arctic. In his statement supporting the filibuster, he didn't talk about anything else." Norm emphasized the same thing, "A lot of the focus on ANWR was due to Wirth. In all his statements and all he wrote, he emphasized that the only thing wrong with the bill was ANWR. . . . Wirth kept saying the rest of the bill is fine; we could have passed this bill months ago if it were not for ANWR and CAFE. . . ." The fear was that at some point Wirth would divide the opposition camp by supporting a Johnston offer to drop ANWR and CAFE.

One of the most dramatic confrontations occurred that same day at the regular Thursday luncheon of the Democratic Policy Committee (DPC). Reportedly, the discussion began with Johnston speaking for about ten minutes, making the case for his bill, followed by presentations by Wirth and Baucus. Wirth focused on ANWR, as he had in the press conference that morning, making the impressive case he had made before the Energy Committee in markup. Baucus, the de facto leader of the rapidly growing core group, repeated the argument he had been using effectively to recruit Democrats into joining the filibuster, that passage of S.1220 would look like a domestic policy victory for the Bush administration. But then, to everyone's surprise, Maryland's Sen. Paul Sarbanes joined the attack. "He has his colleagues' respect," I noted with pleasure in my journal, "and the intellect to change this into a real fight." Suddenly, Mitchell's nightmare of the energy bill debate's erupting into a public battle among Democrats seemed likely. The report of the meeting in *Congress Daily* confirmed this impression: "Supporters and opponents of the bill . . . continued to trade 'make my day' barbs, despite growing fear among Democrats that a bitter intraparty floor fight would prove embarrassing and damaging." Right after the meeting, Mitchell asked Tom Daschle of South Dakota, co-chair of the Senate Democratic Policy Committee, to talk to Johnston and see if they couldn't work something out.

The result of that meeting became known later that afternoon. Daschle called Paul's office to report that he had proposed a "compromise" to separate ANWR and CAFE from S.1220. That evening Johnston announced his acceptance of the compromise.

I was quite disturbed by this development. "The core group must not buy into this ploy," I wrote in my journal; "The Administration and Bennett Johnston will bring back ANWR and a weak CAFE at some later point." What I feared most was that once ANWR was removed, our opposition coalition would lose so much strength that the rest of the bill would pass. Norm and Karl responded differently: "Our first reaction was like yours," they told me. "We shouldn't go for this because it would open the way for the rest of the bill to pass. And ANWR would be brought back later. But then we realized it was in fact a sign of weakness on Johnston's part and that he probably wouldn't be able to carry his allies. The Republicans would consider the deal to be such a sellout that he would lose them, and his solid coalition of Republicans and western conservative Democrats would break up."

On October 22, the reliable *Congress Daily* reported on the state of the negotiations.

> After months of increasingly harsh rhetoric from Democratic opponents of the Senate Energy Committee's "National Energy Strategy" legislation, Energy Chairman Johnston has privately told Senate Democratic Policy Committee Co-Chairman Tom Daschle, D-SD, he is willing to consider a deal to remove the bill's two most controversial provisions—the Alaska [*sic*] National Wildlife Refuge (ANWR) and Corporate Average Fuel Economy (CAFE) standards—in order to bring the bill to the floor without a divisive intraparty fight, according to Senate sources.
>
> Daschle, in turn, has asked leading bill opponents—including Sens. Max

Baucus, D-Mont., Richard Bryan, D-Nev. and Joseph Lieberman, D-Conn.— if they would abandon a threatened filibuster of a motion to proceed on the legislation, the sources said. Under the terms of the proposed deal, Johnston or others could try to re-insert the two provisions once the bill reached the floor. . . .

On October 24, *Congress Daily* reported that agreement had been reached thanks to the support of the "core group of Democratic senators[:] . . . Max Baucus, . . . Richard Bryan, . . . Joseph Lieberman, . . . Timothy Wirth, . . . and Paul Wellstone."

Much to my relief, that deal was not consummated. When Johnston was presented with the official version of the core group's compromise position, he was told that *neither* ANWR *nor* CAFE *could be reinserted at any subsequent point.* Johnston was on the spot. Would removing ANWR cost him support he needed to pass the rest of the bill? If he decided to nix the deal and leave ANWR in, could he muster the 60 votes he would need to shut down a filibuster?

In the end Johnston decided to turn down the "compromise" he himself had been a party to just one week before. Norm's theory: "Johnston couldn't get the backing of the Republicans and others in his coalition for taking ANWR out under any circumstances and the White House wouldn't cooperate, probably hoping for a fight among Democrats." Karl's theory: The central aim of Bush's energy strategy was to get ANWR. If they didn't get ANWR, there wasn't going to be any bill. For Johnston even to suggest taking out ANWR was unacceptable to the White House and other Republicans. Of course, there was another plausible theory: Johnston was confident he had the votes to invoke cloture and shut down the filibuster.

A November Surprise

After Johnston said no, many senators, probably including Majority Leader Mitchell, evidently decided that there was no way out other than to block the bill from coming to the Senate floor. My hunch is that Mitchell had come to see the situation as Wirth had evidently seen it for a very long time, that the key to getting an energy bill passed was the removal of ANWR and CAFE. With these provisions remaining in the bill, the Democratic leadership no longer could say they had substituted a Democratic alternative.

From that day on, the filibuster forces had the feeling things were moving their way. But until the last moment, it was not clear to the filibusterers *when* the vote would be. For instance, at the legislative directors' meeting on Monday, October 28, Mitchell's staffer announced that S.1220 had been changed from a high priority "A" bill to a "B" classification. That same day, Ben Cooper told the Energy Committee L.A.s that S.1220 would not come to the floor that week; maybe next week he said, depending on whether a new "compromise" could be worked out. I speculated that Mitchell was obviously worried about a divisive public fight among Democrats, with no clear Democratic legislative alternative. I did not believe his priority was a far-sighted energy policy, however, but rather maintaining control of the Senate in the next election.

Since Congress would recess before Thanksgiving and not return until January, I entertained the hope that the vote might be put off until the following year, providing the environmental groups with plenty of time to bring home-state pressure to bear on targeted senators. But the very next day, October 29, Norm called: "Urgent, the bill may come to the floor tonight!" It turned out the Republican caucus had put out a rumor that they would interrupt debate on the Civil Rights bill to have a cloture vote limiting the time allowed for debate on the Johnston-Wallop bill. If it passed, our S.1220 filibuster would be stopped before it ever got out of the starting block. The filibuster group immediately went to Mitchell and threatened to slow down the Civil Rights debate and other floor action if he permitted that to happen. But the next day, October 30, a cloture motion was filed, calling for a vote to end the filibuster.

An urgent meeting of the core group late that afternoon reviewed the vote count and discussed how the remaining undecided senators might be approached. Since Johnston needed 60 votes to stop the filibuster, we needed at least 41 votes against cloture to keep the bill from the floor.

When the tally was completed, the core group had identified only 31 sure votes. By their count, Johnston had 39 votes for certain. Then they focused on the most important business, the undecideds, dividing them into two categories, a "B" list that would probably go with Johnston and an "A" list that included senators who were thought either to be leaning toward supporting the filibuster or might be convinced to go our way. There were eighteen senators on the B-list, meaning that even in the most optimistic scenario, Johnston probably had 57 of the 60 votes he needed. As for the remaining twelve, on the A list, Norm had the sense that several of them were there based on wishful thinking more than any solid evidence. Sen. Howard Metzenbaum of Ohio walked out of the meeting shaking his head and saying, "I don't think we've got the votes."

Nevertheless, there was a flurry of activity by the Senate opposition and their environmentalist supporters as the vote drew near. A-list and B-list senators received many calls from their colleagues. One notable caller was South Carolina's Sen. Fritz Hollings. Chair of the Commerce Committee, he had just been enlisted into the filibuster group by two of his subcommittee chairs, Dick Bryan and Al Gore. He was angry about the way Johnston had infringed on his committee's CAFE jurisdiction and vowed to convince members of his committee and other committee chairs to support the filibuster. He was credited with bringing Robb of Virginia, who was on the A list, and Exon of Nebraska, who was on the B list, into the fold. And he may have had something to do with the conversion of the chair of the Environment Committee, Quentin Burdick, who had been expected to vote with his North Dakota colleague, Kent Conrad, and support the Johnston bill.

The environmental groups organized an outpouring of calls and letters to swing senators urging them to vote against cloture. The Sierra Club, for instance, had a bank of ten phones set up every night for three weeks, with volunteers calling members in the states of targeted senators. And the "SAFE ENERGY—*write now*!" campaign organized by the Safe Energy Communications Council, Greenpeace, and the Sierra Club held a press conference three days before the vote to announce the delivery of over a half million postcards and petitions opposing the Johnston-Wallop bill. According to Dave Hamilton, "The Alaska Coalition has to be credited with the most active grassroots toward the end."

Both Florida senators, Bob Graham, a Democrat, and Connie Mack, a Republican, were regarded as swing votes. But the environmentalists in Florida were very well organized in opposition to the Johnston-Wallop provision that would have permitted oil drilling off the Florida panhandle. Through their efforts an outpouring of Floridians contacted their two senators and Governor Lawton Chiles, prompting a letter from the governor asking the senators not to oppose the filibuster and resulting in both voting against cloture.

When gentle persuasion didn't work, there was some arm-twisting. One story involved a Democratic senator running in a special election at the time of the cloture vote. The environmentalists somehow got hold of White House memos suggesting that Bennett Johnston had solicited oil company contributions to that senator's campaign. Suspecting that the quid pro quo would be his vote to stop the filibuster, the enviros threatened to expose the senator. So instead of voting with Johnston, he decided to miss the cloture vote, effectively withholding one of the 60 votes Johnston needed.

On October 31, the debate over whether to approve the motion to proceed, that is, to bring S.1220 to the floor of the Senate, began. The filibuster was underway. The cloture vote calling for an end to the filibuster was scheduled for 10:00 A.M. the next day. My students crowded into our living room in Minnesota to watch the debate on CSPAN.

Tim Wirth realized that if the core group senators waited until the formal 10:00 A.M. starting time, Johnston would be recognized first and put us on the defensive. So Wirth proposed that he and Paul go to the floor early, during what is known as "morning business" preceding formal debate, and get the jump on Johnston. The Energy Committee staffers were furious with this maneuver once they figured out what was happening. Wirth began with his proposed "compromise":

> There are a number of us who feel very strongly that it is wrong for us in the Senate to proceed to the energy bill as it is currently constructed. . . . I have been deeply engaged in working on that energy bill, and as the distinguished chairman of the Energy Committee, Senator Johnston, has pointed out on any number of occasions, much of what is in that bill I wrote, in terms of energy conservation, natural gas regulation, alternative fuels, and so on.
>
> There are many good provisions in the bill. We would have had that bill and those provisions on the floor months ago had it not been for a single title that is enormously controversial. There are many other items in the bill that raise controversy, but the title related to the Arctic National Wildlife Refuge and whether we should be drilling in the Arctic has held up that bill and caused enormous controversy.
>
> A number of us have attempted . . . to offer a compromise strategy for bringing up the energy bill. We have on a number of occasions offered to have the main part of the energy bill come up, to be followed by two separate bills, one on Corporate Average Fuel Economy and one on the Arctic National Wildlife Refuge. . . . I would like to get on with the overall energy policy and have those two controversial elements be dealt with separately. That is what this debate is all about. . . . We would not have this filibuster, we would not have all of this blood on the floor of the Senate, we would not have all this controversy, if the very simple compromise process that I have suggested— having this come up as three separate bills—had been agreed to.[1]

Then came Paul with a scathing critique of the Johnston-Wallop bill:

> I believe S.1220 is so fundamentally flawed that it is not even an acceptable starting point for a rational energy strategy. To begin with, S.1220 is not an energy policy. It is a nonenergy policy. It does not address our two most fundamental long-term energy problems: First, our excessive and growing dependence on imported energy, which in turn threatens our national security and also threatens the health of our economy; and second, the greatest threat to our world environment; namely, the problem of global warming and related climate change that could have devastating effects impacts on the world. . . .

> It is not just the foolishness and greed of destroying the Arctic Wildlife
> Refuge . . . , this bill is fatally flawed from start to finish. It is conceptually
> impoverished; it is totally lacking in vision as to what is possible technologi-
> cally, what is sound economically, what is sensible environmentally, and what
> is sustainable in the future. . . .

He then went on to outline specific defects and giveaways in the bill, explaining the process whereby "the national energy strategy became a wish
list of all the subsidies and regulatory changes that the big energy corporations could think of."

The next speaker was Johnston, who felt he needed to respond directly
to Paul: "Mr. President, we just heard an amazing speech that says that this
bill is nothing but a special interest bill; that the provisions of it that relate
to renewable energy, energy efficiency, alternative fuels, do not amount to
anything. I submit that these provisions are the most far-reaching provisions
on the so-called environmental path—on energy efficiency, on renewables,
on alternative fuels—that have ever been presented to Congress."[2]

Johnston had been making that outrageous claim for some time. Paul
stood up and explained why it was simply not true, and Max Baucus reiter-
ated Paul's analysis, describing Johnston-Wallop as "fatally flawed." At that
point, Johnston posed what he thought would be a very tough question for
Baucus. Essentially, whom do you believe: Wirth, one of the most respected
environmentalists in the Senate? Or Wellstone, a mere freshman who just
got here?

> MR. JOHNSTON: We heard two different descriptions of this bill this morning,
> one from the Senator from Colorado, who abominates the drilling in the
> Arctic, but who said that the rest of the bill was excellent. . . . Another view
> of it was from the Senator from Minnesota, who said this was an awful,
> terrible bill, with almost nothing redeeming about it. I wonder what the
> view of the Senator from Montana is with respect to the rest of the bill. I
> know very well what he thinks about drilling in ANWR.
> MR. BAUCUS: I might ask the Senator if he listened to my statement.
> MR. JOHNSTON: Well, I think what I heard was that he agrees with the Sena-
> tor from Minnesota.
> MR. BAUCUS: The Senator from Montana frankly believes, and I think the
> majority of the Members on this side of the aisle believe, that this bill has
> real problems.[3]

Including Baucus, a succession of twenty-two senators opposed to the
Johnston-Wallop bill, seventeen Democrats and five Republicans, took the

floor before the cloture vote. Twelve senators, four Democrats and eight Republicans, spoke in favor of halting the filibuster. To our satisfaction, of the twenty-two senators who spoke against the bill, only three, Wirth, Lieberman, and Roth, explained their opposition largely in terms of ANWR; the debate, according to Norm Vig, "was much more about basic energy policy than we might have expected."

At 10 A.M., November 1, it was time to vote. I personally was resigned to losing. Norm Vig described the scene on the Senate floor at the time of the vote: The bench around the back of the chamber was crammed with staff. Johnston's people were at one end, carrying thick folders; the filibuster staffers were at the other end. There was no hostility, but there was "icy silence" between them, except for Energy Committee staff economist Karl Hausker and Gore environmental aide Katie McGinty, who later would marry. Ben Cooper was on the floor beside Bennett Johnson.

Lieberman environmental aide Joyce Rechtschaffen and Bryan's chief of staff Jean Neal were keeping track of the vote count: Missouri's Kit Bond, from the B list, Florida's Connie Mack, who had seemed an unlikely choice for the A list, both went our way. So did North Dakota's Burdick, Nebraska's Exon, Virginia's Robb. The filibuster staffers began looking at each other: 38, 39, 40, . . . 41; they had to observe Senate decorum, but they were exchanging smiles of disbelief. Incredible! In the end, the vote was 50–44 for cloture, 10 votes short of the 60 needed.

Bennett Johnston was very gracious in defeat. Recognized immediately after the vote, he said:

> Mr. President, in case anyone wants to know what this vote means, it means we lost. I congratulate those who formed a very strong phalanx against this bill. . . . I certainly have great admiration for those who fought the fight. The environmental groups, I must say, wrote the textbook on how to defeat a bill such as this, and my admiration is to them for the political skill which they exhibited.
>
> Mr. President, we may have defeated comprehensive national energy policy here today, but we have not defeated the problem. The problem remains. . . . I await somebody else's solution. We have done our best, and I give my congratulations to those who, at least at this point in the game, won the fight.

Baucus, the opposition floor manager, responded equally graciously, concluding, "We do want to work with the chairman and other Senators, and we pledge our efforts to do so, so that we can develop an energy policy that makes sense for America."[4]

Paul and Norm stayed around for a while afterward on the floor. In the course of his remarks Johnston had challenged Paul on a charge he had made about the uranium enrichment provisions in the bill. Karl was gathering documents to back up Paul's claim so that, following Congress's weird and misleading practice, the recorder could insert them at the appropriate place in the debate and the next day's *Congressional Record* would have Paul responding immediately to Johnston.

Eventually, Norm left the chamber to seek out Paul's press secretary. As he emerged, he was amazed to find a very large group of environmental lobbyist friends and allies gathered just outside the door. They were jubilant. They all wanted to shake Norm's hand. "That was the greatest feeling of my life," he said later. "They treated us like heroes as we came off the floor. It was a wonderful moment." His walk back to the Wellstone office with the environmentalists was "like walking on air." There was more cheering at the office and then a press conference at the Capitol. The six core group senators were jubilant and spoke about their optimism that U.S. energy policy could now be redirected in a fundamental way. Only Tim Wirth continued to push the notion of separating ANWR and CAFE off and bringing the rest of the bill back immediately.

The rest of the day was filled with celebration. A dozen of the core group staffers gathered at the Union Station grill for lunch. The Wellstone office was inundated with cards, flowers, and balloons from the environmental groups. Exhausted, Karl drove home with some flowers and balloons for his family. Tim Wirth hosted a pizza and beer party, followed by a smaller gathering in Max Baucus's office. Finally, Norm joined some staff and environmentalist friends who were walking over to the Sierra Club for yet another party. On the way, they bumped into Paul and Sheila, who were out for a walk, and convinced them to come too.

Norm recalls going down the stairs to the party in the Sierra Club basement and receiving a big cheer. "Then Paul came down and the place just exploded. . . . A true hero's welcome. There was a sign on the wall, 'We love you Paul.' It was kind of a little love-in for ten or fifteen minutes."

The Seeds of Victory

Only ten months before, when we had arrived in Washington, who would have guessed this could happen? All we knew then was that there was going to be an important debate on an issue we cared about. Now we had scored a stunning, remarkable victory. Why did we win? In retrospect, some of the ingredients are obvious. Within the Senate many Democrats and some Republicans were genuinely uncomfortable with a bill with such far-reaching implications that was so blatantly responsive to, and shaped by, the desires of the major energy industries and counter to the vision of most Americans. As unlikely as it seemed at first, a small group of junior senators who were willing to stand up to a powerful chairman was a sufficient nucleus to spawn a successful revolt.

And, of course, the environmental groups did a superb job mobilizing grassroots pressure where it counted, alerting the media around the country to what was happening, and effectively joining forces with the incipient Senate revolt. ANWR became the symbol around which the most successful grassroots organizing took place, but the environmentalists' concerns about energy policy were much broader and deeper than that single issue.

In the end, bringing together a sufficient number of senators to block the bill required reaching out to some with other concerns, such as the Michigan senators who feared CAFE and others who were concerned about PUHCA reform and some committee chairs who felt Bennett Johnston had trespassed on their turf. And very likely, there were less obvious ingredients as well. Throughout the debate I wondered what role Majority Leader George Mitchell was really playing. Ostensibly, he did nothing but facilitate communications between the warring parties and discharge his responsibility to bring matters to the Senate floor in an orderly, equitable, and expeditious fashion. But Mitchell clearly had two concerns. First, he did not like the Johnston-Wallop bill. Second, he did not want the Democratic senators to end up taking the blame for blocking a comprehensive national energy strategy, with consequent risks of losing Democratic control of the Senate in the 1992 elections.

In 1986, the Democrats had regained control of the Senate when eleven new Democratic senators were swept into office. In late 1991, President Bush was riding high in the public opinion polls and he would be leading the Republican ticket in 1992. The eleven freshman Democrats in the "Class of '86," Adams (Washington), Breaux (Louisiana), Conrad (North Dakota), Daschle (South Dakota), Fowler (Georgia), Graham (Florida), Mikulski (Maryland), Reid (Nevada), Sanford (North Carolina), Shelby (Alabama), and Wirth (Colorado), were up for reelection for the first time, when incumbent senators are usually most vulnerable. By contrast, in 1992 only two freshman Republican senators would be running for reelection.

I believe Mitchell came to see the Wirth "compromise," which I had long thought of as a "divide and conquer strategy," as the way out. If the two most contentious issues—ANWR and CAFE—were separated from the bill and if some more energy conservation measures were introduced, the revised bill could be said to be a "Democratic alternative" to the Bush bill. Mitchell tried to push that compromise at the end when he dispatched Daschle as his intermediary. But when Johnston refused to accept it, Mitchell may well have used his influence to help to bring about our victory with the aim of forcing Johnston to reconsider.

There is even reason to believe that Mitchell had hinted early on to the incipient opposition forces that a filibuster strategy was the way to go. He had been frustrated in March and April when his sixteen-member task force, intended to allow the Democrats to work out their differences in private, was effectively ignored by task force chair Johnston. One well-positioned observer told me that in late spring Mitchell's chief of staff had in effect suggested a filibuster strategy to environmental leaders. According to this source, he had told an officer of one of the leading environmental groups, "It strikes me that what you've got to do is create gridlock; create gridlock on this bill and you can move your own stuff maybe later." The day after the vote the environmentalist called Mitchell's chief of staff and said, I just want to thank you for your excellent advice to us to create gridlock. "Yep. And you did," the chief of staff replied, with obvious pleasure.

Mitchell had previously experienced how a filibuster impasse could create the conditions for a compromise during the protracted 1990 debate over the Clean Air Act amendments. In his floor remarks after the November 1, 1991, cloture vote, Tim Wirth recalled what had happened then under similar circumstances: "It is useful for all of us to remember that there is a very good model for this. We had a Clean Air Act that came to the floor out of the Environment and Public Works Committee, and it was very clear that there were not enough votes to break a filibuster. So that bill got worked out, and we ended up with, I think, a very good piece of legislation. If we can look at that as a model and understand that that kind of constructive history can be used by us here, we can be back very quickly and have an overall energy bill."

In Washington a few days after the surprising victory, I spoke with Norm and asked him about Mitchell's role. He recalled that Mitchell's aide Kate Kimball had made a significant contribution. He noted that Mitchell "was always very sympathetic to this group when they came in and he said some things to Paul on the side which led Paul to think he was really supporting us." Norm's conclusion: "I am convinced that Mitchell was always trying to help us insofar as he could, given his commitment to Johnston to bring this bill up. He never turned on us; . . . When he brought the bill up and announced that he was going to have an immediate cloture vote, you could interpret that as saying, 'Screw you, I've had enough of this; let's just bring it up and see who's got the votes.' But I didn't see it that way. I think that Mitchell had a pretty good calculation of how it might come out and that it probably would be to our advantage to bring it up at that point. He probably stalled it off long enough so that we had enough votes, so we had time to organize the vote. I think he was probably a secret player in this."

Of course, Karl's original theory was that the compromise of removing ANWR from the bill at just the right moment might have been Bennett Johnston's plan. That is, ANWR might have been Johnston's "giant head-fake," a ruse to attract the attention of the opposition. In retrospect, I am skeptical of this interpretation, though I don't rule it out. After all, Johnston did turn down the "divide and conquer compromise" at the crucial moment prior to the cloture vote. On the other hand, he may have thought at that point that he could muster the 60 votes he needed to defeat the filibuster.

And he might have been told in no uncertain terms by ANWR proponents that he had better *not* agree to take ANWR out of the bill. Johnston as much as said this in a later reflection about the debate: "[There] was nothing I could have done to pass ANWR. But having ANWR in the bill initially was absolutely essential to the later success of the bill. I could not have gotten the ANWR supporters, of which there were many, to go along with the bill unless they had the full attempt. And we gave it the full attempt. Also, that enabled the CAFE . . . provisions to be dropped out. So I can't think of much of anything I would have done differently."[5]

So, ANWR may not have been Johnston's giant head fake. What it surely was, however, was the Achilles heel of my strategy, my dream of reframing the debate by first defeating the Johnston-Wallop bill with a filibuster and then, with it dead on the Senate floor, introducing an alternative package. The problem was that the bill could not be killed irreparably. At any point it could be revived by removing ANWR, thereby appeasing a sufficient portion of the opposition that a successful filibuster could no longer be mounted. Tim Wirth saw that early on as the filibuster was developing. And we had to fight off his attempts to push that compromise from the moment he joined the filibuster forces.

What this suggests, of course, is that the November 1 cloture vote was not to be the final battle of the war over the Johnston-Wallop bill.

Losing the War

10

A Sustainable Energy Transition Strategy

From the time we decided to oppose the Johnston-Wallop bill, my expectation had always been that if we succeeded, the next step would be to introduce a sustainable energy transition package. In effect, we would reframe the issue so that the citizens who had mobilized to block Johnston-Wallop would have an alternative to support. The dramatic November 1 vote provided that opportunity.

The ingredients of a sustainable energy transition legislative package would include at least four key elements: the bill introduced by William Roth of Delaware to designate the entire Arctic National Wildlife Refuge a wilderness area off-limits to oil exploration; a modified Bryan bill to promote the development and marketing of highly efficient and/or renewably fueled automobiles; a bill to promote utility regulatory rules that make efficiency and renewables options profitable and attractive; and of course, as a centerpiece, our Sustainable Energy Transition Act, known to its friends as "SETA."

With much help from many people, I had begun working on SETA soon after arriving in Washington. I have described how my first meeting back in Minnesota in March jarred me out of my all-too-willing acceptance of the Washington definition of what was "realistic" and helped to identify the basic concepts of a Wellstone sustainable energy initiative.[1] Most important was our shift of focus from Washington to states and communities across the nation. Years of experience had demonstrated that many kinds of residential, commercial, and transportation energy efficiency programs are best organized at the community level. Because of climate differences, and energy supply histories, energy use patterns are quite different in different regions of the country, so energy efficiency and conservation opportunities differ, too. Renewable energy opportunities also vary widely from one region of the country to another. The generally clear Southwest is especially well suited to solar energy development; the upper Midwest has been termed the "Saudia Arabia of Wind"; and so forth. The positive and negative economic impacts of a sustainable energy transition differ by region as well. As a consequence, it makes sense to rely on states or regional consortia of states to develop sustainable energy transition plans. And it also makes sense for the federal government to collect the revenues to support those plans and distribute the funds equitably.

It wasn't until the summer of 1991 that Karl, Henry, Norm, and I had time to focus on the Sustainable Energy Transition Act. We were greatly aided by a Carleton College senior biology major, Eliot Wajskol, who spent the summer as an intern in our office. By July we began to think seriously about writing a detailed bill. Eliot organized a series of briefings where I described the basic elements of the bill and received useful criticisms and helpful suggestions from friends and associates such as Carol Werner of the Energy and Environmental Studies Institute, her husband, Jack Werner, who headed a group promoting local delivery of energy efficiency services, Ken Bossong and Jonathan Becker of Public Citizen, and Scott Sklar and his associates from the Solar Energy Industries Association. Especially important was Jeff Genzer, general counsel of the National Association of State Energy Offices (NASEO) and its chief lobbyist. While I had talked to Jeff on the phone many times and corresponded with him regularly, I didn't actually meet him until July 10 when at his invitation I attended the NASEO annual meeting in Washington. One of the speakers at the meeting, the deputy director of the Texas Energy Office, Carol Tombarri, caught my attention when she pointed out that in the 1980s the chief source of funding for most of the state energy offices and their conservation and renewables programs had been the money from billion dollar court settlements with major oil companies who had illegally overcharged consumers. That oil overcharge money was about to run out. As a consequence, she warned, many of the state energy offices might have to close down. Several of the state energy directors I spoke with at the meeting echoed this concern. Our bill, with its state sustainable energy transition grants, could not have been more timely from their perspective.

When it came time for actually drafting the bill, in late July, Norm Vig,

Eliot, and I sat around a table one morning in a deserted section of the Senate staff cafeteria. In several hours, we drew up a detailed outline, which Norm took back to the office and refined. The next day we brought the outline to Jeff Genzer's law office across town and briefed him about what we wanted the bill to say. Later, Karl prepared a considerably expanded second draft, so that by the time I returned to Minnesota at the end of August, the bill was taking shape.

A measure of the bill's progress was its enthusiastic reception when Karl, Norm, and I briefed a meeting of the energy policy working group in Paul's Minneapolis office on August 24. Soon our prospective bill began to attract some attention and some enthusiasm in the environmental community, as exemplified by the work of Leigh and Bob Waggoner and Scott Tice, environmentalist farmers who live in rural Wisconsin near the small town of Shell Lake. One day I got a call from Leigh, who wanted to know how they could help mobilize the support of local environmental groups around the country. She even proposed to marshal a contingent to come to Washington to stage a fast on the steps of the Capitol until our bill was passed!

By late summer, we were beginning to come to grips with the difficult issues in the bill. Probably the most problematic was the question of where the money would come from to finance state and local investments in energy efficiency and renewable programs. Since March, I had been thinking in terms of a gasoline tax of a penny per gallon, which would yield just about one billion dollars in revenue annually. Despite a clear public aversion to increased taxes, I was convinced there would be popular backing for a small tax to support renewable energy sources and efficient energy use. Karl argued forcefully for expanding the revenue source beyond gasoline to a full carbon tax, a levy on all fossil fuels on the grounds that they all contribute to global warming. Yet another alternative was a small BTU tax, based on the energy content of fuels, which would apply to nuclear power as well as fossil fuels.

Whatever tax we chose would surely generate opposition; a very strong lobby, led by the truckers and including farm groups, opposed gasoline and diesel fuel tax increases. And a carbon tax was also opposed by powerful and well-placed coal-state members like the chair of the Senate Appropriations Committee, West Virginia's Robert Byrd.

In the end, we decided to go with a "tiny tax" on carbon, amounting to less than a penny per gallon of gasoline and a comparably small amount on coal and natural gas. Such a tax was well within the noise of everyday fluctuations in price and it would raise about four billion dollars a year. Such a small price rise by itself would have minimal effect on consumption in general, but the revenue would fund programs that could produce enormous reductions in energy use and substitution of renewables for fossil fuels.

Early in September, when the Johnston-Wallop bill began to encounter trouble, a Senate Energy Committee staffer who specialized in conservation and renewable issues came to a meeting of Carol Werner's energy efficiency working group. She invited the staffers and environmentalists there to submit proposed language to the committee for energy efficiency amendments to the bill, and she expressed an interest in talking to Karl and Norm about SETA. I wondered what we would do if Johnston offered to include SETA in his bill in return for Paul's support. Such are the everyday temptations of the Senate. Such is the power of a Bennett Johnston who can offer those kinds of deals, though in this case no offer ever came.

Five days after the cloture vote, I flew to Washington for two intensive days of hammering out the final revisions of SETA and Karl drafted a detailed section-by-section summary to be distributed with the bill. Back in Minnesota, I drafted a "Dear Colleague" letter, explaining the SETA bill's rationale and major features to the other senators. My students generated tables showing how much revenue would be derived from each fossil fuel and how much money each state would receive for sustainable energy investments and appended them to the letter. We viewed the state-by-state investment money tables as not very subtle "bait." Each Senate office would find that its state stood to receive tens or even hundreds of millions of dollars a year for urgently needed and politically popular projects.

On November 22 the SETA bill was introduced as S.2020. I was delighted by the fortuitous bill number, which we pronounced "20–20," and announced it was 'The Energy Strategy with a Vision!'[2] And at just that moment, four leading environmental organizations were about to release the major study, *America's Energy Choices,* which laid out a compelling case for change in our national energy policy. It used state-of-the-art computer modelling to show, for instance, that over the next four decades, American consumers could save $2.3 trillion while projected U.S. energy consumption would be cut nearly in half and carbon dioxide emissions would be reduced by 70 percent.

On November 27, the day the study was published, eighteen environmental groups sent a letter to every member of the Senate, describing the principal conclusions of the study and making the case for supporting sustainable energy package instead of proceeding with the Johnston-Wallop bill with ANWR and CAFE removed. It began:

By rejecting consideration of S.1220 on November 1, the Senate has created an opportunity to craft a national energy strategy that is truly in the national interest. This cannot be accomplished by simply removing from S.1220 the provisions related to the Arctic National Wildlife Refuge. Doing so will not make S.1220 the forward-looking energy policy the United States needs.

Deleting the Arctic Refuge Title will only allow attention to focus on the other unacceptable provisions in the bill, such as compromising the rights of citizens and states to obtain a hearing on significant nuclear safety issues once a combined construction and operating license is issued and changes in public utility law that would undermine the ability of states to ensure that utility investments give proper consideration to energy efficiency and are indeed in the public interest.[3]

Unfortunately, at that time, less than a month after the Senate refused to allow the Johnston-Wallop bill come to the floor, the Senate Democratic leadership was clearly moving in the direction of a "compromise," rather than fighting for a sustainable energy transition strategy that might provoke a divisive struggle among Democrats. Tim Wirth's admonition at the post-victory press conference had been an ominous sign: "I think we ought to calm down over the weekend, come right back and work on an energy bill."

The Opposition Core Group Unravels

I began thinking about how to counter what Johnston and Wirth were likely to try next and how to move the Senate to consider a sustainable energy transition package. I proposed to Norm and Karl that Paul take the lead in urging that the November 1 vote be understood as a mandate for a fundamental change in direction of our national energy policy.

With the active support of a now-aroused, energized, organized, and vigilant environmental and consumer constituency, the senators who led this fight should argue that what happened was that Johnston and Wallop and their allies on the Energy Committee and in the Department of Energy tried to rush a special interest bill to the Senate floor and it was soundly repudiated. As a result, the Democratic majority now has an opportunity, indeed a mandate, to take the time to shape its own farsighted national energy strategy with the public interest, not special energy interests, in mind.

I suggested that what was needed right away included: a letter from the core group telling Mitchell that resurrecting the Wirth "compromise" would be unacceptable, and that he should appoint a new task force to come up with a Democratic national energy strategy alternative. On November 4, Norm drafted a memo from Paul to Mitchell opposing the Wirth proposal.

But on November 12, Karl called with bad news. At the Democratic senators' regular Tuesday luncheon, Kent Conrad, Bill Bradley, and Paul Sarbanes had urged Mitchell to support Wirth's proposal immediately and to bring the rest of the Johnston-Wallop bill to the floor before the session ended in late November.

When the core group staffers met later that afternoon, one of Tim Wirth's aides pushed hard for support of the Wirth "compromise," adding a new twist: two other especially controversial provisions would also be removed from the bill, though they could be put back in as amendments when the bill was debated on the floor. If the provisions could be reintroduced as amendments, however, the only effect of this maneuver would be to avoid a filibuster of the bill as a whole. The big surprise was that Senator Joe Lieberman of Connecticut was evidently ready to sign on to the deal; at the meeting, one of Lieberman's legislative aides spoke up in support of the Wirth proposal. Naturally Karl was strongly opposed. In the ensuing discussion, Karl propounded a Trojan Horse theory, saying Wirth was attempting to divide the opposition senators.

The next day began with some good news. At a meeting of the core group senators in Baucus's office, Wirth pushed hard for separating off ANWR and CAFE and bringing the rest of the Johnston-Wallop bill to the floor before the end of the session, but he failed to win support from any of the other senators. However, Lieberman did not back Wirth as we had expected. It wasn't long before we found out why.

That afternoon, nine senators were represented at a meeting of opposition core group staffers in Lieberman's office. But the scene soon turned ugly when Lieberman's aides angrily accused Karl of responsibility for informing the environmental groups that it appeared Lieberman was going to support Wirth on the ANWR/CAFE separation deal.

We learned later that afternoon that Lieberman's office had received several angry calls from Connecticut environmentalists that morning and his staffers denied any intention to support a such a deal. They were furious with Karl and they lashed into him for "unprofessional behavior" in alerting the enviros. They said their office would never work with Wellstone again.

Karl was very upset. He called Environmental Action's Nancy Hirsch and other enviros to try to find out who "leaked" the Lieberman news and arranged the phone calls. Norm wanted to know if I had done it. On reflection, I guess I did play a part. After the disturbing core group staffers' meeting the day before I had called Bill Magavern of U.S. PIRG, and he had notified the Sierra Club. Magavern's colleague Dave Hamilton had also called his U.S. PIRG contacts in Connecticut with the message, "Try to find out what's going on with Lieberman." Then, Karl in continuation of this typical Washington loop, indirectly tipped off Lieberman to the Wellstone office's involvement. After speaking with Karl, Environmental Action's Nancy Hirsch had contacted the Wilderness Society with the message, "Lieberman may be selling us out." When a Wilderness Society official had then called a Lieberman staffer and read her that message, the source in our office was easy to figure out.

To me, the most striking lesson of this tale was the degree to which making this information public had affected Lieberman's position. Of course, it would have been regrettable if my actions had resulted in a permanent breach between Wellstone and Lieberman. But I was confident that would not happen. When told about the charge of "unprofessional behavior," one public interest lobbyist responded, "Where has [Lieberman's aide] been working? It's a given in many offices that industry lobbyists will hear immediately of developments in staff or member meetings. That's the norm of "professional behavior" on the Hill. We're just trying to provide the same sort of information to citizen groups with grassroots connections."

The disquieting thing was that the Wirth proposal to separate off ANWR and CAFE seemed to be getting serious consideration at the highest levels of the Democratic Senate leadership. On November 15, the core group met with Mitchell and Daschle in Mitchell's office. At that meeting, Daschle pushed hard for the Wirth "compromise," perhaps with PUHCA reform and one-step nuclear licensing removed along with ANWR and CAFE. In this formulation of the deal, however, there would be no guarantee that those provisions could not be reinstated in the bill later as amendments.

I hoped Paul would build on his renown as a result of the effort that blocked Johnston-Wallop and lead a highly visible effort in the Senate and in the environmental community to substitute a sustainable energy transition package, thereby changing the fundamental focus of the congressional and public debate to what kind of energy future made sense for America.

To me that seemed to be the obvious next step. We had been instrumental in convincing a great majority of the environmental groups to oppose the Johnston-Wallop bill as a blatant giveaway to the energy industries, an unraveling of important environmental protections, and a failure to take advantage of a rare opportunity to change the direction of our nation's energy course and move toward a sustainable energy future. Those groups with large national constituencies had taken those arguments to their grassroots networks and engaged hundreds of thousands of supporters around the country. Having stopped the bill, the next natural step would be to try to help all those committed people to become involved in a positive campaign in support of a sustainable energy transition package. Paul was in a position to be a leader of a movement for a sustainable energy future.

However, the Senate Democratic leadership was already moving rapidly in very different direction—toward accepting the Wirth "compromise." Tom Daschle and other senior Democrats were also actively promoting the "compromise" in the Senate Democratic Caucus. Majority Leader Mitchell had evidently decided that was the way to go.

At first the environmental coalition tried to hold firm against the proposal. On November 18 Wirth called the environmental groups to a meeting in his office and told them that Bennett Johnston was prepared to guarantee that ANWR would be removed from the bill permanently if they would agree to support the rest of the bill. A great majority of the groups turned him down flat. Wirth backed off and proposed a new task force headed by Bennett Johnston that would come up with a revised energy strategy bill. But late that afternoon, the core group of senators rejected that proposal.

However, the seeds of division had been sown in the anti-Johnston-Wallop coalition. A significant minority of the environmental groups, most notably the Wilderness Society, the Alliance to Save Energy, the Audubon Society, and the Alaska Coalition were interested in pursuing the guaranteed severing of ANWR from the bill. As Brooks Yeager, the NES Working Group co-chair and Audubon society vice president said later, "The Arctic as the strong position with our grass roots is not something we can . . . change."[4] Phil Sparks, the Communications Consortium codirector, agreed: "It was easy to organize around the Arctic, much more difficult to make a sustainable energy future the issue."[5] On Tuesday, there was what Bill Magavern termed a "very bad" coalition meeting, with divisions among the groups and some overt antagonism. By Wednesday, Karl reported that the environmental alliance had lost its cohesion and the commitment of the core group was in question.

Soon thereafter the core group of senators met and agreed that if S.1220 without ANWR (and probably without CAFE), were brought to the floor in February they would not stage a filibuster. At the urging of Mitchell/Baucus staffer Kate Kimball, the staffs of the core group senators then divided up the controversial titles and agreed to take responsibility for developing amendments to improve the Johnston-Wallop bill. Karl and Norm would concentrate on energy efficiency, renewables, and hydropower amendments, Metzenbaum's staffer Ken Rynne on natural gas, and so forth. Although Paul was a party to the agreement, neither Norm nor Karl knew how all this had been decided. As a consequence of the Lieberman debacle, Paul had clammed up to them about what exactly happened at the meeting. The core group had capitulated. A make-it-a-better-bill regime had been reestablished and my dream of introducing an alternative sustainable energy transition package that would compete with Johnston-Wallop had obviously been discarded.

From an inside-the-beltway perspective, this agreement by the core group made perfect sense. Once Johnston decided to accept the removal of ANWR from his bill and to take out CAFE as well, the Johnston-Wallop opposition no longer had anywhere near the 41 votes needed to sustain a filibuster. Mitchell had headed off a divisive fight among Democrats and the core group senators could could claim credit for winning a symbolic victory by creating a "Democratic energy policy." The Arctic National Wildlife Refuge would remain protected, the energy efficiency provisions in the bill, except for automobiles, would be enhanced, the hydropower provisions would be revised. After months of ferment, it was back to business as usual in the U.S. Senate.

In retrospect, we made quite a fight of it. With the help of a nationwide coalition of environmentalists, we had blocked the original Johnston-Wallop bill from coming to the Senate floor, we had an alternative legislative package ready to go; and we had powerful authoritative support in the *America's Energy Choices* study and other analyses of the potential of sustainable energy. In the end, however, the most well-laid plans in Washington, can succeed only if members of Congress act as the agents. But those agents tend not to think of themselves as leaders of movements or even as close collaborators with groups organizing outside of Washington. As usual, the senators, in this case the Democratic majority, were more concerned with maintaining control of the Senate and getting reelected. They decided to go for the symbolic victory.

A Somewhat Better Bill

On February 19, 1992, a month and a half after Congress reconvened, the Senate passed an amended version of the Johnston-Wallop bill by the overwhelming margin of 94–4. Paul was one of the four.

ANWR drilling was gone; so was the language that eliminated federal environmental protections for hydropower and effectively deregulated small hydropower projects. Energy efficiency was enhanced, most notably with efficiency standards for light bulbs, heating and air conditioning equipment, and electric motors. But the efficiency measure that promised by far the most energy savings, CAFE, was no longer even mentioned in the bill. Numerous barriers experienced by the energy industries, including regulations for environmental protection and citizen participation, were struck down by the bill. And large subsidies were provided for coal and nuclear electric power generation.

The environmentalists pointed to the improvements and declared a partial victory. Dan Becker, the global warming and energy program director for the Sierra Club, told me, "We're . . . quietly cheering. . . . We will declare victory at the end because we stopped a bad bill and turned it around substantially. We brought down the Johnston bill, the President's bill, and brought forth a better energy policy." When I mentioned the coal, natural gas, uranium enrichment, nuclear licensing, PUHCA reform, and other provisions, his response was, "those things would have happened [no matter what we did]. . . . We chose our fights very carefully; . . . And on the vast majority of the fights, we won. . . . We turned a bad bill into at least an arguably decent bill."[6]

Brooks Yeager, the NES Working Group co-chair, agreed: "The bill has undergone fairly radical improvements that we would have had a hard time getting [without the November 1 cloture vote]."

When I asked him what he hoped for at the beginning of the debate, he recalled:

> I can't say we had a precise plan going in, but we did have a blueprint in the sense of an idea of where significant progress had to be made. We thought it would be important to achieve major gains in efficiency in the transportation sector, the buildings sector, the industrial sector and so on. We have advocated, though not in a unified way as a [environmental] community, that energy prices be looked at in order to internalize environmental and social costs of the current methods of energy production. . . . For instance, . . . a carbon tax . . . at a level that encourages the economy to move toward energy efficiency and a diversity of fuels. . . .
>
> There should be a major overhaul of how we do energy planning. . . . Right now the federal role in energy planning is largely to accommodate the wishes and the desires of the various energy industries. . . . Government's role ought to be to look ahead and enact environmental guidelines about where you want the energy economy to be in ten or twenty years. DoE clearly doesn't see its role that way. That would be a bold change. . . .

The last thing should be a leveling or an elimination of subsidies for the energy industries that now distort the marketplace.

If you roll those things together—strong initiatives for government leadership in energy efficiency in certain areas like the transportation sector; a new look at energy pricing that might mean the application of a fuels tax or a carbon tax . . . , a way of planning for federal R&D and the application of federal power to influence the energy industries and a roll back or an elimination of the built-in tax and expenditure subsidies for the industries—[these reforms] would look pretty bold compared to what's going to come out of the Senate. . . . On the other hand, it's going to be a lot better than it would have been if we hadn't won that cloture vote.[7]

One thing on which participants on all sides of the debate would agree, however, is that the bill that passed the Senate did not alter significantly the direction of the national energy policy. Margaret Kriz, a reporter for the *National Journal,* concluded her insightful review of the February vote with a judgment that matched my own view: "Johnston triumphed in the war to set the terms of the national energy strategy debate. . . . Johnston has finally put a national energy policy on the table . . . and on his own terms."[8]

Brooks Yeager also emphasized another aspect of the environmentalists' dependence on the senators: "The fact that an alternative is introduced is one thing, but for it to be available for floor action in any meaningful sense, it has to have the imprint of a committee on it. Unless a committee produced an alternative, the reality was that the best we could do was to block Johnston and force him to drop Arctic and negotiate about other glaring problems." The environmentalists were able to get the Commerce Committee to pass Bryan's CAFE bill and Roth's ANWR bill, but they couldn't put together the pieces for overarching alternative legislation.[9]

The person who was left to make the key decision was Bennett Johnston. Some of his closest political allies dearly wanted ANWR. But, as his former aide Bob Szabo, now lobbying out of Van Ness, Feldman and Curtis, later explained, "If he had held out stubbornly for a position unacceptable to the Democratic majority, the legislation could have been controlled by the environmentalists. . . . That's why he had to drop ANWR."[10]

Yeager accepted the far from happy "compromise" bill with resignation, understanding it as the only realistic outcome given the circumstances. "Most of the political juice to defeat cloture was Arctic-related," he said. "With Arctic gone, we didn't have the sheer momentum at the grassroots to block the bill again."[11]

In thinking back, it seems to me the die really was cast when the grassroots organizing focused so heavily on one aspect of the Johnston-Wallop bill. From then on, the most we could hope for, if everything broke just right, was the removal of ANWR drilling from the bill.

To the extent that there was an organized grassroots movement to serve as a countervailing force to the Washington-based energy industry lobbying coalitions, it was the Alaska Coalition's opposition to drilling for oil in ANWR. There was certainly no organized movement united behind the vision of a sustainable energy future, demanding *specific* legislative action.

To put it another way, on the Arctic the Washington environmental generals had an army to back them up with pressure that was felt in the Senate. The outcome of the battle that ended on November 1 reflected that strength. When it came to a sustainable energy future, there was nothing but generals in Washington and a generally sympathetic populace. The arduous task of organizing the troops into an effective sustainable energy army and giving them clear marching orders had not yet happened. The majority Democrats succeeded in keeping this issue from becoming an impediment to their maintaining control of the Senate and they did bring about some significant improvements to the legislation. But they failed to take the next, courageous, possibly risky step, leading the country into the debate we must have soon over a sustainable energy transition for our nation.

A CLEAR
CONFLICT OF INTEREST

It Sure Smells Like
a Bribe or a Shakedown

11

Seized by a Growing Curiosity

As I worked with the Energy Committee on the Johnston-Wallop bill, I was seized by a growing curiosity I strongly suspected I should suppress. Obviously a great many energy and automobile industry lobbyists were pursuing the votes of twenty committee senators. The stakes were enormous and the pursuit was intense. While it was less visible from my vantage point, at the same time committee senators were very likely soliciting—and receiving—significant amounts of money in the form of campaign contributions from those lobbyists and the interest groups they represented.

If I chose to, I was well positioned to satisfy my curiosity. I knew who the lobbyists were. I also knew where to find campaign contribution information. In the course of my research on Rudy Boschwitz's campaign contributions in 1990, I had flown to Washington to consult records at the Federal Elections Commission (FEC). Now the FEC's public documents room was only a short subway hop from my Senate office.

While I did not discuss with Paul or other senior officials in the Wellstone office my desire to see what contributions the Energy Committee senators had been receiving from energy and automobile interest group lobbying coalitions, I had the feeling that such information might be forbidden fruit. I imagined it might be considered improper for Paul or anyone who worked for him to be snooping into campaign contributions to his colleagues on the committee.

Sitting in the hearing room day after day that spring, observing the senators preparing to make very consequential decisions and knowing how much those decisions meant to the corporate lobbyists in the audience, I mentally stepped back to assess the scene. It gave me a very uneasy feeling.

The usual way of talking about money in politics is a bit misleading: the lobbyists pursue the senator's vote and they *give* him or her money. In this way of speaking, the senator's role is portrayed as passive. His or her vote is pursued by the lobbyists and he or she *accepts* money from the lobbyists. In reality, the apt description of the relationship of senators and lobbyists is one of *mutual pursuit*. The lobbyists *are* pursuing the senators' votes, but at the same time the senators are pursuing the lobbyists and asking or demanding the money. The senators pursue because they are dependent on the large contributions the lobbyists can arrange. This mutual pursuit, with the exchange of large amounts of money, is a routine feature of our current campaign financing system.

Finally, my curiosity about the lobbyist-Energy Committee money connections got the better of me, and I decided to do some after-hours detective work. I had discovered in my study of the Boschwitz campaign contributions that the fund-raising had begun in earnest between January and June of the preelection year. That so-called early money, I learned, is the key to launching a successful campaign. It was during the same early money January–June period the year before the 1992 election that the Energy Committee was dealing with the Johnston-Wallop bill.

In the process of doing the Boschwitz study, I had come to know and respect a Washington-based reporter for the *Minneapolis Star-Tribune,* Tom Hamburger, who was also researching Boschwitz's fund-raising. In late April 1991, I told him of my curiosity about the Energy Committee contributions. His interest and encouragement nudged me into action.

Larry Makinson now director of the Center for Responsive Politics, provided me with detailed data on the contributions Senators Johnston and Wallop had received from energy interest group PACs over the previous six years. At a glance, the numbers were mind-boggling. The two senators had been showered with money by virtually every interest group that was lobbying for provisions of their bill. Johnston had solicited nearly a half million dollars from their PACs and Wallop had solicited over a quarter million dollars. As I observed the disappointing results of the markup over the next few weeks, I kept thinking about how inappropriate it would be if money were changing hands while these important decisions were being made. When I explained to Larry the giveaway features of the bill and the surprisingly strong support Johnston and Wallop had on the committee for even its most egregious provisions, he agreed to help me track down the campaign contributions over the previous six years to all twenty the members of the committee from interest groups attempting to influence provisions of the Johnston-Wallop legislation. He was able to coax his computer to cough up the following table of energy and automobile-related PAC contributions to all twenty members of the committee.

Table 1. PAC contributions to the Senate Energy Committee

	ANWR	CAFE	PUHCA Reform
Johnston	$132,500	$116,000	$229,100
Wallop	$104,547	$113,362	$70,830
Other committee members	$571,677	$295,350	$594,585
Totals	$808,724	$524,712*	$894,515

*Includes independent expenditures by AUTOPAC (the political action committee of Automobile Dealers and Drivers for Free Trade, the U.S. lobbying arm of the Japanese auto dealers) of $93,750 for Johnston during his 1990 reelection campaign and $88,862 for Wallop during his 1988 reelection campaign.

Huge amounts of money had been showered on the committee members over the previous six years by those who were now lobbying hard in support of the provisions of the Johnston-Wallop bill. Over 150 PACs affiliated with companies lobbying his committee had given Chairman Johnston between $1,000 and $10,000, including twenty-six oil and gas producers, twenty-three natural gas pipeline companies, and sixty electric utilities. In the memorable words of Senator Sam Ervin when he chaired the Watergate investigation, "These are not eleemosynary [charitable] organizations." They must think they are getting something pretty substantial for that kind of money.

It would have been hard to find a better place to study money in Congress than the Senate Energy Committee at that particular time. Senators serve for terms of six years, but, like Rudy Boschwitz in 1989–90, they concentrate during the first six months of the year before their reelection vote on raising the millions of dollars in "early money" they need to stay in office. Ten of the twenty members of the Energy Committee, moreover, were nearing the end of their terms. And nine of the ten, nearly half the committee, were planning to run for reelection in 1992. As they were deciding the high stakes energy policy issues in the Johnston-Wallop bill during January–June 1991 those nine senators were at the same time heavily engaged in soliciting large war chests of early money.

Six of the nine were Democrats: Dale Bumpers of Arkansas, Kent Conrad of North Dakota, Wendell Ford of Kentucky, Wyche Fowler of Georgia, Dick Shelby of Alabama, and Tim Wirth of Colorado. Three were Republicans: Frank Murkowski of Alaska, Don Nickles of Oklahoma, and John

Seymour of California. I was particularly interested in their campaign contributions during the first half of 1991—the period when the Johnston-Wallop bill was before the committee. However, those data would not be available until the senators submitted their January to June contribution reports on July 15. In the meantime, I spent many hours in the FEC public documents room printing out the 1985–90 contributions to all the Energy Committee senators from PACs associated with the principal groups lobbying on Johnston-Wallop. I was looking for contribution patterns, trying to develop some ideas about what was going on.

"Project X"

I wanted to expose the lobbyist-senator money connections for two reasons. First, the American people should understand the nature and extent of the intervention of money in our lawmaking process; public outrage at what appear to be bribes might spur public demand for appropriate campaign finance reform. Second, the lobbying coalitions and their money were surely influencing the outcome of the energy strategy debate; public exposure of Energy Committee senators' soliciting campaign contributions from interest groups at the same time those interest groups were seeking their votes would give the American people a fuller understanding of how energy policies are decided in Washington.

How could I get this information analyzed and out to the American people? Obviously, Paul would have no interest in releasing it. And as long as I was an employee of his office I couldn't release it myself. The natural choice would be the environmentalists, with grassroots organizations that reach into every state. I began dropping discreet hints that I would be willing to help if an environmental group would do a careful study and publicize the results, but I wondered whether any Washington-based environmental group would be willing to take on incumbents in that way. During Paul's 1990 campaign, a representative of the the League of Conservation Voters had come to Minnesota and sharply criticized the environmental record of Rudy Boschwitz. And Ginny Ying Ling, the director of the Sierra Club's Minnesota chapter, had also endorsed Paul enthusiastically. But she had done so despite the reluctance of the Sierra Club's Washington leadership, because they assumed they would have to work with Boschwitz after his reelection. I imagined that same tension would temper the enthusiasm of many Washington-based groups for exposing the campaign contributions of senators they knew they would be lobbying sometime soon. In that way, the inclinations and the interests of the grassroots memberships of such organizations can be in conflict with the inclinations and interests of their Washington lobbyists.

Eventually, however, I got a positive response from Bill Magavern and Dave Hamilton of U.S. PIRG, who had been leading the environmentalists' lobbying efforts for Bryan's CAFE bill and against one-step nuclear licensing. We agreed to work together on a comprehensive study of campaign contributions from energy industry lobbying coalitions to Energy Committee senators. We dubbed this effort "Project X," where X was shorthand for ECS, "Energy Committee Study," and drafted a research plan. To get some immediate feedback, we sent the plan to a friend who is one of Washington's authorities on money in politics. When I called later to get a reaction, I was told the fax had not been received. I must have misdialed the fax number. With all its references to the Senate Energy Committee, I had visions of copies already on Ben Cooper's and Bennett Johnston's desks, with Paul receiving an angry call at any moment. Thank goodness, that did not happen.

In the process of compiling lists and organizing information about the lobbying coalitions active on the major controversial provisions of S.1220, I realized there was another important issue in addition to the money the Energy Committee senators were soliciting. Chairman Johnston himself had an impressive web of connections to leaders of the lobbying coalitions that were giving large amounts of money to senators on his committee.

I had been alerted to these connections by a 1988 article in the *Congressional Quarterly*.[1] At that time, Johnston had been in a tight race with George Mitchell for Senate Majority Leader. He had established "Pelican PAC," named after the Louisiana state bird, as his own so-called leadership PAC, a pot of money from private sources that he could give to the campaigns of other senators. The article explained the close links between Johnston and his "family" of lobbyist friends, several of whom had worked with him previously as Senate staffers. Studying Johnston's connections to the lobbying coalitions became another focus of Project X.

The Washington-Minnesota Connection

Project X eventually turned into two separate studies carried out by means of a long-distance collaboration: one led by Bill Magavern and Dave Hamilton at the U.S. PIRG office on Capitol Hill, and the other performed by senior political science major Matt Fisher and me at Carleton College after I returned to Minnesota in September. Together we developed comprehensive lists of the PACs associated with the most prominent corporate coalitions active in lobbying for the Johnston-Wallop bill and the relatively few and less affluent PACs associated with the environmental groups in the anti-Johnston-Wallop coalition. With the support of modest grants from Phil Stern's family foundation and environmental activist/donor Jay Harris, Magavern and Hamilton used the computerized data at the Campaign Research Center to study the contributions to Energy Committee senators during the six-year period from January 1985 to December 1990. Matt and I assumed responsibility for the period that interested me the most, from January to June 1991, when I had watched those senators decide the terms of the Johnston-Wallop bill. One difficulty was that the 1991 PAC contributions were not yet computerized; they were stored in filing cabinets at the FEC public documents room. Before we left Washington, my wife, Nancy, copied those lists and on our return to Minnesota, Matt entered them in a computer and analyzed them.

From the beginning, there was a sense of urgency to get the studies done. Johnston was pushing hard to get his bill to the floor. I recall our alarm when at the weekly meeting of Democratic senators on September 17, Majority Leader Mitchell announced that the Johnston-Wallop bill was on the "short list" and would come to the Senate floor soon.

By early October, we began consulting with Magavern and Hamilton about the contents of their report. On October 23, U.S. PIRG released *Abuse of Power: Energy Industry Money & the Johnston-Wallop Energy Package,* at a National Press Club press conference that drew more than thirty reporters.[2] The Associated Press story focused on the enormous amount of money (nearly $3.1 million) the twenty Energy Committee senators had received since 1985 from the energy and automobile interests and highlighted the especially large sums showered on Johnston and Wallop. Headlined "Energy Interests Targeted Senate Committee," it reported:

> Energy and automobile interests have given more than $3 million since 1985 to members of a Senate committee that drafted a pro-industry energy bill, environmentalists said Wednesday. . . . The Energy Committee chairman Democrat J. Bennett Johnston of Louisiana received $449,369 from political action committees affiliated with energy and auto interests, according to a study by the Public Interest Research Group. The 20-member panel's ranking Republican, Malcolm Wallop of Wyoming, got $307,579. . . . Johnston used his personal PAC to give $5,000 each to four key members of his committee as he tried to move the bill to the Senate floor last spring, PIRG said. "If we want cleaner energy we must clean up the political system," said Bill Magavern.[3]

Separate press releases discussing the contributions to each Energy Committee senator were conveyed to the media in their states. The next morning's edition of the *New Orleans Times-Picayune* trumpeted, "Environmental Lobbyists Declare War on Johnston" and went on to say,

A national environmental advocacy group says it will run television ads attacking Louisiana Sen. J. Bennett Johnston for energy legislation it says favors oil and nuclear energy companies that have poured more than $350,000 into Johnston's campaign coffers. . . . At a press conference Wednesday, PIRG attorney Bill Magavern said he wants Louisiana citizens to know how much money Johnston has taken from special interest groups, which he contends are the primary beneficiaries of the senator's energy bill. Debate on the bill is expected to begin next week. "The oil and nuclear industries have filled Johnston's campaign coffers and he has carried their water in the Senate," Magavern said.

Johnston had to respond. He told the reporter, "PIRG has unveiled its own energy policy today. That policy is as follows: oppose any plan that has a chance of lessening America's dependence on foreign oil by promoting domestic energy resources and mount a personal attack on the sponsors of any such effort." He went on to say that PIRG's advertisement "would play better in Baghdad than in Baton Rouge. Our adversaries in the Middle East may take great delight in our growing dependence on foreign oil and our inability to do anything about it. But the people in Louisiana, and across the country for that matter, are fed up with that kind of policy."[4]

The North Dakota papers carried an AP story that focused particular attention on Sen. Kent Conrad: "Conrad, who is up for reelection next year, received $111,000 in campaign contributions from those interests from 1985 through June 1991. . . . Johnston also used his personal PAC to give $5,000 each to Conrad and three other key members of his committee as he was trying to push the bill to the Senate floor. Conrad, who voted against the environmentalists on all but the Alaskan development, has received $48,400 from the nuclear industry and $43,550 from interests opposed to the global warming goals, according to the study. 'Conrad's votes . . . were a big disappointment to environmentalists,' Magavern said."

Conrad's press secretary immediately replied, "He has stood up to the oil industry, he has stood up to the automakers, and he has stood up to the environmentalists. What he wants is a balanced, responsible, reasonable strategy for the nation."[5]

Our effort was quite successful. *Roll Call,* the Capitol Hill newspaper delivered to all congressional offices gave the story prominent coverage the next morning:

> Environmental groups launched a broadbased attack on Senate Energy and Natural Resources Committee Chairman J. Bennett Johnston (D-La) and pro-energy industry forces yesterday, denouncing committee actions on an energy development bill, detailing campaign contributions to committee members by energy interests, and unveiling a television ad that blasts Johnston. In a press conference at the National Press Club, US Public Interest Research Group lawyer Bill Magavern alleged that the bill is a special interest vehicle with little public backing that has been propelled largely by massive energy industry campaign contributions and wheeling and dealing by Johnston. . . . The PIRG ad states that over the last six years Johnston "accepted more than $350,000 in political action money from the auto, oil, nuclear and chemical companies" and details the Senator's alleged anti-environmental activities. . . . At the PIRG press conference, Magavern released a study showing that Energy Committee members who supported industry positions on key committee votes regarding the proposed National Energy Security Act were the recipients of tens of thousands of dollars in energy industry campaign contributions.[6]

Karl Gawell later noted that of all the criticism of the Johnston-Wallop bill, this report bothered its supporters the most, especially because of the possibility that similar media accounts and paid advertisements would appear in their home state papers. We had found a vulnerable spot in otherwise inpenetrable armor.

However, the press reports failed to emphasize the aspect of the campaign contributions that troubled me the most—the spectacle of senators taking money from lobbying coalitions at the same time they were making decisions of acute concern to those interest groups. They also failed to focus on the Johnston connections to the money transactions. To call attention to those issues Matt Fisher and I prepared a separate report on the contributions to the Energy Committee members between January and June 1991. *A Study of Special Interest PAC Contributions to Energy Committee Senators During the Johnston-Wallop Bill Debate, January-June, 1991* was completed in November.[7] "The influence of campaign money from energy and auto industry lobbyists hangs so heavily over this debate that it is almost palpable," we observed. "At the same time that the lobbyists were attempting to influence the outcome of the legislation, a process in which the lobbyists by and large play the active role of approaching the senators, the senators, especially those facing reelection, were seeking large campaign contributions, a process in which, by and large, the senators play the active role of approaching the lobbyists."

The report was in two parts, First we documented the January–June 1991 PAC contributions from energy industry lobbying coalitions with direct, identifiable connections to Chairman Johnston (figure 2).

Second, we documented contributions during that same period to each Energy Committee senator from lobbying coalitions on specific controversial issues in the bill, such as ANWR and CAFE. The results were detailed in a series of tables.

Matt and I had hoped to disseminate this story widely and especially to attract the attention of investigative reporters. Copies of the report were provided to selected reporters interested in money in politics. Tom Baden of the Newhouse newspapers eventually wrote a revealing story on the links between Johnston and the lobbyists. But it was not the timely bombshell that I had hoped would run in a major newspaper just prior to the November cloture vote. Two reporters at the Center for Investigative Reporting planning a public television documentary on the energy strategy debate, were initially very interested in highlighting the chairman's connections to the lobbyists who were giving money to members of his committee. But midway through the project, one left to take another job. When *The Politics of*

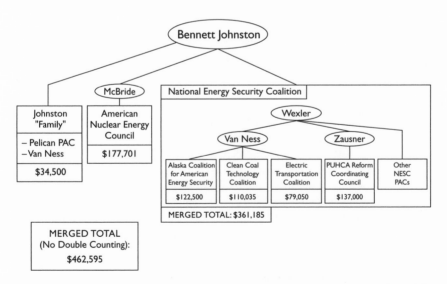

Figure 1. Campaign contributions to Energy Committee senators from energy industry lobbying coalitions with connections to Chairman Johnston

Power aired on the public television series Frontline in October 1992, the money issue had been left on the cutting room floor.

In general, the reluctance of the press to address this issue may lie in the difficulty in establishing causal connections between campaign contributions and a lawmaker's actions. Near the end of its article on the release of the U.S. PIRG study, *Roll Call* provocatively raised an important question:

> The study was to show that Members are beholden to the industry thanks to campaign contributions, but the report was hampered by the classic chicken-or-egg question: Which came first, the contributions, or the support for the industry? For example, Johnston and the committee's ranking Republican, Sen. Malcolm Wallop (R-Wyo), both have a huge regional economic interest in promoting domestic energy production and appear to be supporting the wishes of their constituents. It's almost certain that they would be pro-industry, even if they received not a dime in contributions; to take the opposite position would be political folly in a state like Louisiana. . . . The study makes little effort to show any committee members changed votes or positions based on contributions they received.[8]

Since the PIRG report had been released, I had been intrigued by the chicken and egg problem. The *Roll Call* reporter was right; it *is* impossible to demonstrate from such data alone whether votes follow money or money follows votes. But there is clearly more that can be said about these chickens and eggs, as we argued in the conclusion of our report:

> That begs the key question of where the burden of proof should lie. With a system so open to corruption or appearance of corruption, the burden of proof should not be on the public to demonstrate that votes have been bought with campaign money. For there to be public confidence, senators who actively pursue large amounts of money from special interests while deciding on issues with enormous stakes for those interests, as is clearly true of the Energy Committee senators who solicited contributions from S.1220 interest groups during the first half of 1991, the burden of proof must be on the senators to demonstrate they were not bought. But of course that is an impossible burden. One cannot prove a negative. The results of this study therefore constitute a powerful argument that our system of campaign financing must be fundamentally changed if public confidence in the integrity of our representative democracy is to be restored.[9]

An Unlevel Financial Playing Field

I continued to ponder what these money exchanges mean for our politicians and our politics. It is clear that staying in office is the preeminent goal of most congressional incumbents. These days that means money—millions of dollars every six years for a senator and hundreds of thousands of dollars every two years for a congressperson. In their study of how 1990 congressional candidates spent their campaign contributions, Sarah Fritz and Dwight Morris, reporters for the *Los Angeles Times,* found that on average, Senate incumbents up for reelection in 1990 had spent $4.1 million in the six years since their last election and House incumbents had spent $390,000 in the two years since their last election. On average, Senate challengers spent $1.7 million and House challengers spent $133,000.[10]

In bygone days, candidates depended much more on their political parties for financial support. These days, the candidates raise most of their money themselves. And the situation of incumbents is quite different from the one in which Paul found himself as a challenger. He had a very difficult task raising money and would never have won had it not been for an outpouring of volunteers. Most challengers find to their dismay that their most important function is gathering the money to keep their campaigns going. In April 1992, when Tim Wirth unexpectedly dropped out of his race for reelection, he spoke more freely than usual about his frustrations as a senator, especially the necessity of raising large amount of reelection money. He recalled in an interview with *Time* magazine that when he first ran for the Senate in 1986, "80% of my time was spent raising money—not talking to constituents, not thinking. . . ."[11] I am convinced that most incumbent legislators remember their first congressional campaign with distress and have emerged from it with a strong resolve never to repeat that sort of experience.

When they get to Washington, most soon discover there is a way they *can* avoid the worst aspects of arduous, degrading fund-raising. Fritz and Morris helped to make the scene come alive for me: "Virtually every weeknight in Washington, D.C., the National Democratic Club, the Ronald Reagan Center, the Capitol Hill Club, and various popular restaurants near the Capitol were booked with an endless schedule of fund-raisers for members of Congress. Indeed, even though incumbents often complained these parties were so numerous and so predictable that members of Congress had come to view them as a necessary chore of daily life. . . . 'I don't find it that onerous,' confided Sen. John C. Danforth, R-Mo. 'You just go down to the Ronald Reagan Center, stand around for two hours, shake hands, and collect $50,000 to $100,000.'"[12]

In an article for the *New York Times Magazine* he called "Diary of a Dropout," Tim Wirth was unusually self-revelatory about his decision to quit even though he was favored to win, explaining that, "I have become frustrated with the posturing and paralysis of Congress . . . [and] I even fear that the political process has made me a person I don't like."[13] Wirth had one revealing "diary" entry about energy lobby campaign contributions that led me to try to solve a puzzle I called "The Mystery of the Kissing Pig": "Monday, March 30, was a banner day for the Wirth fund-raising machine. In the morning, my wife, Wren, and I flew from Colorado to Houston, where we secured more than $70,000 in campaign contributions from executives of the natural-gas industry—apparently close to a single-event record for a non-Texan politician." The fundraiser was hosted by the heads of two of the nation's largest natural gas pipeline companies, Tenneco Corporation's Michael Walsh and Coastal Corporation's Oscar Wyatt. According to Wirth,

> I had helped pass a major energy bill that promoted natural gas. . . . The big reception in Houston was a way for the energy industry to say thanks by helping me raise part of the $4 million war chest I thought I'd need for the fall campaign. . . . It was probably just as well that no reporters were in the room in Houston, where earlier in the day I gave a talk to a group of Coastal employees. Journalists would certainly have loved the way Oscar Wyatt had got the group to start asking me questions. Recalling the time his father had taken him to a carnival where one of the sideshows was a kissing pig, Oscar Wyatt said, "C'mon, you only get one chance to kiss the pig, so you better get with it."[14]

Soon after reading this story, I checked Wirth's Federal Elections Commission PAC contribution report to see who had given him the near-record $70,000 at the Houston mansion that day. There were indeed several PAC contributions on March 31, including $5,000 each from the Houston-based Coastal Employee and Tenneco Employee PACs. In all, nine natural gas-related PAC's had reported $19,000 in contributions to Wirth on that date. But Wirth had said in his *New York Times Magazine* piece that he had solicited more than $70,000. The obvious question was: Who else kissed the pig that day?

Wirth left a clue in the article that helped me to probe the mystery. He said he secured the contributions from "executives of the natural-gas industry." According to FEC records, Wirth had solicited $20,150 from twenty-five individuals in Houston. Oscar Wyatt had given him $2,000; Mike Walsh and his wife Joan had added $1,000 each. In all, Wirth had taken in sixteen $1,000 checks from individuals, in addition to his PAC contributions. Ten of the contributors identified themselves with Tenneco. Combined, the $19,000 in PAC contributions and the $20,150 in individual contributions accounted for $39,150 of the more than $70,000 Wirth reported he had received from the natural gas industry that day.

Where did the rest come from? I'm not certain. One possibility is that Tenneco and Coastal hit up less senior employees for contributions. It is not unusual for supervisors at large companies to bring lower level managers together and suggest they write checks to the campaigns of selected senators and representatives. Under the law, a contribution of less than $200 need not be reported to the FEC. Bundles of such contributions can add up to tens of thousands of dollars. One clear lesson of this story is that any attempt to assess the money links between lobbying coalitions and lawmakers that is limited to PAC contributions is likely to miss a substantial part of the total package delivered.

In his well-known book, *Inside Campaign Finance,* Frank Sorauf explains that since the current campaign finance regime was established in the early 1970s, the fund-raising power of incumbents has increased, especially in the House, where incumbent reelection rates had been running well over 90 percent for more than a decade. "As the electoral prospects of challengers slowly diminished," he says, "PAC money deserted them for the certain-to-win incumbents. Incumbents got 60 percent of PAC money going to House candidates in 1980 and an intimidating 81 percent by 1990. . . . As they became more secure in office, House incumbents became more aggressive in their fundraising. PAC managers object more and more vocally to their importunings; they use such words as 'extortion' and 'arm-twisting'. . . . Incumbents . . . became oligopolists in the market, able to extract higher prices than they had in a more competitive market. . . ."[15]

Because of their less certain reelection prospects, many incumbent senators have less leverage with PACs. In a 1992 interview with *Time* magazine, Tim Wirth, had some particularly illuminating things to say: "Congress is awash in money. Interests have emerged that have enormous amounts of cash and that stand between the Congress and its constituency. In my 18 years in the Congress I have seen the denominator of debate get lower and lower, and I think much of that is explained by fear—fear that you will be unable to raise money from a certain group; or worse, that the interest group will give the money to the other guy; or worse still, that the money will go to a third party as a so-called independent expenditure."[16]

I was surprised to see Wirth report that independent expenditures were what he feared the most. He didn't elaborate. I assume that what worried him was that there is no limit on the amounts of money that can be spent via that constitutionally-protected path.

Another member of the Energy Committee, Dale Bumpers of Arkansas, has also noted the fear that senators face. He described how uncomfortable he and many other Democratic senators felt in 1989 when Ted Kennedy insisted on a Senate vote to increase the minimum wage; they knew a vote in favor would hurt them with corporate campaign contributors and even if it passed, President Bush would veto it. According to Bumpers, "A senator tells himself: 'You got an antibusiness reputation and you better work on it.' When it's a money vote—minimum wages, mandatory health insurance, the capital gains tax—and you're perceived as antibusiness, you have to think about it. Even if you know you're not going to get their money, you think about keeping them quiet. You won't get their money, but you can at least tranquilize them."[17] Vin Weber, a former congressman from Minnesota and a close confidant of Newt Gingrich has shed additional light on the fears members of Congress are prone to: "The impact of special interest groups is great[est] when they're organizing voters in your district. Take for example the American Association of Retired Persons or the National Federation of Independent Businesses. Their ability to organize makes them more of a power than the amount of a check they might write."[18]

I would not so casually dismiss the influence PAC and bundled individual checks buy for lobbying coalitions, but relatively speaking, I'd bet Weber is right. The ability to organize people back home is the key to real influence. Members of Congress whose highest purpose is reelection are nervous about even hints of organized efforts to unseat them. Especially frightening is the prospect that groups may organize beyond their membership, with publicity campaigns to mobilize people in their districts. The National Rifle Association's ability to turn incumbents out of office is a well-known example of such power.

What Weber was saying is that congressmen and senators have a nightmare even worse than the three that Wirth mentioned: the possibility that the group will organize constituents in your district against you.

Public interest groups should take this to heart. Their most potent source of power is the threat of organizing back in the districts on issues constituents care deeply about. Paid ads in local newspapers or a barrage of letters-to-the-editor back home can be an effective warning shot, suggesting to the representative that his or her worst fear may be coming true.

Before I went to Washington, I knew the current system of financing election campaigns was in serious need of fixing. Some of the problems I understood well from Paul's campaign. Others I came to understand with greater clarity from what I saw in the Senate. I was committed to trying to develop a campaign finance reform proposal that would speak to the major problems of the system that was in place. Here is my personal list of the most important of those problems:

- First and foremost is the accountability of our elected representatives to a "cash constituency" and the resulting appearance of corruption that undermines public confidence in our representative democracy. Today, most Americans no longer have confidence that their government represents them because they believe that our country's politics is corrupt, that most lawmakers are beholden to special interests.

I find an analogy helpful in pinpointing the challenge framers of campaign reform legislation face. It captures the essence of what was going on as the Energy Committee dealt with the Johnston-Wallop bill. Imagine a trial in which the plaintiffs stood to gain or lose hundred of millions of dollars, depending on the judge's decision. Suppose that one evening while the trial was under way, the judge invited the plaintiffs to his home and solicited thousands of dollars from each of them. If this were known, who could blame people from concluding it was bribery by the plaintiffs or a shakedown by the judge?

Similar behavior occurs every day on Capitol Hill. Members of Congress routinely solicit large campaign contributions from interest groups at the same time they are deciding issues with enormously high stakes for those groups. The analogue of the judge's home solicitation is the member's Washington or fly-in fundraiser, which provides an opportunity for lobbying coalition "rainmakers" to organize tens of thousands of dollars in contributions from PACs, corporate executives, and other employees. This practice is well known to the American people. Who can blame them for thinking it corrupt?

- Second, wealthy contributors have become the gatekeepers of our politics. Unless a candidate is independently wealthy or attractive to rich people and prosperous interest groups, he or she is effectively barred from running for high public office in America today.

- Third, the financial playing field is very often tilted in favor of incumbents. Under the present system, incumbents routinely outspend their challengers many times over. In the vast majority of cases, the Washington lobbying coalitions overwhelmingly support those already in office. Challengers frequently have great difficulty getting their messages out.

- Fourth, the problem most frequently cited by incumbents, is the time and effort it takes to raise the money needed to run. Incumbents tend to be preoccupied with fund-raising throughout the last two years before their re-elections.

- Fifth, money is used in electoral politics to manipulate voters through very expensive, very sophisticated public relations and marketing campaigns. This is one problem incumbents are particularly loath to talk about, because according to the current election financing system, they are generally the candidates best able to gather the money and mount such campaigns.

I have found this list of problems helpful in differentiating real from phony solutions in the years I have spent working on campaign finance reform.

The Essential First Step

12

Kindred Spirits

As the victor in a populist campaign in which his opponent's special interest money connections had become a central issue, Paul Wellstone was well positioned to tackle the problem of money in politics. A precondition of successful efforts to advance significant change on virtually every major legislative front is to break the big money links between lobbying coalitions and lawmakers. Campaign finance reform was already high on the agenda of the 102nd Congress. The immediate question was whether a Wellstone initiative could be ready in time for the 1991 debate.

In the annals of interest group politics, campaign finance reform is an especially thorny issue. When it comes to changing the rules that govern funding of congressional campaigns, those who decide, the incumbent members of Congress, happen also to be the most intensely concerned interest group. Their political futures and the prospects of their political parties may well depend on the legislative choices they make on this issue.

Shortly after the election I sought to organize a Wellstone working group on campaign finance reform and almost immediately stumbled on a promising project already underway. It involved a remarkable combination of highly respected, Washington-based authorities on campaign finance and outstanding grassroots organizers including Larry Makinson, an innovative pioneer in campaign finance research at the Center for Responsive Politics, Ellen Miller, the director of the Center, Randy Kehler, Ben Senturia, Marty Jezer, Phil Stern, and other members of the grassroots campaign finance reform organization, the Working Group on Electoral Democracy.

Randy Kehler was national director of the Nuclear Weapons Freeze Campaign in the early 1980s and I was director of the Minnesota campaign. I don't know of a more highly principled, politically sophisticated practitioner of grassroots politics than Randy. By 1987, he had become convinced that if America's democratic promise of government of the people, by the people, and for the people was to be realized, the system of financing elections by having candidates for public office solicit money from private sources would have to be fundamentally changed. Marty Jezer is a longtime peace and justice activist, a noted author of social history and, I was soon to find, a brilliant writer and political philosopher. He lived on a farm in Vermont, a former commune near Brattleboro, just across the border from where Randy worked at the Traprock Peace Center in western Massachusetts. Ben Senturia, a dynamic, astute community organizer in St. Louis, had been a mainstay of the Freeze movement headquartered there before it moved to Washington and lost its steam.

Randy, Marty, and Ben had been working together since 1987 on developing a campaign for fundamental political reform which, they were convinced would galvanize the public and ignite a national movement just as the Civil Rights movement had. Ellen Miller's colleague Phil Stern, the author of notable books on politics including *Still The Best Congress Money Can Buy* (1992) became the elder statesman and driving force of the Wellstone campaign finance reform working group, with his totally straightforward, no-nonsense style.

The group envisioned the most ambitious kind of congressional campaign finance reform, a system in which all candidates with sufficient demonstrated public support would be eligible for full public campaign funding rather than having to solicit funds from private sources. Ideally this kind of reform would cut the money links between special interests and incumbent lawmakers, making candidacy for high public office accessible to a broader spectrum of American society. It would also offer challengers sufficient resources to make possible a far greater number of truly competitive elections.

Right before Paul took office, Pat Forceia, who had become his chief campaign adviser as the election neared and who became an important adviser immediately after the election, planned a highly visible trip for Paul and an entourage of reporters from Minnesota to Washington on the old Wellstone campaign bus. He wanted Paul to give a ringing speech from the back of the bus just prior to his departure from St. Paul and we agreed the topic would be campaign finance reform.

At my request, Randy asked Marty Jezer to prepare a statement; the result was an eloquent seventeen-page populist manifesto remarkably expressive of Paul's convictions and the spirit of the campaign that had won him the election.

> Conventional wisdom says that as an incumbent I will receive as much money as I need for reelection from fat cats and special interest PACs. All I have to do is quietly play ball with them. But if I am to be the senator that you elected me to be—and the senator that I intend to be—the fat cats and heavy hitting campaign contributors will not be beating down my door. . . . They will be lining up to help my opponent. . . . [Vaclav Havel] earlier this year told Congress that democracy could never be perfect, it will always be no more than an ideal. One may approach it as one would the horizon. . . . The earth turns and the winds of change are blowing. Campaign finance reform is the one reform that encourages other reforms. If we want nuclear disarmament and a balanced budget, laws to protect labor unions and raise wages, job protection and a protected environment, universal health care and progressive taxation, then we are going to have to drive the money changers from the capital, and create a pro-Democracy movement that inspires democratic renewal and a grassroots revival. Total public financing, bold and comprehensive electoral reform is the key to a new era of democratic, popular politics. Let us sail boldly out to meet the horizon.

As January approached, we refined the speech and, at Randy's suggestion, added another element—a personal pledge that Paul would make to the people of Minnesota, promising exemplary behavior in his own dealings with campaign contributions, while fighting for campaign finance reform. However, it soon became apparent that there were major differences between what my friends on the working group thought should be in the pledge and what Pat Forceia had in mind.

For example, Ellen and Randy suggested one alternative: after Paul had paid off his campaign debt, he would declare his own personal moratorium on fund-raising until 1995, two years before his reelection. And, they proposed that in paying off the debt, Paul commit himself to accepting no PAC contributions and limiting individual contributions to no more than $100, possibly only from Minnesota residents.

Forceia, however, opposed any such moratorium. As he put it, that would "neuter" Paul, depriving him of significant opportunities that would flow from continuing campaign activities that the Wellstone Senate office either could not afford or legally undertake, but a Wellstone reelection campaign committee could. He envisioned continuing to raise about $150,000 a year for travel expenses for Paul and for hiring more staff members than the Senate payroll could provide for. He also imagined providing financial support for other progressive Minnesota candidates now that Paul was the highest ranking elected official of the Democratic-Farmer-Labor (DFL) Party in Minnesota. Paul's wife Sheila weighed in forcefully with personal objections to ruling out PACs and limiting individual contributions to $100 while the debt was being paid off. They were a family of modest means, she pointed out, and with a total campaign debt of $160,000 hanging over their heads, she would feel uncomfortable with limits to paying it off. In the end, her reservation prevailed, and Paul's back-of-the-bus pledge committed him to refusing PAC contributions and individual contributions over $100 after the campaign debt was paid off and up until two years before he came up for reelection in 1996. He also promised to fight in the Senate for campaign finance reform.

By giving up the opportunity to collect so-called campaign contributions many years before a campaign we were also, I realized, turning away funds that could help elect other progressive DFL candidates and could also be used as travel money for Paul to mobilize grassroots citizen support for universal health care coverage, campaign finance reform, and a sustainable energy transition initiative. That kind of social movement leadership was at the heart of my vision of Paul's becoming a truly different kind of senator. I came to understand, however, that incumbent legislators routinely succumb to the allure of campaign contributions. By the simple act of establishing a "reelection committee" and registering it with the Federal Elections Commission, an incumbent can gain access to large amounts of money, millions of dollars for a senator, for purposes he or she has wide latitude to define.

From their detailed studies of how congressional candidates spend their campaign contributions, *Los Angeles Times* reporters Sara Fritz and Dwight Morris discovered that incumbents use the money for a broad range of political purposes, including a striking phenomenon: most incumbents use campaign funds to establish what Fritz and Morris termed "gold-plated, permanent political machines." Congressional incumbents, they suggested, were a kind of political entrepreneur, with special interest money their "venture capital":

> Well-funded members of Congress now approach the task of staying in office as if they were starting up a real estate or insurance business. They write

business plans, install sophisticated computers, carry large payrolls, and worry about investments. . . . In fact, 56 percent of the money spent in the 1990 elections had little or nothing to do with what has long been considered the main task of a member of Congress seeking reelection: appealing directly to voters.

Politicians sometimes claim that they raise large sums of money just to scare off potential challengers. . . . But that notion has created the false impression that unopposed candidates simply hoard their funds, never actually spending them. To the contrary, very few incumbent members of Congress—not even those who have gone unopposed for many years—decline the opportunity to spend most of the money available to them. Potential challengers are often less discouraged by the size of an incumbent's campaign war chest than by the political empire an incumbent has built with the money.[1]

Many politician-entrepreneurs become so addicted to and dependent on the continued flow of campaign money for financing their projects and maintaining their permanent reelection machines that raising it becomes a central part of their political lives. For even the most idealistic of public servants, removing such temptation is probably the wisest course of action.

Campaign Finance Rules

The current rules of campaign finance date back to the last reform effort, the 1974 post-Watergate amendments to the 1971 Federal Elections Campaign Act (FECA), as substantially modified by a 1976 Supreme Court decision. The Federal Elections Commission [FEC] was set up to oversee congressional and presidential campaign financing, and rules were established for Political Action Committees (PACs), by means of which employees of corporations and members of labor unions and other organizations can contribute to political candidates. Corporations and unions had long been banned from contributing directly.

The 1974 legislation also established limits on how much individuals ($1,000) and PACs ($5,000) can contribute to the primary election campaign and separately to the general election campaign of a candidate for federal office.[2] The FECA amendments placed limits as well on the *spending* of money to influence the outcome of federal elections. Specifically, the act placed separate ceilings on: (1) spending by a candidate's campaign organization; (2) personal spending on a campaign by the candidate and his or her family; (3) "Independent Expenditures," meaning spending for or against a candidate by individuals, PACs, corporations, labor unions, and so on that takes place without any cooperation or coordination whatsoever with the candidate or the campaign; and (4) spending by political parties in support of their candidates.

However, in a landmark decision, *Buckley* v. *Valeo* in 1976, the U.S. Supreme Court ruled that the first three of those spending limits were unconstitutional. It declared that any limits on political campaign spending, candidates' contributions to their own campaigns, or independent expenditures are violations of the First Amendment right to free speech. That is, in political campaigns limiting spending money limits speech. That controversial ruling significantly changed the campaign financing rules the Congress had passed and has profoundly constrained attempts at campaign finance reform ever since.

The one spending limit in the 1974 FECA amendments that the Court allowed to stand pertained to political parties. Political party committees, including those of national and state political parties, are limited in their spending "on behalf of" candidates to specific amounts as adjusted year-by-year for inflation. In 1990 that limit was $26,500 for the House and for the Senate varying amounts in different states, up to California's $1,166,493. State parties, on the other hand, can spend without limit on "party-building activities," such as voter registration, get-out-the-vote efforts, and the like.

In the years since these rules were established, the candidates and contributors who operate under this system have found loopholes to circumvent the intent of the reforms. Take the so-called Independent Expenditures, for instance, which allow unlimited spending as long as there is no cooperation or coordination between candidates and those who independently spend money in their support. In the last week of Paul Wellstone's 1990 Senate campaign, "Automobile Dealers and Drivers for Free Trade," the PAC of the Japanese auto dealers in the United States, purchased a blitz of television ads favoring his opponent, Rudy Boschwitz. At the time I wondered if there truly had been no contact between them and the Boschwitz campaign, such as suggestions of ad themes to complement the ads the campaign was planning to run.

Fortunately, Oregon's Sen. Bob Packwood spilled some beans about independent expenditures when excerpts from his diaries were made public by the Senate Ethics Committee prior to his forced resignation in 1995. For instance, in 1992, when Packwood was running a close race for reelection against Congressman Les AuCoin, he wrote in his diary of a conversation with his chief of staff, Elaine Franklin, about his own dealings with Automobile Dealers and Drivers for Free Trade. During the last ten days before the

1992 election they poured $65,539 into telephone bank operations urging a vote for Packwood or against AuCoin. It would have been hard to imagine how they would know whom to target with their calls without some cooperation or consultation with the Packwood folks, but in this case one didn't have to imagine. On March 20, 1992, Senator Packwood dictated the following diary entry: "Elaine has been talking to me privately about independent expenditures. Apparently the Automobile Dealers are willing to do some spending against AuCoin. Of course, we can't know anything about it. We've got to destroy any evidence we've ever had of [deleted by the Ethics Committee] so that we have no connection with any independent expenditure." There is an amusing footnote to this story. One bit of evidence he tried to destroy was this diary entry. When the Senate Ethics committee subpoened his papers, Packwood doctored the diary, so the revised entry as submitted read as follows: "We talked about independent expenditures. I said I didn't want to know about that and none of us were to know about that. We want independent expenditures to be truly independent. Those who are going to support us will support us. Those who won't won't. Let's let the chips fall where they may."[3]

A second loophole in the 1974 regulations involves the exemption on "party-building activities." In a frequently used scam, a senator up for re-election prevails on a donor to give money to the Democratic Senatorial Campaign Committee or the National Republican Senatorial Committee in Washington. Using these contributions, or perhaps other unrestricted funds the committee has received, it then sends to the state party an amount far in excess of the amount it can legally give to a senator's campaign, allegedly for "party-building activities" but actually for promoting the senator's re-election.

It is very difficult to track this kind of "soft money," although once again Senator Packwood has given us a nice concrete example. On March 6, 1992, Sen. Phil Gramm of Texas, who was heading the National Republican Senatorial Committee, traveled to Oregon to give a speech plugging Packwood's reelection. After the speech, Gramm met with Packwood and Elaine Franklin, and Packwood's diary recorded that "Gramm again promised $100,000 for Party-building activities. And what was said in that room would be enough to convict us all of something. He says, 'Now, of course you know there can't be any legal connection between this money and Senator Packwood, but we know that it will be used for his benefit'. . . . God, there's Elaine and I sitting there. I think that's a felony; I'm not sure. This is an area of the law I don't want to know." In the doctored version, Packwood described meeting briefly with Gramm after the speech, but the account was considerably less incriminating: "There was the usual argument—I suppose a more polite word for it would be discussion—of how much money the National Committee or Senatorial Committee or any committee was going to give to the state party. . . . When I was county chairman it was how much was the state going to give the county. The lesser unit always wants the greater unit to give them money of some kind. Well, anyway, the discussion ended in a draw." Between April and July 1992, in seven separate transactions, the National Republican Senatorial Committee transferred a total of $96,500 to the Oregon Republican Party.

The loophole known as *bundling,* or at least a particularly popular and effective version of it, was reputedly invented by a Hungarian-born physicist, Leo Szilard, more renowned for his prediction of the nuclear chain reaction, his successful effort to prompt the World War II Manhattan Project that built the first atomic bombs, and his creative but less successful end-of-the-war and postwar efforts to control the use of those terrible weapons. Szilard's idea was a simple one. People concerned about a particular issue could get more bang for their campaign contribution bucks if they pooled and targetted their contributions. When Szilard and his Council for a Livable World wanted to elect members of Congress who favored nuclear arms control, he noted that senators from very small states with relatively modest campaign resources have the same vote as those from large ones. So the highest leverage targets of bundled contributions would be small states where close Senate elections were anticipated. The first test of this idea took place in 1962 in South Dakota, and I was among those who sent a contribution (mine was only $25) to the Council office to have it pooled with many others and shipped off to a little-known candidate named George McGovern. McGovern won by a margin of about 500 votes and he credited the Council contributions for his victory.

The most heralded practitioner of bundling today is probably EMILY's List, an organization that focuses on helping to elect progressive women to high political office by contributing crucial early money to their campaigns. The bundling strategy enables candidates to persuade wealthy donors that they will be able to raise the money to be competitive and thus a contribution to them will not be wasted. Hence the acronym *EMILY,* which stands for "Early Money, It's Like Yeast (It makes the dough rise)." Other players in the bundling game focus more on gaining lobbying access and influence, which often involves bundled contributions to incumbents even if they are likely to win in any event.

Bundling can be a legal way of circumventing the spirit and intent of the campaign contribution limits. It enables lobbyists to gain "credit" with legislators for bundled contributions far larger than the individual and PAC limits. And circumventing some reforms that are contemplated too, such as lowering the cap on PAC contributions; that could be circumvented, for example, by bundling individual contributions from a company's executives and other employees. Bundling of various sorts is rampant in congressional campaign financing today.

Arguments can be made in favor of some kinds of bundling. For instance, the Szilard version of alerting voters to candidates outside their districts who back their issues and encouraging support of their campaigns can be viewed as facilitating informed, positive participation in politics, enabling contributors of modest means to have some clout in a process otherwise dominated by wealthy individuals and PACs. Furthermore, no one could object to a fund-raising event that simply brings together people likely to support a candidate, although such a gathering, of course, would be difficult to distinguish from one that has the additional purpose of giving the organizer of the event credit and influence with the candidate. People of good will are likely to differ over which kinds of bundling ought to be outlawed and which kinds should be permitted.

The campaign finance rules for presidential candidates, as opposed to senators and members of the House, have been in effect since 1976 and are notably different in that they provide for substantial public financing through a fund to which citizens can contribute by checking a box on their federal income tax forms. Once they qualify, presidential candidates receive matching public funds for all contributions up to $250 during the primary campaign and full public funding during the general election campaign if they win the primary and agree to limit their spending to the public funding amount. The general election funding amount is indexed to inflation; it was about $65 million for the 2000 presidential election campaign. As a possible model for congressional finance reform, this presidential campaign financing system represented an intriguing alternative to the proposal that the Wellstone working group was exploring.

A Rocky Start

That congressional campaign finance reform was a high priority for Majority Leader George Mitchell was underscored when he and Sen. David Boren of Oklahoma immediately introduced S.3, the "Senate Elections Ethics Act of 1991" as the 102nd Congress opened. Many were predicting its early consideration, so the Wellstone Working Group was anxious to get started writing its full public financing bill.

That proved to be more difficult than I had imagined. For Paul's first month and a half in office, the Congress was preoccupied with the Persian Gulf war. In addition, since Paul was not a member of the committee that had jurisdiction over campaign finance reform, the Senate Rules Committee, this issue did not automatically appear high on his agenda. Getting up to speed on his two major committee assignments was a higher priority in his early months in office. Then for many months my time was consumed with other matters as well, especially with the Johnston energy policy juggernaut.

While continuing to attend the working group meetings and staying abreast of developments, I enlisted the help of Danny Cramer, a veteran of Paul's 1990 campaign and now one of the three young legislative correspondents in the office. He had worked on Paul's 1990 campaign and had proved to be a superb political organizer. In Washington, Danny increasingly took on the role of staff liaison to the campaign finance reform working group.

The exercise of writing a bill we could back with confidence involved decision points far more daunting than we anticipated. The working group focused on a proposal that involved full public funding in the primary election campaign for major party candidates who demonstrated sufficient public support and in the general election campaign for those who won their party primaries, with lesser amounts for minor party candidates. The plan would later become known by a variety of names: the initial full public financing proposal was called "Democratically Financed Elections." After a strategy to build a nationwide constituency was successfully initiated in Maine in 1996, it and other states that followed have called it "Clean Elections." In coordinating this state-by-state strategy, Washington-based Public Campaign has dubbed the overall effort "Clean Money Campaign Reform."

The fundamentals of Clean Money Campaign Reform (or CMCR for short) are straightforward. To earn full primary election funding, major party candidates who pledge to accept no private money (except a limited amount of "seed money" in donations of $100 or less to get their campaigns underway) would have to agree to voluntary spending limits in their primary and general election campaigns and they would have to demonstrate sufficient public support during a "Qualifying Period," just prior to the beginning of the "Primary Election Campaign Period." Winners of the major party primaries would then qualify for full public funding in the "General

Election Campaign Period." Additional provisions provided for minor party and independent candidates to qualify for full or partial funding.

An example of the thorny issues we had to confront early in 1991 was the test a candidate would have to pass to demonstrate sufficient public support to qualify for public funding. One option was to require a certain number of signatures on endorsing petitions, a test now used in many states for initiatives to qualify to be on the ballot. Another option was to require that a candidate gather a certain *amount* of money, a test of candidate support incorporated in other campaign finance reform proposals. The test that we finally decided on required a candidate to gather a designated *number* of $5 qualifying contributions, an amount sufficiently small so that almost anyone could participate, although that small sum would still be seen by the public as a credible indication of serious support.

While the Wellstone Working Group continued its pursuit of what eventually became known as the Clean Money bill, two other campaign finance reform bills had already been introduced by prominent Democratic senators and were getting all the attention. The prohibitive favorite, of course, was the Democratic Leadership's S.3, the Mitchell-Boren bill; the other was S.128, the "Senate Election Campaign Ethics Act," introduced by three senior Democratic senators, John Kerry of Massachusetts, Joe Biden of Delaware, and Bill Bradley of New Jersey. In the House of Representatives, the Democratic majority leader, Richard Gephardt of Missouri, introduced H.R.3, a companion bill to S. 3., which would move into the limelight later, after the Senate debate.

At least among many Democrats, there seemed to be significant agreement that campaign finance reform legislation should include the following goals, as formulated in the original Clean Money bill: "Eliminate money as the determinant of a person's political opportunity, access, and influence, and give real meaning to the right to vote; create a financially level playing field so that all qualified candidates for the same office have equal financial resources to conduct competitive campaigns; and break the hold that monied interests have over the electoral and governmental processes."

The Supreme Court's 1976 *Buckley* v. *Valeo* decision set the stage for campaign finance reform debates during the last quarter of the twentieth century. Citing the First Amendment, that decision ruled that it would be unconstitutional to require that either a congressional candidate's total campaign spending or a candidate's own spending on his or her own campaign be limited. The currently popular legislative response has been to provide a carrot to candidates in the form of generous public financing of their campaigns if they voluntarily limit their total campaign spending and their spending on their own campaigns. As the Packwood diaries suggest, however, there are likely to be widespread abuses in the use of soft money and independent expenditures. Given the timidity with which the Federal Elections Commission has approached enforcement in the past, there is ample reason to suspect that record amounts of money have been pouring down soft money channels for ends that bear no relation to "party-building activities." The same is true with independent expenditures, which must occur without any coordination or cooperation between the "independent spenders" and the candidates or their campaigns. To see how far lax enforcement has taken us, a court recently found that the political party that nominated and supported a candidate could turn right around and make truly "independent expenditures" on the candidate's behalf.

The two most prominent campaign finance reform bills in 1991 were S.3, the Mitchell-Boren bill, and S.128, the Kerry-Biden-Bradley bill, introduced by Senators John Kerry of Massachusetts, Joseph Biden of Delaware, and Bill Bradley of New Jersey (hereafter the Kerry bill). They both employed the same kind of carrot—public funding—to entice candidates to agree voluntarily to spend less on their campaigns and to limit the amount they personally spend on their campaigns.

To earn that voluntary cooperation, Senate candidates would have to demonstrate public support by raising a designated amount of money in relatively small contributions. The Mitchell-Boren bill would then offer a modest reward in vouchers to buy television advertising as well as reduced rates for both broadcasting and mail. In a state with about average population such as Minnesota, the voluntary campaign spending limit was around $2.5 million (compared to typical Minnesota Senate incumbent spending of about $7 million) and the voluntary cap on personal campaign spending was $250,000. (See table 2 for a synopsis of the Mitchell-Boren provisions.)

The Kerry bill had the same requirements for Senate candidates to demonstrate public support and the same voluntary agreements to obtain public funding, but the Kerry bill had a very different and much more intriguing offer of public financing, patterned after the presidential campaign finance system. Once they agreed to the voluntary spending limits and passed the public support test, major party Senate candidates would receive matching public funds for in-state individual contributions of $250 or less during the primary election campaign. Those who won their party's primary would receive full public funding during the general election campaign, thereby leveling the financial playing field in the final phase of the campaign, at least for the candidates of the two major parties. Contributions during the primary campaign were limited to no more than $1,000 per individual and $1,000 per PAC. (See table 3 for a synopsis of the Kerry bill provisions.)

Judged by my criteria for dealing effectively with the problems that result from the current congressional campaign financing system, both the Mitchell-Boren and Kerry bills were badly flawed. Under the present rules, incumbent lawmakers routinely rely on special interest lobbying coalitions for substantial portions of their reelection campaign funding. This inevitably results in money transfers that have the appearance of corruption and, more generally, the system by which our political campaigns are financed routinely drives lawmakers into financial dependence on lobbying coalitions.

If the Mitchell-Boren bill or the Kerry bill had been enacted, the ubiquitous interest-group-organized Washington fund-raisers where the lobbyists hand over the cash to the lawmakers would have remained a prominent feature of congressional campaigns. Many incumbents would have continued to find it convenient to rely on Capitol Hill fund-raisers for packages of early money that they need to jump-start their reelection campaigns.

Furthermore, incumbents, with years to develop contributor lists and with Washington-based interest groups eager to curry their favor could pass the qualifying test for public financing with ease. Recall that Paul's 1990 incumbent opponent had already received 756 contributions of at least $1,000 a year and a half before the election. Most challengers, especially those with supporters of predominently moderate means, would have a much more difficult time.

In 1991–92, the Democratic House Leadership introduced H.R.3, sponsored by House Majority Leader Richard Gephardt of Missouri, with a different approach to leveling the financial playing field in House races. It provided for up to $200,000 in matching contributions of up to $250 per contributor for all House candidates who passed the test for sufficient public support. However, in recent years, a growing number of House incumbents have found themselves "financially unopposed," meaning that they have many times more money to spend than their challengers. Well over 90 percent of House incumbents get reelected. If many challengers could gain matching public funds of on the order of one or two hundred thousand dollars, many more House races might turn out to be financially competitive. (See Table 4 for a synopsis of the provisions of H.R.3.)

Another problem that looms large in our current system of campaign financing is that wealthy donors have long been the gatekeepers of our

Table 2. Mitchell-Boren Democratic Leadership Bill S.3, 1991–92 and 1993–94

Senate Candidates	Primary Election Campaign	General Election Campaign	Comments
Voluntary spending limit	Average population state: ~ $1 million	Average population state: ~ $1.5 million	The voluntary spending limit is considerably less than typically spent in past elections.
Qualifying test for public funding	Average population state: raise ~$150,000 in $250 or less contributions, at least half from in-state.	Win primary election.	
Public funding		TV vouchers and a grant equal to the remainder of the general election spending limit for General Election Campaign.	More modest public funding than other campaign finance reform proposals. But even that proved to be too much public funding for the incumbent senators to accept. When the bill passed the Senate in 1993, the public funding was removed.
	Low broadcasting and mail rates		
PAC contributions allowed	Up to $2,500 for the Primary Election campaign	Up to $2,500 for the General Election campaign	
	Overall cap on PAC contributions = 20% of total spending limit		
Individual contributions allowed	Up to $1,000	Up to $1,000	
Candidate contributions allowed (voluntary limit)	Up to $250,000		

Table 3. Kerry-Biden-Bradley S.128 (Modeled after the presidential campaign finance system)

Senate Candidates	Primary Election Campaign	General Election Campaign	Comments
Voluntary spending limit	Average population state: ~ $1 million	Average population state: ~ $1.5 million	The voluntary spending limit is considerably less than typically spent in past elections.
Qualifying test for public funding	Average population state: raise $150,000 in $250 or less contributions, at least half from in-state.		
Public funding	In-state individual contributions up to $250 are matched, up to a cap of half the Primary Election spending limit.	Major party primary winners get the General Election spending limit. Minor party primary winners get less (based on past party vote totals.	Generous public funding, with matching funds in Primary and voluntary spending limit in General Election. Minor party primary winners get proportionately less.
PAC contributions allowed	Up to $1,000, with PAC total capped at 20% of the Primary Election spending limit.		
Individual contributions allowed	Up to $1,000		
Candidate contributions allowed	The lesser of $250,000 or 10% of the General Election spending limit		

Table 4. Gephardt Democratic Leadership Bill H.R.3, 1991–92 and 1993–94

House Candidates	Primary and General Election Campaign	Comments
Voluntary spending limit	$600,000	Seemingly designed to fit incumbent fund-raising practice; unlikely that many challengers could raise that amount.
Qualifying test for public funding	$60,000 in contributions of less than $250	
Public funding	The first $200 from any contributor is matched, up to a cap of $200,000. Also, low-cost mail rate.	In the 1993–94 period, when the Democratic president Bill Clinton might sign the bill, many House incumbents were evidently concerned that their challengers could receive $200,000 in public funding and their support of the proposal declined markedly.
PAC contributions allowed	Up to $5,000 for Primary Election campaign Up to $5,000 for General Election campaign	
Individual contributions allowed	Up to $1,000 for Primary Election campaign Up to $1,000 for General Election campaign	
Candidate contributions allowed (voluntary limit)	Up to $50,000	

Table 5. Congressional Clean Money Campaign Reform (full public financing)

Senate Candidates	Primary Election Campaign	General Election Campaign	Comments
Voluntary spending limit	Average population state: ~ $450,000 The exact figure is $(N-1) \times \$50,000 + \$100,000$, where N = # of congressional districts in the state.	Average population state: $750,000 The exact figure is $(N-1) \times \$75,000 + \$150,000$.	This has the lowest spending limit of all proposals examined here. e.g., California ($N = 52$): $6.4 Million Minnesota ($N = 8$): $1.1 Million South Dakota ($N = 1$): $.25 Million
Qualifying test for public funding	Before the end of the public financing qualifying period, collect $(N-1) \times 250 + 1,000$ $5 qualifying contributions.		The qualifying period ends at the beginning of the Primary Election period. The number of $5 contributions required: e.g., California: 13,750 Minnesota: 2,750 South Dakota: 1,000
Public funding	Grant equal to Primary Election spending limit.	Grant equal to General Election spending limit.	
	State-administered, federally funded voter information programs		
PAC contributions allowed	None	None	
Individual contributions allowed	Prior to the end of the public financing qualifying period, "seed money" of up to $15,000 + $(N-1) \times \$2,500$ in amounts less than or equal to $100 can be collected and spent.	None	Total "seed money" allowed in states of different population: e.g., California: $142,500 Minnesota: $32,500 South Dakota: $15,000
Candidate contributions allowed	No more than $100 from each member of the candidate's immediate family.		

politics, in effect determining who will have the financial resources to run competitive challenges to incumbents. As a consequence, many qualified challengers representing a much more diverse spectrum of race, class, gender, and political ideology are effectively shut out.

At this point, I wish to return to consider two campaign finance proposals that I came to believe would resonate much more strongly with people beyond the Washington Beltway. One, of course, was Clean Money Campaign Reform; the other was a variant on the presidential campaign funding model, but one that would be far more accessible to ordinary people. Both have a distinctively grassroots flavor.

First consider the appealing features of CMCR. Under CMCR, elected representatives would not be financially dependent on, and hence accountable to, lobbying coalitions; access to great wealth would not be a determinant of who gets to run for high public office; the financial playing field would not favor incumbent lawmakers; incumbents would not be preoccupied by onerous fund-raising duties; and a provision providing for state-organized Voter Information Programs would at least partially mitigate the problem of campaigns dominated by the expensive, manipulative techniques of electronic media advertising and targetted direct mail. Judged by its ability to deal with the most crippling money-in-politics diseases that afflict American democracy today, CMCR is the most transparently effective cure.

In early March, Danny Cramer and I attended the first 1991 Senate hearing on campaign finance reform, before the Senate Rules Committee. I could see clearly that we were coming into the debate very late. While we were still struggling with some important details of the CMCR bill, two major Senate proposals were already on the table and the most prominent public interest groups with grassroots constituencies active on this issue had been mobilized in support of one or the other. The most influential such organization, Common Cause, had helped to write and was backing the Mitchell-Boren bill. The Kerry bill had the support of three other public interest organizations with links to nationwide grassroots networks, Public Citizen, U.S. PIRG, and Citizen Action. The CMCR bill had not yet been completed; it would not be ready in time for the 1991 campaign finance reform debate.

As I came to realize, none of this really mattered. There was a great deal of hypocrisy surrounding the campaign finance reform debate in the 102nd Congress. A senior aide to Sen. John Kerry assured Paul's legislative director during the debate that "the Mitchell-Boren bill is purely symbolic politics" which even its sponsors would not like to see become law. The point was they did not have to worry about that; whatever campaign reform measure the Democratically controlled Congress passed, the Republican president George Bush was sure to veto. Then the Democrats could blame him for blocking politically popular campaign finance reform when he ran for reelection in 1992. The campaign finance reform fight in the 102nd Congress was largely a cynical charade, an exercise in symbolic politics for partisan political advantage.

Nevertheless, the Wellstone Working Group viewed the campaign finance reform debate as an opportunity for Paul to educate the American people about the difference between genuine campaign finance reform, as represented by CMCR, and symbolic campaign finance reform as exemplified by the Mitchell-Boren bill, thereby setting the stage for future progress on this issue.

By early May, Randy, Marty, Ben, and Phil, assisted by Danny, had fashioned a very rough bill draft. At an evening meeting they pressed Paul to introduce a Clean Money bill, papering over the remaining unresolved issues. Phil Stern and a wealthy friend of his promised Paul a national platform to champion full public financing of congressional campaigns. They were prepared to fund a nationwide public relations campaign in support of a Wellstone Clean Money bill.

Paul was tempted. But it was clear that important loose ends in the Clean Money bill would not be resolved by the time the issue reached the Senate floor. In the end he did not feel he had given the issue and the CMCR proposal sufficient thought.

However, Paul did want to play a role in the campaign finance reform debate when the Mitchell-Boren and Kerry bills came to the Senate floor. During the early April 1991 interlude between the Energy Committee hearings and the markup, I finally found a brief opportunity one weekend to think about campaign finance reform and take stock of progress on CMCR. Over that weekend, I had an idea about how Paul might make a significant contribution to the debate.

As I studied the various proposals, I was struck by the elegance of the presidential campaign financing model, especially by the way primary election campaign contributions were used as the qualifying test for public financing. But the contribution limits in the Kerry bill seemed to be set all wrong. Suppose the following changes were introduced: (1) the limit on individual contributions would be lowered from $1,000 to $100; (2) individual contributions would be limited to in-state (for Senate candidates) or in-district (for House candidates) voting-age residents; (3) PAC contributions would be banned; and (4) candidates' contributions to their own campaigns would be limited to $5,000, rather than $250,000 as in the Kerry bill.

The remainder of the Kerry provisions, including matching public funds for in-state or in-district contributions during the primary campaign and full public funding for general election candidates who have passed the qualifying test, would pertain. Given the 1976 *Buckley* v. *Valeo* Supreme Court ruling, the second, third, and fourth provisions could not be mandated, but candidates would have an incentive to adopt them voluntarily, as they were prerequisites for the public funding.

By eliminating PAC contributions and limiting primary election campaign contributions to $100 or less from in-state or in-district constituents only, this approach, which we labeled the "$100 Solution," would effectively cut the big money links between legislators and Washington-based lobbying coalitions. By sharply limiting the amount candidates could contribute to their own campaigns, the opportunity for wealthy individuals to buy elective office would be precluded. And, as in the Clean Money and Kerry bills, candidates who made it to the general election would compete on a level financial playing field.

Because the $100 Solution had the same structure as the Kerry bill, Paul would not have to introduce his own bill at this point late in the game; he could achieve the same effect with a series of amendments to Kerry's bill. Paul could use those amendments and associated floor statements to demonstrate graphically serious shortcomings of the Mitchell-Boren and Kerry proposals. In this way he could make a significant contribution to the 1991 campaign finance reform debate, even though neither he nor the Clean Money bill were fully prepared.

However, when Danny called Randy and Phil with this plan, they were upset: Yes, let's get CMCR out to the public and widely disseminate it. But no, do not amend the Kerry bill. They were counting on Paul to be the congressional champion of and leading spokesperson for full public financing. They felt strongly that role would be compromised if he amended the Kerry bill.

Then a funny thing happened to the amendments on the way to the Senate floor. While I was preoccupied with the Energy Committee clash over CAFE, the plan for Paul to attach amendments to the Kerry bill that would convert it into the $100 Solution were explored in conversations with other Senate offices. The results were evidently disappointing. In the end, Paul introduced just one amendment: reducing the maximum amount candidates could contribute to their campaigns from the Kerry bill's $250,000 to $25,000.

On the second day of the campaign finance reform debate on the floor of the Senate, Paul gave an excellent speech that Danny Cramer had prepared, and his amendment passed handily. He later presented Danny with a blown-up and framed copy of the speech.

However, members of the working group were very unhappy with what they heard. Their reaction is captured by a letter Phil Stern wrote to me. In his typically direct manner, he laid it on the line:

> My own disappointment . . . is not with the failure to produce a bill: the task of writing a completely new system from scratch proved to be a far more daunting task than any of us had imagined. . . . My principal disappointment lay in Paul's speech. . . . It was a marvelous passionate disquisition that laid out all the evils of the present system—but then failed to make the crucial break from the gradualist approaches that have dominated reform efforts for decades and pronounce his espousal of CMCR. On the contrary, as I understand what he said on the Senate floor that day, the Mitchell and Kerry bills represented steps in the right direction. He made no mention whatever of the notion, which underlay our whole effort, that the only real solution lay in . . . ridding the system of all private money and starting over from scratch. Nor did he make any mention of his work in developing such a solution or any plans he may have to introduce it at such time as his work is complete.[4]

"For Phil"

In my view, the Wellstone office and I had an obligation to the working group to complete the Clean Money bill as soon as possible so that it could be circulated widely for comments and criticisms. I was therefore pleased when Paul called me in Minnesota two days after our November 1, 1991, energy strategy victory, asking with some urgency if I would be willing to help put the finishing touches on CMCR so it could be written up in bill language. He said he wanted to do it "for Phil." The reason for the urgency was this: Phil Stern was a very special person, a man of highest principle, with a deep commitment to building a just society. He personified much of what Paul and I both aspire to. At the time he was urging us on, he was waging a visibly painful battle with cancer and did not have long to live. We both wanted to finish this bill "for Phil."

At that time, Carleton College was about to begin its long Christmas recess. I recruited a senior political science major, Nick Corson, to help. Nick had been an outstanding student in my fall-term class, "Congress, Campaign Money, and a National Energy Strategy"; he had studied the congressional campaign finance reform debate and was already familiar with CMCR. With guidance from Ben Senturia and me, Nick did research during the recess that helped provide credible answers to some important practical questions, including how many $5 or $10 contributions it would be appropriate to require for a candidate to qualify for public funding, how long a qualifying period would be necessary to collect those contributions, and what would be appropriate voluntary spending limits.

The qualifying test is a good illustration of what he found. Since collecting the requisite number of small contributions would be "the key to the Treasury," it was crucial that we get that number right. It would have to be large enough to weed out frivolous candidates, but small enough to allow entrée to a much more diverse range of serious candidates. In contrast, under our present system those who gain access to candidacy-land must either possess great personal wealth or be annointed by the gatekeepers of our politics, big money donors.

Nick tried a number of fact-finding approaches, beginning with consulting congressional campaign managers and ballot-access experts. What proved most helpful was the experience of city council and mayoral candidates in Tucson, Arizona, where for several years matching public funds had been provided to those who collected a certain number of contributions of $10 or more. Since Tucson had a population about equal to a congressional district, that experience was especially illuminating.

Most of those Nick spoke with in Tucson felt that it would be difficult for many serious candidates to collect more than five hundred to one thousand $10 contributions, though with the added visibility and prominence of a congressional seat, one particularly thoughtful respondent felt two thousand might be reasonable. Nick's research at last gave us an empirical basis for choosing and defending crucial numbers in the Clean Money bill. We now had some insight into what was realistic. Nick concluded that we had a bit of a dilemma on our hands. Serious city council contenders in Tucson, with a population about equal to a congressional district, in some cases had trouble raising two hundred to five hundred $10 contributions. "Of course, we are talking about the U.S. Congress as opposed to a city council," he said, "so the requirements should be stricter, but not to the point that they are unachievable. The counterpoint to this is the political reality of not being able to go lower than two thousand and still being credible to the public. Even two thousand may not be perceived as credible; in fact, it probably won't, although I feel strongly that it is a challenging enough number to demonstrate serious support, and I think we can justify it on the basis of the

Tucson model." In the end, we opted for $5 rather than $10 contributions, and the Tucson experience was a very useful guide.

In January 1992, I went to the University of California, San Diego, on sabbatical leave to begin work on this book. At the same time, I helped the working group complete a Model Clean Money Bill. From January to June, Ben Senturia in St. Louis took the lead and organized a series of a dozen or so lengthy conference calls involving Marty in Vermont, Randy in Massachusetts, and me in California. With faxes flying between our conversations, by July we had hammered out the details of a proposal and Marty wrote it up in draft form for circulation to others.

In the course of this work, I developed a particular interest in an issue I believe to be central to campaign finance reform but which had not been well addressed in any of the proposals I had seen. It has to do with the quality of information available to voters both at election time and when their representatives were off in Washington representing them. The two Democratic campaign finance reform bills contained provisions for candidates who agreed to limit expenditures to receive vouchers for television time and reduced broadcasting and mail rates. I was skeptical that encouraging the often manipulative advertising and subsidizing the often deceptive messages of targetted direct mail was a good idea.

Instead, I proposed that a key part of any campaign reform package be state-administered, federally financed Voter Information Programs that would make it easy for voters to acquire the information they wished to know when they voted in the next election and be able to follow easily what their representatives were up to out in Washington between elections. Initially, states would act as laboratories, undertaking Voter Information Programs of their own devising; eventually the most successful elements of those programs could be identified and promulgated nationwide.

From that six-month effort in 1992, I came to realize what an ambitious undertaking this attempt to finance political campaigns completely with public funds would be. I also understood that our original goal of being ready with a total public financing bill for the May 1991 Senate debate had been utterly unrealistic. (See table 5 for a synopsis of the Clean Money bill's provisions.)

While I was helping to complete the Clean Money bill, I began to organize a project that would fulfill another commitment I had made to Paul—to translate the $100 Solution into a comparably detailed bill. In the spring of 1992, I selected eight Carleton students to work with me that fall. In preparation for the project, three of them undertook summer internships.

Of particular relevance were the ideas another fine student, Bert Johnson, worked on at Public Citizen in Washington during the summer of 1992. The basic concepts of the "$100 Solution for Good Government" that Donna Edwards and Craig McDonald were developing for Public Citizen was similar to the "$100 Solution" I had thought about in the Wellstone office. Its basic elements were the presidential financing model with individual and PAC contributors limited to $100 or less and, for qualifying candidates who would agree to voluntary spending limits, 3-for-1 matching contributions from public funds. The research Bert Johnson did for the "$100 Solution for Good Government" paralleled what Nick Corson had done for the $100 Solution. For instance, Bert gained considerable insight by studying the fund-raising experience of a Kentucky congressman, Romano Mazzoli, who only accepted contributions of $100 or less.

That summer I attended a meeting called by Public Citizen in Washington to discuss the "$100 Solution For Good Government" and to try to find common ground among the public interest groups. I found that meeting very helpful.

In June, 1992, I gave a talk on "Congress and a National Energy Strategy" in Orange County, just south of Los Angeles and famed as a bastion of right-wing politics. To illustrate the intrusion of special interest money into the energy debate, I enumerated the campaign contributions received by California's Senator John Seymour, a member of the Energy Committee who was up for election, from lobbying coalitions backing four controversial proposals in the Johnston-Wallop bill.

I suggested they might want to organize a group to publicize Seymour's contributions, to study and publicize campaign contributions on other important issues, such as health care, and to study the various campaign finance reform proposals and prepare to participate in the upcoming debate. A number of people signed up, and one of them, Bill Strahan, volunteered to organize the project if I would help. A physicist who had recently retired from the aerospace industry, Bill turned out to be an enormously resourceful and dedicated colleague. We dubbed the effort "Project Shame," based on one of its principal objectives—to embarrass politicians by publicizing their special interest campaign contributions.

Thanks to Strahan, a group was organized and began meeting every other week throughout the summer. At the second session, I showed a videotape of a Bill Moyers television program about money in politics entitled "Who Owns Our Government?" Strahan immediately recognized its potential as an organizing tool and had many copies made and widely distributed in Southern California.

Soon Project Shame had a mailing list of over three hundred names and substantial attendence at its meetings. At one meeting, Ben Senturia from St. Louis and I presented the Clean Money proposal. Fifty people came to hear Public Citizen's congressional lobbyist, Donna Edwards, describe the $100 Solution for Good Government and the prospects for congressional campaign finance reform.

Prominent among the attendees were local leaders of groups already concerned with this issue, including Common Cause and the League of Women Voters. But also involved were many who were new to the issue. Those meetings pinpointed the problems with the current campaign financing system that bothered people the most. More than anything else, it was the perception of corruption—that special interest money bought special influence. The information-packed *Project Shame Newsletter* was renamed *Money and Politics* when it became a joint venture of Project Shame and Orange County Common Cause. The outpouring of so many civic-minded people in this hotbed of southern California conservatism, well-informed and deeply concerned about the problems of money in politics, reinforced my sense that the timing was right, the issue was ripe, and substantial grassroots constituencies were identifiable.

Why Not Put Your Money Where Your Mouth Is?

13

Bill Clinton's Promise

In 1993 and 1994, the Democrats had control of both the White House and the Congress. They had a rare opportunity to write and pass strong campaign finance reform legislation and have the president sign it into law. During his campaign, Bill Clinton promised to make campaign finance reform a very high priority. According to the statement issued by the Clinton-Gore campaign in the summer of 1992, "American politics is held hostage by big money interests. . . . Bill Clinton and Al Gore believe it's long past time to clean up Washington. As part of their plan to fight the cynicism that is gripping the American people, Bill Clinton and Al Gore will support and sign strong campaign finance reform legislation to bring down the cost of campaigning and encourage real competition. . . . We can't go four more years without a plan to take away power from the entrenched bureaucracies and special interests that dominate Washington."[1]

The document went on to sketch the "Clinton-Gore Plan," which included voluntary spending limits to "level the playing field and encourage challengers to enter the race," opening up the system to candidates who, in Clinton's words, "looked like America." The proposal was to lower the PAC contribution limit per election from $5,000 to $1,000 and reduce the cost of television air time "to promote real discussion and turn TV into an instrument of education, not a weapon of political assassination. . . ." Beyond this one-page summary statement, however, the new president had not yet spelled out what he had in mind. Most likely he and his advisors hoped that even this perfunctory statement would appeal to the angry and disenchanted 19 percent of the voters who had cast their ballots for Ross Perot in 1992.

From November 1992 to January 1993, the transition period before Clinton took office, the newly elected administration began serious discussions with public interest groups and congressional leaders about how to frame its campaign finance reform initiative. Particularly promising to the public interest groups was the fact that Clinton's point person on campaign finance reform was a former colleague, Michael Waldman, an impressive young man who had headed a program called Congress Watch for the Nader-founded organization, Public Citizen. On the surface, campaign finance reform looked like a relatively uncomplicated issue that would gain Clinton points with a key constituency. After all, during the last year of the Bush administration a Democratic Congress had passed a bill by comfortable margins in both houses, only to see it vetoed by the Republican president. What could be easier than reintroducing the same bill, S.3, having it sail through the legislative process, and then taking the credit for a significant reform? But in an ironic twist, Clinton did just fine in the quarter where he might have most expected pressure for more radical change—the public interest community—and was strongly challenged in the quarter where he might have expected support—the Democratically controlled Congress.

A Countervailing Force?

In retrospect, there was plenty of reason to be apprehensive from the start. Many congressional incumbents, probably a majority, would resist significant change in the existing system that had worked so well for them. The public interest groups were the only countervailing force in sight that could lead the fight for breaking the big money links to lobbying coalitions, creating a level financial playing field. But I had not been impressed with the proposals the groups had backed in the previous Congress. Common Cause and the League of Women Voters [LWV] had supported the Mitchell-Boren/ Democratic leadership bill, S.3, while Public Citizen, U.S. PIRG, and Citizen Action had stuck with Sen. John Kerry's alternative.

Beginning in the spring of 1992, those three groups allied with Kerry had been exploring a far more ambitious formulation of campaign finance reform. The time was right to put forward a much stronger bill. They hoped to convince Senators Kerry, Biden, and Bradley to introduce Public Citizen's "$100 Solution for Good Government," whereby qualifying candidates would receive three-for-one matching public funds in return for agreeing to limit their PAC and individual contributions in the primary and general election campaigns to $100. The document outlining this proposal that Carleton student Bert Johnson had helped Public Citizen's Donna Edwards and Craig MacDonald develop began with a call for "bold, comprehensive action."

But even for public interest groups, it seems that once you become an inside "player" in Washington, a self-moderating mechanism kicks in. In order to gain more clout in the negotiations over the Mitchell-Boren and Kerry bills, Public Citizen had joined with Common Cause, the League of Women Voters, U.S. PIRG, and Citizen Action in a working group they called the National Campaign Finance Reform Coalition. Presumably the Kerry bill sponsors had weighed in at that point. By the second week in December 1992, what had been the $100 Solution For Good Government had become only a pale reflection of its bold, comprehensive antecedent. The individual and PAC contribution limits, for example, had increased from $100 to $1,000.

I learned about this debilitating metamorphosis of the $100 Solution when my friend John Bonifaz, then at the Center for Responsive Politics in Washington, sent me a December 11 draft memo he had just received. If Common Cause signed on, joining Public Citizen, U.S. PIRG, the LWV, and others, there would be a formidable coalition behind a new Kerry bill and pressure on Paul to join them.

When I read the memo, I was aghast. In reply, I pointed out that in principle it would be possible under the proposed revision of the Public Citizen plan for as few as four hundred contributors at Washington fund-raisers to provide the entire amount of money a House incumbent would have to raise, with half of it coming from corporate PACs and half from executives of those corporations. "The net effect would be that big money contributions to candidates from lobbying coalitions would continue to be a dominant factor in our politics. Washington-based efforts in support of incumbents who side with lobbying coalitions would remain commonplace." In short, organized money would have a field day if their proposal were enacted.

In dismay, I faxed a letter to several of the key coalition group leaders:

> Pardon my frustration, but after two years of working with many of your groups on campaign finance reform and being very impressed with your efforts, I'm really surprised at the role the public interest organizations seem to be playing. Right now, many Americans are angry and they are primed to get behind a strong campaign finance reform proposal that would really make a difference. Instead, the Democratic leadership is preparing to play symbolic

politics by reintroducing S. 3. And you public interest guys are playing the role of "insiders," trying to figure out "what will sell in Washington." In the process, . . . you have come up with a draft proposal with a loophole big enough for the special interests to drive a Brinks truck through if it ever got enacted. . . . No one is doing what should be the job of the public interest community—making sure a strong, clean proposal is put on the table in Washington that all those concerned and angry people beyond the Beltway could enthusiastically support and organize behind. . . . I ask that you please reconsider your approach at this time of maximum opportunity.

That was not the direction in which they were heading, however. Instead, the coalition undertook an intensive effort to enlist the support of as many public interest groups as they could behind some vague general principles of campaign finance reform. On December 17, a letter signed by leaders of the five National Campaign Finance Reform Coalition organizations and forty-two other prominent public interest groups was sent to the president, followed by a memo spelling out the provisions of the watered-down version of the Public Citizen reform proposal.

At a moment of opportunity like this, in my view the role of public interest groups has to be to back bold, clean, clear proposals that can capture the imagination of their grassroots constituencies and spur them to concerted action. In the case of campaign finance reform, the groups in the coalition had eager, well-informed constituencies in communities all over the country who were committed to meaningful change. But their national offices in Washington had let them down.

I saw the disappointment this created among some grassroots activists when I sat in on a meeting of the Orange County [Calif.] Common Cause chapter the day after Bill Clinton's inauguration in January 1993. There was enormous frustration and even anger at the Common Cause officials in Washington for having lost touch with their local members and failing to press for genuine campaign finance reform. What I was hearing about the Common Cause Washington leadership's being out of touch with their local members was strikingly parallel to the complaints voters nationwide were voicing about elected officials in Washington.

From that perspective there was an enormous vacuum waiting to be filled. The only way meaningful campaign finance reform could possibly pass the Congress would be as a result of massive pressure from the grassroots. But in my view neither the Clinton/Democratic leadership bill, S.3, nor the the National Campaign Finance Reform Coalition's weakened Kerry bill would attract the necessary public enthusiasm when exposed to public scrutiny.

Paul himself was beginning to experience serious pressure to support the latter, including the direct urging of Ralph Nader. It was hard for him to withhold support from a coalition that had set up a "1–800-CLEAN UP GOVERNMENT" number to enlist national grassroots support and had the resources to organize a national campaign.

In many respects, the problem Paul faced was the obverse of the problem faced by a grassroots movement when its leaders come to Washington to press for legislation. These leaders must rely on senators and representatives to be their agents. Yet these people often have agendas that do not coincide completely with those of the groups. Paul, on the other hand, had to rely on the national leaders of Washington-based groups like Common Cause to organize grassroots pressure behind campaign finance reform. In this case, those national leaders also aspired to play an insider role in the Washington negotiations. They, too, had bought into the Washington view of what is realistic. But despite these drawbacks, Paul agreed in early December to work with the National Campaign Finance Reform Coalition on a "common media strategy."

Incumbents Decide the Road to "Real Reform"

When he was inaugurated in January 1993, Bill Clinton announced that political reform was on his "short list" of high priority commitments. One of the most powerful parts of his inaugural address stressed this commitment in eloquent populist terms: "To renew America, we must revitalize our democracy. . . . Let us resolve to reform our politics, so that power and privilege no longer shout down the voice of the people. Let us put aside personal advantage so that we can feel the pain and see the promise of America. . . . Let us give this capital back to the people to whom it belongs."

The new president committed himself specifically to campaign finance reform when he presented his economic program to Congress on February 17: "I think it is clear to every American—including every member of Congress of both parties—that the confidence of the people who pay our bills in our institutions in Washington is not high. We must restore it. . . . I am asking the United States Congress to pass a real campaign finance reform bill this year. . . . I believe lobby reform and campaign finance reform are a sure path to increased popularity for Republicans and Democrats alike because it says to the voters back home: 'This is your House, this is your Senate. We're your hired hands and every penny we draw is your money.'"

Early signs, however, pointed toward symbolic action rather than mean-

ingful change. S.3 was reintroduced in the Senate and H.R.3 was reintroduced in the House. The most notable feature in the Senate bill was a provision setting voluntary spending limits low enough for one at least to imagine
more challengers raising enough money to compete with incumbents. A
House provision that included up to $200,000 in public matching funds
created the possibility that more challengers would become financially competitive.

The same day S.3 was introduced, Kerry, Biden, and Bradley introduced
their bill, which featured the presidential election financing model but with
a $1,000 cap on both individual and PAC contributions (a far cry from the
$100 cap in Public Citizen's original "$100 Solution for Good Government"). Public Citizen in fact, not only supported the bill but also was asking Paul to cosponsor it! The situation at Common Cause made me even
sadder. While nominally urging members to support the principle of a congressional financing system modeled after the presidential financing system,
its national office was very cozy with Democratic leaders in both houses of
Congress. In 1991, Common Cause had enthusiastically backed S.3, and,
as we would soon learn, it was ready to support whatever the Democratic
congressional leadership decided was realistic in 1993. Thus had a behind-
the-scenes process within Washington's public interest community turned
the "$100 Solution," into the "$1,000 Solution" and held in check a grassroots army ready to fight for much more. Meanwhile, as provisions for
meaningful reform either were watered down or discarded altogether, the
rhetoric aimed for public consumption remained the same. Just as the "$100
Solution for Good Government" had been touted as "*real* congressional
campaign finance reform" by Public Citizen the previous summer, the identical term was used in the Campaign Finance Reform Coalition's letter to President Clinton on December 17 to tout the $1,000 Solution. And two months
later, "real reform" was again the president's clarion call in his address to a
joint session of Congress.

As incumbent-biased and as open to very large lobbying coalition contributions as S.3 was, the early signal Clinton received from congressional leaders was that they still would balk. The bill that had easily passed the 102nd
Congress when it was sure to be vetoed by President Bush had suddenly
become much less attractive to the Democratic congressional majority that
had pushed it through, now that the occupant of the White House would
sign it into law. If Clinton had followed through on his campaign promise
to limit PAC contributions to $1,000 per election, he would have encoun-
tered even more resistance. In the previous Congress, the Senate had agreed

to reduce the PAC contribution limit to $2,500 per election. However, the House had refused to accept any lowering of the $5,000 per election limit established in 1974.

Speaker of the House Tom Foley reportedly told Clinton that he doubted the bill would pass the House again, and the other Democratic leaders agreed. Of course, in 1992 Foley had solicited more than $400,000 from PACs, while Majority Leader Richard Gephardt had received over $1 million from the PACs, more than any other House member. In addition, up to $200,000 per House candidate in matching public funds created the prospect of many more financially competitive challenges to incumbents. Gephardt suggested the bill would be more palatable to his colleagues if the public financing were removed, and amazingly, Democratic leaders claimed it was the public who wouldn't support public financing. The lead story in the March 11, 1993, edition of *Roll Call,* the Capitol Hill newspaper, was headlined, "Foley Signals Demise of Public Financing, But Senators Push On," and began,

> In the House, the Democratic leadership is sending out signals that public financing is low on its list of priorities for campaign finance reform this year, even though only last year Congress passed a measure which could have provided more than $200,000 to every House candidate. At his Tuesday press conference, Foley said public opposition made it almost impossible to enact a system with significant public financing. . . . "I still believe in it in principle. I despair of getting it enacted, because the public attitudes are so hostile to it. . . ."

There was plenty of evidence that Foley's assertion that the American people would not support public funding of congressional campaigns was simply not true. For instance, from an opinion poll in December 1992 and focus groups in January 1993, Democratic survey researchers Celinda Lake and Steve Cobble reported:

> Seventy-two percent of voters support extending presidential campaign finance to Congress when we stipulate that the package includes limiting campaign spending and reducing individual and PAC contributions—funded by a voluntary check-off and a new tax on lobbyists. A flat suggestion to extend Presidential campaign finance reform to Congress nets only 28%; adding spending limits to the description bounces support up to 40%. But the full description of reform—extending Presidential campaign finance to Congress, limits on campaign spending, PAC and individual contributions, funded by a voluntary check-off and a new tax on lobbyists—wins big support as almost three fourths of voters support it even though it specifies significant public spending.[2]

Columnist Elizabeth Drew wrote a convincing account in the *New York Times Magazine* of what was going on behind the scenes, aptly titled "Watch 'Em Squirm."

Clinton is now caught in the contradiction inherent in his campaign: he needs to be seen as taking on and reforming an institution—the Congress—on which he is utterly dependent for winning approval of his domestic agenda. As a White House official puts it, "On the one hand, we want to pass campaign reform that's real; on the other we don't want to burn bridges with Congress in doing it". . . . [In 1993] House Democrats are . . . more opposed than ever to serious campaign finance reform. Many of them got the fright of their lives in the 1992 elections. . . . Now House members see incumbency itself as a political liability, and they aren't interested in giving up any of their remaining advantages—the chief one being, of course, fundraising. . . . The real question isn't whether a campaign finance reform bill will pass, but whether the one that is passed will be real or phony. The temptations toward the latter are strong. It now appears that Clinton will put forth some guidelines—but no bill—and that in reality the Senate will write its own bill, the House will write its own bill and the Administration will come up with something about soft money—how serious is anyone's guess. . . . Even if this year's effort falls short of the real thing, there will be a strong temptation on the part of the House, the Senate, the Administration and even some reform groups to declare victory. If Clinton wants to be true to his word, he will have to go on the line—and risk some alliances—to win a bill that truly gets at the corruption in the political system. If he does not, and the result is a phony bill, or no bill at all, the corruption—emboldened by the fact that even a President seemingly determined to get hold of it didn't do so—will be given a new lease on life. So will the public's cynicism.[3]

What most Americans outside of Washington did not know was just how perverse a product emerged from this process. It was shocking how precisely the House leaders had shaped the bill to fit the current incumbent fundraising practices and to perpetuate incumbent financial advantages. For example, the voluntary spending limit for House candidates would be $600,000, with up to $60,000 in fundraising expenses exempted. In their study of 1990 election spending, *Los Angeles Times* reporters Sara Fritz and Dwight Morris had found that on average House incumbents spent $390,000, while those in close races had averaged $557,000. To raise the funds, incumbents had invested an average of $69,000. So the cap fit incumbent practice remarkably well. The maximum amount a PAC could contribute to a House candidate would be $5,000 for the primary election campaign and $5,000 for the general election campaign and each candidate could solicit no more than a total of $200,000 from PACs. The president called the $200,000 limit "a dramatic change in the present system" although Fritz and Morris had found that in 1990, House incumbents had averaged just about that amount in PAC contributions, $209,000. Finally, the first $200 of any individual's or PAC's donation to a qualifying House candidate would be matched in communications vouchers for broadcast, print, and mail, up to a maximum of $200,000. The problem was that incumbents would have no trouble taking advantage of the full $200,000 bonanza, whereas challengers would rarely be able to do so. In 1990, major party challengers who made it to the general election raised an average of only $111,000, an amount far short of what it would take to receive the maximum amount of matching public funds.

That was the context for the 1993 congressional campaign finance reform debate. The major public interest groups were backing vague "principles" and a fatally flawed bill. The Democratic president agreed to let the Senate and House Democrats each write their own campaign finance rules.

The Sorry State of Political Parties

Political parties today need a new model to pursue. Congressional candidates now essentially run their own campaigns, raising much of their own money, hiring their own political consultants and pollsters, producing their own ads, buying their own broadcast time. They function largely like independent entrepreneurs, in most respects quite independent of their political parties.

In his book, *Who Will Tell the People: The Betrayal of American Democracy,* Bill Greider had a particularly devastating critique of a modern political party in a chapter entitled, "Who Owns the Democrats?" He began with the story of what happened when officials at the Democratic National Committee (DNC) decided to plan a nationwide celebration in 1992 to commemorate the two hundredth anniversary of their party's founding and started thinking about whom to invite:

> Naturally, staff officials thought first of the direct mail lists stored in computers—the people who give money to the party more or less regularly. Then, of course, they would include all the elected officials, state, local, and national, who call themselves Democrats. Why not, someone suggested, also invite the many thousands of people who are active in party affairs—the "regulars" who serve on county committees or tend the mechanics of election precincts or campaign operations, the legions of people who faithfully rally around the ticket? But it was asked, who are these people? Where are their names and

addresses? The DNC staffers searched the party's files and discovered that such lists no longer exist. . . . The old lists presumably still existed, but not at party headquarters. They were believed to be in permanent storage at the National Archives—boxes and boxes of index cards from the 1950s and 1960s with the names and addresses of the people who, in that day, made the party real. In the age of television, big money and high-tech candidacies, the "regulars" of party politics have been rendered irrelevant. . . . [The party today] acts neither as a faithful mediator between citizens and government nor as the forum for policy debate and resolution nor even as a structure around which political power can accumulate. It functions mainly as a mail drop for political money.

Greider concluded that there is an enormous vacuum in our politics: "There is no major institution committed to mobilizing the power of citizens around their own interests and aspirations." He mused about what might fill that vacuum: "Imagine, for instance, if the Democratic party devoted a few million each year to party building from the ground up—talking and listening to real people in their communities, hiring organizers to draw people out of their isolation and into permanent relationships with organizations that would speak for them."[4]

I began to think seriously about this in early December 1992. As we were flying back to Minnesota from Washington, Paul told me that Todd Otis, then chair of the Minnesota Democratic-Farmer-Labor Party, was concerned that the DFL's "coordinated campaigns" in support of both state and federal candidates would not be able to function without the support of so-called soft money. This led to a very useful conversation with Otis and DFL coordinated campaign director Todd Rappe on December 14 at the state DFL party headquarters in St. Paul. I told them we would love to find a way to strengthen political parties. The challenge was to figure out how to do that without at the same time leaving a gaping loophole in the campaign financing system. At issue was an abuse of the practice whereby state political parties can receive unlimited amounts of "soft money" from national party collection units for "party building activities," such as get-out-the-vote efforts. The abuse occurs if the soft money is diverted instead to candidate campaigns, creating a channel from contributors to candidates for federal office that can greatly exceed the legal individual and PAC contribution limits.

Otis made it clear from the beginning that the coordinated campaign was the centerpiece of the DFL's electoral organizing efforts. He emphasized his opposition to any measures that would cut off the flow of soft money from the national Democratic Party to the Minnesota DFL. He was concerned that the soft money provisions of the Democratic leadership's reform bill and other campaign finance reform proposals under consideration, including some that Paul's office was looking into, would do just that. At the same time, he expressed his support for reining in soft money abuses. For example, he said he would have no problem with prohibiting candidates for Congress or the presidency from soliciting soft money.

Otis and Rappe were forthcoming in providing data on how much money is needed for a coordinated campaign in an average population state like Minnesota, how that money is spent, and where it comes from. We took as an example the 1990 Minnesota campaign, with one U.S. Senate candidate and eight congressional candidates up for election, along with a full slate of state Senate and House candidates. The total amount spent for the coordinated campaign was $940,000 in 1990, a non-Presidential election year. About one-third of that was spent between the June DFL convention and the September primary and the remaining two-thirds during the general election campaign. This is how the money was spent: polling (15 percent), general administration (10 percent), computer maintenance (5 percent), and phone banks (70 percent).

Obviously the most striking feature is the overwhelming proportion spent on the phone banks, which are used for many functions, including identifying voters' candidate preferences ("Voter ID" in political parlance), polling, persuasion calls to undecided voters, and Get-Out-The-Vote ("GOTV") efforts. I was surprised to learn that virtually all of this was contracted out to professional phone bank operations. The upshot was there is very little reliance on volunteers in the coordinated campaign.

We had a revealing discussion about the possibility of the party's moving strongly in the direction of much greater emphasis on volunteers. I suggested that many people had been turned off by politics, which they rightly viewed as dominated by the influence of big money. In a new campaign finance regime in which the big money links were cut, people would have a reason to become involved again and many more volunteers could be recruited, I speculated. If 70 percent of the budget goes to phone banks, much of that money must be for the salaries of the callers; staffing the phones with volunteers would sharply decrease the amount of money needed for the coordinated campaign and sharply increase the participation of DFLers in election related activities.

Rappe was skeptical. He said they had a volunteer list of two thousand, but they could not turn out volunteers for eighteen phones a night. He discreetly suggested I was out of touch with the times, arguing that in the 1990s people have different responsibilities and priorities than they did a generation ago.

That certainly is possible, but it hasn't been tested, I wrote in a memo to Paul. The pendulum of politics swings slowly but inexorably and right now, I sense, it is beginning to swing back in a direction where people-centered politics will be popular again. My student Bert Johnson, chair of the Carleton Democrats, also was skeptical of Rappe's claim; he said they would have been able to turn out large numbers of students for volunteer phonebanking prior to the 1992 elections.

In any event, I found the conversation quite stimulating. I came away with the feeling that involving many more volunteers could be at the heart of revitalizing political parties. And the significantly lower coordinated campaign expenses that resulted would make it easier to keep political party money in large amounts from undermining the spending limits of congressional campaign finance reform plans.

A White Knight without a Horse

A Wellstone campaign finance reform bill along the lines of the $100 Solution, "The Fair Elections and Grassroots Democracy Act," was finally introduced on May 13, 1993, soon before the Senate floor debate on S.3 began. There had been no serious effort to organize support for it, either in the Senate or among the public interest groups, who found themselves backing bills for which neither they nor their members could muster much enthusiasm. It was lost in the noise of the Senate debate.

I can't say I was particularly surprised that Paul's bill did not attract much attention. My students and I had spent the fall term writing a detailed bill that had the features I had suggested to Paul as a substitute for the Kerry bill. It employed the presidential campaign financing model, with 3-for-1 matching public funds for a $100 or less contribution, with full public financing for the primary victors. I was not taken aback that it did not generate much enthusiasm among the incumbents.

In the meantime, the insider negotiations were concluded. The Senate Democratic leadership had been allowed to write the new Senate campaign finance rules and the House Democratic leadership had been allowed to write the new House campaign finance rules. It was unfortunate that Paul had not submitted his bill earlier or at least been ready to expound on Clean Money Campaign Reform because a few weeks before the debate was to begin he suddenly and unexpectedly found himself in a position where his criticisms would have had great credibility with the media. Because of his courageous stand on a related reform measure, Lobbyist Gift Disclosure, he became overnight the "White Knight of Political Reform" in the Senate. Backed by the new president, with bipartisan support in the Congress, legislation its sponsors dubbed the Lobbyist Disclosure Act had also reached the Senate floor in early May. The bill, a typically overly ballyhooed, watered-down "compromise," would have required lobbyists to disclose the names of their clients, the policies or laws on which they lobbied, and the total amount of money spent on each lobbying effort. One of its principal congressional backers trumpeted that at last the public would be able to see "how lobbying is done in the halls of Congress."

Alerted by Common Cause, the *New York Times* already had launched an editorial page campaign to expose the truth about the bill. An editorial on February 25, 1993 said the bill could more aptly be called the "Congressional Freebies Preservation Act" and accused President Clinton of talking "out of both sides of his mouth" on lobbying reform: "He has launched a verbal assault against 'high-priced lobbyists' while hastily backing the phony reform measure that would perpetuate their undue influence." In truth, the editorial asserted, "The bill's sanitized disclosure rules require revelation by lobbyists of their total expenditures but omit a much more telling member-by-member listing of the expensive meals, vacations, plane rides and other goodies lobbyists dole out in a form of legalized bribery." [5]

Common Cause had sought to add a provision to the bill whereby lobbyists would also be required to report their gifts to individual senators. Specifically, the lobbyists would have to report any gifts exceeding $20—cash, valuables, trips, meals, or anything else—that they gave to senators or staffers. First, Common Cause had approached members of the Senate Governmental Affairs subcommittee that handles such reform to introduce the amendment, but were turned down. Paul then agreed to be the sponsor.

This was not a move likely to endear Paul to his colleagues. Those who would be most embarrassed by public knowledge of the gifts were the senators, not the lobbyists. The day before the lobby bill was to be considered, Paul announced at the Tuesday Democratic Caucus lunch that he would introduce the amendment. The reaction was quite hostile. But on the floor, there was no way the senators could vote against it and on May 5, it passed without objection. Senior senators who had crafted the Lobbyist Disclosure Act spoke against Paul's amendment. They argued that it would be better to ban inappropriate gifts than just to require their disclosure and noted that they were introducing an amendment calling on another committee to prepare such a rule for senators. What they failed to acknowledge was their fear that the passage of Paul's gift disclosure amendment made it much more likely that the Senate would move expeditiously to pass a ban on gifts altogether.

Paul's defiance of his Democratic colleagues was a courageous act; I was particularly impressed that he told the press about the angry response he had received in the caucus. To me, this was a much welcomed declaration of independence from Senate Majority Leader Mitchell. The next day the *New York Times* reported on its front page that "the Senate succumbed today to ethical bombardment by a Minnesota Democrat and voted to bare one of its most tightly held secrets: the size and worth of the gifts, free meals and other perks that are showered on its members by lobbyists. . . . The action guts the Senate's current gift rule, an ingeniously crafted clause that appears to force lawmakers to disclose gifts on their own, but in fact allows them to keep secret any and all perquisites that they can legally accept. . . . It was a startling and complete victory for the amendment's sponsor, a first-term Senator named Paul Wellstone. . . ."[6]

In a May 7, 1993, editorial headlined "The Wellspring of Lobby Reform," the *New York Times* also sang Paul's praise: "[H]is adherence to principle— and his willingness to confront colleagues on a serious ethics issue that is central to influence peddling in Congress—has now shamed the Senate into doing the right thing. . . . Minnesota has long been the wellspring of reform politics. Today the wellspring state has every right to be proud of its Mr. Wellstone."[7]

From that point forward, Paul was the media darling, the senator to interview when it came to ethical matters. It was as if he had been annointed by the *New York Times* as the conscience of the Senate. If his Clean Money campaign finance bill had been ready, he could have blown the whistle on the Clinton proposal and explained how his bill was an appropriate response to the fundamental problems of money and politics. And it would have exemplified the kind of opportunity for reform that should be seized more frequently, especially in the current political climate of citizen distrust and anger. It is not difficult to anticipate debates on timely issues. Given the usual vacuum of appropriate, as opposed to symbolic, congressional responses, it is likely that serious legislators, following their consciences on serious policy proposals and not fearing to speak out forcefully, can find important opportunities falling into their laps.

I hoped Paul would take advantage of the bully pulpit the *New York Times* had built for him to criticize the Clinton campaign finance proposal and to point the way to genuine campaign finance reform. I wrote an op-ed piece exposing the House Democratic leadership's campaign finance "reform" bill in the *Los Angeles Times* on May 23 and Ellen Miller, the director of the Center for Responsive Politics, wrote a similar critique of the Senate bill for the June 28 *Washington Post*.[8] And yet, I noted in my journal, there seemed to be almost a conspiracy of silence from others in Washington.

> There are *thousands* of people in Washington who know how bad this bill is. But they haven't let out a peep. What is really going on, of course, is just the normal workings of the Washington culture. Common Cause, LWV, Public Citizen, etc., all see this through the prism of Washington realism. It's the best bill you could hope to pass; the insider negotiations have tested the limits of reform and this mouse of a bill is the limit. . . . In the meantime, the local chapters of these groups and their members, who care about this issue and could be raising holy hell, have not been mobilized, or if they have, it is in support of the bill. The problem here is there is no appealing alternative on the table in Washington that they could mobilize behind.

Along with John Bonifaz at the Center for Responsive Politics, I resolved to get the attention of the national media with a blockbuster press conference at the Capitol as the Senate campaign finance reform debate began, featuring Paul Wellstone, Ralph Nader, Jerry Brown, and Ellen Miller blasting the Clinton bill. Former California Governor Jerry Brown, who had captured the public's imagination by funding his 1992 presidential campaign with an 800 number and no larger than $100 contributions, said he would be pleased to participate and he flew out to Washington. Ellen Miller said she would come, too, but only if we could get Wellstone and Nader. Nader couldn't make it, and under those circumstances Paul preferred to make his statements on the floor of the Senate.

There was one amusing incident in this otherwise sad story. The Senate Republicans had decided to filibuster the Democratic bill; they believed its campaign spending limits would favor Democrats and many were opposed to any public funding. The floor leader of that opposition effort was the arch-conservative from Kentucky, Mitch McConnell, with whom I rarely agree on anything. When I tuned in on CSPAN at the beginning of the campaign finance reform floor debate on Monday, May 24, McConnell was making his opening remarks. To my surprise, he pointed to a "fascinating article" that had appeared the day before in the Sunday *Los Angeles Times* and quoted it at length about what a perverse product the White House/

House leadership negotiations had produced and how perfectly it fit incumbent fundraising practices and perpetuated incumbent fundraising advantage. He then asked that my entire article be printed at that point in the *Congressional Record*.[9]

As fate would have it, the next scheduled speaker was Paul Wellstone. He said he had some news for McConnell that might surprise him. The author of the *Los Angeles Times* piece was a close friend of his. And while I might agree with McConnell's negative appraisal of the Clinton bill, he said, I surely did not agree with his approach to campaign finance reform. McConnell was somewhat taken aback as Paul launched into his critique of the present system of financing campaigns. Paul did not say, however, that he would oppose the Clinton bill. The reason, he told me later, was that he agreed with McConnell that it was a phony bill, a diversion which for that very reason deserved to be exposed and defeated.

The next day, Paul introduced two amendments. One reduced from $250,000 to $25,000 the amount of their own money Senate candidates could spend on their campaigns and still qualify for public funding. That passed handily, 88–9. The other amendment limited contributions from any individual to no more than $100 per election cycle. In effect, it would have turned the Kerry/Bradley/Biden bill into the $100 Solution. Paul made an outstanding speech on the Senate floor, noting that unless the contribution limit were drastically downsized as he proposed, individual and bundled $1,000 contributions would leave senators just as dependent as before on big money contributors. Confident, however, that with no grassroots attention their vote would go unnoticed, his colleagues overwhelmingly defeated the amendment, 84–13.

The Senate debate/filibuster went on for more than three weeks. The Kerry bill, which had derailed the public interest groups, went down with hardly a wimper and on June 16 the entire debacle ended with the Democrats succumbing to the Republican filibuster and agreeing to remove virtually all the public financing from the Clinton/Democratic leadership bill. The following day, the Senate passed S.3, 60–38, and Paul voted with the majority.

The next week, Paul visited me in San Diego, where he had been invited to speak at a rally organized by the Neighbor-to-Neighbor organization in support of the single-payer approach to health care reform. He explained that he had voted for S.3 because Michigan's Senator Carl Levin had convinced him that the lowered voluntary spending limits in the Senate bill could be a significant advance in leveling the financial playing field for Senate challengers. He agreed the bill would not much alter our politics, but thought it was an improvement.

Clean Money Campaign Reform

After this failed attempt in 1993–94 to get big private money out of politics, I became convinced that the Clean Money approach has decisive advantages, both in substance and strategy, over the $100 Solution and other presidential campaign financing variants. With Clean Money, a sharp, clear line is drawn: Candidates who pass a test of sufficient public support and agree to limit spending, shorten their campaigns, and accept no private money will receive full public financing for their primary and general elections.

In contrast, attempts to get the big money out of politics by drawing the line at a $100 contribution limit, such as in the "$100 Solution For Good Government," opens the discussion to whether a *higher* limit might be more appropriate. Recall how that $100 Solution became a $1000 Solution when the incumbents got their hands on the National Campaign Finance Reform Coalition's proposal. Given the opportunity, they raised the contribution limits to let enough private money in to preserve incumbents' financial advantage over most challengers and thereby compromised the resulting system with big money lawmaker-lobbying coalition links.

I believe that experience provides a crucial insight. The Clean Money approach, with its sharp, clean limits on private contributions in primary and general election campaigns provides the best chance of weaning members of congress from their financial dependence on special interest lobbying coalitions. Meanwhile, throughout the debate in the 103rd Congress over S.3 and its variants, the Working Group on Electoral Democracy had continued to hammer out an alternative proposal, a process we continued after the vote in Congress. We had not yet introduced the Clean Money proposal into the congressional debate, a decision we had made back in 1992 that committed us to a different strategy.

In October 1992, a conference call to plan future strategy took place involving Ben Senturia, Randy Kehler, Marty Jezer, John Bonifaz, Janice Fine in Massachusetts, Pete McDowell in North Carolina, and me. Our first priority at that point was to complete a detailed document laying out all the provisions of a model Clean Money bill. The immediate question, however, was whether the working group would seek congressional sponsors during the 1993–94 debate, or perhaps emulate Public Citizen, becoming a part of the Washington negotiations with other public interest groups to arrive at a compromise proposal for the Clinton bill. The consensus answer to both questions was a decisive no. The notion that kept coming up in that conversation was that in order to achieve real reform, we needed to introduce into the public discourse an "outside-the-Beltway standard" against which the other "inside-the-Beltway" proposals would be measured.

At one point in that conversation, Randy and Ben agreed that above all else, our effort had to learn from the Nuclear Weapons Freeze Campaign and avoid "the Freeze Trap." Randy had been the national director of the Freeze Campaign, Ben had been one of the lead organizers at its national office in St. Louis, and I was the director of the Minnesota campaign. An organizing strategy drawn up in Boston in 1979–80 had a five-year plan for building a nationwide community-based movement against continuing the buildup of nuclear arms. The centerpiece of the strategy was an effort to gather millions of signatures in support of the proposal we had laid out in a short document, *A Call To Halt the Arms Race,* and the decision not to take the proposal to Washington until a grassroots base of such magnitude had been created that it would have to be taken seriously.

However, well before the Freeze campaign had reached the size and strength the five-year organizing plan envisioned, well-intentioned members of Congress decided to introduce a resolution of support in both the Senate and the House. Before the Freeze leaders knew it, the focus of the national debate had become the wording of a congressional Freeze resolution, moving the action from local community organizers to a few members of Congress and their aides in Washington. And to make matters worse, a congressional resolution has no teeth; even in the unlikely event that a strong resolution passed, it would have been a symbolic victory with no binding effect.

Those who fashioned the Clean Money Campaign Reform proposal were determined not to let this effort suffer that fate. They vowed to focus on creating an organizing document to go with the bill and taking it to the people state-by-state, not to Washington. Implicit in this decision was the strong hunch that, unhappily, the incumbents in Washington would not produce meaningful campaign finance reform in 1993–94.

In March 1993, the Working Group on Electoral Democracy published a pair of handsome documents, *A Proposal For Democratically Financed Elections,* consisting of the model bill Ben, Marty, Randy, and I had prepared, and *A Call for Democratically Financed Elections,* which included a summary of the bill and an eloquent statement of its rationale.[10] Around the same time, the intellectual foundation for a reform movement was laid in several articles in scholarly journals and the popular press. An issue of the *Yale Law and Policy Review* was partially devoted to this topic, including two articles (one by Marty, Randy, and Ben and the other by Jamie Raskin and John Bonifaz), and Marty and Ellen published a third article in the *Notre Dame Journal of Law, Ethics, and Public Policy.*[11] One hub of the grassroots campaign was *The Buckstopper* that Ben Senturia began publishing in St. Louis in 1995, reporting on Clean Money efforts underway in many states. Particularly important were the Money and Politics Projects of the Northeast Citizen Action Resource Center with efforts in five New England states, most notably the one in Maine which became the flagship campaign whose success would spark a nationwide movement.

Irresistible Reforms versus Immovable Incumbents

14

Paul's Victory

The Democrats had pledged before the 1992 elections that if they gained control of both the Congress and the White House, they would make political reform a centerpiece of their program. Given the anger in the electorate, it was very difficult for members of Congress to vote against disclosure of gifts they received from lobbyists and their clients, against banning or severely restricting such gifts, and against potentially much more significant measures to reform the way political campaigns are financed. If the Congress were transparent so the public could see what was happening, it might have been easy. But it is anything but transparent and behind the scenes maneuvering led to fierce, protracted struggles on every political reform front.

Paul Wellstone's successful championing of the strictest version of the Lobbyist Disclosure Act led to his becoming a major player in the two-year struggle that followed to pass a law banning all gifts from lobbyists. But just as incumbent legislators proved fiercely protective of their customary practices for financing campaigns, they were equally protective of their lavish, lobbyist-subsidized life styles.

In his 1992 book *The Lobbyists,* reporter Jeffrey Birnbaum noted: "Lawmakers' workdays are filled with meetings with lobbyists, many of whom represent giant corporations. And their weekends are stocked with similar encounters. When lawmakers travel to give speeches, they rarely address groups of poor people. The big-money lobbies often pick up the tab, and their representatives fill the audiences, ask the questions, and occupy the luncheon tables and throng the cocktail parties that accompany such events.

'That's the bigger issue,' contends one congressional aide. 'Who do these guys hang out with? Rich people. If you spend your time with millionaires, you begin to think like them.'" [1]

If you're a member of Congress, lobbyists and corporate executives invite you to dine at Washington's finest restaurants, enjoy the best seats at Kennedy Center performances, join them in their plush boxes at Redskin games, and bring your spouse along on fun-filled "charity" or "fact-finding" excursions to America's fanciest ski, golf, and tennis resorts. These latter junkets had long been disclosed in each member's annual financial statement, but it took investigative television reporting and some celebrated exposés by *20–20* and *60 Minutes* to arouse public outrage. Perhaps the most striking lesson of the gift ban story is how deeply attached many of our public servants have become to the emoluments showered on them by lobbyists, as evidenced in 1993 and 1994 by their remarkably strong reluctance to give them up.

In early May 1994, a bill banning all gifts from lobbyists finally reached the Senate floor. In the extended debate that ensued—recorded in well over a hundred pages in the tiny type of the *Congressional Record*—the principled objections of many senators become almost comically indistinguishable from a frantic effort to protect their lavishly subsidized leisure time.

> MR. [BENNETT] JOHNSTON: My wife is a cochairman of the National Garden Ball. . . . But . . . I would not be able to go to that ball, and indeed she would not be able to go either. . . . Would we be able to go to the Opera Ball? . . . Most of the money comes from lobbyists or companies that are represented by lobbyists. . . . My wife has been chairman of the Ambassadors Ball . . . as have other wives in the Senate. . . . It is paid for indirectly by lobbyists. This bill prohibits gifts provided directly or indirectly by a person registered as a lobbyist. . . .
>
> MR. [PAUL] WELLSTONE: If you were to ask me about the opera, I would say you can go to any opera you want to; you pay for it. Just like regular people pay for it when they go to the opera. It is that simple.
>
> MR. JOHNSTON: This is going to make it much more difficult to do our job as U.S. Senators because we ought to meet with . . . people. Lunches and dinners are the right time to meet with people.
>
> MR. [RUSS] FEINGOLD [WISCONSIN]: I am concerned, as the Senator is, that this bill, however it ends up, does not prevent us from being able to meet with our constituents either here or back in our home states. . . . But there are at least three ways that it is possible for me, even with a rule like this, to have met with them. One is not to have them in connection with a meal. The second is not to eat, not to have lunch. And the third is to pay your own way.

MR. JOHNSTON: For this, bring a brown bag.

MR. FEINGOLD: That is right. . . .

MR. JOHNSTON: It would sure make it a lot more expensive to do things that are ordinary parts of being a Senator as far as I am concerned.[2]

On the subject of subsidized vacation trips, Bennett Johnston took another tack, suggesting that disclosure was as powerful a prohibition as an outright ban:

MR. JOHNSTON: Let us say the tobacco industry goes to wherever you want to go to and they have fun and they do not do any serious work, we will say that is a bad trip. . . . Do you think any Senator is going to go to that sort of thing now, and that [disclosure] is not sufficient protection, rather than trying to get in and, by the sledgehammer when you get that gnat then you have hit the symphony ball and the National Guard dance and all of these other really good charities? . . .

MR. [CARL] LEVIN [MICHIGAN]: Senator [Johnston's] point is, well, why not just disclose that kind of trip? . . . First of all, those trips already are disclosed. Disclosure has not prevented this institution from being held up to public scorn. . . . The problem is that that kind of a trip, where it is paid for by special interests, where lobbyists are present and where, . . . although there may be some work going on in the morning, it is principally recreational, holds the institution up to disrepute and . . . undermines public confidence . . . when that kind of a trip has a broad display in the media.[3]

All this is prologue to a revealing story of how lobbyist gift ban/disclosure legislation that most members of Congress would have great difficulty opposing in public took two years to pass. One aspect of that story particularly attracted my attention. Despite the relative transparency of comments like Bennett Johnston's, most members of Congress would have had great difficulty exposing in public (that is, beyond the pages of the *Congressional Record*) sentiments so blatantly self-serving and defensive. Yet two years would elapse before gift-ban legislation came to a vote, and it finally did so through two notable collaborations involving citizen organizations working with sympathetic lawmakers, each in very different ways aided by particular mass media that reached their core constituencies. One of these collaborations pursued a liberal agenda, the other a conservative one. In each case, the media element attempted to ride herd on the congressional process, mobilizing people of their respective ideological persuasions and using the implicit threat of exposure to influence individual members' actions.

One collaboration included Common Cause, Paul Wellstone, a few other

Senate and House liberals, and the *New York Times* as their citizen mobilizer and media voice. The other included the Christian right, Newt Gingrich, other leading House and Senate conservatives, and talk radio. Throughout 1993 and nearly to the end of 1994, the liberal collaboration held sway. However, as the 103rd Congress drew to a close, the conservative collaboration mounted a swift and effective counterattack.

The day after Paul's lobbyist gift disclosure amendment passed the Senate on May 4, 1993, the senators voted 98–1 for a non-binding "sense of the Senate" resolution sponsored by New Jersey's Sen. Frank Lautenberg saying it intended to enact gift-ban legislation by the end of the year. But by late fall, it was clear that no such legislation was in the offing, so Lautenberg and Wellstone, in consultation with Common Cause, began formulating a gift-ban bill of their own to introduce early the next year.

From the beginning, the *New York Times* was in very close touch with both Paul's office and Common Cause. Staying on top of day-to-day developments and launching a concerted campaign in favor of the lobbyist gift legislation.

For the two years of this debate, *New York Times* editorials alerted readers to what was happening behind the scenes and repeatedly prodded key congressional figures. Those who followed their editorial pages received the kind of detailed intelligence, advance warning, and opportunity alerts on this issue that lobbyists normally provide their clients. According to one lobbyist from Common Cause, the *Times* "did something that newspapers used to do fairly regularly, but television never does; they campaigned for an editorial position."[4]

Near the end of May, in fact, the *Times* extended its campaign to include the House of Representatives.

> Just days after Mr. Wellstone made his brave stand [on the gift ban bill], about 40 House members and their spouses boarded a train for New York City accompanied by lobbyists who paid part of the cost of a four-day fun and fact-finding trip. . . . Such trips are a traditional luxury that legislators just adore. The cost, often involving air travel and tropical resorts, can run into the thousands. The lobbyists . . . are buying access and influence over legislation. But the currently spotty rules often spare members and lobbyists from letting the voters know what they're up to. The public good is now at the mercy of the House leadership. . . . The Democratic chairman of the House Judiciary subcommittee, . . . John Bryant of Texas[,] is strongly opposed to the Wellstone amendment. As leader of the Democrats, [House Speaker] Foley needs to lean on Mr. Bryant to accept the Wellstone language.[5]

In late May, first-term Democratic representatives Karen Shepherd of Utah and Eric Fingerhut of Ohio, working with Common Cause and in close touch with Paul's office, introduced a gift-ban bill in the House. It was eventually folded into a larger bill sponsored by John Bryant of Texas and referred to a Judiciary subcommittee he chaired. In late October the subcommittee seemed to be nearing completion of the bill, but an October 26 *New York Times* editorial, headlined "The Golf and Tennis Caucus Gets Busy" sounded a warning: "Amid compaints from senior Democrats and Republicans, many of whom balked at the idea of having to give up their lobbyist subsidized lifestyles, the subcommittee meeting was suddenly canceled. Speaker Thomas Foley . . . pounced on the dissatisfaction to appoint a committee of Democratic and Republican leaders "to study the issue". . . . The maneuvering has the worrisome feel of an insider cabal to preserve a disreputable status quo."[6] The *Times* quoted Minority Leader Newt Gingrich as saying, in words later echoed by Foley, "I don't see any reason to change . . . [rules that are] honest and reasonable to any fair person."

As the 1993 congressional session neared its close, the *New York Times* kept up its attempt to ride herd on the House collecting intelligence from Common Cause and congressional offices and keeping the pressure on recalcitrant legislative leaders.

> It appears House Speaker Thomas Foley is getting ready to pull a fast one. He's floating a pernicious halfway proposal that would exempt all meals from the new gift limit and allow members to accept free airline tickets and resort vacations from lobbyists, as long as they were disclosed. . . . Mr. Foley may be emboldened to try to push through his phony gift fix in the rush to recess and claim a "reform" victory. . . . He abruptly grabbed the gift issue from Mr. Bryant and handed it to a special new committee of House elders. It's time Mr. Bryant took it back. A lawmaker rarely gets a moment when he or she can turn the tide on an important issue. But Mr. Bryant has such a moment. By calling an immediate meeting of his subcommittee to report out a strict gift ban, he will make it awkward for Mr. Foley and his gift claque to waylay a gift ban. . . . [7]

Three days later, the *Times* reported an impasse in Speaker Foley's bipartisan committee of elders and warned against provisions that would make the reform a "fraud":

> Any measure that emerges from the tense back-room talks will be touted as big "reform." But Americans are well advised to hold their applause until they can read the fine print. Mr. Bryant, for example, favors a $20 limit on the gifts

members may receive from lobbyists—including meals. That sounds terrific. But a loosely worded exemption for "personal friends," including friendly lobbyists, could make the meal restrictions a fraud. Likewise, it would hardly be a triumph for ethics if the House stopped members from taking steak dinners from lobbyists while in Washington, but continued to permit peripatetic members like Ways and Means chairman Dan Rostenkowski to fly gratis to charitable golf tournaments sponsored by interest groups.[8]

When the House finally passed a gift-ban bill on March 24, 1994, they approved legislation that was strong on lobbyist gifts but otherwise full of holes. While no gifts or meals from *registered* lobbyists would be permitted, anyone else could continue to give legislators an unlimited number of gifts of $100 or less. Travel for speeches, fact-finding trips, or other events for legislators, their spouses, and family members, though off-limits for lobbyists, could still be paid by other employees of the lobbyists' corporation. The trips would have to be disclosed, but not their costs, and their purposes were not monitored closely enough to rule out largely recreational junkets. Lobbyists who were personal friends of a legislator could give gifts, with no disclosure required.

Earlier that month, on March 3, 1994, the Lautenberg-Wellstone "Lobbyist Gift Ban/Disclosure Amendment" was announced in the Senate. It went beyond the House bill, extending the ban on meals and entertainment to those from lobbyists and their clients. It banned reimbursements to lawmakers for trips that were substantially recreational, with no reimbursement for family members. And while other trips could be reimbursed by lobbyists, they would have to be disclosed in advance in the *Congressional Record,* not simply after-the-fact in the Senator's financial statement. Lobbyists could give gifts to a legislator "motivated by personal friendship," but they would have to be disclosed and they could not be reimbursed or paid for by a third party.

Initially, Wellstone and Lautenberg intended to attach their amendment to a bill early in the session. But, as I learned from Paul in mid-March, that plan hit a snag. Majority Leader George Mitchell was pressing them to hold off until the Government Affairs subcommittee chaired by Sen. Carl Levin of Michigan could come up with a compromise bill that would avoid a public fight among Democrats. Mitchell had a carrot and a stick. The carrot was his promise to Wellstone and Lautenberg that the Levin bill would come to the Senate floor by May 4, at which time they could have vote on their amendment if they were not satisfied with the Levin substitute. The stick was a parliamentary maneuver that Mitchell could pull to render an earlier effort by Wellstone and Lautenberg to introduce their amendment "non-germane" and hence purely symbolic. Paul had great respect for Levin and that gave him confidence that the outcome would be favorable. As it turned out, the Levin-Cohen bill the committee produced did follow the Wellstone-Lautenberg approach and it was every bit as strong.

The Senate debated the Levin-Cohen bill in early May. Bennett Johnston and Mitch McConnell of Kentucky tried to water down its provisions with an amendment that would have allowed an unlimited number of gifts worth $75 or less to members or staff from any source, including lobbyists and their clients. It would also have permitted lobbyists and their clients to continue to foot the bill for travel, lodging, and other expenses for legislators and their spouses at vacation resorts. The principal "reforms" in the McConnell-Johnston substitute were a lowering of the unlimited gift threshold from $100 to $75 and requiring members and spouses to pay for their own recreational activities at the resorts, such as greens fees, ski-lift tickets, and tennis court time.

That amendment would have gutted the bill, and it almost passed. The official vote tally was 39 for and 59 against, but those on the scene reported a scramble by several senators to change their vote *from aye to nay* at the very end, after it became clear that the amendment would fail. Only four of the twenty-six senators running for reelection in 1994 voted to gut the reform, but others would have been willing to risk voting for the amendment in order to keep their perks. In fact, I believe that the amendment would have passed if it were not for the watchful eye of the *New York Times* ready to expose and castigate the senators who voted in the majority if the amendment had succeeded.

On May 11, 1994, the Gift Ban bill did pass and by an overwhelming margin, 95–4. Bennett Johnston, Mitch McConnell, and many others who had voted for the gutting amendment all joined in voting aye; they could say they had supported lobbying reform. The next day, the lead editorial in Minnesota's largest circulation newspaper, the *Minneapolis Star-Tribune* was headlined "Paul's Victory": "When he was elected in 1990, Wellstone promised to rid Congress of its special-interest taint. Wednesday, he delivered—and did Minnesota proud. . . . Politicians who choose a different path—who come to office as reformers and wind up being part of the problem—won't experience the satisfaction that is Wellstone's today. He delivered on a campaign promise; he shaped a major piece of legislation; and he won respect the hard and lasting way, by challenging his colleagues to live by a higher standard."[9]

It was not till September 22, 1994, as the 103rd Congress neared adjournment, that the Senate and House Democratic leaders finally reached an agreement that reconciled both the *House* and *Senate* bills. The *Minneapolis Star-Tribune* captured Paul's eager anticipation of a long-awaited triumph, reporting that he "predicted that there will be no stopping the lobbying reform legislation, which he said marks the pinnacle of his achievements during nearly four years in the Senate. 'This is the biggest and most important thing I have worked on here,' he said." But as it turned out, Paul's prediction was premature. By September, Republicans in both houses of Congress were sensing the possibility of an historic turnaround in the 1994 elections. It had been forty years since they had had control of the House, and the strategy they chose was to deny the Democrats any significant victories. They figured rightly that they would not be blamed for obstructing the gift ban because Democrats were in control of the Congress and the White House. And they certainly did not want the Democrats to be able to claim credit for a political reform that would be popular with an angry electorate. At the last moment, they devised a clever, if questionable, ploy.

One part of the Lobbying Disclosure Act involved the registration of professional lobbyists, which included disclosure of information about both them and their clients. It is well-known that there are tens of thousands of professional lobbyists active in Washington; one frequently cited estimate is on the order of forty thousand. But the lobbyist registration law was so full of loopholes that only about eight thousand were registered. An important goal of this Act was to close all those loopholes and require all professional lobbyists to register.

In recent years, a deceptive new kind of Washington-based lobbying firm has come into widespread use. Known in the trade as "grassroots lobbyists," or practitioners of "astroturf lobbying," these firms simulate spontaneous citizen concern about an issue. For a hefty price, they will produce any number of constituent phone calls and letters to any member of Congress on any specified issue. The price is hefty; as high as $100 per constituent phone call generated.

The Lobbyist Disclosure Act sought to make sure those firms and their lobbyists registered and that they disclosed their clients. There was no intent to register local citizens involved in *real* grassroots lobbying. But this was the opportunity the Republican strategists seized upon to launch a counteroffensive against the Lobbying Disclosure Act. Some of the problems they claimed to find in the act were patently erroneous; for example, no one would have construed the rules as requiring registration for any citizen who called a member of Congress or traveled to Washington to testify on an issue. And certainly religious organizations, journalists, talk show hosts, and people who phone in to talk shows would not be required to register as lobbyists. But one claim turned out to be justified, the likelihood that legitimate grassroots groups engaged in local political activity that involves contacting their congressperson may have to disclose their contributor and membership lists.

On September 28, the day before the House was scheduled to take up what was now the Levin-Bryant bill, Newt Gingrich denounced it as "a grassroots gag rule," aimed at stifling local efforts of the Christian Coalition and of the so-called religious right, whose views on abortion, gun control, taxes, and other issues were unpopular with the Democratic majority. On very short notice, those grassroots networks had been set into action, with fax machines, computer bulletin boards, and telephone trees getting the word out and generating large numbers of constituent phone calls to congressional offices. One Minnesota congressman reported receiving close to one-hundred calls that day and became convinced that the bill would have a devastating effect on genuine grassroots lobbying and infringe on First Amendment rights. As it turned out, the opposition did not have quite enough time to sink the bill in the *House,* but the Senate debate was not scheduled to begin until October 5, when the real fight was expected. And there the Republicans had a weapon that had worked so well for us in opposing Bennett Johnston's energy strategy bill—the filibuster.

The bill did not reach the Senate floor until a week later, the evening of October 5. That gave the opposition time to mobilize its troops nationwide, with its own very effective mass communications. Rush Limbaugh, in the meantime, was focusing the attention of his three million or so listeners on this bill. Other conservative talk show hosts such as Pat Robertson and Michael Reagan followed suit. Senate offices were deluged with phone calls.[10] Paul's senior policy advisor, Colin McGinnis, described how it felt to be on the receiving end:

> We were caught unawares because for eighteen months we had heard almost nothing from groups that have registered lobbyists in Washington. . . . I think they made the practical political judgment early on that this was a train they weren't going to stand in front of.
>
> In the last ten days you had Gingrich who identified a couple of provisions of the bill that he could mischaracterize and distort. . . . Within two days, he and the other Republican House leadership had sent out hundreds of faxes to all the conservative talk show hosts, the Christian Coalition, and other

conservative groups, with all kinds of wild distortions, saying things like if you are a regular citizen and you call your Member of Congress and urge them to vote a certain way, you will have to register as a lobbyist. Which was utterly preposterous. We began to hear about this stuff on talk radio. We began to get lots of phone calls about it.[11]

When I commented on the ironic parallel between this effort and the success of the *New York Times* in mobilizing public concern, McGinnis answered, with obvious frustration, "And along comes this new media and completely overwhelms us."

To make matters worse, the American Civil Liberties Union agreed that the proposed bill's language would indeed lead to local groups' having to disclose membership and contribution lists, in violation of a landmark 1958 Supreme Court decision protecting the identities of members and supporters of southern Civil Rights groups. The ACLU sent a letter to all senators urging them to reject the bill.

In response, Senators Levin and Cohen offered to delete the grassroots lobbying provisions altogether. At that point, the true motives of the Republicans became obvious. They blocked the move, claiming they had other objections to the bill as well. In anticipation of the Senate debate, Paul had set up a lectern beside his desk on the Senate floor. But as the clerk called the role, it became apparent he would not get the 60 votes needed to defeat the filibuster.

Recall that where we had left off in 1994, with passage in the House but filibuster in the Senate, was legislation that would have completely banned gifts from registered lobbyists and their clients (except for legislators' "friends"), including "substantially recreational" trips. That would have shut down most of the free meals, the free tickets to plays, concerts, operas, and balls, and the most blatant of the free trips to vacation resorts. However, when the 104th Congress convened in 1995, the Republicans were the majority party. Early in the session, the bill that had died the year before had been reintroduced by Paul in the Senate and John Bryant in the House. But soon the senators who had led the fight for a gift ban the year before, Levin, Feingold and Wellstone, decided on two changes in strategy. The first change was to separate the lobbyist registration part, on which there was general agreement except for the grassroots lobbying provisions, from the gift ban part, on which there was considerable controversy. The second was to have the Senate and the House decide separately on their own rules about gifts to their members.

In mid-1995 those issues reached the Senate floor. On July 24, the Senate passed comprehensive lobbyist registration legislation identical to the previous year's bill, with the controversial grassroots lobbying provisions removed. But in a July 22 editorial, the *New York Times* warned of Republican mischief to gut the gift ban: "Senate Republican leaders have chosen an odd way to convince Americans they understand their disgust with Washington. They are preparing to kill a strong gift-ban measure. . . . Cynically, and with the consent of Bob Dole, the Senate Majority leader, they plan to substitute a more permissive measure designed by the G.O.P.'s crafty nemesis of political reform, Senator Mitch McConnell of Kentucky, that would perpetuate much of the old system under the guise of 'reform.'"[12] McConnell proposed a substitute for the Levin/Wellstone/Feingold gift-ban rule that would have allowed an unlimited number of gifts up to $100, prompting Senator Feingold to term it the "all you can eat" bill. It would have perpetuated the pattern of free meals and entertainment from lobbyists and their clients night after night.

At that point, Republican Sen. John McCain of Arizona enlisted the support of several of the newly elected Republican senators behind a compromise modification of the Democratic proposal. It would have established a $50 overall annual limit on gifts from any single source, with gifts of less than $20 not counting toward that limit. Under this formulation, lobbyists and their clients *would* be allowed to give gifts to legislators. However, lobbyists would not be allowed to pay for "substantially recreational" trips or contribute to a senator's legal defense fund.

Then Mississippi's Senator Trent Lott, the Republican Majority Whip, proposed an amendment to increase the annual limit on gifts from a single source to $100, with gifts of $50 or less not counting toward that limit. It would open the door for lobbyists and their clients to wine and dine and provide free entertainment to their favorite senators on a regular basis, and it passed. The *Washington Post* later noted that if that provision had been left unchanged, Washington-area restaurants "could have done a booming business in $49.99 Lobbyist Blue Plate Specials."[13]

Paul then proposed another amendment that pretty much nipped Lott in the bud. It accepted the $100 overall annual limit but said that only gifts of $10 or less would not count toward it. With this amendment, any lobbyist could buy a senator no more than $100 in *substantial* meals and entertainment each year. Paul's amendment also passed. It would cramp the style of individual lobbyists in seeking the favors of particular senators, and it was a significant accomplishment. With thousands of lobbyists in the vicinity, the senators would continue to sup at the lobbyist trough, though if they had a big appetite for that life style they would have to satisfy it with many different lobbyists.

Of course, the gifts to "friends" provision left a gaping loophole, as did the legality of privately funded "fact-finding" missions. Paul, Carl Levin, Russ Feingold, and their allies at Common Cause, Public Citizen, the *New York Times,* the *Washington Post,* and other major newspapers had done all they could to embarrass the Senate into doing the right thing, but a majority of their colleagues were so wedded to a lobbyist-subsidized life style that they seemed beyond embarrassment. At the end of a news conference Levin put his arm around Paul and said, "If I had to pick one thing, it would be the insistence, the persistence, the energy and the passion of Paul Wellstone . . . that brought us to this success that we've achieved." [14]

In the House of Representatives, leadership on this issue came from freshman Republicans who had been elected in 1994 with pledges to clean up Congress. They took a position banning *all* gifts to legislators from anyone except relatives and friends. In the end, Speaker Gingrich was embarrassed into sponsoring the measure himself, although he was privately said to favor a weak alternative measure allowing gifts and charity event trips but requiring full disclosure of all gifts greater than $50.

On November 17, 1995, proposals were scheduled for a vote, with the weak alternative up first. As the roll call proceeded, a majority of Republicans supported it, but near the end, as it became clear that the measure would fail, a stampede of Republicans switched their votes so they would be recorded as opposed, and it was defeated by a 276–154 margin. The complete ban on gifts and charity trips for House members then passed by a 422–6 vote. Almost no one had wanted to go on record against it.

Common Cause and Paul Wellstone deserved particular credit for making the gift ban an issue and diligently pursuing it so that both the Senate and the House *had* to take it up.

Incumbents' Obstruction

In contrast to the gift ban story, the congressional campaign finance reform story ended with a whimper (S.3), not a bang. To paraphrase a comment Sen. John Glenn of Ohio made on the Senate floor during the gift ban debate, even if lobbyist gifts were completely banned and legislators had to refuse a meal or a football ticket from a lobbyist, they still could turn right around and accept a $5,000 PAC contribution from that same person, or a $1,000 personal contribution, and that would be absolutely legal.

In what I have told of the campaign finance reform story so far, I have made no secret of the fact that I was very disappointed with Common Cause's stance on that issue. After the debate was over, I had a lengthy conversation with Jay Hedlund, that organization's lead lobbyist on campaign finance reform. He had a Washington insider's perspective on these matters.

He praised the Senate campaign finance reform outcome in 1993. He was particularly proud of the relatively low voluntary limits on overall spending by Senate candidates. He also stressed the new restrictions on soft money, the reduction to $5,000 in the amount a PAC could give to a Senate candidate, and the cap on PAC contributions to 20 percent of a Senate candidate's total contributions.

Hedlund's major disappointments had to do with the weak restrictions on the bundling of individual contributions and especially the last-minute slashing of the already embarrassingly modest public financing in the bill, with reduced television advertising rates substituted as a sharply weakened inducement for candidates to accept the voluntary spending limits. Common Cause's acceptance of that modification of the bill led many of the most prominent public interest groups to quit the coalition. But Common Cause continued to support the Democratic Leadership positions. Hedlund explained his perspective this way:

> No one's ever claimed this solved all the problems of campaign finance. . . .
> We never claim that. If you can do that, great, but our game is about trying to
> improve the present condition. . . . We would have liked to see more public
> resources; a number of nervous groups jumped ship at that point. It wasn't a
> choice of settling for less public money; it was a choice of trying to get as much
> public resources as we could. . . . The Senate bill was a breakthrough bill. It
> gave the Paul Wellstone's of the world or, more importantly it said to potential
> opponents of those four Senate incumbents who ran without opposition [in
> 1994], the first time ever in the Senate, "you can compete." . . . They're not
> going to be able to spend six or eight million dollars against you."
>
> What you ended up with was a Senate bill and a Senate leadership that
> wanted to do the right thing. . . . And the House kept fighting to keep the
> status quo." [15]

In contrast with what happened in the Senate, Common Cause was not at all happy with what happened in the House. Neither the House Democratic leadership nor most of newly elected Democrats in 1992 were anxious to see dramatic changes in the incumbent-favoring campaign finance rules. Hedlund offered a couple of examples of the House Democratic leadership stance: "Mitchell, Foley and Gephardt met with the President early on and Foley and Gephardt said we're not going to do that; we're not going to cut PACs. . . . The president just removed himself. Foley told him no and Clinton said okay. . . . They had also met earlier with the freshmen in December. They did a series of meetings around the country and essentially said to them, 'If you guys want to get along here, if you want any good committee assignments, then you follow us.'"

The stance of the House Democratic freshmen had surprised Common Cause. Prior to the November 1992 elections, Common Cause chapters nationwide had made a concerted effort to get candidates to pledge to support public funding and plugging the soft-money loophole. A majority of the House had *signed* a very specific pledge. But when they got to Washington, their position changed. Hedlund recalled one particularly disillusioning experience with the freshman Democrats at a caucus in early 1993. One newly elected congressman from Ohio stood up and said, "'My signature there isn't worth the paper it's written on.' . . . A lot of the freshmen liked that." A few freshman representatives, including Karen Shepherd and Eric Fingerhut, did stand their ground, but, Hedlund concluded sadly, by and large "they came in pretty much to be incumbents. That was a real loss."

What were the major factors in the failure of the Democratic controlled Congress to pass campaign finance reform legislation after placing so much stress on it as a major issue in the 1992 election? In Hedlund's view, the House Democratic incumbents were largely responsible: "In the '88, '90, '92 and even the '94 elections," he said, "more than 75 percent of House incumbents ran 'financially unopposed,' with at least twice the resources of their opposition. In more than half those cases, the opponent had less than $25,000. The average figure was something on the order of $680,000 to $30,000. One of the reasons the Democrats in the House were thrown out is they've forgotten how to compete. So they got fat and lazy and they didn't know how to go out and turn on folks."

Common Cause President Fred Wertheimer had been concerned from the time it looked like Bill Clinton would be elected that it would be crucial to push for immediate action on campaign finance reform. He reminded everyone he spoke with that back in 1977, Jimmy Carter had delayed and the Senate killed it with a filibuster. Jay Hedlund recalled, "Fred started saying in October, 1992 to anyone involved in the issue, 'you've got to move quickly. Delay plays into the hands of killing it.'"

But delay is what they got from the House Democratic leadership, who did not care that the President had committed himself during his campaign, and now that the Democrats controlled both the White House and the Congress, the public would hold them accountable: "In February 1993, Fred [Wertheimer] had a conversation with a staff person to a high-ranking House Democratic leader. He asked, 'How can you dig in your heels about PACs? Your President is talking about cutting the PAC contribution limit. You don't use your position to embarrass your President.' The staff person responded, 'We don't give a shit about the President.'"[16]

In order to prevent the Congress from acting, the House Democratic leadership adopted a deliberate strategy of delay. After the filibuster was broken in the Senate and S.3 was passed, Common Cause, at least, had been optimistic that the House Democrats would not want to be the ones to kill it in the conference report (in which Senate and House bills are reconciled). But the House leadership stretched out agreeing on the conference report all the way into September 1994, with adjournment on the horizon. Going into 1994, Common Cause remained optimistic that a campaign finance reform bill they could live with would be passed. But that optimism slowly faded as the months went by without action: "Gephardt's staff guy kept telling Fred [Wertheimer] we're going to do it right up next to President's Day recess in February, we're going to do it right up next to Easter recess in April, we're going to do it. . . . By June we're thinking we are going to have to pull a rabbit out of the hat. We didn't know whether the House bill would be good enough."[17]

In the end, what the House Democrats did, surely deliberately, was to make it possible for the Senate Republicans to kill the legislation. It was not until the fourth week of September, with Congress in a rush to adjourn, that the House and Senate Democratic leaders finally agreed on a bill. By then the House Democrats were well aware of the Republican election strategy to deny the Democrats any congressional victories on issues as politically popular as campaign finance reform. In particular, the Republicans had the votes to sustain a filibuster of the appointment of Senate conferees on the campaign finance bill. Both the Democratic and Republican wings of the congressional incumbent party were firmly in agreement about this one. Don't mess with a campaign finance system that is working so well for us already.

Campaign finance reform was dead. Senate Republicans pulled the triggers, but House Democrats had planned the execution, loaded the rifles, and dragged the victim to the wall.

THE GREAT
HEALTH CARE DEBATE

Outside the Washington Frame 15

From Out of the North

In a domestic policy debate touted as possibly the most important since social security, Paul Wellstone was the Senate sponsor of a bill that a series of authoritative studies and even many advocates of competing proposals conceded would be the most apt and effective remedy for America's health care crisis. During his 1990 campaign, he had endorsed a "single-payer" health insurance system based on the Canadian model, a much simpler, far more efficient, and also more equitable system than the United States currently follows.

In all discussions of health care reform, there is general agreement about the major problems in this country that need to be addressed, from spiraling costs which threaten the economy to our virtually unique position among industrialized nations in failing to provide universal health care coverage. Forty million lower income Americans have no health insurance, and many more have only limited coverage. Health care that most industrialized nations regard as a right of citizenship, like police and fire protection, is routinely denied to American citizens.

For decades, Canada has been providing comprehensive and affordable health care to all its citizens with no restrictions on their choice of doctors or hospitals. At the same time, since implementing its single-payer system, Canada spends 40 percent less per person on health care than the United States does: 9 percent of its Gross Domestic Product (GDP) as compared to our 14 percent.[1]

In the United States, scores of insurance companies in each state offer hundreds of different health care plans to many separately insured groups and are billed for every separate consultation, procedure, and medication. In contrast, in a single-payer system one entity, typically a government agency, establishes procedures for setting limits on what doctors and hospitals can charge. If the U.S. had a single-payer system, each state would have a single insurer providing the same comprehensive insurance plan to everyone, financed by taxes.

Because there is only one insurer, debilitating insurance company diseases that afflict the U.S. system are automatically eliminated. There can be no "cost-shifting," whereby health care providers such as hospitals raise their fees to small insurers to recoup losses from uninsured patients or to compensate for the discounts that large, powerful insurers such as health maintenance organizations are able to demand. There is also no "risk-skimming," whereby insurers try to purge their risk pools of individuals who are likely to need costly medical treatment. One consequence of the sheer size and complexity of the U.S. system is enormous administrative costs for the more than fifteen hundred insurers. At the height of the health care reform debate in 1994, approximately $250 billion of the $1 trillion health care budget was for administrative costs, a far greater percentage than Canada and other single-payer countries pay. For example, in 1990 British Columbia's provincial plan employed 435 workers to cover 3.1 million residents while Blue Cross/Blue Shield of Massachusetts had 6,600 employees for 2.5 million subscribers. In fact, Blue Cross/Blue Shield of Massachusetts had more employees than are required to administer the entire National Health Program in Canada covering 26 million people.[2]

The principles of a single-payer system are fairly straightforward. Every year budgets are negotiated with hospitals and fees are negotiated with doctors. In Canada the arrangement between hospitals and insurers is known as "global budgeting." Each Canadian hospital negotiates an annual budget with the single-payer in its province. Assured of that amount, the hospital plans accordingly. For every patient who receives treatment the hospital simply notifies the provincial office of the total charge. Canada's experience demonstrates that the administrative savings are enough to pay completely for universal coverage. In 1987, Canada spent $.11 for administration out of every health care dollar, while that same year the U.S. figure was $.24. In a 1991 study, the General Accounting Office (GAO) concluded that a U.S. single-payer system would save nearly $70 billion in administrative costs alone. That was enough, the GAO reported, to pay for comprehensive coverage of all those Americans who were uninsured or underinsured. And according to a 1993 study by the Congressional Budget Office (CBO), for all but the very wealthiest Americans, comprehensive health care would cost less than the current insurance premiums and out-of-pocket medical expenses.[3]

Canada has demonstrated that a single-payer system is effective in containing costs. In 1992, *Consumer Reports* magazine estimated potential savings of $200 billion from increased administrative efficiency and avoided unnecessary procedures and services, out of the U.S. total health care costs of $817 billion that year.[4]

A great deal of evidence suggests that a single-payer system has the potential for tremendous popular support in the U.S. A Harris poll in November 1991 asked people's opinion about the Canadian "system of national health insurance, under which the government pays most of the cost of health care for everyone out of taxes and the government sets all fees charged by doctors and hospitals" and asked, "On balance, would you prefer the Canadian system or the system we have here?" Sixty-eight percent of Americans said they would prefer the Canadian system, 29 percent the U.S. system. In July 1992, a New York Times/CBS News Poll found 66 percent of Americans favoring "national health insurance, which would be financed by tax money, paying for most forms of health care," while only 25 percent were opposed.

On the other hand, a U.S. single-payer system has one huge political drawback: the opposition of private insurance companies, who would be phased out of the health insurance business. The largest of those companies are among the wealthiest and most politically influential of America's corporations. As Congress was about to begin the debate on health care in 1993, I was convinced that only a nationwide grassroots single-payer movement could counter such powerful opposition. I was also convinced that no one in the country was better positioned or better equipped to lead that movement than Paul Wellstone.

From out of the White House

During his 1992 presidential campaign, Bill Clinton endorsed a health care concept known as "managed competition," the brainchild of the so-called Jackson Hole Group led by Alain Enthoven, a Stanford University economist, and Paul Ellwood, a physician, and including representatives of the nation's largest health insurance companies. After Clinton took office, Hillary Rodham Clinton's Task Force on National Health Care Reform, which involved hundreds of health policy analysts and others with relevant experience and expertise from government, academia, and health-care-related industries, recommended a modified version of the managed competition plan.

The Clintons unveiled their plan with great fanfare in early fall 1993. According to the president, a bedrock principle was universal coverage. The plan relied on "health care alliances" whereby groups of consumers would choose among competing HMOs or health insurance companies on the basis of cost and quality of services offered. Consumers would receive a payment from their employer or the government with which to purchase insurance, with payments set low enough to give consumers a financial incentive to choose the least expensive health plan available. Because HMOs have a history of enrolling young and healthy people, extracting large discounts from providers, and denying care more aggressively than traditional insurance companies, the Clinton administration assumed that the least expensive health insurance would be that provided by HMOs. One anticipated consequence of the Clinton plan was to coax Americans to enroll in HMOs.

The Clinton plan, however, kept the largest insurance companies in the game—in a big way. With their large capital reserves, they would surely be major players in organizing and operating provider networks and providing the insurance, the basic building blocks of HMOs. Five of the largest insurance companies, Aetna, Cigna, Met Life, Prudential, and Travelers, joined together as the Alliance for Managed Competition to support the Clinton plan. Conversely, the small and medium-sized insurance companies were very nervous about their ability to cobble together large provider networks to survive in competition with the industry giants in a managed competition regime. This potential conflict over health care reform within the insurance industry came to a head when the big five pulled out of the Health Insurance Association of America (HIAA). Seeing itself in a fight for survival, the HIAA then went its own way as a major critic of the Clinton approach, notably with its effective "Harry and Louise" television commercials.

In the meantime, Paul and four cosponsors introduced the single-payer bill, S.491, "The American Health Security Act," in the Senate. A companion bill in the House, sponsored by Rep. Jim McDermott of Washington and Rep. John Conyers of Michigan, attracted the impressive support of over ninety cosponsors.

Once the Clinton bill was unveiled, it instantly set the agenda for the health care debate. In a surprising move, the Clintons went out of their way to dismiss a single-payer system as "politically unfeasible," a judgment that would soon became the conventional wisdom in Washington. Strategically, it might have made sense for the Clintons at least to consider a single-payer plan so that their own proposal offered the "middle ground" and could emerge as the compromise position from what was sure to be a very intense debate. It was obvious that there would be powerful pressures pulling reform back toward the present system and away from universal coverage, with comprehensive benefits and cost containment. One might have expected the Clintons to welcome a single-payer proposal on their "left," with the countervailing pressures it would generate. In retrospect, if they wanted to promote passage of their own plan, they made a fundamental strategic error.

Perhaps the Clintons believed naively that with the power of the presidency to appeal directly to the American people, they did not need a sophisticated political strategy to push through their plan. Or perhaps they felt that in order for their own proposal to look like the obvious path to "simplicity, savings, security, choice and quality" they had to eliminate the single-payer option from the playing field. The single-payer plan was far simpler and easier to understand. It certainly would work in practice to deliver comprehensive health care to every citizen because unlike the Clinton plan— which required a thirteen hundred–page tome just for its description—it had been working in Canada for twenty-five years. And according to the CBO and GAO, the Clinton proposal could promise far smaller savings than a single-payer plan, nowhere near enough to finance universal coverage with expanded benefits. Thus if single-payer had been introduced into the debate, inevitable comparisons of the two proposals might have proved embarrassing to the White House and the congressional Democratic leadership.

Ostracized in Washington

The process by which the health care debate was framed followed the classic pattern. Behind the scenes, before the public debate began, powerful special interest groups helped to shape the legislation. These included the large insurance companies and HMOs that had been a part of the Jackson Hole Group and/or whose employees had worked with the Clinton Task Force on National Health Care Reform. The great pools of capital in the hands of the health insurance giants made it inevitable that they would be among the major restructurers of health care delivery, assembling provider networks and serving as their financial cores.

Of particular interest is the way the Clintons' assertion that single-payer was not a viable option became the conventional wisdom in Washington and among the press. When the health care debate opened, Tom Hamburger, whom I first met when he was researching Rudy Boschwitz's campaign fund-raising for the *Minneapolis Star-Tribune* in 1990, was the paper's Washington bureau chief and was covering the health care beat. An article he wrote in 1993 with Ted Marmor, a Yale health policy specialist, "Dead on Arrival: Why Washington's Power Elites Won't Consider Single Payer Health Reform," began with two stories that illuminated how the Washington debate was framed.[5]

The first suggested the constraints under which the Clinton task force labored. In February 1993, Dr. Quentin Young had been invited to the White House to consult with the task force. A prominent Chicago physician and single-payer supporter, he was pleased that the president's advisors wanted him to participate in framing the Clinton bill and eager to help. But "Young's enthusiasm quickly withered within the White House gates. It turned out, in Young's words, that he had been invited for 'pseudo consultation.' White House staff made it clear that single-payer was off the table. 'Why?' Young asked, amazed. A senior White House health advisor, Walter Zelman, put it bluntly: 'Single-payer is not politically feasible.'"

The second story suggested why seasoned, socialized Washington insiders would readily accept that assessment. Another prominent single-payer proponent, Dr. David Himmelstein of the Harvard Medical School, was also invited to the White House, where he met with Hillary Rodham Clinton. He was taken aback by her response to his presentation on behalf of the single-payer plan that he and his wife, Steffie Woolhandler, also a Harvard physician and the cofounder of Physicians for a National Health Program (PNHP) had been instrumental in developing: "Hillary Clinton had heard it all before. How, she asked Himmelstein, do you defeat the multi-billion dollar insurance industry? 'With presidential leadership and polls showing 70 percent of Americans favor a single-payer system,' Himmelstein recalls telling Mrs. Clinton. The First Lady replied: 'Tell me something interesting, David.'"

How did the press come to buy into the assertion that single-payer was "politically unfeasible" and fail to cover it as an important alternative to the Clinton plan? I could guess the answer. The year before he ran for the Senate, Paul and I had taught a class on "Media and Politics" and had assigned Todd Gitlin's book, *The Whole World is Watching*, which argues convincingly that the norm of the mainstream American press is *not* to challenge conventional wisdom.[6] Reporters who advance in the profession have been effectively socialized into conformity, if not overtly then by a variety of not-so-subtle cues. Knowing Tom Hamburger to be a thoughtful and perceptive person, I sought him out during one of my trips to Washington. He not only told me that Gitlin had it right, but also related an interesting example of the kind of pressures reporters face.

Early in the health care debate, Hamburger had written about the various reform options, including the Clinton plan and managed-competition variants, but also including single-payer, which he treated as a serious option. On the newspaper's computer each story is identified by a "slug," a short descriptive name attached at the Minnesota office, and one small detail on his stories caught his eye: The slug attached was the word *HORSE*. Puzzled and sensitive to possible criticism (was someone hinting perhaps that his health care stories were—horse manure?), he found he wasn't far off. *HORSE* was short for "there goes Tom again, beating a dead horse—single-payer."

Later, my students were the beneficiaries of some fine work of Tom Hamburger and his colleague Eric Black at the *Star-Tribune* who, in an effort to educate Minnesotans, published a special thirty-six-page special supplement about the health care debate, including detailed information about four proposals: the Clinton plan, Tennessee Rep. Jim Cooper's pure managed competition plan, the single-payer plan, the "free market" Heritage Foundation plan.[7] Among the plans, my students and I noticed, only the single-payer presentation was accompanied by a formal rebuttal. I wondered if that was a consequence of *HORSE* and similar cues from the paper's management.

In discussing how the conventional wisdom of the moment is conveyed to the press, Hamburger emphasized the relatively small community of journalists in Washington who cover an issue like health care. They all aspire to be included as part of the in-group invited to elite background briefings such as the Sperling Breakfast Group, organized by Geoffrey Sperling of the *Christian Science Monitor,* and luncheon briefings organized by the *Wall Street Journal.* A regular participant in both, Hamburger had described in his article with Marmor how single-payer had fared in those closed sessions. At a July 1993 Sperling breakfast, Senate Majority Leader George Mitchell had given reporters the inside scoop on single-payer's chances in the Congress. He stated bluntly that "Canada's system may be good for Canada, but 'it will not be enacted' in Washington. Americans want an American solution."

Hamburger and Marmor ended this discussion by speculating why the Canadian and other national health care systems didn't get serious consideration in this political debate: "The short answer is fear. For politicians, this means mostly fear of political attack, fear of taking on powerful American myths, and fear of incurring the wrath of the well-endowed health care and insurance industries. And politicians fear being left out of the game. That means they talk the prevailing talk and think the prevailing thoughts . . . "[8]

Just as Washington reporters are socialized in meetings such as these, Washington politicians and much of the national press get important cues about prevailing political talk and thinking from a few newspapers, notably the *New York Times* and the *Washington Post*. These papers play the role of shepherds in the well-known phenomena of "pack journalism." Their coverage of the framing phase of the health care debate is particularly illuminating. For example, in the six months immediately following the 1992 election, the phrase *managed competition* appeared in sixty-two *New York Times* news stories, while *single payer* appeared in only five. A study in the *Columbia Journalism Review* found that in the twenty-six-month period from May 1991 through July 1993, the *Times* published thirty-five editorials that boosted managed competition as the "best answer" and "blasted" Canada's single-payer system.[9] Subsequently, the *Times,* via their reporter Robert Pear, became a principal conduit for leaks from the White House about what the task force was up to in its private deliberations. An unnamed reporter was quoted in the *Columbia Journalism Review* article: "Robert Pear got leaks, got documents, got scoops, and the *Times* set the agenda for the next day's coverage."

If American politics is ideally a free marketplace of ideas in which citizens are invited to choose among many products on display, the health care debate was in practice a market corrupted by unfair and anticompetitive practices. While the Clinton task force was displaying and advertising one shiny new, but untested, product in the inventory and assuring it was prominently displayed, a stealth campaign succeeded in having another competing product removed from the shelves. The next section suggests that if the American consumers had been allowed to comparison shop, they would likely have found the absent product far more attractive.

A Tantalizing Glimpse of What Might Have Been

This account of the framing ends with a story that suggests how different the outcome might have been if the American people had received adequate information during the 1993–94 health care reform debate. Since the late 1970's, a wealthy, idealistic Minnesotan, Ned Crosby, and his Minneapolis-based Jefferson Center have been experimenting with the "Citizens' Jury" approach to "democratizing" political decision-making. The Jefferson Center brings together a demographically representative group of people who meet for several days to hear alternative options in public policy disputes, question experts, and then arrive at a decision about an appropriate policy response. A report on the jury's debate, deliberations, and decision is then circulated widely.

When I first heard about the Citizens' Jury concept, I very much admired Ned Crosby's intent, but I worried about how and by whom a Citizens' Jury's *judgment options* would be framed, because that could have considerable influence on the outcome.

In October 1993, soon after Bill Clinton described the principal features of his health care plan on national television, the Jefferson Center sponsored a Citizens' Jury on health care reform. Twenty-four jurors from fifteen states, chosen from a random pool of two thousand people broadly representative of the general population in terms of age, gender, race, education, geographic region, political affiliation, and source of health insurance coverage, were brought together for five days in Washington, D.C. They were asked to address two questions: "Do we need health care reform in America?" and "Is the Clinton Plan the way to get the health care reform we need?" In order to prepare a response they received intensive briefings on health care in America and health care reform options, including an entire day of meetings with advocates for the Clinton plan and then with advocates of the Republican plans. Representing the Clintons was Toby Moffett, a former congressman from Connecticut, and his witnesses, including Ira Magaziner, chief of staff of the White House task force that had drawn up the Clinton plan. Vin Weber, a former congressman from Minnesota, and his witnesses spoke for the Republicans. But where, I wondered, when I looked over a copy of the schedule printed in the newspaper, were the advocates for the single-payer option? If the Citizens' Jury was meant to democratize a process which has as one of its most undemocratic features a narrow framing of the issues in private by Washington power elites, how could such an important option be excluded from the outset?

Several months after the health care reform jury had completed its work, I met with Ned Crosby and he acknowledged that the single-payer system had deliberately been excluded because he believed that buying into the Washington frame was the only way to have any impact at all on the debate. "The purpose of [our strategy]," he said, "was to accept the Washington frame and play in their community. We were out to gain legitimacy."[10] Crosby also feared that the Clinton advocate, Toby Moffett, would not participate if single-payer had been an option. Ironically, however, single-payer made its way into the jury's deliberations anyway. Because Minnesota's senators, Dave Durenberger and Paul Wellstone, were members of the Senate Labor and Human Resources Committee and actively involved with the issue, Crosby had invited them to meet briefly with the jurors. Durenberger was a cosponsor of the Cooper-Breaux bill and Paul, of course, was the author of S.491, the single-payer bill. Despite the short time allotted to Paul, his presentation was so persuasive that the jurors voted overwhelmingly to invite him back the next day so they could learn more. As Ned Crosby put it, "in that sense, it was democracy in action."

By the fifth day, it was clear that many of the jurors were inclined to support the single-payer plan. There was significant sentiment among them to modify the original charge which called for a vote only on the Clinton plan and add a vote on the single-payer option. This development evidently reached the White House and made Ira Magaziner nervous enough for him to place a call to Toby Moffett expressing concern and counseling him how to proceed. In the end such a last-minute change seemed too problematic to the jury and they did vote only on the original question—in the negative. Asked whether the Clinton plan was the way to get the health care reform we need, they answered decisively: 19 No, 5 Yes.

According to Ned Crosby, in an informal private session immediately after the formal close of the Citizen Jury's proceedings, Roger Mudd of ABC news, who had been hired to narrate a program about the jury and its conclusions, noted that from their comments at the beginning of the deliberations that morning it was clear that a majority favored the Wellstone plan. According to Ned Crosby, Mudd asked the jurors with evident frustration, "Why the hell didn't you have a formal vote on the Wellstone plan?" Kathleen Hall Jamison of the University of Pennsylvania's Annenberg School of Communications, who had been comoderator of the jury with Crosby, then explored, off the record, which plans the jurors had preferred after their extensive immersion in the health care reform debate. The answer was overwhelming support for single-payer. When Jamison asked, "How many would have voted for the Wellstone plan," seventeen of the twenty-four jurors raised their hands.

This experience supported my hunch that if the American people were able to hear for themselves the cases for the various health care reform proposals, single-payer would likely be the overwhelming popular choice. It also suggested that by using his position as author of the Senate bill and his oratorical gift, and organizing skills, Paul had a remarkable opportunity to help build and lead a national single-payer movement.

Once again, before the public was invited in, an important public policy debate had been framed, with at least one of the most important policy options deliberately left outside the frame. Single-payer was off the table in Washington and, for the most part, in the mass media. On the other hand, a well-defined alternative proposal had been introduced by Wellstone in the Senate and McDermott and Conyers in the House. What's more, by the time the public debate began, substantial single-payer seeds had been planted outside of Washington. Not only did opinion polls consistently show majority support for the single-payer concept, but in many communities, most notably in California, successful grassroots organizing also was demonstrating its popular appeal.

Stirrings in the West

During my time in the Senate, I had not been involved in the health care reform issue. Paul's initial bill for the 102nd Congress was fashioned by Roberta Walburn, an attorney who was his legislative aide on the Labor and Human Resources Committee, and Steffie Woolhandler, the Harvard University physician who, with her husband David Himmelstein, had chaired the physicians' task force that had written its own single-payer proposal. Walburn's successor, Ellen Shaffer, drew up a revised bill for the 103rd Congress.

My own introduction to the subject took place twenty-five hundred miles away, in San Diego, where I was on sabbatical leave at the University of California, San Diego. In April 1993, my wife, Nancy Casper, joined me in California and volunteered to work with San Diego Neighbor-to-Neighbor (N2N), a grassroots political organization. A few weeks before she arrived, I had attended a small meeting about campaign finance reform with former California governor Jerry Brown, where an articulate young community organizer caught my attention with his astute comments. We chatted briefly after the meeting about a demonstration he was organizing at a large insurance company in downtown San Diego to gain media attention for the single-payer alternative. Thinking Nancy might be interested in the Neighbor-to-Neighbor single-payer project, I got his number.

Little did I know that Donald Cohen would soon be renowned as a leader of what became the cutting edge of the national single-payer grassroots movement, and that he and two other San Diego Neighbor-to-Neighbor leaders, Jeanne Ertle and Stephanie Jennings, would become close friends, drawing both Nancy and me deeply into the movement.

Neighbor-to-Neighbor had made a name for itself when it played a key role in the campaign of the 1980s to pressure Congress to stop U.S. funding of the Contras in Nicaragua. At the height of the effort in 1987 to 1988, about fifty organizers were deployed by N2N in targetted congressional districts. With headquarters in San Francisco, it was particularly strong in the Bay Area, Los Angeles, Boston, Chicago, and New York. It played a key role in winning the swing votes that nailed down Congress' close 1988 decision to cut off Contra aid.

In the early 1990s, an N2N organizer who became its National Director in 1993, Glen Schneider, had put his toe in the health care reform water when he lobbied for a single-payer bill in the California legislature. In the spring of 1993, N2N decided to launch a major single-payer organizing effort, focused primarily on the Bay Area through its San Francisco chapter and on San Diego, where a second chapter was being formed. Donald Cohen in San Diego, Paul Milne in Oakland, and Glen Schneider in San Francisco were the instigators of this project and a charismatic organizer, Greg Akili, was hired to lead the San Diego chapter and to work with Donald Cohen in organizing single-payer support there.

Cohen and Milne were formally associated with another organization, the Institute for Effective Action (IEA), which was closely allied with Neighbor-to-Neighbor. Along with Glen Schneider, they were among a handful of idealistic and talented protégés of Paul Milne's father, Crosby Milne, who had worked his way up from the shop floor to the top management of North Island Naval Systems in San Diego, where he was well-known for innovative techniques in industrial management. With his considerable managerial insights, Crosby, along with his son Paul, had developed a model of community organizing that they hoped to apply to progressive social causes. That approach to community organizing is laid out in a widely distributed 1995 booklet, *American Progressives at a Crossroads,* that Donald Cohen wrote with Paul Milne and Glen Schneider.[11]

Donald Cohen had studied physics and astronomy at the University of Michigan, was director of the San Diego Central American Information Center, and attended business school at San Diego State University. Paul Milne had been trained by the legendary community organizer Fred Ross Sr. and had worked as an organizer in the 1970s for Cesar Chavez and the United Farm Workers.

In the spring of 1993, the objectives of San Diego Neighbor-to-Neighbor were to develop public support for single-payer health care, to call attention to the defects of the Clinton managed competition proposal and the role of large insurance companies in backing it, and to convince San Diego's four congressional representatives to support the McDermott/Wellstone single-payer bills. Nancy began working out of an office in the garage behind Donald Cohen's house, as San Diego Neighbor-to-Neighbor gained increasing attention and adherents in the community. Jeanne Ertle supervised the building and implementation of the phone tree, which regularly alerted about two-hundred people to the group's actions, particularly members of Congress, reporters, and the news staffs of radio and television stations. Stephanie Jennings was a vigorous and imaginative media coordinator, and Jeanne Ertle's husband, Bruce, a graphics artist, was the campaign's secret weapon as he repeatedly produced eye-catching alerts and other leaflets on very short notice.

Neighbor-to-Neighbor was a highly professional, highly disciplined operation. The campaign reached out to San Diego with "house meeting" presentations where the single-payer plan was described, phone-bank volunteers were enlisted, and attendees were asked to commit themselves to ongoing contributions to fund the salaries of the organizers. Early that summer the Public Media Center in San Francisco produced a thirty-second television spot for N2N, pointing out what an enormous amount of the money spent on health care in America ends up as profit for private insurance companies. But when local Neighbor-to-Neighbor groups attempted to place the spot on commercial stations in San Diego, San Francisco, and Boston, they ran into a brick wall. Despite their willingness to pay, all but one of the stations simply refused to carry an ad that offended such important advertisers as the large insurance companies. Yet this was just the response N2N leaders had expected. Turning the obstacle to an advantage, they called press conferences in each city and in Washington to denounce the censorship. The result was considerable free media coverage of the single-payer movement and a particular message with a compelling tale of unfair treatment, media bias, and censorship.

In June, single-payer organizing in San Diego got a tremendous boost when Paul Wellstone agreed to speak, and his June 25 appearance became the focus of a major push to increase the number of active participants in the local movement. N2N mounted an intense organizing effort for the event. A flyer announced that Wellstone would deliver a "major address" on "The Coming Battle For Health Care Reform." It described him as "perhaps the most courageous individual and most exciting speaker in the United States Senate today," citing not only his sponsorship of the single-payer bill, but also the effusive praise the *New York Times* had bestowed on him for bucking his

Senate elders and pressing for congressional disclosure of all lobbyist gifts. Jeanne Ertle led an intensive effort involving direct mail and nightly phone bank calls for two and a half weeks, using every likely organization and list she could get her hands on. The result was later referred to as San Diego's "political event of the year." Over seven-hundred people jammed into the Craftsmen's Hall auditorium, which had an official capacity of less than four-hundred. Local political activists were in awe of the effort mounted to draw that crowd and Neighbor-to-Neighbor made good use of the attendee list. The result was enhanced visibility, credibility, and many new volunteers for the budding single-payer movement in San Diego.

At the same time, single-payer fortunes were moving rapidly in the opposite direction in Washington. As the president and Hillary Rodham Clinton turned the managed competition idea into a detailed legislative proposal during the first ten months of 1993, they were able to gather many key Washington players behind their plan. Surprisingly, supporters included many individuals and organizations one might have expected to be in the vanguard of a single-payer movement, such as leaders of organized labor and their unions, several important public interest groups, and many congressional Democrats.

The Single-Payer Movement Splits Apart

The powerful influence of the Washington establishment on even the most unlikely individuals was once again brought home to me by a surprising remark Paul made in early May, before his San Diego appearance. I met him in his St. Paul apartment, brimming with enthusiasm about the grassroots movement in California; he was just in from Washington, where he was enmeshed in the health care reform framing negotiations. In the few months that Hillary Rodham Clinton and her health care reform task force had been in operation, she had met with Paul several times. He told me that they had "very good chemistry" and he felt he had been able to push her a long way toward making the Clinton proposal compatible with implementing a single-payer system in many states. But then he fairly stunned me with an announcement: He thought he might endorse the Clinton plan when it was completed. My immediate distress surprised him. As I later described the encounter in my journal, "My warning light goes on. Paul's caught up in the insider negotiations and feels if they give enough, the *quid pro quo* may be to support them. . . . But there is no way he can take single-payer off the table. He should see himself as an agent of the movement." Fortunately, Paul realized before long that his expectation that the Clintons would give single-payer supporters "75 percent of what they wanted" was not justified and also that it made no sense to compromise at the beginning of the public debate. But Sara Nichols, the lead health care lobbyist for Public Citizen, later told me she sensed the kind of pressure Paul was experiencing around that time. Her surmise was that the chief source was Hillary Clinton: "It seemed that she was personally calling him once every week or so for a time there and he seemed very seduced by it. . . . I think the idea that he had formed this personal relationship with Hillary Clinton was making him not want to do anything that would not be in good faith. He thought it [would be] an act of bad faith to be having these conversations and then to be trashing the Clinton bill. I think that made him really uncomfortable." [12]

What an irony if Nichols were right. When Paul told me he might support the Clinton bill, my first reaction was that he would be letting down a grass-roots movement that was depending on him. From my San Diego perspective, his act would have been the epitome of bad faith. But I could imagine that from the perspective of Paul's Washington world, allegiances might look very different. The net effect of his divided loyalties, however, was a blunting of his effectiveness in the 1993–94 health care debate. Even when Paul spoke on behalf of single-payer in his San Diego speech and elsewhere, he held back from criticizing the Clinton plan.

I agonized for a long time about Paul's demurring. Rep. Jim McDermott, the author of the House single-payer bill, told me that he would be "Mr. Inside," organizing congressional support, and that he hoped Paul would be "Mr. Outside," mobilizing grassroots support. His impression was that Paul was trying to support single-payer, but at the same time he was trying to support the Democrat in the White House too. A leading single-payer lobbyist who liked Paul very much once delivered an apt epitaph to Paul's untimely demise as the single-payer champion: "I think he's trying to dance at two weddings at the same time."

After his San Diego speech, Donald Cohen and I hoped to get Paul back on the single-payer track. In a memo, we urged him to emulate "the San Diego Model" around the country, giving single-payer groups in many cities a similar boost. A key element of our plan was for him to hire an advance team, which would be responsible for planning and implementing appearances in a succession of cities. Paul would seize a rare opportunity to play an unusual role for a sitting senator, carrying the single-payer message to the

American people and leading a social movement. Paul could become a central figure in a historic national debate by doing what he does best, empowering people by helping them to organize in their home communities, supporting and drawing attention to an idea that would make a great difference in the lives of millions of American families. When we first broached the idea, I could see him waver, appreciating the possibilities, the fit with his abilities, his knowledge, his instincts. But in the end, no advance person was hired; no grand strategy to link Paul up with grassroots groups and help to build a nationwide single-payer movement was mapped out. Paul's office never seemed to warm to that idea.

The same kind of inside-the-beltway dynamic had already begun to infect and ultimately split the national single-payer movement. Paul was surely getting signals by early 1993 that key coalitions at the heart of the single-payer movement were wavering under the influence of the seductive charms of the Clintons. That realization may well have dampened considerably Paul's assessment of the likelihood that a single-payer campaign would catch fire and succeed in 1993–94.

For instance, the public interest organization that had championed single-payer longer than any other, both in Washington and around the nation was Washington-based Citizen Action, with activist affiliates in thirty-four states. In Washington, the Single-Payer Coalition was led by Citizen Action's health policy specialist and legislative director, Cathy Hurwit. The coalition included several progressive labor unions that helped to fund Citizen Action, along with Public Citizen and several other groups: the American Federation of State, County and Municipal Employees (AFSCME), the Communications Workers of America (CWA), and the International Ladies Garment Workers Union (ILGWU).

In 1991, Hurwit and Citizen Action had helped Rep. Marty Russo of Illinois draft the very first congressional single-payer bill and both Citizen Action and Public Citizen later assisted in the preparation of the single-payer bill Paul introduced in 1992. Of course, with George Bush as president, the coalition members were outsiders in the health care debate, with no hope that a reform that took private insurance companies out of the health insurance game would ever become law. Single-payer was not even favored by the liberal Labor and Human Resources Committee. When Paul joined that committee in 1991, its chair, Ted Kennedy, who had supported the single-payer approach years before, had bowed to Washington realism and was promoting something called "Pay or Play," wherein employers would either have to arrange for health insurance for their employees or pay into a government-sponsored program.

But after the November 1992 election it was a different story, with a Democratic president committed to health care reform about to take office. At last, an opportunity was at hand. What is more, the new President had enlisted several individuals with strong Citizen Action ties to work with him. At the Democratic National Committee (DNC) were its new chair, David Wilhelm, who had long worked with Citizen Action's Illinois affiliate, and Heather Booth, who had headed Citizen Action's national organizer-training program in Chicago. Later, Citizen Action's president, Bob Brandon, also joined the DNC to work for Clinton on health care reform.

Even though Clinton had endorsed managed competition during his campaign, soon after his election he let it be known he wanted to work with single-payer supporters, inviting some public interest group and progressive union leaders to meet with him at the Governor's Mansion in Little Rock. According to one account, "Clinton was open and conciliatory, telling them he planned to establish a Health Care Task Force in a few weeks, in which the Canadian-style government approach would be seriously considered. . . . Because of his compassionate rhetoric about health, these groups held out hope that Clinton might yet come around during the transition or early in his presidency." [13]

But such hopes gradually were eroded. Sara Nichols, a committed single-payer advocate, told me how she and her organization found themselves taken by surprise. In retrospect, she realized that there were subtle signs of change in some single-payer coalition members even during the transition period prior to the inauguration: "[The progressive union people] all started to temper their remarks—at first very subtly. They started to talk a little less about single-payer and a little more about the 'goals' of single-payer and the principles behind it. . . . Never having had a Democrat in the White House in my adult life and never having operated in that political environment, I really didn't know exactly what was going on at first." [14]

Nichols's vague sense of a weakening commitment to single-payer among the members of the Washington-based Single-Payer Coalition and a strengthening commitment to the president-elect was reinforced at a high-level "pow-wow" at AFSCME (American Federation of State, County and Municipal Employees) headquarters in Washington in late November 1992. Among the twenty or so attendees were leaders of Citizen Action and several unions, including Gerald McAfee, president of AFSCME, Ralph Nader, and Nichols.

At that point, Citizen Action had been pushing for a campaign that would generate an outpouring of a million postcards demanding single-payer health care, to be delivered with great fanfare at the White House gates.

AFSCME's McAfee and others stressed the extraordinary access they had to Clinton after twelve years of being shut out. Sara Nichols recalled:

> The unions said they weren't going to do anything visible, that everything was going to be behind-the-scenes with the president; that they were trying hard to convince him of single-payer, but it was all behind the scenes. And Ralph [Nader] gave a speech about how we have to make leaders do what you want and if they don't feel the heat, it doesn't work. He said, "As far as I can tell, the president wouldn't have gotten elected without your support. If he doesn't understand that he will *lose* your support without going for single-payer and if you don't make that a credible threat, you are squandering the leverage you have with the president." But they said, "We're not going to do that."
>
> Then we discussed the postcards. [A Citizen Action official] presented a prototype of the postcard and the words *single-payer* didn't appear. . . . I was chilled. I said, "What is going on? . . . Why isn't *single-payer* on this post-card?" She said, "Well, it brings in a broader group of people and if you notice that all the principles that are on the postcard, universal coverage, comprehensive benefits, cost controls, access, . . . all these things can only be fulfilled by single-payer, so it really boils down to single-payer. . . . We want the president to introduce a single-payer bill, but he might not call it one." I said, "I think that's very dangerous; I think there are a lot of people who will claim "pay or play" fulfills all these principles or that something else does."

For some months, the Single-Payer Coalition continued to meet, but it was an increasingly uneasy alliance. For instance, in mid-1993, just prior to a meeting between coalition members and Hillary Clinton in Paul's office, they decided to write a letter to her spelling out their position. Sara Nichols recalled, "The first draft was by Citizen Action: 'It is now absolutely clear it's not politically feasible to get a single-payer system.'" Physicians for a National Health Program, the National Council of Senior Citizens, and Public Citizen [all strong backers of single-payer] got upset and it was taken out of the letter.

The rift finally came to a head in June 1993, when an article appeared in the press saying that three coalition members, the National Association of Social Workers, the American Hospital Association, and the AFL/CIO had announced they were supporting a plan introduced by West Virginia's Sen. Jay Rockefeller that was along the lines of the proposal the Clinton task force was reported to be developing. Nichols was taken aback. At the next meeting of the coalition she insisted that if a member of the single-payer coalition was going to support something else, that had to be discussed.

Soon she and her boss at Public Citizen were asked to come to a meeting at the Citizen Action office to discuss the issue. They soon found the purpose of the meeting was to warn them off. According to Nichols, they were told, "'There is no consensus in this coalition to stay with single-payer if the Clinton Administration does something else. Public Citizen is the only group in this coalition that is holding on to single-payer. This is never to happen again or Public Citizen will not be allowed in the room.'"

A few days later, Ralph Nader decided to step in. He invited representatives of both Citizen Action and Public Citizen to his office. This is Nichols's account of what happened:

> Ralph moderated. . . . He was the great patriarch of the public interest movement. It was as if we were appearing before Solomon to work this out. He said he understood how exciting it would be to work with a president after so many years, how seductive it could be to be involved in the inner workings of government. How you often feel you could accomplish a great deal more than you had before because you have the potential of that power behind you and that working relationship and how it could make you reconsider your policy positions in light of your goals. He made it seem as if that was a very natural thing. . . . He was extremely gracious. But he emphasized that there's going to come a point where you're really going to have to cross the Rubicon and you're going to have to make a decision: Are you for them or agin them? There's a bottom line that you've got to have, that you've got to be thinking about here in terms of what really has to be there for you to be to be with the administration and what doesn't. Where are you on that line? At this point a senior official with Citizen Action interjected, "Well, it's complicated Ralph; we're thinking in terms of the actual delivery of universal coverage. . . . [We've] been having deep internal discussions with the administration. It's been at the level of Citizen Action's being courted internally to deliver its support."

I suggested that by then it was very clear Citizen Action had decided to drop its advocacy of single-payer. Nichols replied, "Yeah, it was pretty clear, though they were taking pains to hide it; to this day [April, 1994], they still are, in a way. . . . Even though they are campaigning for the Clinton bill, it's terribly important to them that they be viewed as a single-payer organization." Why is that?, I inquired. She explained that they needed to because much of their grassroots constituency in their state and local affiliates was solidly behind single-payer.

The national leadership of some of the most prominent labor unions was similarly attracted by the prospect of working together with the White House on health care reform. Both Citizen Action and the unions had the problem of explaining and justifying the about-face to other various constituents, grassroots groups, state and local affiliates, union locals and rank-and-file members. The solution was a kind of sleight-of-hand (or sleight-of-mind) that blurred the difference between single-payer and the Clinton approach. By emphasizing the so-called principles of health care reform, they all could support the president, while stressing their commitment to the single-payer concept. For the unions the vehicle for pulling off this ruse was known as the Campaign for Health Security.

The Campaign for Health Security began in early 1993, operating out of the Communications Workers union headquarters and publishing a bimonthly newsletter that was, in Sara Nichols words, "relatively single-payerish." By mid-year, single-payer was being mentioned less and less and the "principles" more and more.

By the beginning of 1994, the Campaign for Health Security—along with other organizations they had succeeded in attracting—were clearly within the Clinton managed-competition bill orbit. In a letter sent to all members of Congress on March 24, 1994, the heads of twenty-seven national organizations, including a dozen major labor unions, explained their common credo: "What guides us in this campaign is our commitment to the underlying principles of real reform: universal coverage, comprehensive benefits, cost control, fair financing and consumer choice. Most of us have supported a single-payer system as the best solution to achieving reform that is truly universal, and we continue to believe that ultimately a single-payer system is the best for our country. However, we all believe that President Clinton's plan meets our principles in substantial ways."[15] Interestingly, when the Clintons' health care legislation was introduced, the title chosen for the bill was exactly the same as Paul's single-payer bill, "The American Health Security Act." Was this a coincidence, I wondered, or a calculated decision to blur distinction even in the name?

In effect, the Campaign for Health Security carved off a major chunk of what might have been a powerful, nationwide single-payer movement. The part they took had tremendous financial resources, with the result that millions of dollars were spent by progressive labor unions on a health care reform plan that came to nothing. Even more important, they neutralized many single-payer supporters around the country, effectively preventing them from participating in unified, countrywide actions their organizations might have sponsored on behalf of the kind of health care reform they believed in.

On occasion, one caught glimpses of what the single-payer movement might have been. On July 17, 1993, Ira Magaziner, the director of the Clinton health care task force, spoke about the emerging Clinton plan at Citizen Action's annual retreat in Chicago. In the audience were about six-hundred Citizen Action door-to-door canvassers from around the country. Their national office was preparing to back the president's managed-competition proposal, but most of them turned out to be strong single-payer advocates. Despite the moderator's suggestion that they give Magaziner a warm welcome, his words were drowned out by a torrent of boos and his entreaties that they work together were dismissed uncategorically.

Taking the Initiative in California 16

An End Run around the Washington Frame

By January 1994, it was clear that single-payer had no chance in the Congress. If there was going to be a fight for comprehensive, affordable, universal health care coverage, it would have to be waged outside of Washington. As it turned out, the Lexington of the movement, where the first shots were fired, was California. Among the leaders of that statewide grassroots movement were Nancy's and my newfound friends at San Diego Neighbor-to-Neighbor.[1]

A January 4 *New York Times* front page story, "Clinton, Defending Health Plan, Attacks Critics Alternatives," typified the message the public was getting from Washington about single-payer via the mainstream media: "At least six health care plans have now been introduced in Congress. . . . Most of the legislation has been offered by Republicans. . . . But one major alternative [to the Clinton plan] has been proposed by a Democrat, Representative Jim Cooper of Tennessee. . . ."[2] There was *no* indication from the mainstream media that single-payer was a legitimate, serious alternative. This despite the fact that as of the day that story was written, the Cooper bill, HR 3222, had attracted the support of fifty-six House cosponsors, while Democrat Jim McDermott's single-payer bill, HR 1200, had ninety-one House cosponsors, nearly as many as the ninety-nine who had signed on to the Clinton bill, HR 3600, introduced by House majority leader Richard Gephardt. The campaign by Democratic leaders to label single-payer "politically unfeasible" had succeeded.

At just that time, California single-payer advocates were deciding on an

248

end run around this Washington frame by going directly to the people. California is one of fourteen states with a "direct initiative" process which can bypass the state legislature to enact statutory legislation. If a sufficient number of registered voters sign an initiative petition, the proposed legislation is put on the ballot. If it receives a majority of the votes, it becomes state law.

Just getting on the California ballot in 1994 was a daunting task for a volunteer organization, requiring the signatures of roughly 670,000 registered voters; in fact, to be sure of sufficient valid signatures after the petitions were checked for nonregistered voters, duplicate signatures, illegible names, incomplete information, and the like, more than a million signatures had to be gathered. Even more daunting was the challenge of winning the election, given the money and other resources that would surely be deployed by the health insurance industry to defeat a single-payer initiative in the nation's largest state. Gathering a million signatures would require an operation estimated to cost between $600,000 and $800,000. Many millions of dollars more would be necessary to wage a competitive ballot campaign if the petition drive were successful.

The genesis of the California single-payer ballot initiative involved the coming together of two different kinds of citizen-activists. Those who wrote the initiative were health care practitioners and university academics. Those who conceived the political strategy and led the signature-gathering and ballot-initiative campaigns were professional community organizers and concerned citizen volunteers, including the California Physicians Alliance, the Congress of California Seniors, California Neighbor-to-Neighbor, and the Institute for Effective Action.

Physicians Write the Prescription

That the initiative came to be written in time was largely the product of the foresight of a husband and wife physician team. Vishwanath (Vishu) Lingappa is an internist at San Francisco General Hospital and a teacher and molecular biology research group leader at the University of California, San Francisco Medical School; Krista Farey is a family physician. In 1992 both were on the steering committee of the seven-hundred member California Physicians Alliance (CAPA), the California chapter of Physicians for a National Health Program founded by David Himmelstein and Steffie Woolhandler in Cambridge, Massachusetts with its national office now based in Chicago.

Along with other CAPA physicians, they become involved in a campaign against a 1992 health care reform initiative, Proposition 166, promoted by the California Medical Association that would have provided neither universal, comprehensive coverage nor effective cost containment. Vishu noted one thing he learned in the process: "I did a fair amount of speaking and found that when I ended with, 'We're going to have our own initiative two years from now,' the audience would go from nodding in agreement to jumping up and down. . . . I realized that when you end with the McDermott-Wellstone bill in Washington, you don't get that reaction. Washington is far away; it's not here; it's not now; it's not ours; it's very abstract."

They decided on their own to write a single-payer initiative, building on a foundation provided by David Himmelstein and Steffie Woolhandler's *National Health Program Book,* as well as an earlier, influential article they wrote for the *New England Journal of Medicine* in 1989 laying out the basic elements of an American single-payer program.[3] They also got useful ideas from an earlier California draft single-payer initiative and single-payer legislation, the Petris bill, that had received majority support in both houses of the California legislature in 1991 but failed to get the two-thirds vote needed to pass a measure requiring new taxes. By December 1992 they had a draft, which they took to the CAPA steering committee for criticisms and ideas.

Vishu also volunteered to represent CAPA at the April 1993 steering committee meeting of Health Access, a broad coalition of California groups that backed universal health care, where a committee was appointed to study the possibility of a 1994 health care initiative. It consisted of Vishu, Glen Schneider, then director of Neighbor-to-Neighbor's San Francisco office and soon to become its national director, and Sacramento-based Howard Owens, formerly president and then legislative director of the Congress of California Seniors, who was a former labor organizer with union contacts throughout the state.

They met for the first time a few weeks later at a restaurant halfway between San Francisco and Sacramento. All three were enthusiastic advocates of single-payer, but Schneider and Owens foresaw one seemingly insurmountable logistical obstacle to a 1994 initiative: how could they possibly get it written in time? Vishu reached in his briefcase, exclaiming "Here it is!" With Vishu's draft legislation and Schneider's and Owens's organizing skills and political connections they were optimistic about putting together a statewide initiative campaign. Thus began a series of biweekly strategy conversations that went on for several months.

Vishu's responsibility was to oversee completion of a polished single-payer initiative for California. Through single-payer strategist Bill Zimmerman, who in 1988 had been campaign manager for the successful auto insurance reform initiative, Prop 103, he got in touch with Karl Manheim, Professor of Constitutional Law at Loyola Law School in Los Angeles. A lawyer for progressive causes, Manheim had defended Prop 103 before the California Supreme Court. But when Vishu first talked to him on the phone, Manheim said he was sorry, but he was just too busy to take on anything else. Nevertheless, Vishu sent him a draft, urging him to reconsider. Soon he got a call from Manheim, who said, "'you know, this could be a lot of fun. I'll be involved, but I can't lead it; I'll get you another lawyer.'" "He ended up not only leading it," Vishu reported, "he worked day and night for months on this thing."

From August through November 1993, Vishu flew from San Francisco to Los Angeles nearly every Saturday to meet with an ad hoc legal team consisting of Manheim and two of his law school colleagues. He later recalled, "The legal team started out with a document that was maybe twenty pages long; I walked in and the chemistry was perfect. Within ten minutes it was like we were old friends." Sometimes they disagreed. For instance, on the subject of mental health the lawyers said, "'You're going to cover this without restrictions? Absolutely no way! . . . Everyone knows mental health is a bottomless pit.' I said, 'We are not going to treat mental health any differently from anything else.' We fought over that one for about four hours until finally Karl said he had an appointment and had to leave right away. I said, 'If you want to go, you're going to have to concede this one.' And he did. It was great because of the rapport. . . . None of our egos got in the way. . . . It was one of the most incredible things I've ever been involved in."

The document eventually went through very many drafts. The direct initiative process puts an enormous premium on getting the initiative language absolutely right at the beginning. Unlike the legislative process, with public hearings, interest group review, floor debate, and other deliberative elements, there is no provision for amending the language if legal mistakes or political miscalculations are later uncovered. Vishu, Krista Farey, Karl Manheim, and their fellow drafters had to approach their task as if they were writing the law precisely as it would go into the books.

Despite an intensive effort for many months, as 1993 drew to a close the starting time for the signature gathering period was fast approaching and the single-payer initiative language was not yet ready. For the campaign to have the full 150-day period to gather signatures, the initiative had to be submitted by the second week in October. Vishu described the sense of urgency they felt: "The time flew by and suddenly it was nearly Thanksgiving.

We were cutting into the 150 days you have for signature gathering. Several times, Karl and I had all-night conference calls, he in L. A., me in San Francisco, both at our computers, reworking sections all night. . . . During November, the pressure to get it done mounted rapidly. Every passing day meant one less day to gather signatures."

In early December, the *California Health Security Act* initiative was finally submitted.[4] It laid out in detail the features of the California Health Security System, providing every California resident with a Health Security Card, providing full inpatient and outpatient care, full mental health and long-term care (without deductibles and with minimal copayments), prescription drugs, and some dental services. The program would be administered by an elected health commissioner with administrative costs capped at 4 percent of system revenues.

Monies from several sources would be pooled to fund the program: funds from current federal, state, and local government programs, such as Medicare and Medicaid (estimated to provide about 57 percent of the total funding); a payroll tax ranging from 8.9 percent for large employers to 4.4 percent for small employers (about 32 percent of the total); a tax on individuals of up to 2.5 percent of taxable income, with an additional surtax of 2.5 percent on income above $250,000 for individuals or $500,000 for families (about 10 percent of the total); and a $1 per pack cigarette tax (about 1 percent of the total).

Organizers Map an Action Plan

In the meantime, Paul Milne and Glen Schneider began to test the waters of public support, meeting regularly to plan the beginning stages of a grassroots campaign. The "Interim Initiative Coordinating Committee" meetings were held in Oakland at the headquarters of the Service Employees International Union [SEIU] Local 250. In addition to Milne and Schneider, participants included Howard Owens of CCS, Vishu Lingappa and Krista Farey of CAPA, Martha Kowalick, a nurse who had been working on health care issues for the Institute for Effective Action since the 1980s, and Steve Schear, an Oakland lawyer who wrote the single-payer initiative draft on which the 1992 Petris bill in the California legislature was based.

Meetings were then held in San Francisco and Los Angeles where representatives of activist organizations were briefed on the initiative and asked to consult with their members about participating. By this time, Lingappa and Schneider had prepared a memo describing the initiative and arguing

that 1994 was the right time to bring it before the voters. Milne and Schneider had drawn up tentative plans for signature gathering and fund-raising
and a proposed institutional structure for the campaign. Soon it became
clear that many organizations would participate with enthusiasm. CAPA,
Neighbor-to-Neighbor, and the Congress of California Seniors, the California Nurses Association, and some progressive labor unions, including the
United Auto Workers and two large Bay-area locals of SEIU, were among
the most prominent.

When the initiative was filed on December 2, fewer than 100 days remained
of the 150 usually available for signature gathering. Only Paul Milne, who
had experience with last-minute signature gathering in his United Farm
Workers days, was confident they could mount the effort necessary to qualify for the ballot. The natural choice for campaign manager, he was more
apprehensive about how single-payer would fare at the ballot in the 1994
political climate. In an early memo he presciently cited some potential
"killer arguments" the opposition was likely to stress, including (1) Big
Taxes; (2) Big Government; (3) Too Big a Risk; and (4) "Gives Money to
Illegal Aliens."

But what Milne worried about most was money. According to his time-
line, participating organizations would have to pledge $200,000 to the cam-
paign by November 15. The most striking feature of this campaign was the
disparity between the financial resources available to Californians for Health
Security, as the initiative campaign was known, and the insurance industry
opposition campaign that soon emerged. From the beginning almost up to
the end, the initiative was a shoestring operation. For instance, the Congress
of California Seniors had pledged $20,000 in November 1993; they put a
staffer on the phone to contact every one of their three-hundred chapters,
pulling in mostly $50 or $100 checks, with a few as much as $500. CAPA
put out a mailing to its physician members; again the money arrived in
mostly $50 and $100 checks, with a few of the officers giving as much as
$1,000. Milne recalled: "This was going on all over the state. A group would
say they wanted to help and then they were pulling in these dinky little
checks from lots of people."

As it turned out, $207,000 was pledged by November 15, but by January
1 only $59,848 had actually arrived. Two hundred and eighty individuals
had donated $46,202 and twelve organizations had given additional $13,656.
Most of the donors were CAPA doctors and CCS seniors.

In trying to understand the campaign's early fund-raising experience, I
got two amusingly different versions of what the November 15 $200,000

commitment meant. Schneider, who eventually assumed responsibility for fund-raising, described the underlying theory as a "Penguin Strategy" to convince organizations to give substantial sums before the campaign started: "Penguins all jump in the water at the same time. Nobody had to write a check, but if we made the commitment goal [of $200,000], then everybody would be asked to write their checks on the same day. Nobody had to feel like they were going to be a fool and lose their money."

Talking with Milne later, I commented that what actually happened didn't sound like penguins to me. He admitted his penguins didn't exactly follow the script: "With penguins, we got the organizations to do it. But it wasn't lots of money and it didn't come right away. It's like the penguins got together and agreed, 'Okay, we're going to jump,' but they were saying 'I left some things back home; it's about twenty miles across the ice floe each way; I'll be back with my stuff in about a month. We'll do it together then, right?'"

Paul Milne's first major responsibility was to draw up a detailed plan for gathering slightly more than a million signatures. The kickoff would be Saturday, January 22, 1994, and the official plan had three distinct components. First, Milne planned to concentrate on volunteer efforts in those areas with strong single-payer support—the San Francisco Bay area, San Diego, Los Angeles, and about ten other cities. Back when he had expected to have 150 days, Milne was estimating at least seven hundred thousand signatures from this volunteer component of the petition drive. Given the late start, he scaled his goal back to three hundred thousand. Second, members of the large organizations and labor unions that had endorsed the campaign would be enlisted to collect signatures among their own colleagues and coworkers with each organization assigned the number of signatures it estimated it could collect. That totaled about 175,000. Third, because of the late start, it was necessary to augment the volunteer efforts with paid help. The remainder of the signatures would come from a professional signature gathering firm based in Los Angeles, called Progressive Campaigns, Inc. In January, the campaign signed a contract with PCI for up to six hundred thousand signatures, at a cost per signature of about sixty-five cents.

This particular initiative campaign was quite unusual in that by the end a large fraction of the signatures had been gathered by volunteers. A central intent of state initiatives when they were introduced early in the twentieth century was to give ordinary citizens the power to force policy proposals onto the political agenda. Until fairly recently, the idealized image of citizen volunteers fanning out into their communities to gather signatures from fellow citizens was fairly close to reality. By the 1990s, however, most initiative proponents had come to rely on money rather than volunteers to obtain petition signatures. With enough money, proponents can qualify almost any initiative for the ballot. Behind that phenomenon is a whole new industry of firms that specialize in gathering signatures, either with paid collectors or through direct mail. A 1990 advertisement for one California firm proclaimed, "Instant Initiative Qualification. . . . We *guarantee* specific numbers of *valid* signatures on a money-back basis." [5]

As January 22 approached, Milne was forced to face the reality that the campaign would have great difficulty raising the money he was planning on for the petition drive. On January 10, the budget was scaled back considerably. Tentative plans to hire a fund-raising director were abandoned, and the posts of media coordinator and deputy campaign manager were eliminated. Schneider estimated the petition drive shortfall could be as large as $150,000, and with Milne threatening to pull the plug on the campaign unless he could be sure they would not run out of cash midway through the signature gathering, Schneider stepped in and said he would personally guarantee that Neighbor-to-Neighbor would come up with as much as $40,000 in loans if that were required to keep the campaign afloat. He said he was prepared to mortgage his house if necessary. He then convinced Vishu Lingappa and Howard Owens to make similar personal commitments with regard to CAPA and the CCS loans. Soon after, it became clear the campaign would run short of cash by the end of February, long before the petition gathering was completed. Once again Glen Schneider took the lead, agreeing to donate $10,000, three or four months of his salary. Other central figures in the campaign, including CAPA cochairs Barbara Newman and John Roark and Steve Schear, a lawyer, contributed a similar amount. Donald Cohen gave $5,000 and, with other individuals kicking in what they could afford, a total of over $50,000 was raised to meet expenses at that crucial juncture.

By late March, as it became clear that the signature gathering was going to go right down to the wire, the campaign was running out of cash again and Milne called in the loan promises. Glen Schneider and his wife took out a $20,000 mortgage on their house, Howard Owens borrowed $10,000 on his retirement account, and Paul Milne lent his daughter's $10,000 college fund.

San Diego Volunteers

January 22 to April 24, 1994, witnessed an outpouring of thousands of committed volunteers. Over half of the slightly more than one million signatures gathered came from volunteer efforts organized in communities and by large organizations and labor unions. Particularly remarkable was the 565,000 signatures collected; 475,000 came from by community-based volunteer programs. It was an inspiring demonstration that grassroots democracy is not dead in America and compelling evidence that a return to the original volunteer citizen initiative spirit is still possible today.

In San Diego County during the signature gathering period, an all-volunteer effort of three hundred citizens collected 74,245 signatures in an intense ninety-three days, a near-miraculous achievement. The effort was led by Donald Cohen and the two remarkable women who would succeed him as Neighbor-to-Neighbor's codirectors later in the initiative campaign, Jeanne Ertle and Stephanie Jennings.

Ertle, one of seven children from a poor Catholic family who grew up in San Diego, dropped out of San Diego State University, when she married artist Bruce Ertle, and eventually graduated as a Latin American Studies major in her early 40's, came to social activism by way of church connections. She was a member of Bread for the World, a Christian lobbying organization concerned with hunger issues, and had organized chapters in all four congressional districts in San Diego County. In the 1980s she chaired the Peace and Justice Commission of the San Diego Catholic Diocese. In 1988 she was hired as coordinator of the commission and subsequently become director of the Diocesan Office for Justice and Peace, dedicated to educating local Catholics about the Church's social teachings and helping them apply those teachings to the issues of their time. Jeanne's leadership of a successful effort to create a multimillion dollar San Diego Housing Trust Fund resulted in her being honored in 1989 as San Diego's "Housing Advocate of the Year."

In 1989, Ertle organized a conference that brought together people from organized labor, churches, and environmental groups and resulted in the formation of "Workers for Environmental and Social Justice." Soon thereafter, however, her work for the Catholic Diocese came to an abrupt end. A coworker's report to the Catholic heirarchy that Jeanne supported birth control resulted in the bishop's requesting her resignation. She then began doing volunteer work with Donald Cohen and the incipient San Diego Neighbor-to-Neighbor single-payer health care reform project.

Like Ertle, Stephanie Jennings came from a deeply religious background. Her father, a specialist in church history, taught at religious colleges in the Midwest and during summers he took his family abroad on archeological digs in the Middle East. She dates her political awakening to a fiery Jesse Jackson speech in which he urged his listeners to commit themselves to the pursuit of social justice. At San Diego State University she joined Amnesty International and became coordinator of the San Diego chapter. Later she became actively involved with the Central America Information Center in opposing U.S. military aid to El Salvador. In 1990 she joined the staff of the San Diego coalition opposing the war in the Persian Gulf. In 1992 she put all of her acquired organizational skills to use as Greg Akili's campaign manager in his unsuccessful run for Congress.

When Akili was hired by Neighbor-to-Neighbor to direct the San Diego single-payer campaign, Jennings became its media coordinator. Unfortunately, she was to learn first-hand the virtues of single-payer health care. Soon after the campaign she had kidney failure, became seriously ill, received dialysis, and underwent a successful transplant operation. To that point, she admitted, "It seemed like just another policy issue to me—kind of dry. But soon it became real." Anyone in the U.S. who experiences renal failure is eligible for dialysis under Medicare, a single-payer system for the elderly and disabled.

By the end of 1993, Donald, Jeanne, and Stephanie had become discouraged about the prospects for passage of single-payer by the Congress. An initiative seemed a much more promising way to organize single-payer support. A tremendous outpouring of public enthusiasm for a single-payer initiative in California, the nation's most populous state, would put the lie to the Washington claim that this reform was "politically unfeasible."

Donald Cohen feared the organizing capacity required to overcome the enormous money disadvantage they would face in an initiative campaign had not yet been laid; Neighbor-to-Neighbor was quite strong in the San Francisco Bay area, but he would have preferred two more years of intensive organizing to create a comparable base of supporters statewide. He was especially troubled that they had not yet become a "movement of the uninsured," with the personal stake and moral force of the Civil Rights and anti-war movements of the previous generation. But larger forces had determined that 1994 was to be the year for confronting health care reform in America.[6]

The goal Paul Milne had assigned San Diego Neighbor-to-Neighbor in his initial plan was 50,000 signatures. The campaign began with about 150 volunteers on hand for a kickoff rally on Saturday, January 22 and almost 2000 signatures were collected that day. An intensive effort that would involve hundreds of San Diegans had begun. The N2N office became a beehive of activity, where the volunteers would report, pick up petitions, clipboards, and literature, and fan out to prime sites for signature gathering. Remembering the remarkable dedication of the volunteers and the spirit of the campaign, Stephanie Jennings recounted this vignette in her inimitable down-home style:

> I remember the time this proper attorney in her late forties, early fifties came in. She dresses like a school marm, really proper and conservative looking. And there's this guy named Ed who lives on a boat and drives a motorcycle and he's got hair coming out of his ears and they came in and got paired up to get signatures. He looks like a motorcycle guy, wears scruffy clothes. He's an alternative lifestyle kind of person and she's definitely not. She picks up her ironing board [used as portable tables for signature gatherers] and there she goes armed with this ironing board and this box and they're going to meet each other at the grocery store 'cause he's going to ride his motorcycle and she's going to drive her car. The thought of these two people giving two or three hours out of their day at five o'clock at night, when it's dark in the wintertime, and meet this man at a grocery store and stand out there and ask strangers to sign the initiative petition is phenomenal. It was just amazing to see that people would be willing to do that. What it makes me think is that people really want concrete ways to make a difference in the world.[7]

The seemingly incongruous image of a middle aged lawyer paired with a biker was emblematic of an effort that brought together people of widely varying ages and backgrounds who had little in common except their strong conviction and passion for social justice—a bond, of course that overrode superficial difference. Allen McAfee was a computer wiz from Austin, Texas, whose brand-new employer wanted him so badly that he agreed to hold the job for the three months of the petition drive and provide him with health insurance in the meantime. Allen was so adept and so dedicated that he personally collected an astounding 5,205 signatures. Donald Cohen once remarked, "If we ever do achieve single-payer, it will be because of the Allen McAfee's of this world."

Another volunteer was JoAnn Koppany, a quiet, committed woman who became the keeper of the petitions, taking on the responsibility of painstakingly checking every one of the signatures to make sure that all information required on the petition was provided properly. This became her personal project, which she approached with skill and diligence. She had her own office at the Park Boulevard headquarters and she worked full time, eight hours every day.

Ken Thurston was an eighty-one-year-old retired painter who lived in a mobile home park in Chula Vista. A member of the Gray Panthers, he was, according to Stephanie, "a radical, really radical." He would sit under his umbrella out in front of Chula Vista grocery stores gathering signatures for hours everyday. They didn't hear from him for three or four weeks, but then he returned with six hundred signatures. "Donald's eyes went bugging out," Stephanie recalled. By the end of the petition drive, Ken had brought in nineteen hundred signatures. Kathy Wodehouse commuted an hour and a half every day from her home in rural Ramona in eastern San Diego County, where she and her husband owned and operated the Witch Creek winery. Blunt, articulate, and assertive, Kathy achieved considerable renown within single-payer circles when the congressional health care debate was unraveling in the summer of 1994. Kathy called the National Public Radio "Talk of the Nation" program, and the host, Ray Suarez, was so intrigued by her passionate and well-reasoned advocacy that he kept her on the line for several minutes; it was the voice of reason calling from another planet with a view that hadn't been heard from in the public debate.

A couple from Chicago in their late seventies, Harvey and Norma Mader, became Nancy's and my dear friends. A retired labor lawyer and alumnus of Carleton College, Harvey is the epitome of an effective political activist. Relentless in his pursuit of whatever he's after, he became very much committed to single-payer. This led him to pursue the substance and the politics of the national health care debate with his characteristic thoroughness and enthusiasm. I became the beneficiary of his health policy research, in the form of frequent phone alerts and periodic large packages of newspaper clippings, magazine articles, government documents, and books.

From the beginning, the San Diego effort was right on track with the approximately four thousand signatures a week necessary to reach the 50,000 goal. It was arduous work and Donald kept the pressure on. Jeanne and Stephanie, along with a young woman who was paid by the state campaign, Gregory Ormsby, worked day and night to line up volunteers to keep the operation running like clockwork. The first four week's totals were 3,977, 4,194, 4,105 and 3,989, right on the 4,000 signatures per week mark. In mid-February, with the large organization/union numbers lagging, campaign manager Milne raised the San Diego target to 60,000. Like a machine put into a higher gear, the weekly average signature rate lept up to 5,000.

In order to spur them on, the state campaign leadership fostered competition among the organizers, which Stephanie and Jeanne found oppressive. Stephanie referred to it derisively as the "IBM World" of the state leadership. As Jeanne put it, "We really felt strongly it was just wrong. We should be be supporting each other, not competing."

Midway through the signature gathering they rebelled. They refused to compete and began to work together. In retrospect, Jeanne noted, this did not at all represent a change in the state campaign's philosophy. "*We* changed," she asserted with satisfaction. As a consequence, their morale improved markedly. The weekly signature totals, which had declined for a couple of weeks in early March, turned sharply upward. Around the beginning of April, Paul Milne jacked up the San Diego target again, from 60,000 to 70,000. And once again the volunteers met the challenge, increasing the weekly average to 6,000. At that point, though, the statewide signature total was lagging significantly behind the original statewide schedule that had been drawn up in January. The petition drive nominally ended Sunday, April 17, but Milne had built in a cushion—seven days that could be added on at the end, if necessary. It certainly was necessary; as of April 17, the total was still 90,000 signatures short of the number needed to qualify.

Early Saturday morning, when I arrived at the Park Boulevard N2N headquarters for the final weekend push, the place was already alive with activity. I had heard reports, but it was still quite a surprise to see for myself how far San Diego Neighbor-to-Neighbor had come in little more than a year. An impressive signature-gathering machine, a political force, had been created. Among the dozens gathered in the room that morning, there was a pervasive sense of purpose and a powerful feeling of confidence and momentum.

In late April, after a brief orientation, I joined the campaign and was assigned to work with Ellie Batt, a social worker who had taken a leave from her job and was by then an experienced veteran of two weeks of signature gathering. The trick, of course, was to go where we were likely to encounter lots of people—supermarkets, large discount stores, and shopping malls. We drove about an hour north to the Price Club, a huge discount store in San Marcos, arriving at about 10 A.M. It was a very hot day and it soon became apparent that most people were not overjoyed to see us. Our approach had to be brief, understandable, and nonintimidating. For about seven hours we asked customers approaching and exiting the store, "Would you sign this petition to help us put health care reform on the ballot this November?" Most didn't want to be bothered; they saw me as an obstacle and would do their best to avoid eye contact, while maneuvering to avoid interception. Of those curious enough to listen to me, few were interested in pursuing the matter further, and far fewer signed the petition.

It was a frustrating business, to put it mildly. I had been told by my briefers that thirteen to fifteen signatures an hour was typical, but after a few hours in the sun with a somewhat below average rate of ten an hour, I began to get discouraged and a little bit resentful of the people who were passing me by. While I began to fade badly, my partner seemed to pick up confidence and energy as the hours went by. After five hours, I went back to the car to rest. When I returned through the parking lot, I saw Ellie in the distance and realized that while I was exhausted, she was on a roll! She was like a magnet, with hardly anyone getting by her without signing. She kept going for two more hours; by the time we left, she had set a new single-day San Diego single-payer record: 205 signatures. I had collected 51.

The next day, Sunday, April 24, was the climax of the ballot-qualifying effort. We were so close that if the weather held it seemed certain we would go over the top. My assignment was a quite different venue, an environmentalist celebration in Balboa Park, "Earth Fair '94" commemorating the twenty-fourth anniversary of the original Earth Day. It was a setting that attracted many single-payer sympathizers, and I did considerably better than one day before. Many people were eager to sign my petition, including two women with college-age kids who turned out to be nurses at a large San Diego hospital. They were up in arms against managed care and unalterably opposed to the Clinton managed competition plan, which promoted the creation of large managed care networks. They were often frustrated, even infuriated, by the interventions of "utilization review" personnel, former nurses now employed by HMOs and other managed care networks, countermanding what they and the doctors they worked with felt to be appropriate and necessary treatment of their patients.

Around noon I was privileged to witness yet another striking example of the volunteer work that got single-payer on the ballot. While I was having a sandwich on a bench near one of the main entrances to the park, I spotted Miriam Goldberg, a slight woman in her early eighties, one of the most politically perceptive and consistently reliable single-payer activists in San Diego, in the distance with her clipboard. She had planted herself at the top of some steps leading down into the park, in a perfect position to intercept large numbers of people. Like Ellie the day before, she had a commanding presence that somehow made it difficult for people to pass her by. I marveled as she gobbled up the signatures.

That evening back at the San Diego Neighbor-to-Neighbor office, there was an air of excitement and elation. The volunteers based there had collected more than 74,000 signatures, well over their final assigned target of 72,000. And the word from Oakland was that the campaign statewide had comfortably surpassed the seemingly unreachable 1,025,000 target set 93 days before. Universal, affordable single-payer health insurance, shunned in Washington, was on the ballot in California! It was now labeled Proposition 186.

On April 26, the petitions were turned in around the state, with press conferences in San Diego, San Francisco, Los Angeles, Sacramento, and Fresno. I stayed for the press conference at the office of the San Diego County Registrar of Voters, where boxes after boxes of petitions were hauled in and piled high. In the room were dozens of people who had contributed enormous efforts to gather those 74,000 signatures because they believed, or at least fervently hoped, what the banner held high proclaimed: "When the People Lead, the Politicians Will Follow." We were celebrating a tremendous accomplishment and eagerly anticipating what the coming months would bring. At that moment we all felt nothing could stop us.

The story was page one news in America's leading newspapers. The *Washington Post* article, headlined "'Single Payer' Alive, Kicking," noted the national significance of the accomplishment: "As congressional leaders working on health reform legislation have been moving toward the right in search of moderate Democratic and Republican votes, 1,078,000 Californians have signed petitions to turn the debate in the opposite direction."[8] The *San Francisco Chronicle* editorialized,

> Whether one supports it or not, the single-payer, Canadian-style health-care reform initiative that was submitted for California's November ballot last week is just what the doctor ordered to inject some life and substance into the faltering debate over President Clinton's national health-care proposals. . . . In the end, whether the measure wins or loses, Californians will have moved far beyond the meager boundaries of the national health-care debate—a fact that could influence that debate in profound ways. . . . What many people may find over the next six months is that the single-payer system of health-care financing, long-regarded in America as "socialized medicine," has some very attractive features compared to either the present system or the president's alternative.[9]

Like the *Chronicle*, I was hopeful that the demonstrated support for single-payer in California could spark a turn-around in the national debate. On the plane back to Minnesota that afternoon, I felt I had witnessed something very important, the birth of a grassroots social justice movement.

An Unlevel Playing Field

17

A Difficult Transition

In April, I had left a budding California single-payer movement with tremendous momentum—a volunteer army with thousands of committed activists experiencing the euphoria of a hard-won victory. When I came back just a month and a half later in mid-June to work on the campaign for the summer, I expected to find that signature gathering army hard at work on the ballot campaign. Instead, the ebullient spirit, the confidence, and the enthusiasm had evaporated. The N2N office was subdued and figuring out what to do with all the volunteers was said to be a problem and a similar mood had taken hold all over the state. The momentum of the signature gathering phase had somehow been lost.

Stephanie Jennings recalled this period with dismay: "People were spinning their wheels and doing a lot of work that wasn't real work." Both she and Jeanne Ertle were uncomfortable because they sensed their job during the late spring and much of the summer was basically holding the volunteers back while the state leadership got its act together. Literature distribution, public education, and the like were put on hold for months while they were told to wait for just the right messages to be developed by media professionals hired by the campaign.

By the time we went back to Minnesota in August, I could see some promising signs. I assumed that eventually the pieces of the campaign would fall into place and the volunteer army would march again as the November election approached. Then, I imagined, single-payer volunteers throughout San Diego would be involved in precinct-by-precinct organizing, educating people at house meetings, identifying single-payer voters, and getting them to the polls on election day.

When I returned five days before the election, I expected to see that final get-out-the-vote effort in full swing, but there had been *no* precinct-level organizing in San Diego. In fact, there was very little for the volunteers to do besides dropping literature in residential neighborhoods and holding signs by the side of the road for commuters to see. I found that very puzzling, though months later campaign cochair Glen Schneider gave me at least a partial explanation: "Even on local initiatives, the signature gathering usually is the high point. Because there's a measurable goal, people will sacrifice; people will take off work. The answer is building a good precinct-level, grassroots get out the vote operation. To me one of the big embarrassments of the campaign is that we didn't build one successfully."

Naturally, I was curious as to how and why that happened. Schneider demonstrated he understood just why I was puzzled. He said, "You thought, 'These people would do that.' Right? If anybody's going to do it, it's this crowd. Right?"

The solution to this mystery sheds light on serious problems with initiatives as they are now practiced, at least in very populous states like California. It also reveals a difficult, questionable decision by the state campaign leadership as the ballot campaign was planned. Given the down-to-the-wire character of the signature gathering, it is not surprising that the transition to the ballot phase was not given very much attention until the million signatures had been collected.

In retrospect, Donald Cohen lamented that more attention had not been paid to strategic planning for the ballot campaign. If the grassroots momentum generated by the signature gathering was to be sustained, highly focused critical tasks for volunteer activists during the transition period had to be thought through and planned ahead of time. An obvious central component of such a program was a precinct-level operation. Given the dire financial straits the campaign found itself in at that point, another important task for volunteers was phone-banking—getting on the telephone and asking likely prospects for money.

In planning the ballot phase of the campaign, there were two obvious objectives. One was winning a single-payer victory at the polls in California on November 8. The other was building a single-payer movement that would carry on after the election. In May, just after the million-signature goal had been met, the campaign was riding a wave of euphoria. Naturally, the immediate focus was on the election, although the strategy adopted to pursue the goal of winning the election might greatly affect the strength and complexion of the movement that would emerge at the end of the ballot campaign.

The political conditions for substantially advancing the movement's base of supporters through the initiative campaign were surely there. But whether the initiative could be passed in 1994 was much more problematic. To be realistic, we were up against one of the most powerful interest groups in America. It would surely take many years of movement building and protracted struggle. That certainly was the case with the fights for Social Security in the 1930's and America's single-payer model, Medicare, a generation later. In each case, victory was achieved only after repeated defeats.

On May 21, Paul Milne sent out a confidential strategy memo, noting that it would take roughly 4 million votes to win. Published polls suggested 65 to 70 percent of California voters would favor single-payer if they understood what it was, he noted, but a substantial portion of that support was obviously "soft." Single-payer support dropped markedly when the polling questions associated it with unfavorable buzzwords such as "higher taxes." Milne's educated guess at that point was that the "hard" support Proposition 186, the single-payer initiative, had when it was certified for the ballot, was only about 30 percent of the voters, or 2.4 million. The focus of the campaign would be to "harden" the support of at least 1.6 million more voters by educating them so they would stick with their support in the face of the anticipated all-out attack.

As one major element of the campaign strategy, Milne had very high expectations for free media, television, radio, newspapers, and talk shows. The campaign would "conduct professional message research and development, . . . contract with a team of professionals for the development of all public materials, bring on a staff of publicists to coordinate press relations, systematically recruit, train and deploy speakers." Based on his experience in 1988 with Prop 103 the auto insurance reform initiative, political consultant Bill Zimmerman had told Glen Schneider, "You get this on the ballot, you're going to be beating the media away with a stick."

A second means to reach voters was via large organizations that endorsed Prop 186. Milne described this as the "most credible channel of communications." A critical task would be to "get the endorsement of large membership organizations and then work with their leadership to educate their members about Prop 186 and to get out those votes on election day." At the top of the large organization wish list was California's largest union, the Service Employees International Union (SEIU), which represented hospital workers, among others. SEIU's influencial state political director, Dean Tipps, had been outspokenly skeptical of the single-payer effort, fearing it would be overwhelmed by the insurance industry opposition. But once the signatures were submitted, SEIU immediately endorsed Prop 186 and Tipps joined the campaign's executive board, where he played an influential role, including arranging the money for polls and focus groups and personally overseeing the crafting of the public relations campaign messages.

Donald Cohen was tapped to lead that statewide effort to collect other major endorsements. Milne predicted that free media and large organizations would secure on the order of one million additional votes.

A third element of Milne's overall strategy involved paid media, television and radio advertising in the final weeks of the campaign. As a tactic this one was, at best, a major compromise, a coming to terms with the reality that the campaign did not have the money for television advertising at any earlier point. According to Milne's initial calculations, the campaign needed at least $1 million in the bank to come roaring out of the blocks in the ballot phase. Instead, it was over $200,000 in debt. An indicator of the sad financial state of the campaign at the end of the petition drive was that numerous paid local organizers, including some of the sparkplugs of the signature gathering operations in Orange County, Long Beach, westside Los Angeles, the San Fernando Valley, Fresno, San Jose, Santa Cruz, San Francisco, Berkeley, Marin County, San Bernardino, San Diego, Sacramento, and Sonoma had been laid off for lack of funds. The campaign was well-organized in San Diego, the Bay Area, and in some other northern cities, but otherwise it had huge gaping holes, most notably in the state's largest population center, the Los Angeles basin, and elsewhere in the South. There were enormous demographic holes as well, most notably among Hispanics, blacks, and the poor. The key to filling those crucial gaps was organizers, but the campaign could not afford to pay their modest salaries.

The fourth major channel to the public was described in the strategy memo as a "massive grassroots voter education program." The goal was to mobilize volunteers in five thousand precincts throughout the state in a grassroots campaign to persuade, identify, and get to the polls at least a half million swing voters. It would begin with the distribution of a million plastic "Health Security Cards" simulating the wallet card that every California resident would receive if the initiative passed; getting a quarter to a half million bumper stickers on cars; posting fifty thousand lawn and house signs; and distributing at least five million pieces of campaign literature. It would culminate with intensive Voter Persuasion, and GOTV (Get-Out-The-Vote) programs between Labor Day and Election Day in each of the five thousand targeted precincts. The goal was to provide precinct leaders with a list of two hundred swing voters and charge them with identifying and producing one hundred single-payer votes on election day.

This would be the main grassroots field program, with a sequence of specific outreach tasks that would engage the volunteer signature gathering army and many new volunteers in contacting and persuading voters throughout the state. It would be an enormous effort, comparable in scope and intensity to the petition drive. Requiring a large number of organizers to reach new regions and constituencies, it had the potential vastly to expand the base of single-payer supporters in California. Martha Kowalick, who had organized and supervised the signature gathering, would be in charge.

However, as a consequence of the dire cash-flow situation, an unexpected and far-reaching decision was made by the campaign leadership. Of the four basic programs described in Milne's memo, two were relatively inexpensive. Less than $200,000 was budgeted for free media and publicity and $50,000 for organizational endorsements. With paid media, the sky was the limit, of course, with a minimum of $1.5 million required and an additional $3 to $6 million needed to be "competitive." As for the program to mobilize citizens in five thousand precincts statewide, $750,000 was budgeted in Milne's original plan and $1 million or more would have been required to do it very well. As the crucial decisions that shaped the strategy for the ballot campaign were considered in late May and early June, it became agonizingly clear that given the financial situation, GOTV had two different possible meanings, and that a choice would have to be made between them: either Get On TV or Get Out the Vote.

According to Donald Cohen, the campaign leadership felt enormous pressure to win or at least make a credible showing, which was generally agreed to be at least 40 percent of the vote. The period between the signature gathering and ballot phases of the campaign was marked by ongoing tension between those who felt "this has to be a grassroots campaign from the bottom up . . . and those who felt the need to figure out what it's going to take to win." Glen Schneider stressed that to win in California you have to be on television. Others on the steering committee, most prominently CAPA chair Barbara Newman, representatives of the California Nurses Association, and some leaders of local single-payer groups, favored a large investment in organizers and Get Out the Vote activities, especially the precinct-level effort to involve the signature gathering activists. To them, winning in 1994 was an important goal, but using the campaign to build a strong and diverse single-payer movement was absolutely essential.

At the end of May, according to Paul Milne, the grassroots campaign was simply "pulled out of the plan, . . . just clipped right out." Instead of running that effort, Martha Kowalick was put in charge of house parties to pay for the media ads. "This is a case," Milne said, "where a lack of money was deadly."

When it came time to decide on a plan, the campaign was nearly $200,000 in debt. To put into place a precinct-level operation would have involved hiring a large number of local organizers *in the next month or two*. They simply did not have the money at that time. In Donald Cohen's words, "The realities of the situation determined what we could and could not do. When you are in deficit, you cannot hire organizers."

Television ads were different; the campaign leaders decided to hold off on TV until the last two weeks before the election and see if they could raise enough money for that. This meant that for a campaign field operation, the statewide precinct Get-Out-The-Vote program was replaced by an ambitious fund-raising effort to pay for the television advertising. That fund-raising effort involved hiring many organizers to arrange "house parties." In the end, it was quite successful, raising nearly a million dollars for television advertising. But for months there was great concern about whether even that would succeed. Cohen recalls meetings as late as September, "when it wasn't clear we were going to have even $200,000 for TV. In which case, there was not even going to be any TV either! That was very real. I looked at some of those fundraising projections and I thought 'Never going to happen.'"

The upshot was that the centerpiece of the ballot campaign plan ended up being fund-raising house parties to pay for a last-minute television advertising blitz. Of course, in June when the decision was made, the leadership was anticipating a great deal of press and other "free media." At that point there were high hopes for Donald's large organization endorsement project too. If organizations like the three million–member California AARP could be convinced to endorse the initiative, that in itself could lead to large-scale member education programs and Get-Out-the-Vote efforts. But there was no money available to pay for organizers to work with the organizations to make that happen.

So, in the end the part of the plan aimed at activating volunteers was cut entirely out of the state campaign budget. Although there was no formal announcement of this decision within the campaign, the message got out and it sent out shock waves to the grassroots. Stephanie Jennings in San Diego recalls how she and Jeanne Ertle reacted: "We both knew that what we needed was a precinct operation and we needed something on the level of the signature gathering. But Donald insisted that precinct operations didn't win elections. . . . Advertising was the thing that won campaigns."

In retrospect Donald regretted that they had not thought through a "win-win" strategy—aimed to win the election and come out of the campaign with a greatly strengthened single-payer movement, ready for a protracted struggle in the years ahead.

A Formidable Foe

On May 16, three weeks after the petitions were submitted, the enemy was sighted. It was a formidable foe indeed. Calling itself "Taxpayers Against the Government Takeover" (TAGT, or the "No on 186" campaign), the opposition hit the ground running. Just by introducing itself, it pushed what early polls and focus groups had identified as the two most effective anti-single-payer hot buttons—"run by big government" and paid for by enormous new taxes. The campaign was headed by Kirk West, president of the California Chamber of Commerce; and lurking out of sight in the bushes and bankrolling the effort was the American insurance industry. One early indication that it was taking the single-payer challenge very seriously was the immediate hiring of Goddard*Claussen/First Tuesday, the media consultants who had made the potent Harry and Louise ads that were widely credited with undermining public support for the Clinton health care proposal.

One clear lesson from past California initiatives for change was their vulnerability to well-financed attack advertising. To defeat an initiative, opponents simply had to plant sufficient seeds of fear and doubt in enough voters' minds about what the change would bring. Studies of previous initiatives had shown that an opposition with enough money to mount a concerted fear-mongering campaign via television ads, targeted direct mail, and other tools of modern marketing almost invariably defeated initiatives for change, usually quite decisively. In this case, the health insurance industry had plenty of money and it was prepared to spend whatever necessary to defeat an initiative that threatened its very survival.

The contrast between the financial resources available to the opposing forces on this initiative was truly remarkable. In the next six months, TAGT raised ten million dollars, most of it coming from a very few large insurance companies and HMOs, which are insurer-provider combinations. The largest TAGT donor, at $1,672,035, was the Health Insurance Association of America (HIAA), a Washington-based lobbying coalition of most of the smaller health insurance companies. Next, totaling $1,655,722, came a group of five California HMO giants, led by PacifiCare's $525,470 and Blue Cross/California Care's $500,250. After that came our "good neighbor," State Farm, who was there with $994,988 to help defeat universal health care coverage for Californians. Then came another Washington health care lobbying powerhouse, a consortium of the five largest insurance companies known as the Alliance for Managed Competition; four of them from New England, Boston-based Prudential and Hartford-based Aetna, Met Life and Travelers, gave California's TAGT $966,428. Three more big players in the Washington insurance lobbying community, Connecticut General Life, the American Council on Life Insurance, and the American Insurance Association contributed a total of $833,509. Then came the California Hospitals Committee on Issues with $709,681 and the California Physicians Insurance Corporation with $555,000.[1] The grand total for those fifteen TAGT contributors was $7.39 million, almost three-quarters of the more than $10 million the "No on 186" campaign ended up spending. Fourteen of the fifteen were insurance providers or insurance industry lobbying coalitions.

By contrast, the largest source of funds for the "Yes on 186" campaign was house parties. The campaign's principal field operation, directed by Martha Kowalick and employing 19 area organizers and 282 volunteer speakers, arranged 1,455 house parties that attracted 22,000 attendees and grossed $978,000, the bulk of that coming in October, just in time to pay for nearly $750,000 in television advertising the ten days before the election.

In addition, county and grassroots organizations such as San Diego Neighbor-to-Neighbor contributed a total of $427,000, much of it in "in-kind" contributions to pay the salaries of local organizers such as Donald Cohen, Jeanne Ertle, and Stephanie Jennings and underwrite the local campaigns, though Donald went on the state campaign payroll during the summer. More conventional fund-raising approaches were employed as well, such as soliciting from large organizations, primarily labor unions and AARP, and from wealthy individuals.

In the end, $3.2 million was raised by Californians for Health Security, a fairly impressive sum, though far short of the $10 million or so typically spent in winning senatorial or other statewide campaigns in California. However, the late arrival of most of the money greatly influenced the character and diminished the effectiveness of the campaign. As campaign cochair Glen Schneider remarked in retrospect, "We needed to push everything back about three months! And the lack of money in any kind of an effort really kills off the creativity."

Seven weeks into the opposition campaign, by June 30, 1994, the money was pouring in to Taxpayers Against the Government Takeover. Twenty-one companies and lobbying coalitions had already contributed $510,000 in amounts ranging from a low of $5,000 to three $100,000 contributions; polls and focus groups had been conducted; some of California's leading media and political consultants had been hired; and an "expert" study of the impacts Prop 186 would have on the California economy had been completed.

In the meantime, the single-payer ballot campaign was having trouble getting out of the starting blocks, with one impressive accomplishment, but several dark clouds spotted on the horizon.

An Impressive Accomplishment

The big early success of the "Yes on 186" campaign was organizational endorsements. The campaign strategy was to concentrate on a few prominent organizations with very large memberships that could be reached through those organizations' newsletters, magazines, slate cards, and forums. The strong encouragement of the organizational leaders could win many votes.

Because of the lack of financial resources, during the critical first three months of the ballot campaign, Donald Cohen had almost sole responsibility for this statewide assignment while he continued to direct San Diego Neighbor-to-Neighbor. Only in August did the state campaign find sufficient funds to hire him as Director of Coalition Building. Some prominent organizations had already given their endorsement. Beth Capell of the California Nurses Association (CNA) and N2N's Glen Schneider were co-chairs of the "Yes on 186" campaign. The California Teachers Association, the California Professional Firefighters, the state AFL-CIO executive committee, the Service Employees International Union (SEIU), the Oil, Chemical and Atomic Workers Union, the International Longshoreman's and Warehousemen's Union, the California Council of Churches, the Gray Panthers, the Older Women's League, and the Congress of California Seniors had already endorsed by August. With single-minded determination, Donald set out to expand that list.

The two most sought-after organizations were the three million–member California affiliate of the American Association of Retired Persons and the California League of Women Voters. In seeking their endorsements, Donald had to contend with reservations or outright opposition of their national leadership. Both of their national offices had joined the Campaign for Health Security that was backing the Clinton plan in Washington and they were not enthusiastic about the prospect of their California affiliates supporting single-payer. A separate strategy, with a specially tailored lobbying plan, was developed for winning the support of each organization.

To gauge member sentiment about Prop 186, the AARP state leadership announced that its State Legislative Committee (SLC) would sponsor a series of mid-June hearings, in San Diego, Los Angeles, and San Francisco, with the final decision scheduled for the regular SLC meeting on June 21 in Sacramento. Knowing that single-payer had a major base of support among senior citizens and organizations like the Congress of California Seniors, the Gray Panthers, and the Older Womens' League, the "yes" campaign packed the hearings in each city with elderly supporters and spokespersons who lined up in advance to testify and make key points.

The campaign also collected intelligence about how each SLC member was leaning on this issue and what concerns each one had about single-payer; they each received appropriately crafted messages via mail and telephone. At the same time AARP leaders in both Sacramento and Washington received a barrage of a thousand letters and phone calls. Finally, exceptionally articulate and effective spokespersons were prepped for the Sacramento meeting of the full committee at which the decision would be made. In particular, they were prepared to counter the arguments against single-payer by representatives of the California State Employees Association, CSEA, which offers its own health insurance plan. When CSEA reps claimed as expected that they offered a better benefits package than Prop 186, they and the committee were offered such convincing evidence to the contrary that it took the wind out of their sails. The SLC voted overwhelmingly to endorse the initiative, as did the League of Women Voters after a similarly intense lobbying campaign. In July, these two organizations lent their prestige to the campaign as two of the three official signatories of the pro-186 ballot argument distributed to all California registered voters.

There were other important endorsement successes too. Dozens of labor union locals throughout the state signed on; so did the largest statewide teachers union, the California Federation of Teachers. A striking phenomenon was the endorsement of many national organizations like Consumers Union, Church Women United, Citizen Action, the National Association of Social Workers, the Screen Actors Guild, and state and local affiliates of unions like the Communications Workers and Service Employees, all of whose national offices were part of the Campaign for Health Security that was lobbying for the Clinton bill in Washington but whose local membership strongly favored single-payer.

Generally speaking, the effort to garner organizational endorsements was a great success. The combined memberships of the endorsing California organizations was between five and six million voters. However, given the limited resources available to the campaign, translating those membership numbers into votes would prove to be very difficult.

Dark Clouds

Meanwhile, the campaign was receiving a series of ominous signals. The complete results of polls and focus groups commissioned by Dean Tipps of the SEIU found that while substantial majorities of those polled liked the physician choice, universal coverage, and cost containment provisions of the initiative, they were very fearful of an increased role for government in health care and of the increase in taxes to pay for it, despite the promise of significantly lower overall health care costs to most families. Probing further, the studies found many people dubious that the promises of the initiative would really materialize. They knew their taxes would go up but were skeptical that their over-all health care costs would go down, and they feared they would encounter a much greater degree of bureaucratic control. Two other strong fears also emerged in the polls and focus groups. One was that since the program would cover undocumented immigrants unless the legislature decided differently, it would make California a magnet for them. The other was that the program would adversely affect the fragile California economy, driving out businesses and reducing jobs.

One thing that surely wasn't going to swell our vote total was what people would see first when they went into the polling booth and turned to Proposition 186. The California Attorney General's Office had given it an off-putting title: Health Services. Taxes. The SEIU surveys found that going by only the information printed on the ballot, 27 percent of respondents indicated they favored the initiative and 40 percent were opposed. This was very scary news, as Glen Schneider explained: For an initiative to succeed, a comfortable majority of voters has to support it before the campaign even begins. A campaign, he explained, does not generally succeed in moving an issue forward; if all goes well it has succeeded in heading off the other side trying to tear it down. The rough rule of thumb, according to Schneider is: You've got to begin the campaign with more than 60 percent to have a chance of winning.[2]

In July, when the campaign received the opposition's ballot arguments, it was clear that their polls and focus groups had uncovered the same vulnerabilities ours had. The first claim in their ballot argument was that if Prop 186 were to pass, "most Californians would lose private health coverage and instead be forced to get coverage through a massive new government-run bureaucracy—a completely untested and experimental system in the United States." The second claim was that Prop 186 "would cost $40 billion in new taxes, including huge increases in income taxes and payroll taxes. That's the biggest tax increase in California history and there are no limits on how high taxes could be raised!" And third, "Spectrum Economics, a respected economic consulting firm, concludes that over 300,000 jobs could be lost over the next four years because of the huge new costs of the payroll tax. Small business would be hit hardest and many could be forced to go out of business, lay off employees or leave California." The ballot argument was signed by the president of the California Taxpayers Association, the director of the Organization of Nurse Executives/California, and the state director of the National Federation of Independent Businesses.

Leaders of the single-payer campaign decided immediately that they needed at least one well-known, highly respected individual to be associated in the public mind as its symbolic leader—someone who would lend instant legitimacy and credibility to the Yes on 186 effort. Ralph Nader and former Surgeon General C. Everett Koop came to mind. Nader's organization, Public Citizen, was the leading backer of single-payer health care in Washington, and he had played just that kind of symbolic role in the successful 1988 Proposition 103 initiative to reform California auto insurance. Koop had enormous moral authority as well as the benevolent appeal of a physician. But neither, unfortunately, was interested.

The third name on the short list was the California Democratic Party's gubernatorial candidate, Kathleen Brown. With her backing and the backing of her party, Proposition 186 would be sure to be a central issue in the 1994 California election. Brown was approached soon after the primary election and asked to support Prop. 186. At that point, however, she had a substantial lead in the polls and it was evidently the judgment of her advisors that supporting Prop 186 would only hurt her, both in political support among the electorate and in fund-raising support among influential segments of corporate California.

The big surprise was that Brown chose to go beyond refusing her support. I recall vividly the shock at San Diego Neighbor-to-Neighbor when the draft of the opposition ballot argument was received. It led with quotations from two prominent California politicians. Republican Governor Pete Wilson's assessment of Prop 186 was unsurprising: "'This initiative is exactly the wrong medicine for California's recovering economy. It's a budget buster and a job killer.'" The shocker was the other one: "'We all want to achieve universal health care coverage for Californians, but this measure is not the right way to go.' [signed] Treasurer Kathleen Brown."

Brown's campaign manager had specifically authorized the quote. Having Brown come out publicly against Prop 186 was a severe blow and it hung like a very dark cloud over the campaign all the way to November.

Kathleen Brown's motivations remained a mystery. As Paul Milne noted, "That was a real surprise. I expected her to be opposed, but not vocally. Why split her constituency?" Then he recounted an ironic footnote to the Brown episode. Very soon thereafter, in early July, Milne was approached by the Brown campaign field director, Scott Washburn, whom he knew well from past work together. Scott said, "'You've got the leadership for a massive state operation; we have the resources. We're planning to put three, four million dollars into this. So, why don't we work together on this?' I said, 'There's a little sticky point here, Scott. Your candidate is opposed to our measure. She's quoted in the ballot argument. How are you going to make that work?' He acted very surprised." Milne later reflected wistfully on what might have been: "Had she been for it, the 186 constituency and forces would have spearheaded the Kathleen Brown grassroots organization throughout the state. . . . We could have created organizations in 20,000 precincts."[3]

To make matters worse, a dark cloud of bitter internal controversy of the campaign leadership's own making came to hover over the ballot initiative. It had to do with the issue of whether or not undocumented immigrants would be eligible for Prop 186's health care benefits. The initiative drafting group had attempted to finesse this issue with language that said in effect that all California residents would be eligible unless and until the legislature decided otherwise. But a raging political controversy had arisen around another initiative, Prop 187, which would deny "illegal aliens" and their children access to public education, nonemergency public health care, and other public social services and require health care workers, educators, social workers and other public employees to report anyone they suspect to be undocumented immigrants. The Republican candidate for governor, Pete Wilson, had come out in favor of Prop 187, Kathleen Brown, to her credit, had come out against it and a sizeable movement in opposition to Prop 187 had been organized.

The internal controversy within the Prop 186 campaign arose from a decision by the thirty-five member steering committee to insert a single word in the "Yes on 186" ballot argument. The crucial sentence was "With

Proposition 186, your coverage can never be taken away, as long as you are a legal California resident." The steering committee was sharply divided on whether or not to put *legal* in. Dean Tipps of the SEIU urged the steering committee to include the word, arguing that allowing opponents to connect Prop 186 to Prop 187 and the "illegal aliens" issue would hurt the election prospects of 186. The steering committee agreed to insert the word *legal* in the ballot argument. Barbara Newman, cochair of CAPA and a member of the committee who had voted against the decision, led a fight to reverse it. She had organized meetings between the executive Board and Latino and Asian professionals as the language was being drafted; only two members had appeared and the full Legislative Board voted to retain the language in question. "Specifically, they rejected these people's offer to promote 186 in their organizations and communities, in return for changing the ballot argument wording," she wrote in a memo to the leadership. "In my judgment, they honestly felt that *the use of anti-immigrant rhetoric was necessary to secure a victory for Prop 186.* This is racism. This is the cynical abandonment of the concerns of people of color for short-term political goals, without regard for long-term consequences. . . ." Even in the short run, the decision had unfortunate results: Most campaign workers [were] caught up purely in winning the election, not, as I believed was essential, in building a movement. This also explained the lack of a program to use the many volunteers who'd gathered all those signatures. . . . With no centralized grassroots component to the campaign, who needed them? If they couldn't give or raise money for the paid political commercials, there was nothing for them to do.[4]

Donald Cohen later described the agonizing effect this had on him and others in the campaign: "It was bad. . . . We looked like we were liars because in the initiative we said *California resident* and [in the ballot argument] we said *legal resident.* There were lawyers arguing back and forth. There were debates. People tried to overturn it. It went through September. It was really terrible."[5]

Meanwhile, the campaign focus had shifted to raising money for television and radio advertising. Jenning's continued, "Money was the thing. That's what [the state campaign leadership] talked about; we had to raise money." House parties were to be the main activity. In San Diego, organizing and speaking at house parties became Stephanie's and Jeanne's principal preoccupation. They did virtually all the house parties. But that did not engage the activists.

In San Diego, as elsewhere, the activists became restive as it become clearer and clearer that there was little for them to do. A few of the San

Diego volunteers did make important contributions to the endorsement project and the San Diego speakers bureau which sent volunteers to house parties was a serious effort. Many volunteers hosted fund-raising gatherings, solicited local business endorsements, wrote letters to the editors of local papers, and improvised other useful projects. However, there was also quite a bit of what seemed to Jeanne and Stephanie to be "make-work" to keep the volunteers occupied. There was nothing like the focused, statewide effort with important, well-defined goals, as in the petition drive.

Finally, late in the summer a bit of a rebellion broke out among the San Diego volunteers. "They started calling us." Jeanne said, "and telling us we were doing the wrong thing. They said, 'We need things to distribute! Where's the literature?' We kept being told [by the state office] that we would get it by a month or two before the election, . . . [that] the message hasn't been honed yet. As a result we started to do our own literature and we started running it off. It wasn't THE message, but it was what the volunteers needed." Stephanie continued, "The problem was we didn't have any guidance. . . . We just decided to do what we had done during signature gathering—pass out literature at events and street fairs, places where there would be people." The San Diego group by then had also modified the state model for house parties and were using those events primarily for education, not fund-raising: "By this time it can safely be said we had broken away from the campaign," said Jeanne. "We weren't waiting for them to tell us what to do. We paid attention to our activists." . . . Stephanie added, "In retrospect, we should have organized a Get-Out-The-Vote campaign ourselves. We could have done it, but the house parties were all consuming."[6]

A Sophisticated Propaganda Campaign

During the three months from July through September, Taxpayers Against the Government Takeover solicited $5.2 million, mostly from the insurance industry, and they spent the entire amount. Their media firm, Goddard*Claussen/First Tuesday, spent a total of $4,266,114 in those three months, and they were pros. Clearly the "No on 186" campaign had learned from its polling and focus groups what we had learned from ours, that among the messengers the public trusted most on health care reform were nurses. But while the California Nurses Association had endorsed the "Yes" campaign, and Beth Capell was a cochair, what Californians saw and heard repeatedly in the months leading to the election were actresses representing nurses in television and radio ads with "No on 186" messages.

In thirty-second television spots, for example, "Jane Clair Walsh, R.N.," speaking from the stage-set of a nurses' station, warned the public: "Believe me, we know health care reform is critical. . . . But Proposition 186 isn't the reform we want. . . . 186 will force most of us to give up our private health coverage . . . and push us into a government run health care bureaucracy . . . controlled by an elected politician, not a doctor or a nurse. . . . This kind of government takeover is bad medicine for California." As she spoke, dire warnings flashed on the screen: "Government Health Care Takeover"; "Health 'Czar' Controls Health Care; "No on 186."[7]

The first half of TAGT's widely aired sixty-second radio spot also featured nurses. Two of them meet in the hall of a hospital. One, whom the other describes as "our floor health care reform expert," says she's looked into Prop 186, but "it's not the reform we want; it pushes most people out of their private health care plans and into a government system." The other nurse replies, "Politicians don't know what kind of health care people need!" An announcer then intones, "But many nurses do," and the segment ends with the voices of a group of women saying in unison, "NO on 186."[8]

In the three months from July through September, Goddard*Claussen/First Tuesday spent 2.8 million dollars to buy television and radio air time. All the major media markets in California were saturated with those spots.

Outraged, by this and other misleading advertisements, the California Nurses Association, by far the largest professional and labor organization in California representing registered nurses, called a press conference in San Francisco. They condemned the "No on 186" campaign and the California Organization of Nurse Executives, representing relatively small numbers of supervisory nurses which had sponsored the spots and implied that nurses in general opposed the initiative. But the press conference received very little coverage, and the advertising was so effective that when San Diego's major newspaper, the *Union-Tribune,* carried a story about the initiative, the reporter listed the California Nurses Association as one of the groups opposed to Prop 186. And from early summer until Election Day, surveys noted a steady shift in popular opinion toward mistrust of government and greater confidence in the ability of insurance companies to run the health care system.

Taxpayers Against the Government Takeover's second major method of contacting voters was direct mail from insurance companies and HMOs. A major feature of direct mail is that it is a private channel of communication, with no easy way of making it likely that false or misleading information will be countered. In October, for example, PacifiCare, California's largest

HMO, sent out a glossy, multicolored, eye-catching brochure put out by Tax-payers Against the Government Takeover. Inside was cartoon featuring a man and a woman with their eyes bugging out, the looks on their faces suggesting they had just seen something horrible; in their hands they held a paper labeled "Prop 186 TAX BILL, $40 Billion, Government Run Health Care."

An accompanying letter from PacifiCare's president and CEO encouraged the public's greatest fears. For instance, Prop 186 "would turn over full control of every aspect of the health care system to the state government . . . [and] devastate California's economy with heavy new taxes on individuals and businesses. . . . *A married couple with 2 children and an annual income of $32,000 would be subject to a state income tax increase of over 200 percent.*"

His first claim, that government would be in full control of health care, was patently false. In the proposed single-payer system, the management of health care delivery would remain in the hands of private doctors, hospitals, and clinics. Day-to-day decisions about treatment would be decided by physicians and nurses in consultation with their patients and possibly HMO insurers. To contain health care costs, however, the government would macromanage the provider system by negotiating annual physician and clinic fee schedules and hospital global budgets.[9]

His second claim, a family income tax increase of "over 200 percent," was true, but grossly misleading. The family he described would have paid $296 in California income taxes in 1993. Under Prop. 186, comprehensive single-payer health insurance would cost that family an additional $680, in fact an increase of 230 percent. But to stress that was to mislead and frighten. Under the current system, a typical family with one breadwinner earning $32,000 and working for a large employer, who typically pays 80 percent of the employee's health care premium, would pay about $1,700 annually for the remaining part of the insurance premium and out-of-pocket costs. Under the Prop 186 single-payer plan, that family would find its total annual health care costs lowered by nearly half to $930. What is more, the employer would find its contribution reduced from $4,400 annually to $2,848.[10]

Soon thereafter, in mid-October, the State Farm Insurance Company spent $833,051 on letters to approximately 2.5 million California policyholders, personally signed by their local insurance agent, who wrote: "Dear Neighbor: As your State Farm agent, I'm responsible for helping you make good insurance decisions. . . . I plan to vote "No" on Prop 186, and here's why. . . ."[11] In effect, the policyholders' own insurance premiums were being used to persuade them to oppose Prop 186.

In response to all the negative publicity, the California Physicians Alliance published a booklet called "Who Do They Think They Are Fooling? Response to the Lies About Prop 186: A Resource for Speakers and Debaters." Knowledgeable and articulate spokesperson for Prop 186 were available for debates from the "Yes on 186" campaign and from CAPA and its national parent organization, Physicians for a National Health Program. Authors of several studies commissioned by the "No on 186" campaign would have been natural debate opponents. Unfortunately, the debate was never joined. In-depth media coverage was essential if California citizens were to be able to sort out the conflicting claims. However, the media did not seek out and disseminate the information voters needed to make informed judgments about Prop 186. With a few notable exceptions, such as Susan Duerksen's excellent reporting in the San Diego *Union-Tribune,* California's newspapers did not appear to feel that was their responsibility. Besides, the chief source of news for most Californians is not newspapers, but television and radio, and the demise of the fairness doctrine and equal time requirements in the 1980s had virtually eradicated their statutory responsibility. Now it is mostly talk shows that masquerade as forums for public debate, most prominently talk radio with its overwhelmingly right-wing bias.

In short, the expectation that the California media would flock to cover a critical, controversial debate over an issue that was at the center of the nation's public policy agenda in 1994 simply never materialized. Glen Schneider reflected later that "We thought we were going to be the big show in town in a raging debate. Instead, we were basically ignored. . . . Some of it was because the hard-headed polls, the *LA Times,* the Field poll, were showing us badly behind. The press decided we had no chance, so they decided not to cover it. [Another factor was] the economics of the press—the insurance companies are big advertisers; they have a self-interest in keeping this quiet."

Whatever media coverage Prop 186 did manage to get in newspaper editorials and radio and television commentaries was overwhelmingly superficial and negative. Virtually all of California's daily newspapers editorialized against 186. In the San Diego area, the *Union-Tribune* opposed "a government takeover of the state's health care system, financed by massive new taxes. . . ." Radio station KNSD claimed that "Proposition 186 would bring socialized medicine to California, . . . kill the economy with a huge burden of new taxes, . . . create a monster bureaucracy, . . . cost us tens of billions of dollars and hundreds of thousands of jobs. . . ." In some cases the editorials went beyond misleading information to outright lies. According to Dr. Vishu Lingappa, "A [leading California] newspaper came out with an editorial against us that was loaded with lies, like this initiative is bad because it doesn't cover long-term care. . . . The reporter [on that paper] called me, . . . embarrassed by the transparency of their lying [and saying] he [had done] everything he could to prevent that cheap shot. . . ." A radio station that had similarly lied about the provisions of Prop 186 offered Lingappa a taped sixty-second rebuttal to their "No" editorial. "You understand I'm not just asking for the rebuttal time," he told them, "but I am bothered by the fact that what you said in your editorial was not factually true. . . . As far as they were concerned, they were discharging their entire responsibility to the truth, to morality, by giving me a sixty-second response. . . . I said I would like to meet with your editorial board because I can prove to you that what you said was not true. . . . They were not interested in pursuing that discussion." Reflecting on such experiences, Dr. Lingappa later wrote, "The media abdicated any responsibility for conveying the truth. . . . Moreover, by recklessly cramming complex issues into thirty and sixty-second sound bites, and by not following up contradictory statements, the media typically garbled and confused what little information they did present on Prop 186. . . . Whether due to ideological hostility, collusion of editorial boards with their insurance industry advertisers, laziness on the part of news anchors and reporters, or for other reasons, most "no" voters received a wildly distorted image from the media of what was contained in Prop 186."[12]

Just as the campaign strategy to educate voters via free media coverage fell far short of expectations, the attempt at using endorsing organizations to get out their members to back 186 did not fare much better. The endorsing organizations allowed their names to be used as backers of Prop 186, but generally speaking, they did not expend very much of their own resources promoting it. The California AARP, for instance, did arrange for activists to speak, pass out flyers, participate in phone banks, and the like. But when AARP officials from Washington and California were urged to include a strong endorsement from their leadership as an insert or a wrap-around in a national publication that reached all three million California members, they told the campaign that they were unwilling to incur such an expense. At most their efforts reached one hundred thousand AARP members, about 3 percent of the California total.

In retrospect, Glen Schneider felt that the way senior citizens were treated in the initiative had been a tactical error. Had Prop 186 passed, seniors would have been folded in with the rest of the population and would have received a better benefits package than the current Medicare provides. But that approach made it possible for the opposition to tell seniors that Prop

186 would "take away your Medicare." A better approach, Schneider believes, would have been to leave Medicare as a separate program and to include the extra benefits for seniors as a supplementary benefits package in California. In any case, the "No on 186" campaign spent so much money striking fear in the hearts of senior citizens that no altered tactics would have been sure to succeed. Although their health benefits would have been substantially increased, only 27 percent of the seniors who went to the polls voted for Prop 186 in November.

The remaining element of the campaign strategy, paid media, was the focus of much of the fund-raising and expenditures in the ballot campaign. Martha Kowalick's house party fund-raising program was substituted for precinct-by-precinct organizing as the campaign's field operation. The part of that program that was run out of the state headquarters in Oakland grossed $978,000, the bulk of the money coming in near the end of the campaign, just in time to pay for television and radio spots during the ten days before the election. To run this program, the state campaign invested $353,000. A complementary "Radio Phone Bank" fund-raising program that Glen Schneider conceived and Donald Cohen and Ingrid Smith executed brought in an additional $157,000. That involved phone banks of volunteers calling supporters to ask for money to fund radio ads that both spread the 186 message and prompted additional contributions.

There is no doubt that the house party program was a shining light of the campaign, ranking alongside the campaign's other field operation, the signature gathering. However, the principal use of the money the house parties raised, a last minute television and radio advertising blitz, had little impact on the outcome. One reason was surely the lack of sufficient money early on, as opposed to the "No" campaign that was able to flood the airwaves with ads from late summer on. Ten days before the election was simply too late for even the most brilliant ads—and the two Prop 186 television spots surely were not that—wouldn't have been able to rescue Prop 186. The last-minute advertising blitz was almost like flushing a hard-earned $750,000 down the drain.

By the time I returned to San Diego a few days before the election, there was nothing left to do but play out the final scenes of a very sad drama. Out at the N2N headquarters, people were trying to stay upbeat, hoping at least for a respectable showing. In the final hours, on the evening before and the morning of Election Day, I stood on a busy street downtown with Bruce Ertle and others holding up a large "YES ON 186" sign. With a marker, I added a second message to my sign: "and NO ON 187." Election evening, back at the headquarters, I joined friends who had for nearly a year put everything they had into Proposition 186. What began as a party ended more like a wake when the 1994 California Single-Payer Initiative garnered only 27 percent of the vote. Adding to the gloom, the anti-immigrant initiative, Prop 187, passed handily.

Prop 186: What Went Wrong?

In reflecting on the reasons Prop 186 went down to crushing defeat, it is useful to distinguish two kinds of effects: systemic factors relating to the initiative process, and particular circumstances pertaining to this specific campaign. Of course, even in examining these factors, many accomplishments stand out as having gone "right." First was the exemplary way doctors and lawyers from two academic institutions, the University of California, San Francisco, and the Loyola University Law School in Los Angeles, and professional associations, the California Physicians Alliance, and the California Nurses Association, supported the campaign as spokespersons, speakers, pro bono technical consultants, financial contributors, and grassroots organizers, activists, and leaders in the rest of campaign.

A second accomplishment was the citizens' role in framing of the debate. Because of the late start, the signature gathering period was reduced from the normal 150 days to 93 days. In those 93 days, volunteers managed to gather nearly 570,000 signatures. At that rate, they would have been very close to a million signatures in the full 150 days. This campaign provides strong evidence that a return to the original initiative spirit of volunteer citizen efforts framing public policy debates is still possible today.

A third major accomplishment was the campaign's generating a successful grassroots fund-raising model, with house parties and volunteer phone banks netting close to $1 million. In 1994, the money was far too little, far too late, but with a considerably earlier start and a much larger initial base of support, the next California single-payer initiative can reap the benefits of these very powerful fund-raising tools.

However, the Prop 186 campaign also reveals features of initiative campaigns as presently conducted that give one pause. Although in this case citizen-volunteers won a place on the ballot for Prop 186, the initiative process also can allow for corporations or other groups with lots of money to buy their way onto the ballot with the services of the paid signature gathering industry, bypassing citizen involvement altogether. Another such systemic problem is the striking asymmetry between what it takes to defeat an initiative for change and what it takes to pass such an initiative. The task for opponents with substantial financial resources such as Taxpayers Against the Government Takeover is straightforward—to create enough doubt and fear in voters' minds that they lack the confidence to vote yes. There are plenty of high-priced consultants ready to help them out with polls and focus groups to identify the fears and doubts and the hot buttons and strategies best suited to trigger them. Television and radio are ideal media for reaching voters and manipulating their minds with sophisticated techniques to plant the appropriate, focus group–tested seeds of doubt and fear.

The task for the proponents is much, much harder—overcoming those doubts and fears. That is difficult even when you have loads of money, as did Philip Morris, Inc., in promoting its losing 1994 initiative attempt to overturn local and state ordinances banning smoking in indoor public places. It is especially difficult when you lack sufficient money to reach voters effectively and when institutions such as the press and other media feel little or no responsibility to promote the public discussion and debate necessary for an informed electorate.

Another systemic problem is the typical disbalance of financial resources in a case like Prop 186 when citizens propose a change that runs counter to the interests of large corporations. A certain amount of money is necessary to run a competitive campaign against an incumbent politician or a well-heeled opponent of an initiative for change. The operative word is *competitive* and in California, where extensive use of electronic media for voter contact is essential unless you have a tremendous grassroots base or extraordinary media support, the figure is probably $10 million or more. An investment of $10 million is peanuts for a health insurance industry with tens of *billions* at stake. But it is out of sight for most grassroots citizens efforts like the 1994 Prop 186 campaign. Here it should be noted, however, that California is an extreme case. Its population of over thirty million is far greater than any other state; in fact, it is greater than many countries. A state like Minnesota, with about the national-average population and one large metropolitan area where 60 percent of the people live, is much more amenable to grassroots organizing and statewide media reach is far less expensive. The competitive figure there is more like $1 or $2 million.

Looking back on the Prop 186 campaign, Vishu Lingappa marveled at how tiny an investment, a few tens of thousands of dollars, is necessary for corporate lobbying coalitions to gain special access to, and significance influence with, a congressional or state officeholder and similarly how tiny an investment relative to what is at stake is necessary to thwart a California initiative for significant change.

A final systemic problem with initiatives is the dearth of effective institutions dedicated to an informed citizenry. California makes a step in the right direction with voter information pamphlets that offer pro and con arguments—and opportunity for rebuttals—on every initiative. In practical terms, however, to reach voters effectively the print and electronic broadcast media must contribute. Right now they do a miserable job. And the recent trend is in precisely the wrong direction with the demise in the 1980s of the fairness doctrine and the equal time rule.

The most charitable explanation of the media's failure to inform voters about the single-payer initiative is that they never took it seriously because they looked at the early poll numbers and concluded it didn't have a chance; it was not a "story." Of course, that is a real "Catch 22" for an underfunded initiative campaign. The media cover *viable* initiative campaigns, but in critical respects the media are essential to *creating* viable campaigns by covering them. This paradox has important consequences for initiatives like Prop 186 that challenge the established order. Recall, for instance, that television stations from coast to coast even refused to carry single-payer *paid advertising* in 1993. There is obviously a built-in structural tendency for the media to narrow the frame, squeezing such initiatives out.

From Paul Wellstone's experience with the Citizen's Jury, there is good reason to believe that with in-depth media coverage, the single-payer poll numbers would have soared. Vishu Lingappa liked to say that all Prop 186 needed was one hour of every voter's time.

New approaches to informing citizens are clearly needed. A part of the answer may lie in the flip side of Lingappa's insight about interest groups' small investments reaping enormously greater gains. Relatively modest public investments and/or regulations could create a framework of incentives and/or obligations for all the broadcast media, print and electronic, to use their power to educate to help make our nation the effectively functioning democracy it is supposed to be. On the other hand, like many others involved in the Prop 186 campaign, Lingappa came away with jaundiced expectations of the privately owned media in a future single-payer initiative strategy: "To the extent that the media give us coverage or opportunities, we'll be happy to take it. But we have to have a strategy that doesn't depend on them. Either we rely on a house-party, grassroots kind of approach and/or here's this multibillionaire who's prepared to put whatever it takes behind our campaign. Ideally both."

Of course particular circumstances of the Prop 186 campaign also contributed to its overwhelming defeat. Given what was known in January 1994, opting to go for a single-payer initiative that year was probably the right decision. Enormous public attention was focused on health care reform that year and the initiative campaign could have been an excellent vehicle for building a single-payer movement. Paul Milne's confident judgment that ninety three days would suffice to gather a million signatures was a gutsy call that was ultimately confirmed. But the fund-raising for the campaign and the planning for beyond the signature gathering suffered as a consequence of the late start. By the end of the petition drive, the campaign was deeply in debt and far behind in strategic planning. The next California single-payer initiative campaign will need a year or more to build a financial war chest and map a strategic plan before the signature gathering begins.

In addition, the large debt and failure to map a smooth transition to the ballot campaign had disastrous consequences. Lack of money to hire organizers led to the extreme measure of dumping the program of the initially proposed strategy with the greatest constituency expanding, movement building potential, precinct-level organizing. A strategy aimed at raising $1 million or more and shooting the entire wad on two weeks of television ads at the very end may have fit the financial circumstances, but it was doomed to fail.

The state and national political leadership also created problems for Prop 186. When Kathleen Brown decided not to endorse and indeed chose actively to oppose Prop 186, the single-payer issue was denied easy entrée to political legitimacy and media coverage as a central controversy of California's 1994 electoral politics. At the same time, President Clinton's success in dividing the single-payer movement in Washington had the effect of delaying disastrously the support and cooling the eventual ardor of some of Prop 186's most prestigious and best-heeled California backers, including important labor unions and the AARP.

And then 1994 turned out to be perhaps the worst time in fifty years to be running a single-payer initiative. Polls and focus groups that summer showed that people reacted extremely negatively to government control and higher taxes. In the case of Prop 186, in which the government would run the insurance program but private health care providers chosen by the consumers would continue to decide the appropriate treatment, the term the opposition chose to use in its advertising and direct mail, *government run health care,* was patently misleading. The term *huge tax increase* to characterize taxes that replace considerably higher private insurance premiums and out-of-pocket expenditures was similarly misleading. What most Californians knew about Prop 186 was the frightening drumbeat from television and radio advertising and targeted direct mail: "government run health care" requiring a "huge personal tax increase."

Since 1994, the American public's rejection of Newt Gingrich's extremism probably is a promising sign. However, it would not be wise to count on the Democrats in Washington for courageous leadership. The best hope for laying the groundwork for universal health care coverage in the United States probably lies in a strategy of a series of single-payer state initiatives, beginning with states with more modest populations than California.

In the end, I think the largest mistake of the Proposition 186 campaign was the decision to sell single-payer as basically a better insurance product. What moved most Prop 186 supporters to commitment and action was the opportunity to be a part of a movement for social justice—a movement for universal coverage. Presenting the single-payer approach as the practical path to affordable, comprehensive, universal health care coverage is, I believe, the key to winning this struggle. The foreseeable trends are only likely to heighten the visibility of this issue. Cutbacks in Medicare and Medicaid spending on the federal level and closings of local hospitals and clinics that serve the poor are going to result soon in a great deal of pain for many families and a sharp swelling of the ranks of the uninsured. Donald Cohen was right to emphasize the striking absence of families without health insurance at the core of a single-payer movement. That is the immediate challenge and the key to ultimate success.

This issue will not go away. By mid-1994, as her proposed reform was being torn to shreds in the Congress, Hillary Rodham Clinton issued a prophetic, thinly veiled threat to the insurance companies about the whirlwind they would reap if they deserted her cause. In a speech to the Economics Club of Washington on June 28, 1994, she "predicted that if Congress does not pass a health reform bill this year, public pressure will build for a single-payer system, where the government will pay for all health care. 'There will be a grass-roots movement that sweeps the country that will achieve a single-payer system,' she said, 'possibly around the year 2000.'"[13]

Hillary Rodham Clinton may well prove to have been a better prophet than a leader of health care reform.

FINDING THE WAY BACK TO DEMOCRACY IN AMERICA

The Capital and the Countryside 18

Capturing Our Capital and the Nation

In his provocative book, *Who Will Tell the People. The Betrayal of American Democracy,* William Greider makes a persuasive case for viewing public policy-making in America as a contest of "organized money vs. organized people."[1] At this juncture, organized money clearly has the upper hand. Concentrations of political power in Washington, aided and abetted by special interests with their enormous wealth, routinely overwhelm the popular will, making a mockery of the ideals of representative democracy. In effect, our capital has been besieged and captured by the forces of organized money.

We have examined at length the often decisive effect of campaign money on election outcomes and consequently on the ideological tilt of our government. But funding for political campaigns is just the tip of the organized money iceberg. Also crucial in creating opportunities for organized money to work its will in Washington is the disposition of power in Congress. Soon after going to work there, Henry Kelly, one of the nation's leading figures in the move to sustainable energy, said he felt as though he had "left the twentieth century and entered a bizarre feudal system." For example, there are a few *legislative lords*—Bennett Johnston–like figures who set the agenda on the most important issues, senior members of Congress who have been permitted by their colleagues to aggregate and exercise such great individual authority that they are de facto lords of their realms. There are also lobbying coalitions on nearly every important issue that aggregate enormous resources and target them for maximum effect. Because Congress delegates authority on each issue to specialized committees, the lobbying coalitions have a relatively small number of "targets" to zero in on. As typified by the Senate Energy Committee, the great majority of committee members tend to be in synch with the dominant lobbying coalitions and they learn it pays to be pliant supplicants of the lords of their realms.

Perhaps the most striking feature of the Washington political culture is the way the legislative lords become locked in symbiotic embrace with the lobbying coalitions, providing each other with services and sustenance aimed at mutual survival and prosperity. By bringing complementary strengths to their liaison, they are able to exercise exceptional power in the mutual pursuit of their goals.

It is clear what considerable strengths the legislative lords bring to these symbiotic partnerships—extraordinary control over the framing and legislating processes and over their committee members' behavior. It is also clear what complementary strengths the lobbying coalitions contribute. Unlike ordinary citizens, institutions with lobbyists have a permanent presence in Washington aimed at anticipating and influencing events. What we saw in the energy strategy and health care reform debates is a typical pattern: corporations with common policy objectives tend to organize into large lobbying coalitions, enabling them to combine resources and coordinate strategies.

On any given issue, there is a relatively small community of public and private players in Washington. It is helpful to think of the lobbyists as very talented, well-connected, full-time organizers within each community, with loads of money to spend and lots of time to think, enabling them to plan and execute sustained, relentless campaigns.

One or more legislative lords are at the center of the framing and legislating action in each community, but their prospects for success depend on the organizers from the lobbying coalitions. Working closely with the legislative lords and their staffs and with experts from their parent organizations, the lobbyists fashion policy proposals and initiatives, create strategies to sell the initiatives within the community, recruit authoritative support, execute media strategies, gather intelligence, and target undecided legislators for appropriate persuasion. In his book *The Lobbyists: How Influence Peddlers Get Their Way in Washington,* Jeffrey Birnbaum makes an insightful observation: "Over time, the sheer pervasiveness of corporate lobbyists has had a major impact on government policy, beyond just the lucrative margin of legislation. The fact that lobbyists are everywhere, all the time, has led official Washington to become increasingly sympathetic to the corporate cause. This is true among Democrats as well as Republicans. . . . Lobbyists provide the prism through which government officials often make their decisions."[2]

Infiltrating the Countryside

To have any chance of challenging the corporate public policy agendas, ordinary citizens have to move the political struggles away from the capital and out to the country at large. Unfortunately, they will find that the lobbyists have thought of this too; having captured the capital, the lobbying coalitions are already increasingly focusing their resources beyond the Beltway. They have developed potent ways of using their vast financial resources to reach beyond Washington into states and congressional districts to shape local public opinion through media campaigns and to put pressure on selected members of Congress by creating floods of phone calls and letters from folks back home.

In 1991 such a media campaign was hatched by the nuclear industry to counter public resistance to a congressionally mandated plan to build a permanent radioactive waste depository in the Yucca Mountain in Nevada. Recall the vehemence of the opposition when Nevada's Governor Bill Miller and the entire Nevada congressional delegation came before the Senate Energy Committee and blasted the plan in 1991. We know a good deal about the media campaign because a document dated September 1991 addressed to the American Nuclear Energy Council and stamped *Confidential* was leaked to the press. Entitled *The Nevada Initiative: The Long Term Program,* the document noted that "by a clear majority of 61 to 35 percent (with 4 percent undecided) the Nevada public at large opposes a repository." In addition, "powerful political adversaries [are] confronting the industry— including two former influential governors, the present governor, the state nuclear waste office, the state's second largest newspaper, and the U.S. congressional delegation, led by outspoken Senator Richard Bryan. The Nevada Resort Association remains precariously uncommitted." The report warned that "without an effective campaign to neutralize the political resistance, public opposition to the repository will be increased and reinforced." "It is critical," it concluded, that the industry put its resources behind a concerted three-year referendum-style effort that incorporates all the elements of a comprehensive modern campaign."[3]

Thus a three-year, "multi-faceted political marketing plan" got underway in Nevada in January 1990 to which electric utilities with nuclear generating plants nationwide contributed $9 million. The first of several key campaign

elements was the creation of a "political team" of Nevada political professionals, led by Kent Oram, a key advisor to Governor Miller from the public
relations firm Oram, Ingram and Zurawski, which did the commercials for
Gov. Miller's 1991 election campaign. The focus was on Bill Miller and the
entire congressional delegation that had testified vehemently against the
Yucca Mountain project before the Senate Energy Committee in March 1991.

Another focus was on the Nevada media. They trained several Department of Energy scientists to act as a "Scientific Truth Response Team" and
hired a "media response team" that would be "the vehicle for generating
positive free media coverage and conversion of the press away from its opposition to the repository." According to the memo, "two highly respected investigative reporters and anchormen have been identified and will be able to
deal with the working press as peers. . . . They also enjoy wide recognition
and high credibility with the general public." By the time the document was
written, a year and a half into the project, significant progress was reported
on this front: "The Las Vegas *Review-Journal* had begun to take a more
objective look at the Nevada siting issue and has called for a discussion of
negotiated benefits in a ground-breaking editorial."[4]

At the same time a major advertising offensive was launched. As the confidential document put it, "the industry must address the major obstacle to
ultimate success: public attitudes, particularly as they relate to safety. Political networking, media relations, one-on-one negotiations and stressing the
benefits that the repository can bring will not assuage these fears. Major
shifts in public perceptions and attitudes are achievable only through a sustained advertising program. . . ." For this they hired the firm that had produced commercials for Governor Miller in his successful 1990 campaign to
come up with a strategy: "The bulk of the television advertising messages
will stress safety. Roughly 70% of the messages will be delivered by scientists. . . . Once public sentiment swings, the next phase of the campaign will
focus on the merits of nuclear energy. The primary target audience will be
women, aged 25 to 49—the group with the highest statistical potential for
favorably affecting polls if they can be informed, reassured and moved. . . ."[5]

The advertising would continue for twenty-four months, to "reduce the
number of negative leaning Nevadans and drive them into the undecided
camp, where they will be more receptive to factual information. By softening
public opposition, the campaign will provide 'air cover' for elected officials
who wish to discuss benefits. Additionally, the advertising components will
act to encourage politicians to be much more cautious in their attacks."

Other features of this coordinated, multifaceted campaign included regular polling and tracking to provide "an up-to-date roadmap to navigate the communications campaign," using the science and attack/response teams for editorial board visits, talk shows and so forth.

The campaign leaders were optimistic. They viewed the campaign as "a domino theory, in which the many pieces will fall into place. . . . As each move is made, one or more of the targeted adversaries will begin to surface, move our way, fight us and then, eventually dialogue with the industry. It is through this strategic game of chess that the campaign will ultimately prevail and move to checkmate anti-nuclear forces in Nevada. Our projections are that within 24 months Nevadans supporting the repository will be at or near a majority . . . while a solid majority, about two of every three voters . . . will be in favor of the [Yucca Mountain site]. . . ."[6]

The projected budget for the three-year campaign was $3.8 million in 1992, $3.5 million in 1993, and $1.4 million in 1994, for a three-year total of $8.7 million. Of course, those citizens opposing the repository had no such resources available to them. The nuclear power industry, with much at stake, was preparing to overwhelm its opposition with money, much as the health insurance industry would overwhelm Proposition 186 proponents with money in California in 1994.

Ironically, convincing citizens of Nevada that a Yucca Mountain repository would be safe for them and their families proved to be a very hard sell, given the legacy of distrust in Nevada about nuclear safety and the government's past false assurances. However, this organized campaign gives a frightening glimpse of how important public policy issues can be removed from the realm of democracy and public debate.

"Grassroots Lobbying"

As noted, a powerful new tool for organized money to manipulate the outcome of congressional debates has burst into prominence in the 1990s. The technique known as "grassroots lobbying" builds on the premise that most important goal of congressional lawmakers is reelection. Their nightmare is that well-organized constituents might catch them voting against the popular will and organize against them at the time of the next election.

Of course, grassroots organizations have long known about this weakness and taken advantage of it. In the energy strategy debate prior to the November 1, 1991, Johnston-Wallop cloture vote, the Sierra Club and other groups targetted swing senators with a phone-bank and direct mail operation alerting environmentalists in their districts, resulting in an avalanche of phone calls and mail to their offices. But clever lobbyists have realized that with enough money they can simulate the same effect. The fastest growing segment of the Washington lobbying industry now consists of offices poised to generate instant constituent communications from the grassroots, in support of just about anything and directed to selected members of Congress. The going rate for each constituent phone call may be on the order of a hundred dollars.

A pioneer in this business is Jack Bonner and Associates. According to a remarkable story in the *Chicago Tribune,* Bonner was hired to undermine an amendment passed by the Senate in 1992 to require banks to lower the interest rate on credit cards. Despite the lack of public opposition to such a measure the banking industry told Bonner to fan opposition among influential people in the congressional districts of ten carefully selected members of the House Banking Committee, "to try to make sure this popular provision would never see the light of day in the House."[7]

Bonner put his staff of two hundred bright, young "unemployed policy junkies," who are "available only in Washington's unique labor pool," to work the telephones. In a four-day period they made over ten thousand phone calls to selected constituents of the ten House members. Most of the Bonner staffers had worked in politics or government; "they knew how to construct an argument and fervently pitched the banking industry position. The callers' argument was that if the amendment became law, millions of people might have to give up their credit cards. (The bankers association now concedes it had no firm evidence to support the claim.) They also argued that small businesses would suffer because the number of credit buyers would drop. . . . If the telephone pitch worked, Bonner's people immediately patched the voters through to their representative's office or persuaded them to write a personalized letter." The American Bankers Association paid Bonner at least $400,000 for that four-day effort.

The result: "Collectively, Bonner and other bank lobbyists created a fog so thick that Congress did what it usually does when faced with enormous pressure: preserve the status quo. The amendment died in a House-Senate conference committee."[8]

Many other firms and interest groups are also taking up the grassroots lobbying tool. For instance, one interest group that was active on many fronts in supporting the Johnston-Wallop bill, the U.S. Chamber of Commerce, has opened a computerized phone bank that connects to its more than two hundred thousand members and alerts them to issues of interest to the organization. Those answering the phone are able to press *1* to have a mailgram or letter sent in their name to their representative, to press 2 to record a voice-mail message for the representative, and to press 3 to be connected immediately by phone to his or her office. Used to target swing votes, this is a powerful tool to generate pressure on selected congressional offices.

Certain Bonner-like services, if available and affordable to all, such as advance information about what is going to happen in Congress, who the swing votes are, and so on would be a contribution to the democratic process. But as long as such capability is by and large available only to well-heeled interests, it perpetuates the opposite of democracy. It strengthens the already excessive advantage of organized money over organized people and appropriates to the wealthy the relatively few levers of power ordinary Americans have. Phone calls from local citizens working together can now be drowned out by a cacophony of voices artificially generated by a boiler room telemarketing operation on behalf of whatever interest group has the hundreds of thousands of dollars required. In addition, these grassroots efforts expand the influence by threat that special interest money can buy. Not only can lobbying coalitions implicitly threaten to move their campaign money from an incumbent to his or her challenger, they also can credibly threaten to organize constituents against targetted members at election time, buying local advertisements with money from outside the district, and mobilizing local citizens in support of his or her opponent. I expect to see such election-time actions emphasized in Phase II of grassroots lobbying companies.

One of my students stumbled across further evidence of just how attractive "grassroots lobbying" is likely to become for Washington influence peddlers. During our campaign finance reform project's deliberations, Frank Sorauf of the University of Minnesota, an authority on campaign finance, came to Carleton to discuss reform options. He was asked his opinion of what would happen to all the available PAC money (over $150 million in the 1990 races) if PAC contributions were eliminated. Sorauf had a nice analogy for thinking about money in politics as a hydraulic system filled with a fluid—money—trying to reach the candidates at the center. If certain channels or loopholes are plugged by campaign finance reform, the fluid will naturally seek other ways of getting to the candidates or otherwise influencing political outcomes.

Our Carleton campaign finance reform project had suggested two possible alternative channels whereby what had been PAC contributions could support candidates: independent expenditures on behalf of candidates or in opposition to their opponents and bundling of individual contributions

from executives and other employees of corporations that previously channeled money to candidates through PACs. Sorauf suspected that bundled
individual contributions would be the preferred course of action. Candidates
generally do not like independent expenditures; they have no control over
the content of this sort of advertising and yet they constitute highly visible
links between the candidates and the interest groups responsible for it. On
the other hand, tracking down the connections between bundled contributions and interest groups is generally a difficult task. Sorauf had seen internal
PAC memos that showed they were already preparing for bundling contributions if PAC money were cut off or severely limited by campaign finance
reform legislation.

In Washington on a congressional internship, Carleton student Bert Johnston posed the same question to a prominent political consultant: Where
would the PAC money go? The consultant replied that he believed a significant portion of it would be channeled into buying grassroots constituent
communications to pressure Congress to pass the legislation the interest
groups wanted. What an unintended consequence that would be! One hundred fifty million dollars would generate a lot of phone calls and local ads.

We should not underestimate the political potency of the high-priced
campaigns these mercenaries can wage. On the other hand, there may be
some cause for optimism. Real grassroots organizations outside of Washington have the formidable advantage of superior numbers; if they organize
effectively, they have a fighting chance. And grassroots organizations have
the potential of using to great advantage a political advertising tool known
as the "issue ad" that was ushered in by the 1996 campaign. The law now
recognizes that as long as an ad does not explicitly advocate a vote for or
against a political candidate, an organization can call attention to that candidate's position on issues and voting record with no requirement that the
identity of contributors or amount of the contributions be disclosed. Some
see this as opening an avenue that will amount to little more than thinly
veiled advocacy of the election or defeat of candidates without requiring
contributor disclosure or contribution limits. Others, including myself, see
it as a legitimate exercise of the First Amendment right to free speech that
is likely to become an increasingly important tool in holding candidates accountable for their campaign promises. Of course, the ability to use this
particular tool will vary greatly, depending on the wealth of individuals and
institutions. My view, however, is that any new channels for holding candidates accountable to their positions represent a welcome development. The
challenge is to make the tools available to ordinary citizens as well. To win

the struggle for democracy, ultimately we will have to retake Washington. But I am convinced a winning strategy must focus until its final phases primarily on mobilizing and empowering ordinary people where they live.

It is especially important that the major public interest groups understand this. They usually stand astride the boundary between capital and countryside, with their headquarters and lobbyists in Washington while most of their members live elsewhere. Too often their leaders have become creatures of the Washington culture, seduced by their proximity to power and, even when reluctant, accepting the Washington definitions of what is politically possible. Too often, they sell their members short, settling for symbolic lip service they can call a victory, when they could be a much more influential political force if they would only trust and rely on their members around the nation to organize in their communities behind reforms they believe in.

Throughout the 1990s, from around the time of Paul's first Senate election, I have sensed that we are at the dawn of a new populist era. I believe that the greatest hope for our democracy would be some straightforward changes in the rules of America's political game, aimed at drawing ordinary people back into participating effectively in our representative democracy at a time when more and more citizens don't see why they should or how they can.

Changing the Rules to Revitalize American Democracy   19

A Hollow Ideal

Democracy is now a hollow ideal in the country that is supposed to be its leading champion. Most Americans have come to realize they are powerless to influence policy on issues they care about. They are effectively shut out of the policy-making process. They know that a wealthy and powerful few have far more influence than ordinary citizens on laws that are passed by Congress and state legislatures and on the ways those laws are implemented by bureaucracies and enforced by the courts. They are not fooled when lobbyists and lobbying coalitions claim that large campaign contributions merely gain them "access." They can see that the two major political parties have lost their constructive purpose. They understand that most elections are charades, in which politicians are packaged and sold like soap, by the same kinds of ad agencies using the same kinds of focus groups, usually running on platforms that have little or nothing to do with what happens when elections are over. In a nation founded on the notion that government is of, by, and for the people, this is intolerable.

In pursuit of a platform for a movement to revitalize democracy in America, let us reflect on the lessons of the three policy debates recounted in this book. Three features of current American political practice stand out as subverting essential expectations of representative democracy by giving enormous advantages to economic and political elites and rendering ordinary citizens relatively powerless.

The Incumbent Addiction Problem

Members of Congress have become addicted to periodic fixes of cash to satisfy their reelection needs every two or six years. They are routinely driven into financial dependence on a relatively few special interest lobbying coalitions and very wealthy individuals. As a consequence, on most issues they are far more accountable to power elites in Washington who are the secure sources of those fixes than they are to their constituents back home, especially to those who provide the crucial "early money" for their campaigns. As I discovered by studying Rudy Boschwitz's reelection fund-raising in 1989–90, direct mail and telemarketing operations funded by the early money can be used to reach voters with targetted messages and turn hundreds of large and often out-of-state contributions into tens of thousands of small in-state contributions.

The Elite Framing Problem

A second major challenge to the democratic process are the tight networks of legislative lords, lobbying coalitions, and executive branch allies that shape the agenda of virtually every important issue debate, in the process routinely eliminating proposals for change that would be the most attractive foci for grassroots citizen organizing efforts. In the debate over the national energy strategy, for instance, the resulting Johnston-Wallop legislation fulfilled the dreams of the major energy industries who had been very well represented behind the closed doors. On the other hand, that bill was a nightmare for environmental groups, who had been effectively left out of the framing process.

The Challengers' Resource Problem

The grassroots citizen organizing efforts that are the key to challenging the power elites in Washington usually are starved for the funds needed to compete effectively in legislative debates or ballot initiatives—money for organizers, networking, public education, and so on. Commercial news media and government-supported information channels hardly take up the slack, failing miserably in communicating timely intelligence and in promoting the public education and open debate needed to foster the informed and involved citizenry that is essential to representative democracy.

The 1994 California Proposition 186 campaign illustrates well the challengers' resource problem. In debt after the successful petition drive, the single-payer campaign leadership was forced to curtail sharply its statewide field operation for the ballot phase of the campaign. That decision was reluctantly agreed to because money was not available in time to pay the modest salaries of full-time professional organizers. This left the campaign even more dependent on the commercial news media for educating California voters about the pros and cons of single-payer health insurance. With a few notable exceptions, the media simply failed to take that responsibility seriously.

With these three problems in mind, what would constitute an appropriate program of systemic reforms for an American democracy movement. The extent of current disillusionment with American democracy is astounding. A September 1994 Gallup poll found that 84 percent of Americans strongly [39 percent] or partially [45 percent] believed "that our present system of government is democratic in name only. Special interests run things."

An essential first step is to change the rules for funding political campaigns so the American people no longer have good reason to believe that most elected representatives are financially beholden to special interests.

We must deal head on with the addiction of incumbents to special interest money. That is the central aim of Clean Money Campaign Reform. It makes the cleanest cut of the big money links between lobbying coalitions and lawmakers, with the least opportunities for loopholes and the greatest likelihood that candidates who opt out will find that decision a serious liability on election day. Clean Money Campaign Reform would also remove big money donors from their current role as the gatekeepers who decide who gets to run for public office and who does not. In particular, it would open the door to candidates who are not wealthy or annointed by the wealthy. It holds the greatest promise of becoming the campaign finance proposal that will galvanize a social movement. Many of the best community organizers in the country already have been drawn into this effort. There is no better evidence of its appeal than the success it has already achieved. Beginning with the 1997 breakthrough in Maine, citizen organizing has passed Clean Money Campaign Reform for state office candidates in four states, and very impressive efforts are well under way in dozens of others.

Bear in mind that candidates cannot be *required* to participate in this system. That would mandate campaign spending limits, which the Supreme Court ruled to be an unconstitutional violation of the First Amendment in its 1976 *Buckley* v. *Valeo* decision. So candidates can choose to *opt out*, accepting as much special interest money as they like, spending millions of their own money, and leaving the sky as the limit on campaign expenditures. But in so doing, there's a good chance it will cost them their elections; they are likely to be viewed as undermining the best chance of getting special interest money out of America's electoral politics.

There is a second major challenge facing a movement to take back our democracy, every bit as important as campaign finance reform. Can the rules of the political game be changed so that a deeply disaffected and widely cynical citizenry will participate with enthusiasm in a new, truly democratic issue politics? It would begin by confronting directly the fact that ordinary citizens are now effectively shut out of the policy-making process. The challenge, I believe, is finding appropriate responses to the Elite Framing and Challengers' Resource problems.

In responding to that challenge, the experiences described in this book lead naturally to an initial focus on the framing stage of congressional policy debates—the anti-democratic early period where ordinary citizens are most decisively shut out. After a brief recap of the three policy debates, I will describe an idea for inviting ordinary citizens to become involved in the democratic framing of congressional policy debates. At first this idea seemed to be simply a straightforward way to circumvent the dominence of elite Washington circles in setting the congressional agenda. But it turns out to be much more than that. I believe that a seemingly small change in the political process would *naturally* catalyze a grassroots-based citizen-involving politics with a rich yield of democracy-enhancing consequences. Among the important consequences would be to give political parties vital new purpose and to draw many citizens into participating in their communities in a reconnected issue and electoral politics, rather than shutting them out and alienating them. The remainder of this book explores the likely consequences of instituting this citizen-involving policy process idea and democratically financed elections. The pursuit of these changes in the rules of American politics leads to surprisingly fertile ground.

Issue Politics: The All-Important Frame

We now have a political system in which a public policy proposal can have enormous popular support and the potential to garner an electoral majority, but it may not even get a fair hearing, much less a vote, in the Congress or anything approaching adequate coverage in the media. With a framing process dominated by elite networks in Washington, the values that prevail are the short-term, bottom-line values of those power centers—the survival and prosperity aspirations of lobbying coalitions and their executive branch allies and the power game preoccupations of legislative lords. The public policies that result tend to keep the country barrelling down the same old tracks, in the directions we have been heading. Policies to promote orderly transitions to new directions are effectively resisted in such a system; it typically takes a crisis to bring about a substantial change in course.

From these power centers, webs of influence reach out and manage to create self-serving definitions of what is "politically realistic" and what is not. Within this political culture, Washington-based agents of change find themselves inhibited and constrained, especially public interest group leaders and reform-minded legislators who can hardly avoid becoming entrapped in these webs.

When the energy strategy debate began in early 1991, for example, a survey showed three-quarters of the American people favored an energy policy that emphasized improved energy efficiency and greater reliance on renewable energy sources. But a year and a half framing process dominated by Bennett Johnston, the Senate Energy Committee staff, energy industry lobbying coalitions and allies at the Department of Energy, and in the White House produced a bill aimed at *removing* barriers the traditional energy supply industries had encountered. Most of those barriers were a result of two decades of overwhelming public support for protecting the environment. Bowing to "political reality," the environmentalists resigned themselves to working within the framework already introduced, trying to improve the bill a bit but mostly trying to eliminate its worst features, including opening up the Arctic National Wildlife Refuge to oil drilling. Paul Wellstone, Dick Bryan, and a few other "core group" senators pressed instead for rejecting the bill altogether. But along with the environmental groups, we found that our most promising options were basically those negative, oppositional ones. Given the locus of power in Washington, it is far more difficult to mount a positive, constructive effort such as one aimed at changing our nation's energy course and redirecting it toward a sustainable energy future.

Unless, of course, there were tremendous public pressure from beyond the Washington Beltway. The nationwide organizing by environmental and consumer groups against the Johnston-Wallop bill gave a strong hint that a powerful movement might have been mounted behind a positive proposal. Unfortunately, after blocking the bill in November 1991, the coalition of environmental groups and their congressional allies failed to seize the moment and move swiftly into a national campaign behind a sustainable energy transition legislative package.

Similarly, a poll taken on the eve of the 1993 congressional campaign finance reform debate showed that a substantial majority of the American people wanted to change the campaign finance rules to give challengers without huge financial resources a chance to compete against incumbents. But after months of private negotiations with the Clinton White House, in which the leading public interest groups had their say, the Democratic congressional leadership framed the debate with S.3, the Mitchell-Boren bill, a glaringly inadequate and incumbent-protecting piece of legislation.

A strong alternative bill never was put forward by the coalition of public interest groups in Washington or conveyed to their member chapters as the basis for a nationwide grassroots movement. A coalition led by Public Citizen made some moves in the right direction with its ambitious "$100 Solution for Good Government." But in the end the coalition bowed to the Washington view of "political reality." Local organizers were encouraged instead to rally support behind some general principles of campaign finance reform. That left their local affiliates around the nation without a sharp, positive focus, a piece of legislation they could rally behind with enthusiasm.

Nor did the press alert the public in a timely fashion. It was not until after the House passed its own particularly egregious version of reform, H.R.3, that mainstream pundits like David Broder began telling the public the truth. Referring to the bill the House passed as a "joke," Broder observed, "officials in the good-government groups argue that these rotten ingredients can somehow be cooked into a nourishing reform meal in a House-Senate conference committee. Don't bet on it. The pattern suggests clearly that the closer a campaign finance bill comes to enactment, the more the Democrats drain it of elements that might seriously inconvenience their incumbents. This is reform? Give me a break."[1]

The health care reform story also includes a classic case of an important policy proposal denied a place in the public debate. Despite strong public interest in the single-payer approach, the Clintons and their White House task force, supported by the insurance industry, removed single-payer from the game as an unviable option. The one ray of hope came from California, where committed citizens and community organizers began the painstaking task of building a single-payer movement. In spite of the disappointing outcome of the 1994 ballot initiative, tens of thousands of active single-payer supporters were identified by election day.

When we went to the Senate, I had a notion that Paul Wellstone and his staff would be democracy-enhancing agents of change. By introducing legislation, we could put strong policy proposals on the table in Washington around which community-based movements could rally. And Paul could use his senatorial position and his oratorical and organizing skills to become a leader of such movements, helping to support and strengthen them in close collaboration with the public interest groups that represent grassroots movements in Washington. The most striking lesson of the three Wellstone initiatives is that the would-be agents of change tend to be thwarted from the beginning, unable to get a fair hearing, much less a vote, in the Congress and unable to avoid being dismissed much less receiving serious unbiased reporting, in the mainstream media.

During the time of these three initiatives, the Democrats were in control of the Congress. In each case, I found myself angry and frustrated with their failure to take advantage of their opportunity to provide bold national leadership, as narrow self-interest calculations of political advantage took precedence over major opportunities for historic policy change.

A second observation is the disturbing degree with which the national leaders of some of the older and more established public interest groups have become so focused on being players in Washington's insider power games that they have sold short their activist constituencies beyond the Washington Beltway.

The net effect in the campaign finance reform and health care reform debates was to concentrate the efforts of progressive public interest groups in the "realistic," "responsible," "respectable" center of the dialectical spectrum, instead of mobilizing their grassroots members to demand much more at those rare moments of maximum opportunity.

Senators and representatives who come to Washington committed to progressive social change and leaders of citizen advocacy groups with Washington lobbying operations and national networks of political activist members are caught in the middle. On the one hand, they expect to live and work in Washington for a long time. Naturally, they hope to be considered serious "players." And they are there to serve grassroots constituencies or memberships, who want their representatives in Washington to be effective. That generally means buying into the Washington frames. However, on those rare occasions when they could challenge the elite frames and spur social movements for significant change, they often seem reluctant to lead. Over time, many become creatures of the Washington culture and inhabitants of the dialectical center. Perhaps they must to be able to survive and prosper there under the current rules of the political game.

The question is, what would it take to liberate them?

The Missing Link

There is a crucial missing link in our politics today. With great effort, citizens can organize together, become well informed about an issue they care about, link up with other like-minded groups organized about that issue around the country, develop apt policy proposals, and establish effective ways of monitoring what their representatives are up to in Washington. But why bother if powerful networks of legislative lords, lobbying coalitions, and their executive branch allies that frame Washington debates can shut them out? The crucial missing link is the ability of ordinary citizens organizing together where they live to circumvent the dominant framing system and force onto the national agenda policy proposals they can support with enthusiasm.

In each of the three policy debates described in this book, elite insider networks, with their permanent, relentless, affluent Washington presence, were able to get their policy proposals to center stage in the Congress, while alternative proposals with the potential for strong popular support were shunted aside. Mounting a democratic challenge to the dominance of those powerful networks will require opening alternative paths for organized citizens to frame congressional debates.

That realization was an important advance for me. Focusing on the framing obstacle to effective citizen participation leads to a deceptively simple, but surprisingly powerful, reform idea. It not only speaks directly to the framing problem, but, more important, its implementation would have many far-reaching, democracy-enhancing consequences, pulling the nation toward a new citizen-involving politics. What is more, in this new way of thinking, democratic financing of elections is an *essential corollary* to a democratic response to the framing problem.

The idea is a "National Citizens Agenda-Setting Initiative" (or "National Citizens Initiative" [NCI]), with a "Democracy Fund" to facilitate citizen financing of grassroots efforts. The basic concept is a simple one: If a designated percentage (say, 3 percent) of registered voters in a designated fraction (say, one-third) of congressional districts signed a petition saying they wanted a certain proposal considered and voted on, Congress would have to hold full and fair hearings and both houses would have to vote on it. This procedure would have the obvious consequence of giving ordinary citizens the opportunity to frame the congressional agenda, putting on the table proposals that they could unite behind. Less obvious and more important, it would naturally encourage and support a vital new kind of efficacious, citizen-involving politics. It is a politics from the bottom up, which emphasizes people organizing together in the communities where they live on issues they care about and joining in state and national networks behind policy initiatives they believe in.

Such a citizens' initiative plank of the platform of an American democracy movement would naturally require a parallel provision for democratic financing of congressional elections. It would make no sense to leave decision-making on citizen initiatives in the hands of a Congress financially dependent on lobbying coalitions for reelection funding and widely perceived by the citizenry as bought by special interests.

The rationale for this proposal begins with an analysis of the strengths and weaknesses of the direct ballot initiative, which has two distinct parts: (1) the initiative qualifying test, where a certain number of petition signatures are required to get a legislative proposal on the ballot; and (2) a popular vote, where gaining a majority will make the proposal a law.

The ballot initiative has an appealing ring, at least to someone with a progressive-populist bent. Many years ago, when I ran for public office in Minnesota, our ticket endorsed the direct initiative for my state. But I subsequently came to be troubled by problems with this idea in practice. The problems relate to the popular vote. Experience in California and other states has demonstrated a fundamental asymmetry between what it takes to defeat an initiative for change and what it takes to pass one. In the campaign for Prop 186, for example, the task for initiative opponents was comparatively easy—create sufficient fear and doubt in voters' minds so that they will be inclined to vote no. Modern public relations techniques are well suited for that. Overcoming fear and doubt is much more difficult.

The experience of Prop 186 in 1994 was not an aberration. Another much-remembered California initiative, Prop 128, the 1990 "Big Green" campaign. A comprehensive package of environmental reforms backed by the Sierra Club and other environmental groups, it prompted a massive corporate-funded opposition campaign. Over $13 million, 99.5 percent of the opponents' money, came from business interests led by three oil companies—ARCO with $947,500, Chevron with $811,800, and Shell with $600,000. Over $8 million came in contributions between $100,000 and $1,000,000 and more than half the opposition money, 55 percent, came from outside the state. Nearly three-quarters of the opposition spending went to broadcast advertising and media consultants. Big Green proponents raised a lot of money themselves, almost six million dollars, but they were overwhelmed by their opponents' media blitz. As with Prop 186, the initial public support withered under the onslaught of the business-funded public relations attack, and Prop 128 was defeated by a decisive 2 to 1 margin.

In the 1990 California initiative contests overall, two-thirds of the more than $100 million raised came in contributions of $100,000 or more from just 141 donors and 37 percent came from donors of a million dollars or more. One beer company, Anheuser-Busch, company spent over $8.3 million and another, Miller Brewing Company, added over $3.2 million in a successful attempt to crush an alcohol tax initiative.

One clear lesson of the ballot initiative experience in California is that an overwhelming amount of money against an initiative for change can usually carry the day. In significant part, this is because most important issues require careful deliberation. It is certainly possible for ordinary citizens to understand the nuances of legislative proposals and decide where they stand, but that takes a substantial commitment of time and effort. Otherwise, they are susceptible to manipulative advertising campaigns.

Of course, this is not a new issue. To provide for deliberation, the authors of our constitution consciously opted for representative democracy, not direct legislation by popular vote. But the representative democracy concept assumes that constituents can follow what their representatives in Washington are up to and hold them accountable at election time. As the three issues described in this book well illustrate, that is now a dubious proposition at best.

That is where my experience with the California Prop 186 single-payer health insurance campaign was useful. Wary of the initiative, I began casting around for alternative ways of circumventing the ability of the Washington power elites to shut out good ideas with much popular appeal. It soon occurred to me, however, that this might be throwing out the baby with the bathwater. The part of the initiative I had been especially attracted to in the first place as a remedy to the framing problem was qualifying an initiative by signature-gathering and forcing a vote. But if it were the Congress that would have to vote on the legislative proposal citizens had developed, this would enhance rather than supplant representative democracy.

The signature gathering should be carried out by citizen-volunteers. In San Diego, I witnessed scores of dedicated volunteers participate in the Prop 186 petition drive. Their spirit of camaraderie and sense of efficacy in working for a cause they believed in was inspiring. It invited ordinary citizens to participate in the political process in a difficult, but immensely satisfying, way. Anyone who was there when boxes after boxes of petitions in favor of Prop 186 were carried in and presented to the San Diego County Clerk could feel the extraordinary sense of accomplishment it evoked. I thought to myself, this is what politics should be about.

But would there be sufficient money and other resources for citizens to participate effectively in framing the congressional agenda by gathering signatures across the nation? Surely the elite circles that currently dominate issue debates in Washington will continue to have the necessary resources and the insider avenues of access to get their proposals onto the congressional agenda and to lobby effectively for them. If an alternative agenda-setting avenue involving organized efforts of ordinary citizens countrywide is to come close to achieving its democracy enhancing potential, the initiative efforts require a great deal of money. Even largely volunteer petition campaigns are enormous tasks requiring large budgets—for staff, organizers, research, volunteer recruitment, citizen education, communications, networking, and so on.

What's more, getting an initiative on the congressional agenda would be just the beginning. Given the gross disparities in the distribution of wealth in our society, without a mechanism to facilitate financing a National Citizens Initiative could give ordinary citizens a chance to participate and then take it away by failing to provide sufficient resources to compete with wealthy and well-connected elite interests.

Where could that kind of money come from? William Greider puts forward an intriguing possibility in *Who Will Tell the People:* curtailed tax deductions for corporate politics, a modest tax on the assets of foundations, and an annual tax credit of $100 or $200 to every citizen for the purpose of political expression in any form. "Any citizen would be free to contribute the money to any political activity—parties, candidates, issue organizations, local political clubs, whatever—and then be reimbursed at tax time. Citizens themselves would have an independent resource base for inventing their own politics—defining political goals and strategies in their own terms—without the need to beg for funds from beneficient patrons. Political reforms such as this," Greider concludes, "speak to real questions of who has power."[2]

A variant of this idea seems well-suited for the financing of National Citizens Agenda-Setting Initiative campaigns. Suppose a Democracy Fund were established by the federal government, with revenues from an appropriate tax. Each year, every registered voter would receive Democracy Fund vouchers for $50 that could be given to the initiative campaigns of their choice. In this way, organized citizens nationwide, not just elite issue networks in Washington, would really be invited to join in framing the congressional policy agenda.

There is precedent for providing public funds to citizens to support their political participation. Alaska and Oregon provide tax credits to reimburse contributions to initiative campaigns, up to a total of $50 in Alaska and $25 in Oregon. Some states also provide tax credits to reimburse contributions to candidates for state offices. Minnesota provides up to $50 per year in immediate reimbursements of campaign contributions to candidates for public office. But vouchers have an important advantage over tax credits or reimbursements in that they allow individuals to contribute who can't afford to advance $50 to initiatives. On the other hand, a voucher system might be more difficult and expensive to administer; for instance, it might be more vulnerable to black-marketeering. Though I use the term *vouchers* in the subsequent discussion of Democracy Fund contributions, consider that shorthand for one of several possible methods for funding citizen involvement, including tax credits or rapid reimbursements.

A Cornucopia of Democratic Consequences

With financial support from individual citizens, who could contribute up to $50 a year to the initiative campaigns of their choice, a National Citizens Initiative program would likely have consequences that would radiate throughout our politics, with the promise of creating vital new political life in our communities. Ordinary citizens would be invited to participate where they live in an open, pluralistic process to shape the policies that affect their lives. They would be motivated to do so because they could not be shut out; they could not be told it's too late by power elites in Washington; instead, through concerted action, they could force proposals they believe in onto the congressional agenda.

The less obvious but more crucial point is this: in the process, people would naturally organize, first in their communities, then in congressional district, state, and national networks to reach consenses on legislative proposals and to obtain the requisite number of signatures in congressional districts around the nation. Most important, when their representatives in Washington were forced to consider and vote on those proposals, they would do so under conditions that rarely pertain today—they would know that they were being closely watched by constituents back home, with the support of national networks, and that they would be held accountable for their actions when they ran for reelection.

There would be at least four distinct phases in National Citizen Initiative efforts with Democracy Fund support: (1) citizen development of initiative proposals, (2) citizen organizing of congressional district petition drives,

(3) congress watching and citizen lobbying during congressional debates; and (4) incumbent accountability at election time. Like-minded individuals and groups of very different political persuasions and concerns, with ideologies and agendas across the full political spectrum, would find opportunities to work effectively within the political system for public policies they believe in.

For example, it is reasonable to imagine that with NCI, colleges and universities would be drawn into important roles in service to their communities. Working closely with local citizens and citizen groups they could organize informational meetings on timely issues such as the farm financial crisis, welfare reform, health care reform, a sustainable energy transition strategy, and campaign finance reform. College and universities also could provide expertise to assist citizens in formulating initiative proposals, preparing critiques of those proposals, and planning and implementing community-based education efforts including public debates. In this way, policy ideas truly could emerge from the people. A good example of that was the participation of local farmers in Carleton College's 1985–87 Crisis in Agriculture Project, which pointed the way to the Fair Credit Plan, a very different approach to restructuring family farmers' debts from the proposal the leading agricultural lenders had already put on the table in Washington and subsequently to the National Farmers Fair Credit Campaign testimony before the House Agricultural Committee and the inclusion of the Fair Credit Plan as the debt-restructuring title of the Agricultural Credit Act of 1987. A more recent example of a debate in which such a resource would obviously have been useful is welfare reform. In that 1996 congressional debate and the state legislative debates that followed, the most affected constituencies, the recipient families, those with the greatest insight into the consequences of alternative reform options and the greatest stake in the outcome, were excluded from effective participation in discussions of how to reshape the welfare system.

Colleges and universities could also serve as local hubs in state and national information and communications networks to help keep local groups informed about developments on their issues and to facilitate ongoing discussions and planning about legislation, strategy, tactics, and so forth. The rapidly evolving Internet/World Wide Web environment has the potential for effectively linking like-minded people and groups around the country, providing them with the capabilities for sharing timely information and for organizing concerted action. Corporate lobbying coalitions have those capabilities already. The resources of colleges and universities can assist in bringing comparable capacity to ordinary citizens in their communities, helping to sort out and make intelligible a myriad of information, and sponsoring community forums for bringing people together in the same room to share important information, develop policy ideas, and organize collective action.

As previously noted, the collective action accessible to ordinary citizens often tends to be negative and oppositional. That is largely because they are invited to participate only after public policy debates have been framed. The National Citizens Initiative would change that dramatically, enabling citizens to work positively and constructively for policies they have conceived.

At a time when public faith in American democracy is dangerously on the wane, colleges and universities can help to facilitate this kind of political empowerment of ordinary people in their communities. A principal rationale for the practice of tenuring faculty is to insulate them from politically motivated reprisal, thereby enabling them to function as social critics. But that function is only rarely exercised. At this critical juncture in American history, it is time to elevate that function to the status of a social responsibility of colleges and universities to their communities.

The National Citizens Initiative would also naturally attract support from local organizers and affiliates of sympathetic state and national organizations. Leaders of Washington-based nonprofit public advocacy groups with members nationwide would have an attractive alternative to playing the Washington insider game, with the great constraints that places on what they can accomplish. A National Citizens Initiative would allow them to work for passage of legislation they and their members would find worth fighting for. They would have an incentive to invest heavily in community organizers to build much stronger, more activist-minded grassroots organizations needed to compete with the now dominant interest groups in battles beyond the Washington Beltway. In addition, reform-minded senators and representatives, now held in check by Congress's feudal-like system with its legislative lords, would be liberated to become national leaders of revitalized grassroots constituencies. The new politics of the post-2000 period could begin with alliances between populist lawmakers and local organizers and groups around the nation. Together they could work with citizens to develop initiatives that have widespread support and to mobilize constituencies in congressional districts nationwide.

In this way, members of Congress and citizens groups could develop their own strong grassroots power bases and challenge the tyranny of Washington's power elites.

With regard to tyranny, one probable consequence of the NCI is curbing the power of legislative lords. Early exercises of citizen initiatives would very likely encounter such egregious examples of abuse and arrogance of power among senior legislators that dealing with this anti-democratic problem would soon become a major issue. Direct curbs on the power of committee chairs and term limits are likely to be among the remedies considered.

One other very important natural development of an NCI regime would be the repair of the current disconnect between electoral and issue politics. On the issues people care about most, there would be organized constituencies in congressional districts nationwide, closely watching what their representatives do, holding regular accountability sessions back in their districts and remembering and reminding their community in a highly visible fashion at the time of the next election. The present state of primary accountability of congressional lawmakers to the power elites depends on the people back home not being able to follow easily what's going on in Washington. New mediating institutions naturally would emerge to remedy that when citizen initiatives come into widespread use because of the citizen interest in particular legislative proposals generated by local organizing associated with country-wide signature-gathering efforts. The ideal in this regard is to provide ordinary citizens with the kinds of timely information that lobbyists now provide to their clients.

A particularly intriguing and possibly the most significant consequence of a National Citizens Initiative regime is the effect it would likely have on political parties. My hunch is that when people are able to participate in setting the congressional agenda, use of the National Citizens Initiative would naturally fall into the rhythm of the election cycle. Before elections, the NCI process could be used by citizens to establish the content of the major legislative battles in the next Congress. Since the content of specific legislative proposals in the next session would be known, candidate commitments would naturally be sought. In this way, there would be direct connection between candidate-citizen dialogues during campaigns and important policy choices elected representatives would face in office.

In such a situation, political parties would find vital new purpose. Permanent organizations of like-minded citizens in every congressional district would provide a base for nationwide citizen initiative efforts. Such organizations might include the present political parties; they might also include new multi-issue organizations of like-minded citizens that might eventually become new political parties, given their utility in this new political environment. Institutions, like people, become inflexible and eventually moribund in their old age, primarily preoccupied with their own survival and prosperity. That is certainly true of the Democratic and Republican parties. American politics would benefit from the nimble flexibility, youthful enthusiasm, and creative ideas of new parties to challenge the same old dance of the ancient duo. As discussed shortly, the formation and flourishing of new parties would be facilitated by replacing America's current winner-take-all electoral system with one based on proportional representation elections for Congress and state legislatures.

Unintended Consequences

Whenever the rules of the political game are changed, individuals and institutions adapt, sometimes producing consequences that are neither intended nor welcome. It is therefore important to try to anticipate such consequences of an NCI regime and shape the rules to avoid or mitigate them.

For instance, one might suppose that a National Citizens Initiative would exacerbate the tendency toward single-issue politics. It is true that single-issue organizations are likely to find an NCI regime to be a fertile field. It could well be that early on in an NCI regime, some existing single-issue groups would be especially well-prepared to take advantage of the citizen initiative opportunity. For example, organizations of the religious right, such as the Christian Coalition, might well promote an abortion-ban initiative. Groups already organized in many states are likely to back a term-limits initiative, a flat-tax initiative, an initiative similar to one that passed in Colorado in 1992 depriving gays and lesbians of anti-discrimination rights, a balanced-budget constitutional amendment initiative, and so forth. At the moment, as the above list suggests, the conservative side of the political spectrum seems to be best organized for grassroots action. But organizations such as Handgun Control, Common Cause, the PIRGs, Citizen Action, the Sierra Club, and other environmental groups also have considerable potential for grassroots leadership and organized grassroots action.

To the extent that single-issue politics are encouraged and supported by an NCI regime, it would lead to pluralistic competition in a national marketplace of ideas. An anti-abortion initiative would prompt a prochoice initiative in response; a flat-tax initiative would likely prompt a wealth-tax initiative for the richest 1 percent, the multimillionaire households that hold more than 40 percent of the nation's wealth; a single-payer initiative would probably be one of several in the health care realm, along with another for breaking up oligopolies of HMOs, another mandating a patients' bill of rights. A sustainable energy transition initiative would be countered by a safe and clean nuclear power transition initiative; a Clean Money Campaign

Reform initiative would share the field with an initiative that bars any public funding for politicians' campaigns. The NCI would naturally pull the policy battles and the issue debates and organizing beyond Washington into the American heartland, and provide a way for citizens of all persuasions to participate.

Some kinds of initiatives do worry me, however, most notably those that would deprive minorities of civil or human rights, such as the Colorado anti-gay and lesbian initiative. When I ran for public office in Minnesota, our ticket endorsed a direct initiative program in the state but explicitly excluded any that would deprive minorities of fundamental civil or human rights. The courts will provide some protection, but my hunch is that such a provision is an essential ingredient of a National Citizens Initiative statute.

In the long run there would probably be such a premium in an NCI regime on permanent nationwide organizations that need constant exercise to maintain vitality, multi-issue organizations, most notably political parties, would likely come to play the leading role.

Of course, I do not pretend to have anticipated all the important consequences of instituting a National Citizens Initiative, nor have the details been worked out fully. Nevertheless, I am confident that the NCI can set the stage for many disenfranchised groups to compete in an inviting new public policy arena. In order for less affluent constituencies have a fighting chance, however, Democracy Fund vouchers are needed to ensure that citizens from across the socioeconomic spectrum can contribute financially to our political life.

Looking Forward 20

Building a Movement to Take Back Our Democracy

For a quarter century, the American public's trust in government has been plummeting and real wages for American workers have fallen steadily, while at the same time the proportion of the nation's wealth held by the richest 1 percent of households has been soaring upward. Historically, that kind of inflammatory mix of political and economic conditions has produced potent progressive-populist movements. As the twenty-first century begins, we can see the outline of such a movement beginning to take shape once again.

When the Clean Money Campaign Reform model bill came off the drawing board in 1993, the Working Group on Electoral Democracy was committed to building a network of state-based Clean Money organizations around the nation. By the year 2000, considerable progress had been made toward that goal: Six states had enacted Clean Money Campaign Reform for state offices, about twenty-five more states had vital Clean Money statewide coalitions, a dozen or so more had incipient efforts under way, and a fully functioning national organization, Public Campaign, was providing resources and coordination to regional networks of state coalitions, in close cooperation with regional centers and state campaigns.

A plausible vision of what could happen: The campaign would first achieve Clean Money victories in several states. Eventually, when it achieves sufficient strength, the effort will refocus on Washington, winning decisively in Congress and emerging energized and powerful as the heart of a nationwide "Movement to take back our democracy." Equally critical for inviting ordinary citizens back into effective participation in American politics would be enactment of the NCI/Democracy Fund proposal. That would provide a tool both for mobilizing citizens behind specific legislation such as a sustainable energy transition and universal, comprehensive, affordable health care, and behind further important democracy enhancing political reforms, such as the None-Of-The-Above ballot option, proportional representation elections, overturning of *Buckley* v. *Valeo,* reinstituting the Fairness Doctrine and Equal Time provisions, thereby ushering in an historic new era of revitalized democracy in America.

November 5, 1996, may well be remembered as D-Day in the effort to break our elected representatives of their addiction to special interest campaign contributions. A historic beachhead was established in Maine when voters went to the polls and changed profoundly the rules by which their state elections will be financed. By a 56 percent to 44 percent margin they passed Question 3, the Maine Clean Elections Act, a state version of Clean Money Campaign Reform.[1]

In 1992 the Northeast Citizen Action Resource Center [NECARC] started a Money and Politics Project directed by Nick Nyhart in Hartford and funded by a two-year MacArthur Foundation grant and began working with local activist groups on studies of the financing of candidates for state offices in five New England states and New York City. The Maine study was the most detailed examination of that state's campaign contribution patterns ever undertaken, giving the project instant credibility with the press and other media.

In 1995, "Maine Voters for Clean Elections," a coalition of such statewide organizations as the League of Women Voters, Common Cause, AARP, the AFL-CIO, the Natural Resources Council of Maine, Peace-Action Maine, the Dirigo Alliance, and the Maine People's Alliance decided to back a full public financing approach for gubernatorial and state legislative campaigns patterned after the Clean Money model, while adding a number of innovative ideas. Unlike the situation in California in 1994, the qualifying number of registered voter signatures required in Maine was just over fifty thousand, less than 10 percent of those required in California. What's more, in sharp contrast to the lengthy California signature gathering drive, it was conceivable in Maine to try to gather all the signatures on one day. The obvious candidate: Election Day the year before the vote. Eleven hundred volunteers from coalition organizations turned out at about 225 polling places on Election Day 1995, and by the time the polls closed, they had collected sixty-five thousand signatures.

Another difference was that California has the more common "direct initiative," whereby the requisite number of signatures automatically puts the proposal on the next election ballot. Maine is one of nine states with the "indirect initiative." Once the signatures are gathered the initiative goes first to the legislature; if the legislature fails to pass the initiative into law, it goes on the ballot. A Clean Elections bill had been introduced in the Maine legislature and voted down in 1993 and 1995. That experience convinced the coalition to go the initiative route.

The first step was a hearing before a legislative committee, where it was expected that Question 3 would be defeated and then proceed to a vote of the people. When the hearing was held before the Legal and Veterans Affairs Committee in early 1996, many committee members were hostile. Some members argued they would be better off keeping the initiative "in their court" so they could amend it. The notion that the legislature might pass the bill so it could gut it the next year hung heavily over the hearing. Initiative leaders soon learned that was precisely what was planned. When Question 3 overwhelmingly passed the committee by a vote of 12 to 1, many supporters reacted with deep concern.

It had become clear that legislative passage would likely be a trap. The indirect initiative allowed the legislature in effect to assume ownership of their proposal, derailing the vote of the people and putting the legislature in a position to attach crippling amendments later. So, instead of celebrating victory, Question 3 supporters sounded the alarm. Within days, four Maine newspapers warned that a perfidious plot was unfolding at the legislature to undermine a democratic reform with a "pass it to repeal it" strategy. Exposed, the committee reversed itself, rejecting the proposal 11 to 2. Subsequently the Senate passed Question 3, but the House voted it down.

Maine's Question 3 seemed vulnerable to a campaign of fear and doubt similar to the one California's single-payer initiative had faced. It could be tarred and feathered as "welfare for politicians" or "taxpayer funding of politicians' campaigns." Although the coalition anticipated such opposition from interest groups and incumbent politicians, it was slow to materialize. Consequently they were able to frame the debate and define their initiative for the public in favorable terms.

For instance, anticipating the "taxpayer funding" charge, the initiative drafters had arranged for the Clean Elections program to be funded in such a way that no new taxes would be required. The estimated $2.3 million per year for Clean Elections candidates would come from a combination of voluntary $3 contributions on state tax returns, the $5 qualifying contributions collected by Clean Elections candidates, and, in large measure, from relatively small reductions in legislative and executive branch administrative budgets. In this way, they effectively blunted the taxpayer funding issue.

Furthermore, the Question 3 campaign strategists had carefully shaped their message to direct attention to what the initiative would accomplish: In a nutshell, the message was: "Too much money in politics? Clean Elections will set spending limits. Wealthy special interests playing too much of a role? Clean Elections will cut private contributions. Campaigns going on too long? Clean Elections will shorten them. Is the political system tilted against ordinary citizens? Clean Elections will level the playing field for all. The name "Clean Elections" by itself was very important; it "kept the focus of public debate on the issue of cutting the power of wealthy special interests in elections."[2] The one poll they could afford, in July, 1996, suggested that this explanation boosted public support from around 30 percent to more than 60 percent.

Another crucial element of the strategy was enlisting the support of highly respected organizations and individuals. Leaders of the League of Women Voters, Common Cause, and AARP were often put forward as spokespersons, and prominent individuals from beyond those groups and across the ideological spectrum were sought out to serve on a campaign advisory committee. While popular Governor Angus King did not support Question 3, business leaders on the committee convinced him not to wage a campaign against it.

However, the campaign never had reason for overconfidence. In an eerie parallel to Prop 186, ambitious plans for a statewide volunteer field operation were scaled back dramatically early in the summer of 1996 because of a financial crisis. In July 4, just four months before the vote, the Question 3 campaign bank account had shrunk to $3,200; the coalition shifted the campaign's emphasis away from the grassroots field operation to raising money for paid media advertising. The July poll showed Question 3 ahead, but only narrowly: 43 percent to 34 percent, with 23 percent undecided. With support well short of a majority, a substantial voter persuasion effort was needed. As in California at just about the same point in the campaign, the emphasis in Maine suddenly changed to urgent, relentless fund-raising in the hope of obtaining $200,000 for radio and television advertising in the final weeks.

The field effort was not shut down altogether, but it was cut back and targetted on the most densely populated region, in the South, where the poll showed least support, around 39 percent. A coordinated letters-to-the-editor and op-ed piece campaign framed the debate and inoculated voters against anticipated opposition arguments, as did door-to-door canvassing by the Maine People's Alliance. That targetted field effort paid off with 60 percent of the region's vote on election day.

The intense fund-raising effort resulted in an ironic twist for an initiative dedicated to ridding Maine's politics of large contributions from wealthy individuals and interests. The initial campaign budget target was $420,000, with a goal of 80 percent of that from Maine donors. By July, however, it was clear that in-state goal was totally unrealistic.

At that point, Janice Fine, NECARC's dynamic, articulate, and persuasive organizing director, stepped up to lead the fund-raising enterprise. National interest was beginning to focus on Question 3 as a crucial test of the political viability of an attractive campaign reform concept. With aggressive pursuit of financial supporters wherever they could be found, the fund-raising goal was achieved. But in an initiative dedicated to ridding Maine of political domination by the wealthy and whose initial goal had been 80 percent in-state contributions, more than half the money raised, 54 percent, came from just thirteen donors who each gave more than $15,000. Another 32 percent came from fifty-five donors who gave between $1,000 and $15,000. So 86 percent of the Question 3 funds came from 68 donors in amounts of $1,000 and greater, and 73 percent of the total amount of money raised came from outside the state of Maine. From August on, direct mail and paid phone bank solicitations, which net relatively little money, were employed primarily to raise the number of Maine donors to 66 percent, though most of these new contributions were in small amounts. Only one news story was written about the out-of-state fund-raising; it never became an issue.

Six weeks before the election, a poll by one of Maine's leading newspapers found 78 percent opposed to "taxpayer financing" of elections, suggesting Question 3 was vulnerable to an opposition media advertising campaign. Maine Voters for Clean Elections had an effective ad ready to go in response to the taxpayer financing charge. But the long-anticipated last minute anti-Question-3 media blitz simply failed to materialize.

Of course, media advertising is very expensive, to the point that raising money for it can become the central focus of an initiative campaign. The Maine Clean Elections campaign ended with two weeks of unanswered pro-Question-3 television and radio ads, spending about $215,000, just under half the total campaign budget, to counter an expected media blitz from the opposition. Mysteriously, it never materialized. Nevertheless, the funding predicaments encountered by both Maine's Question 3 Clean Money campaign and California's Prop 186 single-payer campaign suggest that to reach voters, citizens initiative campaigns need access to additional public funding sources and/or access to free or low-cost media. The possibility of involving new government-subsidized channels for informing the public about initiative proposals should also be considered.

Question 3 won because it had the backing of a broad coalition of organizations as well as bipartisan support of prestigious political players, a judiciously targeted field operation, and adequately funded media advertising. By and large, media editorials were supportive and in-state press exposés of interest group campaign contributions to Maine legislators as well as national reports about White House and Democratic National Committee fundraising practices added saliency to Question 3's call for dramatic change in campaign financing. Of course, the failure of the expected opposition media campaign to materialize was a huge plus. Speculations about why that happened include opponents' mistaken confidence that public financing of political campaigns would never win at the polls or, if it did, that the legislature could reverse it later.

Mounting evidence suggests that the American people are fed up with the corrosive effects of special interest money on our democracy. Clean Money Campaign Reform will obviously eradicate the most troubling practices relating to campaign financing and probably create a climate of public opinion that will not tolerate use of the few remaining loopholes. The Maine victory showed that organizing behind Clean Money Campaign Reform can be an effective way to capture the imagination of a disaffected American electorate.

A Nationally Coordinated Grassroots Strategy

State-by-state initiatives can set the stage for building national movements and influencing national policy debates. Maine's Question 3 was proposed in a relatively small state with a population of 1.2 million. Nonetheless, the Maine victory was a tremendous shot in the arm for an incipient Clean Money Campaign Reform movement, catapulting it to instant national credibility. California's Prop 186 was put forward in the nation's most populous state. This was a challenge the health insurance industry took *very* seriously, and a win would have given the movement for single-payer health care an enormous boost nationwide.

It is not difficult to imagine organizing similar initiatives in many states, catalyzing coalitions of organizations across the nation, giving them the ability to choose when and where the early battles will be fought and the opportunity to demonstrate that an idea initially labeled "politically unfeasible" in Washington can actually attract widespread popular support. In that sense, state citizen initiatives can serve as incubators of social movements in America. In August 1996 the Center for Responsive Politics commissioned a telephone poll of eight hundred adults, who were given an explanation of the Maine Clean Elections option and asked if they would favor it for congressional campaigns. The results were overwhelmingly positive: Democrats favored it by a margin of 74 percent to 19 percent, Independents by 71 percent to 19 percent, Republicans by 61 percent to 30 percent, and self-identified conservatives by 66 percent to 27 percent. The most popular provisions of the proposal were campaign spending limits, with 78 percent in favor, and a level financial playing field, with 71 percent in favor.[3]

In early 1997, buoyed by the victory in Maine and buttressed by polling in several other states, Ellen Miller of the Center for Responsive Politics founded a new organization, Public Campaign, dedicated to building a nationwide movement behind Clean Money Campaign Reform.[4] The Public Campaign strategy had three principal objectives: "reversing the conventional wisdom among journalists, lawmakers, and pundits that systemic, comprehensive reform that involves public financing is unacceptable to the American people; assisting non-profit, non-partisan organizations in building grassroots support for systemic reform at the state level . . . ; and finally, establishing a presence in Washington, D.C., to convince key decision-makers and opinion leaders of the necessity for systemic reform and the public's willingness to support it."[5] On June 12, 1997, the Vermont legislature passed the Maine-like "Vermont Campaign Option" by a comfortable margin. Shortly thereafter, Connecticut was the site of a near-miss, when the governor convinced two legislators to change their votes at the very last minute. By mid-1997, several other states, including Massachusetts, Arizona, Missouri, Michigan, Idaho, Oregon, Washington, Illinois, Wisconsin, North Carolina, and Georgia, as well as New York City had substantial Clean Money campaign organizations in place. In three of those states, Arizona, Massachusetts, and Missouri, voters favored Clean Money Campaign Reform by a margin of greater than 2 to 1.[6]

The vitality of an incipient national movement was on display in Raleigh, North Carolina, in July 1997 when Public Campaign assembled 140 Clean Money advocates from forty states for its first strategy planning conference. Paul Wellstone was the keynote speaker at that conference. As a series of workshops demonstrated, the state representatives included large numbers of sophisticated, successful grassroots organizers. Ellen Miller had assembled a top-notch staff for Public Campaign, a combination of out-standing Washington operatives, with experience and contacts in the Congress and skills in media and public relations. What is more, before the campaign began, Miller had accomplished the prodigious feat of gathering a war chest of about $9 million.

The year 1998 was a crucial test. Sufficient signatures to get Clean Money initiatives on the ballot were obtained in Massachusetts, Arizona, and Missouri. Maintaining the momentum at this crucial early stage would require an unbroken string of state-level victories. On November 3 an outpouring of six thousand volunteers in Massachusetts and a strong coalition of citizen groups propelled Question 3, "The Clean Elections Law" to an overwhelming 66 to 34 percent victory. In Arizona the vote was expected to be close, but the Arizona leadership had put together an excellent coalition of supporting groups and an outstanding volunteer signature gathering effort. Kaia Lenhart, the political director for Arizonans for Clean Elections, noted the significance of the 51 to 49 percent victory for Proposition 200, "The Citizens Clean Elections Act": "Even in a conservative western state, people are ready to embrace comprehensive campaign finance reform. It . . . clearly sends a message to Washington that citizens will vote for measures that are much more sweeping than are currently being debated inside the beltway."[7] In Missouri a strong grassroots coalition had been mobilized and the major newspapers in the state had come out in support of the Clean Money initiative, but it became clear it would face substantial organized opposition. To make matters worse, a familiar obstacle blocked the path: gathering the requisite 120,000 signatures had left the Missouri campaign treasury very short of cash as of early July 1998. After much discussion, it was decided to put off the initiative there until the 2000 election and spend two years on intensive voter education and fund-raising. New York City residents had also gathered enough signatures to get on the 1998 ballot, but political maneuvering by Mayor Giuliani resulted in postponement of the vote.

You could just feel the momentum swinging our way. By the day of the Massachusetts and Arizona votes, major newspaper endorsements of the Clean Money approach included the *Boston Globe*, the *St. Louis Post Dispatch*, the *New York Times*, *USA Today*, *Newsday*, and the *Milwaukee Journal-Sentinel*.

The early successes of Clean Money initiatives put the lie to the notion that people would never support public financing of political candidates' campaigns. The 1998 election also shattered the myth that campaign finance reform is not a winning issue for candidates. For years, Congress's archenemy of campaign finance reform, Sen. Mitch McConnell of Kentucky, had been fond of saying that no one ever lost an election by opposing campaign finance reform. However, Sen. Russ Feingold of Wisconsin won a tight race for reelection in 1998 by taking a strong, principled stand in favor of campaign finance reform.[8] The *New York Times* reported that "a Republican lobbyist in Washington said confidently, 'Mitch [McConnell] will spend what it takes in Wisconsin.' And a Republican Senator said Mr. McConnell recently told him: 'Don't worry about campaign reform. Feingold's going to be dead meat by Christmas.'"[9] But Feingold fought back effectively by pointing out that most of the targeted soft money had come from outside the state and framing the issue as an attempt by out-of-state interest groups to buy a Wisconsin election. Feingold made campaign money the issue, and he won.

By 1998 it was clear that a failure of the leading public interest groups to achieve consensus was a major barrier to success in campaign finance reform. At the time of the Raleigh conference, there were honest differences among the organizations. Two of them, Common Cause and Public Citizen, were championing the McCain-Feingold bill, which banned unlimited "soft money" donations to political parties, while Public Campaign was organizing in many states for the Clean Money approach. To foster unity among the groups, Public Campaign agreed to put considerable resources behind McCain-Feingold in 1998. This substantially increased the likelihood that the groups would pursue a unified campaign finance reform strategy in the future.

A Liberated Politician

In November, 1996, Paul Wellstone was reelected to a second term in the U.S. Senate. He had been number one on the hit list of the National Republican Senatorial Committee [NRSC]. The much-feared political consultant Arthur Finkelstein, known in the trade as "the Terminator," was hired to design and implement a million-dollar anti-Wellstone television ad campaign.

His approach wasn't very subtle, but a nearly identical campaign designed by Finkelstein had propelled Sen. Alfonse D'Amato to victory in New York in 1992. With clever visuals, including animated cartoon Wellstone figures and other bizarre but effective attention grabbers, the ad series had a very primitive goal—to pin the label *liberal* on Paul in 1996. According to one count, these Republican ads and an extension of that series paid for by Paul's opponent, Rudy Boschwitz, called Paul *liberal* seventeen times, *ultraliberal* eleven times, *embarrassingly liberal* five times, and *unbelievably liberal* and *too liberal* twice each. I must admit there was poetic justice in this. Just before Paul debated Boschwitz in 1990, he was prepped by a lawyer-friend, wise in the ways of political debate. In the debate Paul, heeding his advice, had labeled Boschwitz *incumbent, incumbent, incumbent.*

This kind of simplistic labeling is typical of what happens when candidates are sold like soap. Paul was reelected in Minnesota anyway, in large part because of the support of a grassroots campaign that mobilized many volunteers. In part, Paul also won because he raised and spent lots of money. After considering various restrictions on his campaign fund-raising, he decided he would not "unilaterally disarm"; given the current system of financing campaigns, that would amount to senatorial suicide. Even the best intentioned senators—and Paul is surely one—are trapped by the necessity of raising millions of dollars just to compete. So it was full speed ahead, and by election day 1996 he had solicited and spent nearly $7.5 million, about what Boschwitz had spent against Paul in 1990 when he was the incumbent.

An amusing footnote: The fact that Finkelstein was hired by both the National Republican Senatorial Committee and the Boschwitz campaign to mastermind their respective ad campaigns against Paul posed a bit of a problem to the Republicans. The NRSC reported its advertising as "issue ads," meaning that legally there could be no cooperation or coordination between the NRSC and the Boschwitz campaign with regard to the content and timing of the ads and the NRSC did not have to report where the money came from. A columnist from the *Minneapolis Star Tribune,* Doug Grow, asked Boschwitz's campaign manager if there was a violation of the campaign finance law, since the same individual had been hired to oversee both ad campaigns. Is it possible for one person to avoid cooperation and coordination with himself? The campaign manager explained that while "we are legally prohibited from contact, . . . they've basically set up a firewall . . . [Finkelstein] doesn't touch things [at the national level] that have to do with things he's touching [at the state level]. . . . It seems implausible there'd be this firewall, but it's a routine thing. Every Senate candidate in the country has this sort of linkage."[10] It's hard to imagine a more blatant violation, but no sanctions were imposed. This is a good example of the joke that enforcement of campaign finance laws has become.

By the time he began his second term, Paul was convinced that Clean Money was the way to go in campaign finance reform. On June 17, 1997, the twenty-fifth anniversary of the Watergate break-in, he and Senators Kerry (Massachusetts), Glenn (Ohio), Biden (Delaware), and Leahy (Vermont) introduced the "Clean Money, Clean Elections" bill. Paul's senior policy advisor, Brian Ahlberg, played a key role in drafting that legislation, in consultation with the other sponsoring senators' offices and with Public Campaign and the Working Group on Electoral Democracy.

By November 2000, more states are likely to have joined Maine, Vermont, Massachusetts, and Arizona in passing Clean Money reform for state government posts, with a vital nationwide movement off to a very promising start. Public Campaign should be well along in pursuit of its goals of creating a national constituency for Clean Money Campaign Reform and at the same time laying the groundwork for the passage of CMCR in many more states and eventual passage of CMCR in congressional elections as well. Perhaps this will be the beginning of a movement to take back our democracy, with a considerably broader democracy reform agenda.

Even before his reelection, Paul was in a fight-back mood. When the punitive but popular federal "welfare reform" bill, based on one of the ten planks of the 1994 Republican "Contract With America," came to the Senate floor two and a half months before the 1996 election, Paul was the only senator running for reelection who voted against it. Many other politicians, right up to the president himself, were afraid to oppose it. Paul's vote was widely hailed as an act of political courage. In retrospect, rather than hurting his reelection chances, it reinforced his reputation in Minnesota as a senator who stood up for what he believed in. Anyone familiar with his work in the early 1970s as a leading community organizer for welfare rights in rural Minnesota never had any doubt how Paul would vote. He knew too much and cared too much about women and children on welfare to support that bill.

Before the election Paul also announced he would undertake a national "poverty tour," speaking out to highlight the predicaments of low-income families and exploring their views about ways government and the private sector could make it possible for them to escape from poverty and achieve economic self-sufficiency. It was an attempt to substitute the circumstances of real families trapped in poverty for misleading stereotypes that fear-trapped politicians were afraid to challenge. Paul was urged to undertake this effort by Richard Goodwin and Peter Edelman, who had been close advisors to Robert Kennedy at the time his own "poverty tour" was cut short by his assassination. They hoped Paul would be the leader to rekindle the idealism the Democratic party and the American people have lost, with a vision of a positive role for government in search of a just society.

Increasingly, Paul signaled his independence of the White House. He was one of only three Democratic senators who refused to vote for the 1997 balanced budget deal the president had cut with the Republican congressional leadership. Paul denounced it as "unfair to the vast majority of working Americans who deserve real tax relief, but will not get it in this bill because most of its benefits go to the wealthiest 3 or 4 percent of taxpayers and profitable companies." Richard Goodwin and others urged Paul to go one big step further in gaining public visibility for his views. They believed the prospects for his getting serious media coverage would be greatly enhanced if he hinted that he might run for President in 2000. A sign that he was seriously considering it soon appeared in early 1997, when Paul made the astonishing announcement that he would give up his seat on the Energy Committee to join the Foreign Relations Committee, chaired by Jesse Helms. Just before he took office in 1990, Paul had created a minor flap by telling a reporter that he "despised" Helms. The only sense I could make of this committee shift was that if Paul really wanted to run for president, he would have to fill a gaping hole in his resumé with some legitimate foreign policy credentials.

In early 1998, Paul began planning an exploratory campaign for president, provided he could raise the money and expand the terms of the debate beyond the mushy middle of Clinton, Gore, Gephardt, and other self-styled "moderate Democrats." As Paul was fond of putting it, he represented "the Democratic Party wing of the Democratic Party."

For the thirty years I have known Paul, one central characteristic is that when he takes on a quest, he doesn't do it halfway. By mid-1998, Paul had obviously warmed to the idea of using a presidential candidacy to spark a movement and he was ready to plunge in. Unfortunately, his recovery from back surgery the previous December took longer than expected and the pain bothered him more than he let on. His back and some other nagging problems distracted him and conspired to make him realize that a presidential run in 2000 was not in the cards.

NCI/Democracy Fund: Preparing to March on Washington

Beyond Clean Money Campaign Reform, in my view the next essential step is the National Citizens Agenda-Setting Initiative, with Democracy Fund financing. It would open the door to a revitalized American politics that invites people to organize together and provides them with access to the resources to compete effectively in the political arena to promote policies they support, in the process building the strong constituent accountability links which our representative democracy needs to flourish.

The NCI is much more than just a framing tool. Gathering signatures is only one way citizens will participate. Drafting initiatives, building coalitions, educating the public, lobbying lawmakers, watching them closely, and holding them accountable at the next election will be equally important functions of citizens in an NCI regime.

In this era of "New Federalism" when Congress frequently mandates programs with federal money provided to states that develop and implement plans consistent with federal guidelines, federal and state actions often complement each other. Examples of this pattern abound. The core idea of the Wellstone Sustainable Energy Transition Act (SETA) was federal funds for implementing state or regional sustainable energy transition plans consistent with the guidelines in the bill. The core idea of the McDermott/Wellstone health care legislation was a federal mandate of fifty state-organized single-payer programs.

A popular complementary idea is the notion of "states-as-laboratories." Within the bounds of the federal guidelines, the states often have considerable discretion in implementing federally mandated programs and much can be learned from their diverse approaches. That was sure to be true with SETA, where different states have very different climates, different renewable energy resources, different kinds of electric generating capacity already in place, and so forth.

This approach was a promise of the "Healthy Americans Act" Wellstone introduced in 1998, whereby a state would be eligible for federal funding for health care only after it had developed its own plan for universal coverage, comprehensive benefits, insurance portability, and regulation of insurance companies.

A National Citizens Initiative and state ballot initiative or state legislative opportunities would galvanize organizing at the local, congressional district, and state levels behind complementary state and federal proposals. The beauty of this is that much of the organizing, educating, and debating would necessarily take place outside of Washington. Ideas bubble up from the bottom with initiative or legislative victories in one or several states, with the possibility that they will spread to catalyze national movements. With the National Citizens Initiative and the Democracy Fund, organized citizens would have the keys for unlocking doors to framing forums that had previously been the exclusive domain of elites. National Citizen Initiative campaigns would gain them the opportunity to compete for Democracy Fund vouchers. In effect, the Democracy Fund would establish a nationwide pluralistic funding consortium, which might be thought of as the "Every Family

Foundation," in which every household with a registered voter or two would have access to $50 or $100 to give each year to support initiative campaigns.

The vanguard of such movements would be the grassroots activist component, and having an NCI/Democracy Fund regime in place would introduce two important new opportunities: the ability of a movement to use Democracy Fund vouchers to fund organizers, offices, and activities in congressional districts throughout the nation; and the opportunity to use the National Citizens Initiative at the appropriate moment as the focal point for mobilizing public support for congressional legislation the movement has written and applying pressure from citizens nationwide for passage of that legislation.

Enactment of the National Citizens Initiative/Democracy Fund would also be the key to advancing crucial additional elements of the political reform agenda of a general movement to take back our democracy. One such reform proposal that has long appealed to me as a preferable alternative to term limits is NOTA, short for "None of the above." A problem with term limits is that it is such a blunt instrument. The voters are not given a choice; it takes out able, honest, diligent, genuinely popular incumbents along with a host of those who have long since worn out their welcome and deserve to move on. Under a NOTA plan, the voter could choose "None-of-the-Above" instead of a candidate in any general election. In the cleanest version of NOTA, a vacancy for that office would be declared if NOTA won, and a special election would be called, with the previous candidates—often including the incumbent—prohibited from running in the second election. So far, NOTA bills have been introduced in four state legislatures, but only one, in Colorado in 1993, would pertain to congressional candidates. It seems very likely that neither state legislatures nor Congress would respond positively. But NOTA *initiatives* could well be a different story, since term limit initiatives for congressional representatives and senators have passed in twenty-one of the twenty-two states plus the District of Columbia where they have been introduced.[11]Along with NOTA, probably the most important and far-reaching political reform beyond those previously mentioned would be the introduction of proportional representation elections into the electoral system of the United States. Most democracies have consciously rejected the American winner-take-all system in favor of some form of proportional representation. While several variants of proportional representation systems are in use, they all have the result that for any given office—for example, the state senators from a particular region of a state—the proportion of candidates for that office elected from each political party would mirror the pro-

portion of votes for state senate candidates of that party in that region. For
example, if ten state Senate seats were up for election and the Republicans
got 50 percent of the vote, the Democrats 30 percent, and the Greens 20
percent, then the top five Republicans, the top three Democrats, and the top
two Greens would be elected. Such a system encourages the formation of
more political parties representing a much broader spectrum of political
ideas and programs than those provided by the Republicans and Democrats.

One consequence is that the legislature would more closely mirror the full
range of political preferences of the electorate. A second consequence is that
most voters would cast votes that actually elect candidates, giving voters a
much greater sense that their vote counts. A third is that it would give voters
viable alternatives to the two now dominant political parties and make it
much more likely that when they go to the polls they would find they can
vote for and elect viable candidates they support with enthusiasm. A fourth
is that women and minorities would be more likely to achieve fair representation in our legislatures. A fifth—judging from other Western democracies
with proportional representation—is that the embarrassingly low voter turn-
outs in U.S. elections would become a thing of the past. A sixth is that positions on issues would naturally assume a much more prominent role in electoral politics than they do now.[12]

Yet another much-needed change in the rules is overturning the *Buckley*
v. *Valeo* 1976 Supreme Court ruling. The basic claim of the Buckley ruling
is that in the political arena, spending money is equivalent to speaking out;
therefore, the First Amendment's free speech protection prohibits any limits
on spending by a candidate's campaign, on spending by a candidate on his
or her own campaign, and on independent expenditures for or against a
candidate. But limits on contributions to a candidate's campaign were allowed on grounds that there would be a risk of corruption or perceived corruption if private contributions from interested parties were permitted to get
too large.

Following Buckley, the courts have ruled out any limits on expenditures
for or against initiatives and any limits on expenditures to qualify an initiative, including attempts to prohibit or limit the use of paid signature gather-
ers. What's more, in the case of an initiative there is no risk of corruption or
perceived corruption because the contributions are given to initiative proponents or opponents, not public officials, so the courts have ruled there can
be no limits on the size of contributions for or against initiative campaigns.

However, more recent Supreme Court rulings suggest that the Court
may be more receptive in the future to limiting large initiative contributions

or expenditures on the grounds that large corporate spending might "unfairly distort" political campaigns, or undermine "democratic processes" or "the confidence of the citizenry in government." [13] All three of those antidemocratic diseases seriously afflict both candidate elections and ballot initiatives in America today and the *Buckley* v. *Valeo* decision is blocking appropriate cures.

One very promising development was a U.S. Supreme Court ruling in the case of *Nixon v. Shrink Missouri Government PAC* on January 24, 2000, the majority opinion written by Justice David Souter. It acknowledged the oft-cited assertion of the 1976 Buckley ruling that in politics free speech implies no spending limits, but it emphasized what it identified as an even more important principle of political efficacy—that citizens must have the tools, including the financial resources, to be able to work together effectively in pursuing political goals in a democratic marketplace of ideas. According to Souter's ruling, a state could set whatever contribution limits it wants unless they are "so radical in effect as to render political association ineffective, drive the sound of a candidate's voice below the level of notice, and render contributions pointless." A natural consequence of the Supreme Court's majority opinion is the following test of contribution limits: they must not be set "so low as to impede the ability of candidates to amass the resources necessary for effective advocacy." [14]

I cannot resist noting at this point that there is a much more fundamental political free speech issue than the notion that in politics free speech equals unlimited spending. From the early days of radio, the Fairness Doctrine and equal time provisions required broadcasting stations to set aside a reasonable amount of time for discussion of controversial issues of public importance, to make available opportunities for opposing views to be aired, and to provide time for persons attacked in such discussions to be allowed to respond. Those legal responsibilities of radio and television broadcasters were abandoned in the 1980s. One consequence of this is the speech impediment that third-party candidates usually labor under: the media ignore them. Of course, those candidates are free to say what they like, but without amplification by the media, they are not heard.

An especially important development is the normal practice of excluding third-party candidates from candidate debates. In May 1998, the U.S. Supreme Court ruled that even state-owned public television and radio stations are not obligated to invite "marginal" candidates to take part in the debates they sponsor. That fall, when the gubernatorial debates were being negotiated between the Republican and Democratic party nominees in Minnesota, the Democrat, Hubert H. Humphrey III, pushed for including the Reform Party candidate, Jesse Ventura. All the pundits were saying Ventura had no chance of winning, but Humphrey was calculating that the libertarian Ventura would take more votes from the Republicans than from him.

Given the opportunity to be heard in the debates, however, the blunt-spoken Ventura outshone the other two and his support in the polls began to rise dramatically as the election neared. Those normally prone to sit out elections voted in surprisingly large numbers, Ventura won, and Humphrey, initially the heavy favorite, finished third. Could it be that there are "third party" gems in many races, but they are locked in soundproof "third party" closets by the media? In my judgment, that is surely true.

The failure of the media to inform the public adequately about public policy debates and political candidates is near the top of the list of problems facing American democracy today.[15] So add to the list of important political reforms reinstatement of the Fairness Doctrine and equal time provisions. And that's just the beginning.

A central claim of this book is that if they only had the tools, many Americans today would be attracted to a movement aimed at taking back our democracy and undoing the obscene concentration of power in the hands of the wealthy, and the steadily worsening concentration of wealth. The NCI/Democracy Fund can be a vital new tool for extending this effort beyond political reform to become a modern-day progressive-populist revival of a movement for political equality and economic justice that takes aim on the political and economic consequences of the unequal distribution of wealth and income in America.

The pursuit of a compelling vision of economic justice in America will have many components beyond the specific reforms recommended here. Comprehensive, affordable health care for all is one critical need, for which the groundwork has been laid. Looking out for future generations with an orderly transition to a sustainable energy future is another. Universal access to living-wage jobs, adequate, affordable food, clothing, housing, and education surely are important goals as well. It is especially important to focus on those families with the least resources. A 1996 letter of the National Conference of Catholic Bishops on economic justice put it very well when it stressed that "all economic life should be shaped by moral principles" and admonished our nation to keep in mind that "a fundamental moral measure of any economic system is how the poor and the vulnerable are faring."[16] That statement could not have been more timely, coming as it did in the wake of the U.S. Congress's and President Clinton's renunciation in their August

1996 welfare reform bill of our nation's longstanding commitment to the notion that all our people are entitled to the basic necessities of life.

It is immoral for the richest nation on earth to renounce its obligation to provide the basic economic necessities to its people. Americans need to appreciate the maldistribution of wealth and income in our society and the human toll it takes. For the past twenty-five years, public policies have been shoveling wealth and income from the bottom to the top of America's economic ladder. If we have the courage to look at our economic face in the mirror, we could not be proud of America today. We have so much family wealth and income at the very top that all we need is the political will to design a wealth and income redistribution that would match our egalitarian values and restore our national pride.

Historically, in times like these, the progressive-populist heart of America has been moved to political action to elevate the questions, Who Benefits? Who Sacrifices? Who Decides? to the summit of national debate. The answers to the first two questions are obvious. Our country has been the victim of a hostile takeover by the wealthiest among us, to their material benefit, while the great majority of American families experience sacrifice in the form of economic insecurity and, in the case of the poor and most vulnerable, material deprivation.

Of course, this is not the first time. Our nation's history has been punctuated by periodic outbursts of excessive greed by the wealthiest few, which set the stage for inevitable backlashes in the form of populist movements to take back our democracy. It is our good fortune to live in an exciting time when such a struggle for political equality and economic justice in America is once again beginning to take shape. What better way to start than by joining the vanguard of the movement and liberating elected officials with Clean Money Campaign Reform and empowering ordinary people with a National Citizens Agenda-Setting Initiative and Democracy Fund support?

Notes

1. Has American Democracy Lost Its Way?

1. These 1994 data are from a telephone poll of eight hundred adult Americans taken for *Time*/CNN on August 17–18 and September 1, 1994, by Yankelovich Partners, Inc. Figures for 1964 and 1984 are from University of Michigan tracking. Data provided by the Roper Center, the University of Connecticut.

2. Edward N. Wolff, *Top Heavy: A Study of the Increasing Inequality of Wealth in America* (New York: The New Press, 1996), figures 3–4 and 5–1.

3. Edward N. Wolff, 1992 table of wealth (marketable net worth) distribution in the United States; private communication.

4. Lester Thurow, "Why Their World Might Crumble: How Much Inequality Can a Democracy Take?" *New York Times Magazine*, November 19, 1995, 78.

5. Wolff, ibid.

6. Thurow, "Why Their World Might Crumble."

2. "We Don't Let Strangers In"

1. Paul D. Wellstone, *How the Rural Poor Got Power: Narrative of a Grassroots Organizer* (Amherst: University of Massachusetts Press, 1978).

2. Barry M. Casper and Paul D. Wellstone, *Powerline: The First Battle of America's Energy War* (Amherst: University of Massachusetts Press, 1981).

3. Barry M. Casper, "Technology Policy and Democracy: Is the Proposed Science Court What We Need?" *Science* 194 (October 1976): 29–35.

4. See Barry M. Casper and Paul David Wellstone, "The Science Court on Trial in Minnesota," *The Hastings Center Report*, August 1978.

5. Dennis McGrath and Dane Smith, *Professor Wellstone Goes to Washington: The Inside Story of a Grassroots U.S. Senate Campaign* (Minneapolis: University of Minnesota Press, 1995).

6. Ed Garvey, "It's Money That Matters: A Candidate Looks Back In Anger," *The Progressive*, March 1989, 17–21.

7. See John Bonifaz, *Challenging the Wealth Primary: Continuing the Struggle for the Right to Vote* (Cambridge, Mass.: National Voting Rights Institute), April 1995.

8. Gina Campbell, et al. "Where Rudy Boschwitz Got His Crucial Early Money," a study prepared for the 1990 Wellstone for Senate Campaign, Northfield, Minn, November 1989.

10. Barry M. Casper, "To Wealthy Out-Of-Staters, Boschwitz Fits the Bill," *Minneapolis Star Tribune*, October 31, 1990.

11. Michael Barone and Grant Ujifusa, *The Almanac of American Politics 1992* (Washington, D.C.: National Journal, 1991), 657–58.

3. Into the Realm of a Legislative Lord

1. Barry M. Casper, "Scientists on the Hill," *Bulletin of the Atomic Scientists* (November 1977): 8.

2. Solar Energy Research Institute, Henry Kelly, Project Director, *Building a Sustainable Future*, U.S. House Committee on Energy and Commerce, 2 vol. (Washington, D.C.: United States Government Printing Office, 1981).

3. I must confess my own initial bias about nuclear power. Like many of my generation, I originally was an enthusiast. What's more, my father worked for the Atomic Energy Commission in Washington for the ten years following its inception in 1947, so I was more familiar than most with the early developments in nuclear power. When I graduated from college in 1960 I received an AEC fellowship in nuclear science and engineering, which supported me during my first year of graduate study in physics at Cornell University. However, in the 1970s I became increasingly skeptical of the dream of nuclear power and increasingly drawn to the vision of a sustainable energy future.

4. Barry M. Casper, "Impact of Super Energy Committees," *Minneapolis Tribune*, Dec. 14, 1976; reprinted as "Congress and the Cozy Triangles: The Case of Energy," *Bulletin of the Atomic Scientists* (May 1997): 5.

4. How the Energy Strategy Debate Was Framed

1. Ford Foundation, *A Time to Choose: America's Energy Future*, final report by the Energy Policy Project of the Ford Foundation (Cambridge, Mass.: Ballinger Publishing Company, 1974); *Energy In Transition, 1985–2010*, final report of the Committee on Nuclear and Alternative Energy Systems, National Research Council, National Academy of Sciences (San Francisco: W. H. Freeman, 1980); Solar Energy Research Institute, *Building a Sustainable Future*.

2. A fuel cell is an electrochemical device in which chemicals react to produce direct current electricity. It is comprised of a fuel electrode (anode), an oxidant electrode (cathode), and an electrolyte. The simplest fuel cell uses hydrogen as the fuel and oxygen (or air) as the oxidant. Other chemicals containing hydrogen can also be used as fuels, including methyl and ethyl alcohol.

3. Alden Meyer, et al. *America's Energy Choices: Investing in a Strong Economy and a Clean Environment* (Cambridge, Mass.: Union of Concerned Scientists, 1991). The Union of Concerned Scientists, the Natural Resources Defense Council, the American Council for an Energy-Efficient Economy and the Alliance to Save Energy commissioned the Boston-based Tellus Institute to do this study.

4. The Alliance to Save Energy and the Union of Concerned Scientists commissioned Vincent Breglio, project director for Research/Strategy/Management, Inc., and Celinda Lake, project manager for Greenberg/Lake, Inc. to do this opinion survey, entitled "America at the Crossroads: A National Energy Strategy Poll," which was conducted in early December 1990.

5. U.S. Department of Energy, *National Energy Strategy: Powerful Ideas For America* (Washington, D.C.: GPO 1991); available from National Technical Information Service, Springfield, Va.

6. U.S. Department of Energy, *Interim Report: National Energy Strategy, A Compilation of Public Comments* (Washington, D.C.: GPO, 1990), 4; available from National Technical Information Service, Springfield, Va.

7. Memo dated June 1, 1990 from Treasury Department official Ray Squitieri to Bob Marley, Director, DoE Office of Program Review and Analysis, June 1, 1990, reprinted in House Committee on Science, Space, and Technology, *The National Energy Strategy,* Hearing Before the Subcommittee on Investigations and Oversight, October 16, 1991, 100.

8. Vito A. Stagliano, DoE Associate Deputy Under Secretary for Policy Analysis, Hearing on *The National Energy Strategy* before the Subcommittee on Investigations and Oversight, House Committee on Science, Space, and Technology, October, 16, 1991, 117.

9. Ibid., 19.

10. Ibid., italics added.

11. *National Energy Security Act of 1991,* 102nd Cong., 1st sess., S.341. The bill was introduced by Senators Johnston (D-LA) and Wallop (R-WY) on February 5, 1991.

5. The Johnston Juggernaut

1. U.S. Dept. of Transportation, *Summary of Fuel Economy Performance* (Washington, D.C.: National Highway Traffic Safety Administration, February 1, 1991).

2. For a discussion of S.279, the CAFE bill Senator Bryan resubmitted in the 102nd Congress, see Senate Committee on Commerce, Science and Transportation, *Motor Vehicle Fuel Efficiency Act,: Hearing before the Consumer Subcommittee of the Senate Committee on Commerce, Science, and Transportation,* 102nd Cong., 1st sess., February 21, 1991.

3. Quoted in Margaret E. Kriz, "A Savvy Veteran of Hill Energy Wars," *National Journal,* March 16, 1991, 655.

4. For a discussion of PG&E's strategy, see Greg Reuger's testimony on the *National Energy Security Act of 1991* [NESA of 1991] in Senate Energy and Natural Resources Committee [SENRC] Hearings on S.341, pt. 2, 102nd Cong., 1st sess. February 6, 1991.

5. For a glimpse of Senator Johnston's attempt to discredit the Bryan CAFE bill, see ibid, pt. 4, February 28 and March 20, 1991.

6. For the flavor of Senator Johnston's attempt to promote ANWR drilling, see ibid, pt. 8, March 12, 1991.

7. For insights into the high stakes battle over revising the 1935 *Public Utilities Holding Company Act,* see ibid, pt. 9, March 14, 1991.

8. For an informative debate over changing to one-step nuclear licensing, see ibid, Pt. 5, March 5, 1991.

6. Why Not an Alternative?

1. Meyer, et al., *America's Energy Choices.*

2. Margaret E. Kriz, "Showdown Over Arctic Oil," *National Journal,* March 9, 1991, 606.

3. Barry M. Casper and Paul David Wellstone, "Perpich Can Lead on Energy Reforms," *Minneapolis Star Tribune,* March 5, 1983.

4. George J. Mitchell, *World on Fire: Saving an Endangered Earth* (New York: Macmillan Publishing Company, 1991).

7. The Tide Turns

1. "Minority Views of Senator Wellstone," *National Energy Security Act of 1991: Report of the Committee on Energy and Natural Resources, United States Senate, to Accompany S.1220 together with Additional and Minority Views,* Report 102–72, June 5, 1991, 432–59.

2. "Minority Views of Senator Bradley," *National Energy Security Act of 1991: Report of the Committee on Energy and Natural Resources, United States Senate to Accompany S.1220 together with Additional and Minority Views,* Report 102–72, June 5, 1991, 430–31.

8. Preparing for Battle

1. Historically in a filibuster, one or more senators opposing a bill may decide to try to "talk a bill to death" by speaking continuously for such a long time (hours or sometimes days) that the bill's sponsors eventually will give up and remove their bill from consideration by the Senate. According to Senate rules, the proponents can call at any time for a "cloture" vote; if at least sixty senators vote for cloture, the filibuster is over and the bill must come to a vote. If the bill's sponsors fail to get 60 votes and see no way they *can* get 60 votes, then they will generally remove their bill from consideration. In the Senate in 1991, the filibuster/cloture procedure employed by Senate Majority Leader George Mitchell had the same effect, but did not involve speakers droning on for hours to keep a bill from coming to a vote. Instead, when a filibuster was announced, a moderate amount of speechmaking was allowed, but then up to two cloture votes were taken. If those wanting the bill to come to the floor could not muster the necessary 60 votes to invoke cloture and halt the filibuster on either vote, then the practice was to remove the bill from consideration.

2. John Egan, "Growing Senate Opposition to Johnston's Energy Bill," *The Energy Daily,* June 19, 1991, 1.

3. Thomas W. Lippman, "Senators Try to Light a Fire on Energy Bill," *Washington Post,* June 27, 1991, A21.

9. Winning the Battle

1. *Congressional Record,* 102nd Cong., 1st sess., Vol. 137, S15600, October 31, 1991, S15600.

2. *Ibid,* S15600.

3. Ibid.

4. *Congressional Record,* November 1, 1991, 102nd Cong., 1st Sess., S15755.

5. *Nuclear Energy* (1993), 12.

10. Losing the War

1. The basic elements of the Sustainable Energy Transition Act were first outlined in an April 11, 1991, memo entitled "Energy Transition Trust Fund/State Energy Transition Grants, a Key Element of a National Energy Sustainable Energy Transition Strategy," from Sen. Paul Wellstone to the sixteen members of the Democratic Energy Policy Task Force organized by Majority Leader Mitchell.

2. The Sustainable Energy Transition Act, S.2020, was introduced by Sen. Paul Wellstone on November 22, 1991. For the text of the bill, a summary of its provisions, and the carbon tax funding mechanism, see *Congressional Record,* 102nd Cong., 1st sess., 1991, 137: S1760.

3. Letter dated November 27, 1991, signed by eighteen major environmental groups, advocating an alternative to the Johnston-Wallop energy package and describing the principal conclusions of the Tellus Institute's study, *America's Energy Choices.*

4. Brooks Yeager, telephone interview with author, February 12, 1992.

5. Phil Sparks, telephone interview with author, July 1, 1993.

6. Dan Becker, with author, Washington, D.C., November 7, 1991.

7. Ibid.

8. Margaret Kriz, "The Power Broker," *National Journal,* February 29, 1992, 499.

9. Brooks Yeager, interview.

10. Robert G. Szabo, quoted in Kriz, "The Power Broker," 494.

11. Yeager, interview.

11. It Sure Smells Like a Bribe or a Shakedown

1. Joseph A. Davis, "'Family' Raises Energy Funds For Pelican PAC," *Congressional Quarterly,* October 8, 1988, 2779.

2. David Hamilton and Bill Magavern, *Abuse of Power: Energy Industry Money and the Johnston-Wallop Energy Package* (Washington, D.C.: U.S. PIRG, October 1991).

3. The press conference about the U.S. PIRG study attracted a great deal of press coverage. The Associated Press ran a long article about PAC contributions to Energy Committee senators from interest groups lobbying on behalf of the Johnston-Wallop bill during the previous six years. Overall, Energy Committee senators had received more than $3 million from energy and automobile interests. Johnston himself had received $449,369 in that six-year period.

4. Another element of this strategy was to alert the media in the Energy Committee members' own states to the special interest money they had received by sending out press releases to key reporters back in their home states. What's more, U.S. PIRG announced at the press conference that it planned to run television ads highlighting Johnston's special interest contributions and his anti-environmental record in his home state of Louisiana. The *New Orleans Times-Picayune* picked up on the story and Johnston felt compelled to respond. He said the ad campaign "would play better in Baghdad than Baton Rouge."

5. Philip Brasher, "Energy Interests Target Conrad, Senate Committee," Associated Press, October 23, 1991.

6. Glenn R. Simpson, "Nader Group, Greenpeace Launch Assault on Johnston Over Energy Development Bill," *Roll Call*, October 24, 1991, 20.

7. Barry M. Casper and S. Matthew Fisher, *"A Study of Special Interest PAC Contributions to Energy Committee Senators During the Johnston-Wallop Bill Debate, January–June, 1991"* (Northfield, Minn., Carleton College Technology and Policy Studies Program, November 1991).

8. Glenn R. Simpson, *Roll Call*, 20.

9. Casper and Fisher, "A Study of Special Interest PAC Contributions," 9.

10. Sara Fritz and Dwight Morris, *Handbook of Campaign Spending: Money in the 1990 Congressional Races* (Washington, D.C.: *Congressional Quarterly*, 1992).

11. Quoted in "Mr. Smith Leaves Washington: Three Members of Congress Who Decided Not to Seek Reelection Explain Why They Grew Disillusioned—and How to Change a Stalemated System," *Time*, June 6, 1992, 64.

12. Fritz and Morris, *Handbook of Campaign Spending*, 4.

13. Tim Wirth, "Diary of a Dropout," *New York Times Magazine*, August 9, 1992, 16.

14. Ibid.

15. Ibid, 26.

15. Frank Sorauf, *Inside Campaign Finance* (New Haven: Yale University Press, 1992), 67–68.

16. "Mr. Smith Leaves Washington."

17. Greider, *Who Will Tell the People: The Betrayal of American Democracy* (New York: Simon and Schuster, 1992), 195.

18. "Mr. Smith Leaves Washington."

12. The Essential First Step

1. Fritz and Morris, *Handbook of Campaign Spending*, 15. Fritz and Morris attribute the entrepreneurial image to Alan Ehrenhalt, *The United States of Ambition: Politicians, Power and the Pursuit of Office* (New York: Random House, 1991).

2. Individuals can give $2,000 and PACs $10,000 "per election cycle," the two years between elections for House candidates and the six years between elections for Senate candidates. In addition, each year any individual is limited to no more than $25,000 in total contributions to candidates and political action committees. Party Committees can also contribute to candidates, with a limit of $5,000 per candidate per election cycle, except for the Democratic and Republican Senatorial Campaign Committees, which can each contribute up to $17,500 per election cycle to Senate candidates.

3. This and the subsequent excerpts from Senator Packwood's original and doctored diaries are recorded in appendix C, Senate Committee on Ethics, *Summary of the Counsel's Report Regarding Documents Related to the Investigation of Senator Robert Packwood,* 104th Cong., 1st sess., September 7, 1995. See also volume 3 of *Documents Related to the Investigation of Senator Robert Packwood.*

4. Phil Stern, letter to author, May, 1991.

13. Why Not Put Your Money Where Your Mouth Is?

1. Undated one-page memo on campaign finance reform issued by the Clinton/ Gore campaign during the summer of 1992.

2. Celinda Lake and Steve Cobble, Campaign Finance Reform opinion poll, December 1992.

3. Elizabeth Drew, "Watch 'Em Squirm," *New York Times Magazine,* March 14, 1993, 33, 50, 56, 74.

4. Greider, *Who Will Tell the People,* 247.

5. "Indecent Disclosure," *New York Times,* February 25, 1993.

6. Michael Wines, "Senators Bow on Disclosing Lobbyist Gifts," *New York Times,* May 6, 1993, 1.

7. "The Wellspring of Lobbying Reform," *New York Times,* May 7, 1993.

8. Barry M. Casper, "Rules Change but the Game's the Same," *Los Angeles Times,* May 23, 1993; Ellen S. Miller, "The Senate's Sham Reform Plan," *Washington Post,* June 28, 1993.

9. *Congressional Record,* May 24, 1993.

10. The Working Group on Electoral Democracy, *A Proposal for Democratically Financed Elections* and *A Call for Democratically Financed Elections* (Deerfield: Mass., 1993).

11. Marty Jezer, Randy Kehler, and Ben Senturia, "A Proposal For Democratically Financed Elections," *Yale Law and Policy Review 11,* no. 2 (1993), 333; Marty Jezer and Ellen Miller, "Money Politics: Campaign Finance and the Subversion of American Democracy," *Notre Dame Journal of Law, Ethics and Public Policy 8,* no. 2 (1994), 467; Jamin Raskin and John Bonifaz, "Equal Protection and the Wealth Primary," *Yale Law and Policy Review 11,* no. 2 (1993), 273.

14. Irresistible Reforms versus Immovable Incumbents

1. Jeffrey H. Birnbaum, *The Lobbyists: How Influence Peddlers Get Their Way in Washington,* (New York: Random House, 1992), 4.

2. *Congressional Record,* 103rd Cong., transcripts of the Senate gift ban/disclosure debates of May 4, 1994, S5146–S5198, and May 5, 1994, S5208–S5289.

3. Ibid, S5151–S5153.

4. Jay Hedlund, conversation with author, Washington, D.C., December 16, 1994.

5. "The Gift Horse's Mouth," *New York Times,* May 1993.

6. "The Golf and Tennis Caucus Gets Busy," *New York Times,* October 26, 1993.

7. "Mr. Bryant's Moment," *New York Times,* November 15, 1993.

8. "End Congressional Freebies Now," *New York Times,* November 18, 1993.

9. "Paul's Victory," *Minneapolis Star Tribune,* May 12, 1994.

10. The Republican's successful effort to block the lobbying bill is well-described in Katharine Q. Seelye, "Conservatives Hobble Lobbying Bill," *New York Times,* October 7, 1994, A13.

11. Colin McGinnis, conversation with author, Washington, D.C., December 16, 1994.

12. "Republican Gift Fraud," *New York Times,* July 22, 1995.

13. "Freebies Vote," *Washington Post,* July 25, 1995.

14. Pam Louwagle, "Senate Tightens Its Policy on Gifts," *Star Tribune,* July 29, 1995, 1A.

15. Hedlund, conversation with author.

16. Audiotaped interview by author with Common Cause lead lobbyist Jay Hedlund at Hedlund's office at Common Cause's national headquarters in Washington, D.C.

17. Hedlund, conversation with author. Gephardt's office kept delaying, setting the stage for inevitable failure.

15. Outside the Washington Frame

1. For extensive data and other information about the U.S. and Canadian health care systems, see David U. Himmelstein and Steffie Woolhandler, *The National Health Program Book* (Monroe, Me.: Common Courage Press, 1994). Also see John Canham-Clyne, Steffie Woolhandler, and David Himmelstein, *The Rational Option for a National Health Program* (Stony Creek, Conn.: The Pamphleteer's Press, 1995).

2. U.S. General Accounting Office, *Canadian Health Insurance: Lessons for the United States,* (Washington, D.C.: GPO, June 1991).

3. Congressional Budget Office, *Single-Payer and All-Payer Health Insurance Systems, Using Medicare's Payment Rates* (Washington, D.C.: GPO, April 1993).

4. *Consumer Reports,* The Health Care Crisis: "Wasted Health Care Dollars," July 1992, 435–49; "Are HMO's the Answer?" August 1992, 519–31; "The Search For Solutions," September 1992, 579–92.

5. Tom Hamburger and Theodore Marmor, "Dead on Arrival: Why Washington's Power Elites Won't Consider Single Payer Health Reform," *Washington Monthly,* September 1993, 27–32.

6. Todd Gitlin, *The Whole World is Watching* (Berkeley: University of California Press, 1980).

7. Eric Black and Tom Hamburger, eds., "Seeking a Cure: Looking For Answers to America's Health Care Woes," *Minneapolis Star Tribune*, October 26, 1993.

8. Hamburger and Marmor, "Dead on Arrival," 29.

9. Trudy Lieberman, "Covering Health Care Reform Round One: How One Paper Stole the Debate," *Columbia Journalism Review*, September/October 1993, 33–35.

10. Ned Crosby, interview with author, Washington, D.C., April 1994.

11. Donald Cohen, Paul Milne, and Glen Schneider, *American Progressives at a Crossroads: A Challenge to Lead and Govern the Nation*, The Institute for Effective Action, San Diego, 1995.

12. Sara Nichols, interview with author, Washington, D.C., April 30, 1994.

13. Charles Lewis, et al., *Well-Healed: Inside Lobbying for Health Care Reform* (Washington, D.C.: The Center for Public Integrity, 1994).

14. Nichols, interview. Nichols is also the source for the subsequent account of the breakup of the Washington-based Single-Payer Coalition.

15. John Sweeney, et al., to Members of Congress, March 24, 1994. The letter was written on Campaign for Health Security letterhead, and signed by twenty-four heads of organizations, including John Sweeney for SEIU, Owen Bieber for the United Auto Workers, Ira Arlook for Citizen Action, and Rhoda H. Karpatkin for Consumers Union. The letter enumerated seven essential ingredients of health care reform, including universal coverage and the elimination of unreasonable barriers to state enactment of single-payer systems.

16. Taking the Initiative in California

1. In 1993 I came to know many of the key figures in the emerging statewide single-payer movement in California. In 1994 I was back home in Minnesota, but I remained in close touch with leaders of the movement in San Diego. I had a brief taste of the signature gathering phase, a several-month immersion in the ballot initiative phase during the summer, and an opportunity to join in the debriefing exercise just after the vote in November. Much of what I know comes from personal experience, but quite a bit came from a series of interviews after the campaign was over. I learned a great deal from those taped interviews, to which I refer repeatedly in this account:

Dr. Vishu Lingappa, San Francisco State University molecular biologist, coauthor of the concepts and language of the ballot initiative. Interviews: March 25, 1995, San Diego; August 17, 1995, College Park, Md.

Paul Milne, Prop. 186 Campaign Manager, telephone interview, August 11, 1995.

Glen Schneider, Prop. 186 Co-Chair, in San Diego, July 24, 1995.

Donald Cohen, San Diego Californians for Health Security Campaign Director and later Director of Coalition Building for the statewide campaign: August 2, 1994, August 12, 1994, November 6 and 7, 1994; July 29, 1995, and August 23, 1995, San Diego.

Jeanne Ertle and Stephanie Jennings, who succeeded Cohen as Co-Directors of the San Diego Californians for Health Security campaign in August 1994: August 2, 1994, August 16, 1995, and August 22, 1995, San Diego.

2. "Clinton, Defending Health Plan, Attacks Critics' Alternatives," *New York Times*, January 4, 1994.

3. D. U. Himmelstein and S. Woolhandler, "A National Health Program for the United States: A Physician's Proposal," *New England Journal of Medicine* 320 (1989) 102–8.

4. Lingappa, interview, March 25, 1995.

5. Advanced Voter Communications, "Instant Initiative Qualification" (advertisement), California Commission on Campaign Financing, reprinted in *Democracy By Initiative* (Los Angeles: Center for Responsive Government, 1992).

6. Cohen, interview, August 2, 1994.

7. "Single Payer' Alive, Kicking," *Washington Post*, April 26, 1994, 1.

8. "Single-Payer Plan," *San Francisco Chronicle*, May 1, 1994.

17. An Unlevel Playing Field

1. Contributions to Taxpayers Against the Government Takeover and to Californians For Health Security were provided by the Office of the California Secretary of State, Sacramento.

2. Schneider, interview.

3. Milne, interview.

4. Barbara Newman, "Class, Race, Gender in the Proposition 186 Campaign, or, The 70 Kilogram Man's Syndrome," a memorandum to the Proposition 186 Campaign leadership.

5. Cohen, interview, July 29, 1995.

6. Jennings and Ertle, interview, August 16, 1995.

7. Goddard*Claussen/1st Tuesday, Script for "NURSE," (thirty-second television spot), August 23, 1994.

8. Goddard*Claussen/1st Tuesday, script for "PEOPLE SAY," (sixty-second radio spot), August 1994.

9. Jeff Folick, president and CEO of PacifiCare HMO, letter to PacifiCare subscribers, October 6, 1994.

10. See K. Grumbach and T. Bodenheimer, *Financing Single Payer Health Insurance: An Economic Analysis of the California Health Security Act*, July 6, 1994. In these calculations, I used estimates of the family's out-of-pocket costs and the employer's share of the employee's insurance payments from this very useful and instructive paper.

11. "Dear Neighbor" letter to California's 2.5 million State Farm Insurance subscribers, signed by their local State Farm Insurance agents.

12. Lingappa, interview, August 17, 1995.

13. *Los Angeles Times*, June 29, 1994, 1.

18. The Capital and the Countryside

1. Greider, *Who Will Tell the People*, 28ff.

2. Birnbaum, *The Lobbyists*, 4.

3. Kent Oram and Ed Allison, *The Nevada Initiative: The Long Term Program:*

An Overview, Proposal to the Nuclear Energy Council, Washington, D.C., September 1991.

4. Ibid, 2.

5. Ibid, 13.

6. Ibid, 18.

7. Christopher Drew and Michael Tackett, "More and More, Lobbyists Call the Shots in D.C.," *Chicago Tribune,* December 6, 1992, 1.

8. Ibid.

19. Changing the Rules to Revitalize American Democracy

1. David Broder, *Minneapolis Star Tribune,* December 6, 1993.

2. Greider, *Who Will Tell the People,* 52–53.

20. Looking Forward

1. Much of what I know about the 1996 Maine Clean Elections initiative, Question 3, is from conversations with Question 3 Campaign Manager David Donnelly and his insightful account, *As Goes Maine* (Hartford, Conn.: Northeast Action, 1997).

2. Nick Nyhart and Janice Fine, internal memo entitled "The Maine Money and Politics Victory," November 20, 1996.

3. The Mellman Group, Inc., commissioned by the Center for Responsive Politics, surveyed eight hundred adults by telephone, August 18–22, 1996.

4. Public Campaign, *New Organization Launches $9 Million Effort For Comprehensive Campaign Finance Reform,* press release dated April 8, 1997.

5. Public Campaign, *Background Paper,* December 1996.

6. Public Campaign, Arizona, Massachusetts, and Missouri surveys were conducted by the Mellman Group in May/June 1997.

7. Chris Moeser, "Voters Opt for Radical Campaign Reform; Candidates to Receive Public Funds," *Arizona Republic,* November 5, 1998, A18.

8. Randy Kehler's Pre-[St. Louis] Conference Discussion Paper, November 1998, cites counterexamples in the 1998 U.S. Senate elections to the conventional wisdom that a candidate's stand for or against campaign finance reform will not be decisive.

9. R. W. Apple Jr., "The 1998 Campaign: Wisconsin," *New York Times,* October 23, 1998, 1A.

10. Doug Grow, "Political Turnabout Makes for a Finkel," *Minneapolis Star Tribune,* October 31, 1996, B2.

11. For an illuminating discussion of NOTA and term limits, see the entire issue of the *Valpariso University Law Review* 29 (Fall 1994), 361. See also Craig Holman, "None of the Above Voter Empowerment Act of 1998" (Los Angeles: Center for Governmental Studies, 1998).

12. See Douglas J. Amy, *Real Choices, New Voices: The Case for Proportional Representation Elections in the United States* (New York: Columbia University Press, 1993).

13. California Commission on Campaign Financing, *Democracy by Initiative*, 293, 295.

14. Linda Greenhouse, "Justices Uphold Ceiling of $1,000 on Political Gifts," *New York Times*, January 25, 2000, 1A. For key quotes from the U.S. Supreme Court's historic majority ruling in *Nixon v. Shrink Missouri Government PAC*, see also Derek Cressman, The State PIRG's Political Reform Update, undated, but the lead report is titled "U.S. Supreme Court upholds low contribution limits," available from U.S. PIRG, 218 D Street SE, Washington, D.C. 20003, (202)-546-9707, <cressman@ pirg.org>.

15. See Ben Bagdikian, *The Media Monopoly* (New York: Beacon Press, 1997), xxxiii.

16. See for instance, the editorial on the 1996 letter of the National Conference of Catholic Bishops on economic justice, "A Homily For the Left," *In These Times*, December 23, 1996, 2.

Index